GLOBAL TAX FAIRNESS

Global Tax Fairness

Edited by

THOMAS POGGE AND KRISHEN MEHTA

OXFORD
UNIVERSITY PRESS

OXFORD
UNIVERSITY PRESS

Great Clarendon Street, Oxford, OX2 6DP,
United Kingdom

Oxford University Press is a department of the University of Oxford.
It furthers the University's objective of excellence in research, scholarship,
and education by publishing worldwide. Oxford is a registered trade mark of
Oxford University Press in the UK and in certain other countries

First Edition published in 2016
Impression: 1

Published in the United States of America by Oxford University Press
198 Madison Avenue, New York, NY 10016, United States of America

British Library Cataloguing in Publication Data
Data available

Library of Congress Control Number: 2015943022

ISBN 978–0–19–872534–3 (hbk)
978–0–19–872535–0 (pbk)

Printed in Great Britain by
Clays Ltd, St Ives plc

Table of Contents

List of Figures

List of Tables

List of Contributors

Reuven S. Avi-Yonah is the Irwin I. Cohn Professor of Law and Director of the International Tax LLM Program at the University of Michigan Law School. He teaches the basic course on taxation and courses on international taxation, corporate taxation, tax treaties, and transnational law. He has published numerous articles on domestic and international tax issues, and is the author of *Global Perspectives on Income Tax Law* (Oxford University Press, 2011) and *International Tax as International Law: U.S. Tax Law and the International Tax Regime* (Cambridge University Press, 2007). Professor Avi-Yonah graduated *summa cum laude* from the Hebrew University in 1983, received a PhD in history from Harvard University in 1986, and received a JD *magna cum laude* from Harvard Law School in 1989. From 1989 to 1993 Professor Avi-Yonah practiced tax law in Boston and New York, specializing in the international tax aspects of mergers and acquisitions. He has served as consultant to the US Treasury and the OECD on tax competition issues, and has been a member of the executive committee of the New York State Bar Association Tax Section and of the Advisory Board of Tax Management, Inc. He is currently a member of the Steering Group of the OECD International Network for Tax Research and Chair of the AALS Tax Section, an International Research Fellow of the Oxford University Centre for Business Taxation, a Trustee of the American Tax Policy Institute, and a member of the American Law Institute.

John Christensen has worked in offshore finance and between 1987 and 1998 served as economic adviser to the government of the British Channel Island of Jersey—a major tax haven satellite of the City of London. Since 2004 he has directed the global activities of the Tax Justice Network, a leading global network of experts with a research and advocacy focus on tax havens, tax avoidance, and tax wars between nations engaged in beggar-thy-neighbor tax policies.

Lee Corrick is Senior Advisor to the OECD Tax and Development Programme working on transfer-pricing capacity-building in developing countries, particularly in Africa. He is also Technical Adviser on transfer pricing to the African Tax Administration Forum (ATAF) and an associate lecturer in international tax at the School of Advanced Study, University of London. Lee previously worked as the Senior Specialist for Transfer Pricing at the South African Revenue Service (SARS) and advised National Treasury on changes to the South African transfer-pricing and thin capitalization legislation. Lee was also South African delegate to OECD Working Party 6. Before working for

SARS Lee was Assistant Director for Transfer Pricing at HM Revenue and Customs (HMRC) in the UK with responsibility for HMRC's transfer pricing including its litigation work. He led HMRC's work on its largest and most complex transfer-pricing disputes and led the HMRC litigation of the DSG Retail Ltd transfer-pricing dispute. He had responsibility for HMRC's transfer-pricing Mutual Agreement Procedure cases and for the HMRC Advanced Pricing Agreement Programme. He also led the UK delegation at OECD Working Party 6 and was a member of the Working Party 6 Bureau.

Michael C. Durst has been an attorney for more than thirty years; he has taught and written widely in the field of international taxation, with a special interest in problems of developing countries. BA 1975 Williams College; MS (Econ.) 1978 M.I.T.; JD 1981 U.C. Berkeley; LLM 1985 Harvard.

Lorraine Eden is Professor of Management and Mays Research Fellow at Texas A&M University, College Station, Texas. She has a PhD with distinction in economics from Dalhousie University. Her research focuses on two areas: the economics of transfer pricing and multinational (MNE) strategies in "hot spots" (e.g., conflict zones, corrupt economies, tax havens). She was editor-in-chief of the *Journal of International Business Studies* for 2008–10. She was elected a Fellow of the Academy of International Business in 2004, and received the President's Award from the Academy of International Business in 2012.

Itai Grinberg joined the Georgetown Law Faculty after serving in the Office of International Tax Counsel at the United States Department of the Treasury. At Treasury, he represented the United States on tax matters in multilateral settings, negotiated tax treaties with foreign sovereigns, had responsibility for a wide-ranging group of cross-border tax regulations, and was involved in international tax legislative developments. Prior to joining Treasury, he practiced tax law at Skadden, Arps, Slate, Meagher & Flom LLP, where he focused on a wide range of international tax controversy and planning matters. In 2005, Professor Grinberg served as Counsel to the President's Advisory Panel on Federal Tax Reform, where he advised a bipartisan presidential commission that made sweeping proposals to restructure the US tax code. Professor Grinberg earned his BA from Amherst College and his JD from Yale Law School.

James S. Henry is a US economist, attorney, and investigative journalist who has written extensively about global banking, debt crises, tax havens, and economic development. In the corporate world, Henry served as Chief Economist, McKinsey & Co. (NYC global HQ); VP Strategy, IBM/Lotus Development Corporation (Cambridge); Manager, Business Development, the Chairman's Office (Jack Welch), GE (Fairfield); and Senior Consultant, Monitor Group, the international consulting firm. As Managing Director of Sag

Harbor Group, a strategy consulting firm, his clients have included such enterprises as ABB, Allen & Co., AT&T, AT Kearney, Calvert Fund, Cemex, ChinaTrust, the Scotland Yard/FBI Task Force on Caribbean Havens, IBM/Lotus, Intel, Interwise, Lucent, Merrill Lynch, South Africa Telkom, Rockefeller Foundation, the Swedish Power Board, TransAlta, UBS Warburg, Volvo, and Monitor Company. A member of the New York Bar, he has served as a pro bono cooperating attorney for the NYCLU on First Amendment issues, and as Vice President, New York Civil Liberties Union—Suffolk County. He is author of the acclaimed investigative economics book *The Blood Bankers,* and his articles and citations have appeared in *The New York Times, The Wall Street Journal, New Republic, The Nation, The Conference Board, The Washington Post, Harper's Magazine, Fortune, Jornal do Brasil, Manila Chronicle, La Nación*, and many others.

Edward D. Kleinbard is the Ivadelle and Theodore Johnson Professor of Law and Business at the University of Southern California Gould School of Law, and a fellow at The Century Foundation. Professor Kleinbard joined USC Gould in 2009. Before joining USC Gould, Professor Kleinbard served as chief of staff of US Congress's Joint Committee on Taxation. The JCT staff are the nonpartisan tax resource to Congress, helping legislators to formulate legislation, writing analyses of legislative proposals or tax issues of interest to the Congress, and estimating the revenue consequences of legislative proposals. Prior to his appointment to the staff of the Joint Committee on Taxation, Kleinbard was for over twenty years a partner in the New York office of Cleary Gottlieb Steen & Hamilton LLP. Professor Kleinbard received his JD from Yale Law School, and his MA in history and BA in medieval and renaissance studies from Brown University.

Krishen Mehta completed his thirty-year career with Pricewaterhouse Coopers in 2008 having served in its New York, London, and Tokyo offices. While at PricewaterhouseCoopers, he was responsible for PwC's US tax practice in Japan, Singapore, Malaysia, Taiwan, Korea, China, and Indonesia, and worked with over 140 American companies conducting business in Asia. Krishen is currently an advisor to Aspen Institute's Business and Society Program, and is a member of the Asia Advisory Council of Human Rights Watch. He is also a Trustee of the Korbel School of International Studies at the University of Denver, and of the Institute of Current World Affairs in Washington, DC. Krishen has taught at a number of universities, including American University and the Fletcher School of Law and Diplomacy at Tufts University in Boston. He has been an invited speaker at the Global Justice Program at Yale University, and has conducted Capstone workshops for graduate students at the School of International and Public Affairs at Columbia University. From 2010–12, Krishen was Co-Chairman of the Advisory Board of Global Financial Integrity, a division at the Center for International Policy in Washington, DC.

Richard Murphy is a UK chartered accountant. He was senior partner of a practicing firm and director of a number of entrepreneurial companies before becoming one of the founders of the Tax Justice Network in 2002. He now directs Tax Research UK and writes, broadcasts, and blogs extensively, the latter at <http://www.taxresearch.org.uk/Blog/>. Richard created the country-by-country reporting concept and has been credited with creating much of the debate on tax gaps in the UK and Europe. He also defined the term "secrecy jurisdictions," now widely used in debates on offshore. Richard was named the seventh most influential person in international tax by the *International Tax Review* in 2013.

Sol Picciotto has been a professor at Lancaster University since 1992 (emeritus since 2007), previously taught at the University of Dar es Salaam (1964–8) and Warwick University (1968–92), and Scientific Director, the Oñati International Institute for the Sociology of Law (2009–11); founding editor and editorial board member of *Social & Legal Studies* since 1992; Senior Adviser, Tax Justice Network since 2003; member of the Advisory Group of the International Centre for Tax and Development at Sussex University, and coordinator of its research program on Unitary Taxation with Special Reference to Developing Countries (2013–14), and Applying International Corporate Tax Reforms in Developing Countries (2014–15).

Thomas Pogge received his PhD in philosophy from Harvard and is now Leitner Professor of Philosophy and International Affairs and founding Director of the Global Justice Program at Yale. He holds part-time positions at King's College London and the Universities of Oslo and Central Lancashire. Pogge is a member of the Norwegian Academy of Science as well as President of Academics Stand Against Poverty (ASAP), an international network aiming to enhance the impact of scholars, teachers, and students on global poverty, and of Incentives for Global Health, a team effort toward developing a complement to the pharmaceutical patent regime that would improve access to advanced medicines for the poor worldwide (http://www.healthimpactfund.org). Pogge's recent publications include *Politics as Usual* (Polity, 2010), *World Poverty and Human Rights* (Polity, 2008), *John Rawls: His Life and Theory of Justice* (Oxford University Press, 2007), and *Freedom from Poverty as a Human Right* (Oxford University Press and UNESCO, 2007).

Nicholas Shaxson is a writer and researcher who has specialized in the oil-producing countries of West Africa and, more recently, on international financial centers and tax havens. He is author of the critically acclaimed *Treasure Islands*, and has written regularly for the *Financial Times*, *The Economist*, *Vanity Fair*, Reuters and many others.

Erika Dayle Siu is a tax research consultant and has worked for the United Nations and the International Centre for Taxation and Development. Her research with the UN Tax Committee focused on proposing recommendations for the UN Model Convention on the taxation of profits from emissions trading. At the UN Office for South–South Cooperation, Erika worked on a project to exchange successful tax practices among developing country tax administrations. Her most recent work with the ICTD analyzes unitary taxation approaches with a focus on developing country regional economic communities. Erika is a graduate of New York University Law School's Graduate Tax Program and member of the New York Bar.

Vito Tanzi received his PhD from Harvard and was Professor of Economics at American University (1967–74). He was Chief of Tax Policy Division (1974–81) and Director of the Fiscal Affairs Department (1981–2000) at the IMF. Professor Tanzi was Senior Associate at Carnegie Endowment for Peace, State Secretary for Economy and Finance in the Italian Government (2001–3), and Senior Consultant to the Inter-American Development Bank. In 1990–4 Professor Tanzi was President of the International Institute of Public Finance, which has its secretariat at the University of Munich. Author of about twenty books and of hundreds of articles in professional journals, he has an economic effect, the "Tanzi effect," named after him.

Harald Tollan is Senior Advisor in the Norwegian Ministry of Foreign Affairs, with a focus on development, financial transparency, tax, and natural resource governance. Tollan chaired the International Task Force on the Development Impact of Illicit Financial Flows, leading to the establishment of the Financial Transparency Coalition. Amongst a range of transparency initiatives he has served on the International Board of the Extractive Industries Transparency Initiative and as a technical advisor to the African High Level Panel on Illicit Financial Flows. Tollan is an economist by profession and has worked on international issues for twenty years in the Norwegian Ministry of Justice, the Norwegian Agency for Development Cooperation, and the Ministry of Foreign Affairs.

Peter Wahl studied political economy, sociology, and roman languages in Mainz, Frankfurt, and Aix en Provence. From 1977 to 1989 he worked as Secretary General of the German Solidarity Committee for Africa, Asia, and Latin America, based in Frankfurt dealing with North–South relations. From 1990 to 1993 he was coordinator of the European NGO-network ANPED (Alliance of Northern People for Environment and Development). In 1990 he was co-founder of the German NGO World Economy, Ecology & Development Association based in Berlin. In 2000 he took the initiative to set up Attac Germany and served as member in its federal leadership until 2007. Today he is chairman of World Economy, Ecology & Development Association in Berlin.

Johnny West is the founder of OpenOil, a Berlin-based publisher. He has a Shuttleworth Foundation fellowship to explore the potential of open data systems to improve accountability and management of extractive industries worldwide. In 2012 he convened a group to write the first book explaining petroleum contracts to the general public which has been downloaded 75,000 times. He has advised the United Nations, development agencies, governments, and civil societies in over twenty countries on extractives governance issues. Johnny West was a Classics scholar at Balliol College, Oxford and covered oil markets as a correspondent for Reuters in the Middle East. He speaks Arabic and Farsi, as well as French and Spanish.

Introduction

The Moral Significance of Tax-Motivated Illicit Financial Outflows

Thomas Pogge and Krishen Mehta

New Year's Day 2016 marks the beginning of the era of the Sustainable Development Goals, which are to guide development efforts until 2030. It also marks the expiration of their predecessors, the Millennium Development Goals (MDGs), which have been used to track progress against human deprivation over the period of 1990–2015. Although some MDGs will not be achieved globally and none will be achieved for all countries and regions, there has been significant human development, especially in China. And yet, incomes in the poorest three deciles of humanity remain quite low indeed—ranging up to the purchasing power equivalent, per person per month, of about $60 in the United States in 2005 (PovcalNet, n.d.). At such low incomes, we cannot be surprised to find how precarious the human rights of the world's poor still are. Of the 7.3 billion people alive today, 805 million are officially counted as chronically undernourished (FAO, IFAD, and WFP, 2014: 8, 11, 40), well over 1 billion as lacking adequate shelter (Rolnik, 2014: 1), 748 million as lacking safe drinking water (Too-Kong, 2014: 47), 1.8 billion as lacking adequate sanitation (Too-Kong, 2014: 25), around 1.1 billion as lacking electricity (World Bank, n.d.), more than one-third as lacking reliable access to essential medicines (Nyanwura and Esena, 2013: 208), 781 million over age 14 as illiterate (UNESCO, 2014), and 168 million children (aged 5 to 17) as doing wage work outside their household—often under slavery-like and hazardous conditions: as soldiers, prostitutes, or domestic servants, or in agriculture, construction, textile or carpet production (ILO, n.d.). During the first decade of the new millennium, easily a third of all human deaths were due to poverty-related causes, some 50,000 daily (WHO, 2008: 54–9 Table A1).[1] For the entire decade, severe poverty

[1] The figure in the text is derived by counting deaths from causes that occur almost exclusively in the poor countries, such as diarrhoeal diseases, hepatitis, HIV/AIDS, lower respiratory

killed at least 180 million people, three times as many as perished in the Second World War.

Severe deprivations suffered by so many people constitute a massive deficit in social and economic human rights as summarized in Article 25(1) of the 1948 *Universal Declaration of Human Rights*: "Everyone has the right to a standard of living adequate for the health and well-being of himself and of his family, including food, clothing, housing and medical care and necessary social services, and the right to social security in the event of unemployment, sickness, disability, widowhood, old age or other lack of livelihood in circumstances beyond his control." But these same deprivations also entail massive deficits in civil and political human rights. Very poor people are substantially more vulnerable to violence, for instance, because they lack the protection of a secure home and because others—including police and other state officials—can with impunity ignore their needs and even mistreat them. Severely deprived people also are generally poorly equipped to fend for their legal rights and interests: many of them are physically or mentally stunted due to malnutrition in infancy, many are poorly educated or even illiterate, and most are in addition heavily preoccupied with their family's survival and thus find it very hard to defend, individually or collectively, their legal rights to political participation and due process. Especially in rural areas but also in relationships of domestic service, employers, landowners or local officials find it easy to entrap poor people—often from an early age—in relations of abject servitude and personal dependence, which in turn perpetuates their poverty, often over generations.

In centuries and decades past, most human deprivation may have been unavoidable. In more recent times, however, humanity has quite clearly come to possess the economic, technological, and administrative capacities to avoid such severe poverty. Just consider the current distribution of global household income: the poorest three quarters of humanity have merely 15 percent, the poorest half have 4.4 percent and poorest quarter 1.22 percent.[2] Global wealth inequalities are even more dramatic, with the 66 richest people on Earth owning as much wealth—0.6 percent—as the poorer half of humanity (Moreno, 2014).[3] Surely we could implement institutional reforms that would raise the share of the poorer half enough at least to realize their human rights. If this required raising their income share from 4.4 percent to 7 percent, and if this raise came entirely at the expense of the richest ventile's

infections, malaria, maternal conditions, measles, meningitis, nutritional deficiencies, perinatal conditions, pertussis, tropical-cluster diseases, and tuberculosis.

[2] These 2011 data on the distribution of global household income at market exchange rates were kindly provided by Branko Milanovic, City University of New York.

[3] The webpage concludes with a later update saying that the wealthiest 66 people now suffice to match the wealth of the poorer half.

income share, these richest 5 percent of humanity would still capture over 40 percent of global household income.[4]

The foregoing reflections alert us to the obvious point that development efforts are not the only factor affecting the evolution of the global income distribution. These efforts are, in fact, of comparatively minor significance: easily overwhelmed by stronger opposing forces that favor the most affluent segment of humanity and disfavor the world's poor. Prominent among these opposing forces are structural features of the existing global economic and financial order which, shaped under the influence of the more powerful multinational corporations (MNCs) and banks, industry associations, hedge funds, and billionaires, tends to serve the interests of these powerful agents.

The present volume focuses on the global financial system and, in particular, on some of its important structural features that facilitate so-called illicit financial flows, which disproportionately drain the economies and state budgets of the developing countries. Illicit financial flows are movements across international borders of funds that are earned or transferred or utilized in violation of law. Often motivated by the desire, and followed by the result, of avoiding taxes, duties, and other fees, such flows severely diminish government revenues in poor countries and also deprive these countries of much-needed capital. The present volume offers a set of essays that analyze various aspects of this phenomenon and discuss plausible reform ideas. It is our shared hope that these discussions will contribute to the success of ongoing efforts—in the OECD, the G7 and the G20, for example, as well as within countries and regional groupings of countries—to curtail illicit financial flows and will also help ensure that these efforts are responsive to the needs and interests of the poorer countries.[5]

The first-line responsibility for poverty-related human rights deficits lies with the governments of the countries in which severe poverty persists. But most of these governments are also poor. While the advanced industrialized states have annual government revenues in the order of $20,000 to $50,000 per person, India has annual revenues of barely $200 per person and many other governments are poorer still. These large international discrepancies are due to two factors: the *per capita* gross domestic products of poor countries are much smaller; and these countries also raise a much smaller proportion of their gross domestic products (GDPs) as government revenues, typically below 20 percent as compared to an OECD average of well over 40 percent.

It is difficult for poor-country governments to raise income or consumption taxes from the poor majority of their population—such taxes are unpopular, costly to collect and aggravate the very human rights deficits they are supposed

[4] According to Milanovic, the richest ventile captured 42.8% of global household income in 2011.

[5] A valuable predecessor to our volume is Reuter (2012).

to alleviate. But such governments also encounter difficulties in imposing taxes on those who could pay. Through sophisticated efforts, wealthy citizens of these countries, and corporations operating there, escape taxation to an extent that would be unthinkable in an affluent country with political clout and a highly sophisticated and well-funded tax administration. Boston Consulting Group estimates that 33.3 percent of all private financial wealth owned by people in Africa and the Middle East and 25.6 percent of such wealth owned by Latin Americans—some $2.6 trillion in total—is kept abroad; while the analogous estimates for North America and Europe are 1.8 percent and 7.9 percent, respectively (Boston Consulting Group, 2013: 4, 11). To collect taxes on the income and capital gains produced by this wealth, poor countries must largely rely on the honesty of their taxpayers as they lack access to information about their citizens' overseas holdings.

MNCs also reduce their tax burden significantly, typically by creating additional subsidiaries in tax havens and then having their poor-country subsidiaries contract with their tax-haven subsidiaries into arrangements that diminish the taxed profits of the former while increasing the untaxed profits of the latter—arrangements involving trade misinvoicing, abusive transfer prices, or inflated consulting or trademark fees, for example (Hearson and Brooks, 2012). Global Financial Integrity estimates that corporate tax abuse accounts for 80 percent of all illicit financial outflows from less developed countries, or about $6.6 trillion during the 2003–12 period and $991 billion in 2012 alone (Kar and Spanjers, 2014: vii). These illicit outflows constitute 3.9 percent of the GDP of the developing countries (5.5 percent in Africa) (Kar and Spanjers, 2014: 11), are larger than incoming total foreign direct investment (Kar and Spanjers, 2014: 12) and also vastly larger than the sum total of all official development assistance flowing into these countries, which officially amounted to some $127 billion in 2012 (UN, n.d). Christian Aid calculates that, through these profit- and tax-diminishing capital outflows, governments of less developed countries have lost tax revenues in the order of $160 billion annually—or about $2.5 trillion for the 2000–15 period. "If that money was available to allocate according to current spending patterns, the amount going into health services could save the lives of 350,000 children under the age of five every year" (Christian Aid, 2009: 3).[6]

Clearly, massive reductions in existing human rights deficits could be achieved by allowing poor countries to collect reasonable taxes from MNCs and from their own most affluent nationals, assuming the resulting revenues

[6] Intense national and international efforts are underway toward improving current government spending patterns in poor countries, which are often distorted by corruption, bloated security apparatuses, and indifference to the poor. Insofar as such efforts are succeeding, additional revenues would have an even larger human rights impact than Christian Aid is calculating.

were appropriately spent.[7] One might fault various groups of agents for poor countries' current inability to do so and for the resulting human rights deficit. There are the secrecy and tax haven jurisdictions (including Switzerland, Ireland, the UK, and the US) that structure their tax and legal systems so as to encourage tax abuse and also typically protect bank secrecy against the tax authorities of less developed countries. There are the individuals and corporations who erode the tax base of poor countries by using tax havens to dodge or reduce taxes on their wealth and profits. And there are many bankers, lawyers, accountants, and lobbyists who devise, implement, and "legalize" these schemes. Moreover, the jurisprudence of the European Court of Justice has made it difficult for countries in the largest integrated economic area on Earth to enact legislation to address some of these concerns. While all these agents surely share responsibility, it is quite unrealistic to hope that the problem can be meaningfully reduced through their morally motivated self-restraint. Even if many of them could be convinced to desist, their business would continue to thrive so long as it provides attractive and safe rewards. Realistically, tackling the problem of illicit financial outflows from the poor countries requires concerted action on the part of the more powerful rich-country governments, which currently all too often encourage the tax dodging of their MNCs abroad[8] and use strong-arm tactics to get tax havens to cooperate with their own tax enforcement efforts without ensuring that poor-country governments receive similar cooperation.[9]

The current draft of the Sustainable Development Goals agrees that we should "by 2030 significantly reduce illicit financial and arms flows" (Open Working Group for Sustainable Development Goals, 2014: Target 16.4). But it falls miserably short of recognizing what the most powerful states within the

[7] See also International Bar Association (2013).

[8] Shifting profits out of developing countries would not be so lucrative for MNCs, if their home countries taxed such profits while granting a tax credit for profit taxes already paid abroad. But most such home countries do not do this, allowing MNCs to pocket the taxes they dodge in poor countries as pure profit. The US is an exception by imposing a 35% tax on funds that MNCs repatriate from tax havens while granting a tax credit for taxes already paid abroad. But there are ways of getting around this tax. Thus the US Congress granted a "tax holiday"—misleadingly named the *American Jobs Creation Act* of 2004, which temporarily enabled US-based MNCs to repatriate profits accumulated in tax havens at a discounted 5.25% tax rate (Alexander, Mazza, and Scholz, 2009: 401–57). A coalition of 93 corporations spent $282.7 million on a concerted effort to get this Act passed by the US Congress, and these same corporations then repatriated over $200 billion while realizing a total of $62.5 billion in tax savings—$221 for every $1 they had invested in lobbying. The losses fell mostly on the populations of the less developed countries from which these MNCs had shifted their profits into tax havens; without the prospect of circumventing profit taxes in their home country, MNCs would have little to gain from such profit shifting.

[9] Even the OECD's new landmark model agreement on automatic exchange of financial information is likely to exclude many less developed countries from its benefits because they lack the resources to set up the data collection arrangements required to qualify as a reciprocating partner.

global financial system would need to do in order to accomplish this task. All the Open Working Group (OWG) draft demands of them is that they "strengthen domestic resource mobilization, including through international support to developing countries to improve domestic capacity for tax and other revenue collection" (Open Working Group for Sustainable Development Goals, 2014: Target 17.1).

The key to reducing the tax gap and consequent human rights deficit in the poor countries is global financial transparency: the abolition of shell companies and anonymous accounts, automatic exchange of tax information worldwide, and the requirement that, in their audited annual reports and tax returns, MNCs report their sales, profits, and taxes paid country by country for each jurisdiction in which they operate.[10] Adding such targets to the SDGs would open the door for policy reforms that are essential to curbing illicit financial flows which, by draining less developed countries of capital and tax revenues, are a great impediment to sustainable development. Such policy reforms would not merely advance tax justice but would additionally protect human rights by also curtailing the activities of criminals such as terrorists, money-launderers, and traffickers in persons, drugs, and weapons.

A major break-through for financial transparency is now within reach. To achieve it, the citizens of the countries that are home to the world's major financial centers must keep up the pressure on their governments to carry forward the needed institutional reforms and to shape these reforms so that the populations of the poor countries, whose basic human rights are at stake, participate fully in their benefits.

Let us now take a quick overview of the chapters that constitute this anthology. We start with the more conventional, better-known smaller reforms that developed countries can implement without a lot of international coordination and then ascend from there to deeper more systemic reforms that would require these same countries to build, and then to subject themselves to, substantial global institutional mechanisms. We then follow a similar approach for the developing countries, again ascending from smaller, more conventional ideas to larger and more radical ones.

Itai Grinberg's chapter proposes a system of Automatic Exchange of Information (AEI) that is uniform and multilateral in order to tackle tax evasion through the use of offshore accounts. This is premised on the role that financial institutions can play as tax intermediaries to facilitate government-to-government exchange of tax information. There is precedence for this, as Grinberg explains in his chapter, and also some progress through the OECD. But creating a uniform multilateral automatic information exchange system that benefits the developing countries that need it most, and not just

[10] Extensively discussed in the present volume, these are among the key ideas emerging from a recent Delphi study conducted by Academics Stand Against Poverty (ASAP, 2014).

the major developed economies, requires much more intensive investment in institutions as well as a refined technical architecture. Developing countries should have a stronger voice in the substance of the information exchange, which should not be controlled on a selective basis by the developed countries that are the recipients of much of the developing countries' wealth. The overall objective of information exchange also requires continuing progress on practicable mechanisms for identifying beneficial owners of financial accounts.

Jim Henry's reform proposal is startling in its simplicity. Very simply, he argues for taxing anonymous wealth at a modest rate of 0.5 percent per annum. This would only be for accounts that prefer to remain private, and where the beneficial owner is not publicly known or disclosed by choice of the true owner. Much of this money is now invested by way of the burgeoning global tax haven industry. The levy would be administered by the financial institutions and could generate billions of dollars each year. An international trust fund can then be created to channel this revenue directly to valuable projects, like helping poor countries adapt to climate change, recover from so-called natural disasters, prepare for epidemics, deploy the infrastructure required for clean water and smarter power grids, lower the outrageous fees they now pay for remittances and finance, and backstop the First World's shrinking budgets for development aid.

Richard Murphy's chapter proposes a reform of the current corporate accounting practices and converging to a country-by-country reporting model. This would require multinational corporations to report their profits and losses in every jurisdiction where they operate rather than providing one consolidated balance sheet for all operations. The current system enables companies to use tax havens and hide abuse of the arm's length pricing method of transfer pricing, thereby reducing the amount of tax they owe in both developed and developing countries. Country-by-country reporting would provide an accurate picture of actual corporate performance in each jurisdiction, would bring transparency to the incentives or treaty benefits that have been agreed and would empower institutional investors and civil society to have credible information on the true corporate performance. The inevitable consequence of this would be a more equitable tax system that would be fair to all jurisdictions.

Reuven Avi-Yonah proposes doing away with tax deferrals in their entirety. His chapter proposes that each OECD member country impose a tax at its normal corporate rate on the entire profit of multinationals that are managed and controlled from headquarters within it, with a foreign tax credit allowed for taxes paid to other jurisdictions. An approach such as this would reduce tax competition among countries and also diminish the propensity of MNCs to keep offshore trillions of dollars that are not subject to current taxation. This proposal offers an important and thoughtful solution to the faults of the current system, which is widely seen as conducive to massive tax avoidance.

The proposal treats the multinational corporation in the same way it is treated for financial reporting purposes—as a single unified entity controlled by the parent. In the modern world, this is a much more realistic and equitable approach to taxation, in comparison to taxing each entity separately and allowing profits to be deferred.

Edward Kleinbard's proposal argues for a fundamental reform of international tax norms that produce stateless income, that is, income that is earned by MNCs but not taxable in any jurisdiction. The stateless income phenomenon is large and amounts to lost tax revenues in excess of $100 billion each year to both developed and developing countries. It leads to government budget shortfalls, and it distorts a multinational firm's incentives as to where to invest as an economic matter. Options considered as solutions by Kleinbard include formulary apportionment—where a corporation's global profit is divided up and attributed to each jurisdiction where it has a taxable presence based on specific (economic?) factors, and taxed accordingly. Another option is to limit territorial tax models, under which only source countries tax business arising in those countries, to cases where it can be convincingly demonstrated that the source country is the nexus of business income ("geographic nexus"). This would require more precisely defining geographic nexus in terms of actual business activity. Kleinbard explains these concepts quite simply and eloquently in his chapter.

Lorraine Eden proposes policies for improving, rather than replacing, the current Arm's Length Standard (ALS) in order to limit transfer pricing abuse. The arm's length standard is designed to answer the question, "What would independent enterprises do?" Eden argues that this criterion requires MNCs and governments to search for arm's length comparables; a search that is problematic both in theory and practice. Eden suggests a variety of remedies to fine-tune the methods and processes currently used to implement the search for comparables. These remedies, several of which are currently being discussed as part of the OECD's BEPS initiative, would eliminate most of the incentives for abusive behavior that riddle the international tax system today.

Lee Corrick's chapter takes us into the real world of reforms currently under discussion among governments and within the relevant international agencies, and how this is a global issue requiring global solutions. He provides an update on the OECD's Base Erosion and Profit Shifting (BEPS) project, its genesis and the progress made thus far. At the core of BEPS is the premise that international tax rules have not kept pace with the changing business environment and that urgent action is needed to correct the resulting distortions. The paper discusses the current fault lines in the international tax system, the action plans that seek to address them and the solutions and compromises that are emerging as of this anthology's date of publication.

Peter Wahl's reform proposal seeks to rekindle the ongoing debate about a Financial Transaction Tax (FTT) and supports the proposal made by the European Commission toward implementing such a tax. This proposal is currently being considered by the European Parliament. The FTT has been advocated by civil society for years, but it was not until the financial crash of 2008 that the proposal gathered momentum as many policymakers realized that the current system is not working and that tax evasion is rampant. The FTT proposal derives additional support from the need to regulate finance as an instrument of society and to reduce some of the currently existing volatility in financial markets. In these ways, an FTT would also serve financial institutions as well as society at large. The success of the civil society movement pushing for an FTT can also serve as a useful example and provide valuable lessons for other movements.

Sol Picciotto's chapter proposes reorienting international tax rules so that multinationals are treated as single firms rather than as a collection of separate and independent entities. His reform proposal envisions the adoption of a system of unitary taxation with combined reporting and profit apportionment for multinational companies. A basic premise in Sol Picciotto's chapter is that the current international tax system is so flawed that it is unlikely to be corrected by applying further patches to the existing rules. What is clearly needed is to reorient the rules at a more fundamental level, specifically so that multinationals are treated for tax purposes as single firms rather than as a collection of separate and independent entities. This idea is known as unitary taxation, and such a system would have three components: combined reporting for the firm as a whole, including consolidated worldwide accounts, profit apportionment (as explained in Kleinbard's contribution), and a resolution procedure for resolving conflicts between states. Picciotto argues that such reform would place international taxation on a much sounder foundation, and would address most of the egregious tax avoidance practices by multinationals.

Harald Tollan's chapter proposes the creation of an International Convention on Financial Transparency that would require countries to modify current regulations and practices that facilitate financial secrecy within their own countries and across international borders. It would provide legally binding rules for financial transparency, and a framework for strengthening the global community's commitment to such transparency. The basic principle underlying the Convention is that financial secrecy undermines the sovereignty of other jurisdictions (their right to collect taxes) and must be addressed head-on if it is to be abolished over the longer term. Rather than international regulation tolerating the existence of financial secrecy and other harmful structures and adapt to it, the Convention would address the root cause of the problem and attempt to do away with secrecy altogether.

Vito Tanzi's reform proposal argues for the creation of a World Tax Authority (WTA) that would have the objective of making the tax policies of a country with global implications a global business and not the exclusive business of that country alone. A WTA would identify and report on problems in taxation at the international level and propose solutions. It would also establish a system of monitoring the use of the tax policies of the various countries to identify egregious practices that cannot be condoned. Vito argues for a WTA that would be like an influential and competent global mentor that can work toward the implementation of tax reforms that benefit all countries. The WTA would provide a forum for discussing tax policies with cross-countries implications and also serve as a forum for tax disputes for resolving tax disputes among countries. It would do for the area of taxation what the World Trade Organization does for the trade area.

The chapter by Nicholas Shaxson and John Christensen addresses the promotion by many politicians around the world of so-called "tax competitiveness." It proposes that this ideologically driven phenomenon is reframed as "tax wars" and suggests a set of recommendations for how developing countries can respond to such economic warfare. It also argues for the creation of a think-tank whose mission would be to counteract tax competition as an ideology, that is, as a belief system that falsely promotes tax competition as a demand of economic realities. The world understands now that offering tax incentives to tempt investment, hot money and individual wealth shrinks the tax base, distorts markets and results in a "race to the bottom" in which nobody (except for the very richest people) wins. Tax competition has nothing to do with market competition and is more like a trade or currency war. The chapter makes a compelling case for ending the race to the bottom since it harms sustainable development while also undermining democratic governments and diminishing human rights.

Johnny West's proposal makes a strong argument for reforming the current tax structure of oil and mining contracts between companies and governments. We have all heard of the "resource curse" affecting many developing countries that benefit little from the wealth extracted from their territories, wealth that ought to enhance the welfare of all their citizens. West proposes a new framework for extractive industry contracts directly linking taxation to the "internal rate of return" used by the companies to measure profitability. This would result in a more equitable economic return to developing countries where the extraction is taking place. In many poor (but resource-rich) countries today, there have been decades of super-profits for extracting companies and little or no revenue for the citizenry of the countries concerned. This paradigm is not sustainable over the long term and needs to shift. Johnny West's essay provides a solution and a way forward.

Michael Durst takes the position that action is needed in both developed and developing countries if the goal of tax justice is to be achieved. In the developed world, there is a clear need for strengthening some of the international Controlled Foreign Corporation (CFC) rules—which, roughly, subject certain kinds of income transferred from a subsidiary to one in a zero-or-low tax jurisdiction to the MNC's home country's tax rate. Developing countries, in turn, need to take action to limit taxpayers' ability to move income to zero- and low-tax countries through various kinds of deductible payments, including interest and excessive payments for goods and services. Developing countries also should protect their tax bases through more substantial withholding taxes on deductible payments—an approach with historical precedent but which has tended to atrophy in recent decades. Durst argues that both the wealthier countries and developing countries will need to muster greater political will to take the measures necessary to protect the world's tax bases. In particular, the wealthier countries will need to be willing to enforce tax payments by their home-based multinationals in their competitive activities around the world, and developing countries will need to be willing to collect taxes effectively from inbound investors even at the competitive risk of deterring some investment. Overall, Durst suggests, the key to effective action against base erosion lies more in the realm of politics, and particularly in countering the forces of tax competition, than it does in the technical intricacies of tax law.

The final essay by Erika Siu and Krishen Mehta addresses an important and sensitive issue, that of tax sovereignty. How can developing countries take control of their own tax destinies and still not risk losing foreign direct investment? In this paper, Siu and Mehta present ten steps that developing countries can take, within the existing tax norms and practices, to significantly improve their tax revenues as a percentage of GDP. These steps include caution about signing tax treaties, avoiding tax competition and incentives, adopting safe harbors to simplify tax administration and compliance, adopting a wider use of the profit split method in determining source country taxation, adopting more disclosure and attestation rules, taxing the black economy, and so on. These steps are fully within the developing countries' control and are not subject to challenge under international tax laws and practices. It is therefore important that developing countries not miss these opportunities while they pursue and support a more just and equitable global tax system.

ACKNOWLEDGMENTS

The editors would like to give special thanks to Esther Shubert, graduate student of philosophy at Yale University, who has collaborated closely with us on the editorial tasks and, through her careful and highly competent work, has greatly contributed to the quality of this volume. In particular, Ms. Shubert has reviewed and commented on drafts of each chapter, communicated with authors about their chapters and paperwork, communicated with the OUP editors, formatted the reference sections of the draft manuscript for compliance with OUP's style and for consistency (in some cases creating abstracts and keywords, in some cases providing assistance with reviewing the copy-edited chapters), obtained copyright permissions for images and figures, and given useful input on the table of contents, title, and other matters. We have been truly fortunate to have had such a bright and versatile collaborator.

We are deeply grateful also to Norway's Ministry of Foreign Affairs, to the German Friedrich Ebert Stiftung, and to Academics Stand Against Poverty for recognizing the importance of this volume and helping us cover the costs of producing it.

REFERENCES

Alexander, Raquel M., Stephen W. Mazza, and Susan Scholz, 2009. "Measuring Rates of Return on Lobbying Expenditures: An Empirical Case Study of Tax Breaks for Multinational Corporations," *Journal of Law and Policy* 25 (4): 401–57.

Academics Stand Against Poverty, 2014. "Policy Options for Addressing Illicit Financial Flows: Results from a Delphi Study." <http://academicsstand.org/wp-content/uploads/2014/09/Policy-Options-for-Addressing-Illicit-Financial-Flows-Results-from-a-Delphi-Study.pdf> accessed 15 July 2015.

Boston Consulting Group, 2013. *Global Wealth 2013: Maintaining Momentum in a Complex World.* <http://www.bcg.de/documents/file135355.pdf> accessed 31 December 2014.

Christian Aid, 2009. "False Profits: Robbing the Poor to Keep the Rich Tax-Free." <http://www.christianaid.org.uk/Images/false-profits.pdf> accessed 15 July 2015.

FAO, IFAD, and WFP, 2014. *The State of Food Insecurity in the World 2014. Strengthening the Enabling Environment for Food Security and Nutrition.* Rome, UN Food and Agriculture Organization.

Hearson, Martin and Richard Brooks, 2012. "Calling Time." Action Aid. <http://www.actionaid.org.uk/doc_lib/calling_time_on_tax_avoidance.pdf> accessed 15 July 2015.

ILO, n.d. "Child Labour." <http://www.ilo.org/global/topics/child-labour/lang–en/index.htm> accessed 15 July 2015.

International Bar Association, 2013. "Tax Abuses, Poverty and Human Rights". London. <http://www.ibanet.org/Human_Rights_Institute/TaskForce_IllicitFinancialFlows_Poverty_HumanRights.aspx> accessed 15 July 2015.

Kar, Dev and Joseph Spanjers, 2014. "Illicit Financial Flows from Developing Countries: 2003–2012." Global Financial Integrity. Washington. <http://www.gfintegrity.org/report/2014-global-report-illicit-financial-flows-from-developing-countries-2003-2012/> accessed 15 July 2015.

Moreno, Kasia, 2014. "The 67 People As Wealthy As The World's Poorest 3.5 Billion," *Forbes.* 25 March. <http://www.forbes.com/sites/forbesinsights/2014/03/25/the-67-people-as-wealthy-as-the-worlds-poorest-3-5-billion/> accessed 30 December 2014.

Nyanwura, Edmund Mohammed and Reuben K. Esena, 2013. "Essential Medicines Availability and Affordability: A Case Study of the Top Ten Registered Diseases in Builsa District of Ghana," *International Journal of Scientific and Technological Research* 2 (8): 208–19.

Open Working Group for Sustainable Development Goals, 2014. "Outcome Document." <http://sustainabledevelopment.un.org/content/documents/4518SDGs_FINAL_Proposal%20of%20OWG_19%20July%20at%201320hrsver3.pdf> accessed 15 July 2015.

PovcalNet, n.d. "PovcalNet: An Online Analysis Tool for Global Poverty Monitoring." The World Bank. <http://iresearch.worldbank.org/PovcalNet/index.htm?1> accessed 15 July 2015.

Reuter, Peter (ed.), 2008. *Draining Development? Controlling Flows of Illicit Funds from Developing Countries*. The World Bank. Washington.

Rolnik, Raquel, 2014. *The Right to Adequate Housing*. Office of the United Nations High Commissioner for Human Rights. Geneva.

Too-Kong, Tessa (ed.), 2014. *The Millennium Development Goals Report 2014*. United Nations. New York.

UN, n.d. "Millennium Development Goals Indicators." <http://mdgs.un.org/unsd/mdg/SeriesDetail.aspx?srid=569&crid=> accessed 15 July 2015.

UNESCO, 2014. "International Literacy Data 2014." <http://www.uis.unesco.org/literacy/Pages/literacy-data-release-2014.aspx> accessed 15 July 2015.

WHO, 2008. *Global Burden of Disease: 2004 Update*. World Health Organization. Geneva. <http://www.who.int/healthinfo/global_burden_disease/2004_report_update/en/> accessed 30 December 2014.

World Bank, n.d. "Energy." <http://www.worldbank.org/en/topic/energy/overview> accessed 15 August 2015.

1

Building Institutions for a Globalized World

Automatic Information Exchange

Itai Grinberg

> Developing countries should have the information and capacity to collect the taxes owed them—and other countries have a duty to help them.
>
> —G8, Lough Erne Declaration, June 18, 2013

1.1 INTRODUCTION

Approximately $8.5 trillion, representing more than 6 percent of all global wealth, is managed through offshore accounts (The Boston Consulting Group, 2013). Beginning in 2008, well-publicized cross-border tax evasion scandals focused political attention on offshore tax evasion in the world's major economies. The details read like a thriller. Bankers smuggled toothpaste tubes full of diamonds across borders, while governments bought stolen disks that identified tax evaders and handed new identities to the informants.

For the large developed economies, the spectacle of some residents blatantly evading their tax obligation to the state threatened to undermine many more residents' commitment to voluntary compliance with their own tax obligations, while putting in doubt whether the burden of maintaining government was distributed fairly. Politicians responded swiftly to the offshore tax evasion scandals in light of the budgetary pressures brought on by the financial crisis. Presidents and finance ministers uniformly insisted on improved transparency to combat offshore tax abuses. Projects proposing various approaches to enhance cross-border tax cooperation based on automatic information exchange were launched by the United States, the OECD, the European

Union, and the United Kingdom, France, Germany, Italy, and Spain, operating largely independently of the European Commission. Finally, the G20 endorsed automatic information exchange ("AIE") and asked the OECD to produce a proposal for a new multilateral reporting standard for AIE, which the OECD released in February 2014.

But relatively little attention has been paid to the fact that emerging and developing economies are the most affected by offshore tax evasion. More than one-quarter of all Latin American household wealth, and one-third of all Middle Eastern and African wealth, is held in offshore accounts (The Boston Consulting Group, 2013). By contrast, although the United States undertook the most forceful response to addressing its problem with offshore tax evasion, only about two percent of the household wealth of US residents is managed offshore. For many emerging and developing economies, it is exceedingly difficult to constrain residents from using offshore accounts to evade domestic tax liability on income from capital, whether earned domestically or abroad. Various experts have suggested that the revenue losses are of a similar magnitude as all official development assistance worldwide (totaling $120 billion per year).

In many emerging and developing economies, a general inability to collect tax on capital income of the wealthy—in significant measure because of the prospect of offshore tax evasion—severely threatens the broader administration of the domestic tax system (Grinberg, 2012; Prichard, 2010). Offshore tax evasion can also raise major concerns about the equality of citizens and taxpayers' engagement with the polity—not only in the face of the taxing authority, but more generally—particularly in countries characterized by a legacy of legal impunity for the elite. Weak tax administrations lacking vigorous enforcement programs with respect to both offshore and onshore tax evasion contribute to a state of affairs in which tax evasion carries very little moral opprobrium and low tax morale translates into reduced confidence in government more generally. Moreover, revenue losses from offshore tax evasion can hurt the poor by reducing funding for social programs. For this author, the outright illegality associated with tax evasion also distinguishes the concerns described in this chapter from the other issues addressed in this anthology because the question is one of enforcement rather than substantive tax policy.[1]

[1] The motivating theme of this volume—finding ways to facilitate domestic resource mobilization in the developing world in order to address abject poverty—has received insufficient attention in the past. I believe that all those interested in international tax policy should focus on this issue with greater intensity. However, I am concerned that many of the substantive international tax policy proposals described in other chapters of this volume could be counterproductive to promoting domestic resource mobilization, while also raising other tax policy concerns.

Effective tax administrations play a central role in promoting the legitimacy of government institutions in emerging and developing countries. For these countries, from a state-building perspective it matters both how *much* revenue a government raises, and also *how* the government raises that revenue (Organization for Economic Cooperation and Development, 2011; Prichard, 2010; Moore, 2007). For example, some scholars suggest that visible, progressive taxation of capital income and closely held business income at the top of the income distribution is a necessary symbol of the commitment to fairness in a liberal democracy (Scheve and Slaughter, 2007; Bird and Zolt, 2005; Cavanaugh, 2003). Others point out that imposing taxes on mobile assets in a transparent manner encourages collective bargaining with the sovereign and thus promotes the emergence of more representative and classically liberal government (Ferguson, 2002; Levi, 1988; Bates and Lien, 1985). Addressing offshore tax evasion is therefore particularly important for the rapidly developing economies that are increasingly important sources of offshore private wealth, but that still have large numbers of extremely poor people. Especially in these countries, the tax administration both provides the lifeblood of the country's government and can shape citizens' perceptions of evolving national institutions more broadly.

1.2 REFORM PROPOSAL

Addressing the problems caused by offshore tax evasion requires information. The availability of relevant information is the starting point for governmental processes and systems designed to collect any tax. If information regarding the income flows into offshore accounts were reported to residence-country tax administrations using taxpayer identification numbers or dates of birth, systems could eventually be devised in many countries to electronically match information received from cross-border exchange with taxpayer returns. That matching of information with taxpayer identities is in turn the starting point for enforcement: for making sure that the use of hidden accounts by the few does not raise the burden of taxation on the many.

In terms of providing workable technical architecture and international regulatory and compliance momentum, the most important catalyzing step in the shift toward automatic information exchange was the United States' 2010 enactment of legislation known as "FATCA." FATCA requires foreign financial institutions to report the account balance or value of each US account and the amount of dividends, interest, other income, and gross proceeds from the sale of property credited to such accounts. In order to "force foreign financial institutions (FFIs) to disclose their US account-holders or pay a steep penalty for nondisclosure," FATCA imposed a withholding "tax"[2] on specified payments received from US sources on FFIs that did not comply and become a participating FFI (Levin, 2010). In the United States Congress, FATCA was enacted with bipartisan support as a result of the shocking details of the offshore tax evasion scandals and the understanding that failing to pay taxes legally due was a "law and order" problem, as opposed to an attempt to increase the legal tax burden on one constituency or another.

However, FATCA as enacted required FFIs to report information directly to the US government, close certain account-holders' accounts, and/or withhold on payments made by a FFI to another non-US person. As a result, compliance with FATCA in the manner provided for in US legislation would have required foreign financial institutions in many jurisdictions to violate contractual relationships as well as the data protection, bank secrecy, and other laws of the jurisdiction in which they are located (Polayes, 2011). This untenable situation spurred negotiations in which the five largest economies in Europe (France, Germany, Italy, Spain, and the United Kingdom, together the "G5") agreed to cooperate with the United States through intergovernmental processes that solved the conflict of law problems while simplifying the FATCA rules.

After the G5 completed negotiations with the United States, they relatively quickly agreed among themselves to adapt the FATCA rules into a proposal for a multilateral FATCA-style pilot project. Then the G20, largely spurred by these same European members, moved towards a commitment to support automatic exchange of information as a new, global standard for cross-border tax enforcement with respect to offshore accounts. By enacting FATCA unilaterally rather than negotiating from the outset for a multilateral solution, the United States reinvigorated a longstanding multilateral discussion about addressing offshore tax evasion that otherwise would likely have remained moribund.

However, the compliance architectures proposed for the various approaches to AIE—whether FATCA as legislated, FATCA under bilateral agreements, or the OECD's new Common Reporting Standard (CRS)—do not take emerging and developing countries' concerns fully into account. The prospect of these countries benefitting from automatic information exchange turns heavily on the question of whether any new regime provides for uniform or fragmented compliance by financial institutions, and whether sufficient technical support is provided to developing countries so that they may participate effectively in the regime. Even mildly inconsistent sets of rules for automatic information exchange promulgated by the United States and European Union Member States could limit the set of countries that eventually benefit from those rules.

[2] FATCA is not a conventional withholding tax. It is better understood as a penalty regime intended to force foreign financial institutions to disclose information to the IRS.

The issuance of the CRS provides a possible solution for the problem, but does not in and of itself alter the potential for fragmented compliance—both as between FATCA and the CRS and as regards differential implementation of the CRS. The result may be a fragmented international architecture for cross-border tax administrative assistance. A fragmented regime would ensure that the benefits of automatic information exchange are largely limited to the developed economies, with little or no benefit for tax administrations in emerging and developing economies. In contrast, a uniform multilateral automatic information exchange system could positively affect their ability to address offshore tax evasion and, further, could serve to improve the structure of their domestic tax information reporting and withholding regimes more generally. Such a regime would, moreover, substantially reduce the rents available to asset management jurisdictions from facilitating offshore tax evasion.

Meanwhile, for the large majority of multinational financial institutions that do not benefit substantially from facilitating tax evasion, a uniform system remains essential if compliance costs associated with the new international automatic information exchange standard are to be contained. Financial institutions would rather collect information on all account-holders in one way than on various subsets of account-holders in a dozen slightly different ways.

Finally, the large developed economies themselves would also benefit from a broadly multilateral, truly uniform regime. At a narrow level, supporting tax administration in countries with more severe offshore tax evasion problems is necessary if the large developed economies are to rely more extensively on other tax administrations for the administrative assistance required for automatic information exchange. More importantly, there is a moral rationale for devoting resources to achieve broad participation in automatic information exchange, as offshore tax evasion deprives governments of developing countries of revenue they might otherwise use to meet the basic needs of their citizens.

If a uniform multilateral automatic information exchange system is to succeed it requires both an efficacious institutional architecture and a single standardized technical architecture. Two key issues lie at the intersection of the institutional architecture and the technical architecture: the incentives to ensure that financial institutions and governments choose to join the system, and the manner in which the system verifies that financial institutions comply with the rules. In the remainder of this chapter I sketch out the necessary institutional and technical architectural features. I also address the purported privacy objections to automatic information exchange. I conclude by noting that offshore tax evasion raises fundamental fairness issues in a globalized economy that create an imperative for a coordinated international response.

1.3 INSTITUTIONAL ARCHITECTURE

Across an array of subfields of international financial regulation, organizations that lack any formal international legal force nevertheless successfully regulate complex cross-border financial matters. They typically possess highly developed institutional structures with membership and decision-making rules and processes (Brummer, 2012). The Basel Committee, the Financial Action Task Force (FATF), and the Financial Standards Board (FSB) provide just a few examples.[3]

Successful soft law cross-border financial regulation generally includes four common features, in one form or another: a standard setter, a monitoring (verifying) body, enforcement mechanisms, and mechanisms to help developing countries take advantage of the system. For multilateral automatic information exchange to work, the G20 will need to use its powers of convocation to establish a governance structure for automatic information exchange that effectively incorporates these four features.

1.3.1 Standard Setter

To succeed, a uniform automatic information exchange system must include a mechanism for setting and subsequently refining standards for the key technical features of a multilateral AIE system. Further, that standard setting must be accomplished with the cooperation of a body that can obtain support and buy-in from developed, emerging, and developing countries alike. Thus, the standard-setting process for the FATCA-style multilateral exchange system embodied in the CRS should ideally be continually refined by subject matter experts from both OECD and non-OECD governments working together. The Global Forum on Exchange of Information for Tax Purposes (Global Forum) brings together over 120 countries and could serve this function, but currently is slated to play only a peer review rather than a standard-setting role with respect to the CRS. Thus, the appropriate way forward may involve moving ongoing refinements to the CRS and international standards for AIE out of the OECD's working parties and into the Coordinating Body of the Multilateral

[3] The Financial Standards Board is focused on standards for macro-prudential regulation; the Basel Committee on Banking Supervision is most well known for its standards of capital adequacy at the individual institutional level; and the International Organization of Securities Commissions is known for setting standards for international securities regulation. None of these organizations has any formal legal basis in the sense of traditional international law, but each has deep influence on international regulatory coordination in member and non-member states alike. Other "soft law" financial standard-setters have narrower mandates, including, perhaps most notably, the Financial Action Task Force (FATF), which focuses on combating money-laundering and terrorist finance.

Convention on Administrative Assistance in Tax Matters (Multilateral Convention). The Multilateral Convention facilitates international cooperation to combat tax avoidance and evasion and provides, among other things, a legal mechanism for multilateral automatic information exchange. Further, its Coordinating Body has the capacity to adopt expert opinions that can set technical guidelines for automatic information exchange that have formal recognition under international law. In 2010 the Multilateral Convention was opened to signature by all countries, with particular emphasis placed on including developing economies so that they might benefit from a "new cooperative international tax environment" (G20 Leaders, 2009). Developing countries that join the Multilateral Convention gain the right to participate in the Coordinating Body, and are steadily signing the Convention.[4] Once adopted, Coordinating Body guidelines would, in effect, become new international standards with legal force that carry the imprimatur of an ever-growing number of the world's governments. If the Development Working Group of the G20 mandated that the Coordinating Body review the CRS with the interests of developing countries in mind, and allowed for modifications to international standards that addressed developing countries' distinctive needs and pushed developed countries to meet them, it would help avoid the currently quite real possibility that the CRS will only be implemented in G20 jurisdictions, their dependencies, and other major financial centers.

1.3.2 Monitoring

The next step in developing an international institutional infrastructure for automatic exchange is to establish a system that efficaciously monitors and verifies compliance with technical standards set internationally. The G20 has already asked the Global Forum to establish a mechanism to monitor and review implementation of an emerging international standard for automatic information exchange (G20 Finance Ministers, 2013). Review of whether countries have appropriate laws on the book to meet the standard are scheduled to begin in 2016, with review of implementation in practice beginning in 2019.

The Global Forum will, for instance, examine whether taxpayer information is being used properly and kept private by jurisdictions benefitting from AIE. Such monitoring is key because misuse of information in a way that facilitates extortion, kidnapping, or worse could destroy a multilateral automatic information exchange system in its infancy. For this reason, ensuring that exchanged information is only used for legitimate tax administration

[4] As of August 2015, seventy-two countries have signed the revised Multilateral Convention, with many more signatures expected.

purposes, especially by countries that may have less experience with tax information exchange, is a key concern of many developed economies.

To ensure that monitoring is effective, the Global Forum should also develop a mechanism by which financial institutions' compliance with agreed standards in the automatic information exchange area could be reviewed. There are many more financial institutions in the world than the Global Forum would ever wish to review. However, a risk-based process (including a limited right for countries to nominate institutions for potential review) should be established. The reputational and commercial consequences associated with a potential review that could be negative would have a strong compliance effect on financial institutions, thereby achieving many of the benefits of more intrusive verification with relatively little effort.

1.3.3 Enforcement Mechanisms (Participation Incentives)

A multilateral regime that realistically intends to ensure global compliance with the CRS should also require all participating jurisdictions to impose some measure to encourage participation by other countries and institutions. A coercive mechanism imposed by multiple sovereigns will be needed to ensure compliance with—as opposed to nominal commitment to—a multilateral automatic information exchange system like the CRS. Otherwise, non-cooperative jurisdictions and institutions will benefit from defecting from the emerging regime, because they can become repositories of choice for tax evaders' assets without paying a significant price for making that business decision. As long as the United States is the only country exercising coercive authority to ensure compliance (through FATCA's withholding tax), defecting from the emerging regime remains possible. Willingness on the part of other concerned countries to exert some coercive effort is also needed if the United States is to be encouraged to participate in a truly multilateral regime rather than relying on FATCA, which was built to serve the United States alone.

Unlike the United States, most jurisdictions lack sufficient leverage (via the threat of withholding or other penalties on inbound investment) to unilaterally force cross-border financial institutions to change their due diligence and reporting procedures with respect to their nationals. However, in a multilateral system, not all countries would need to employ the same level of coercive force. Withholding along the lines of FATCA or denial of treaty benefits for investors using non-compliant financial institutions may be realistic sanctions for use by some jurisdictions. Important parts of the financial industry have also suggested that access to improved systems for reduced withholding at source for legitimate treaty investors could be limited to multilateral FATCA-compliant-financial institutions as a way of encouraging participation in a uniform automatic information exchange regime (Bennett, 2013; Lawson, 2013).

Some jurisdictions may fear deleterious consequences on inbound investment and therefore express interest in less onerous defensive measures. More graduated sanctions to be used by some jurisdictions would be possible in a compliance architecture that featured standard-setting and monitoring bodies and therefore could invoke reputational sanctions and more graduated penalties. Broadly imposed "outcasting" mechanisms and threats of sanctions can also help to enforce a multilateral AEI regime (Hathaway and Shapiro, 2011).[5] Nevertheless, a working system of incentives and penalties that most participating countries help to maintain in some way is the key to ensuring that automatic information exchange does not simply shift tax evader accounts to a few recalcitrant jurisdictions and financial institutions.

1.3.4 Enabling Participation

Establishing robust technical systems and governance structures for the developed economies to engage in automatic information exchange among themselves and receive information from asset management jurisdictions is not enough to address the concerns of those countries most deeply affected by offshore tax evasion. A huge amount of additional work remains to ensure that AIE provides benefits to those less developed tax administrations that face big challenges from offshore tax evasion. In July 2013 the G20 recognized this fact when it asked the World Bank and the OECD's Task Force on Tax and Development to identify developing countries' needs for technical assistance and capacity building in order to benefit from automatic information exchange.

Three key issues need to be addressed. First, in order for automatic information exchange to improve enforcement of tax obligations, tax administrators must be interested in taxing income from capital and opposed to impunity for wealthy tax evaders. Not all officials in all countries will meet this test. However, even in a country where finance ministry or tax administration leaders are beholden to elites who take advantage of offshore tax evasion opportunities, availability of and access to information about offshore accounts may empower honest individual administrators who are battling with other state actors to improve tax administration.[6]

[5] Being labeled as a non-cooperative country can carry real costs; to provide just one example, Standard & Poor's changed Liechtenstein's outlook from stable to negative when Liechtenstein was blacklisted by the FATF.

[6] Even in the case where finance ministry officials who are responsible for entering into automatic information exchange arrangements in the first place are uninterested in addressing tax evasion as an a priori matter, when compelled to agree to exchange information on non-residents' domestic accounts as part of a multilateral automatic information exchange system, those officials find it politically awkward to ask not to receive information on their own residents' offshore accounts.

Second, the availability of exchanged information about offshore accounts does not necessarily mean that tax administrations will be able to use the data. Meaningful information exists only when the information is provided in a form that a tax administrator can access, and the tax administrator has the information technology tools and trained personnel to make use of the information. However, technology will continue to alter the ways in which various governments seek to collect tax revenue. Colombia, for instance, trumpets its recently developed ability to match reported taxpayer information with taxpayer records and to use statistical-sampling models and other risk-based indicators to select cases for audit (Franco, 2010). Providing IT tools must be part of the burden of the large developed economies that desire a global automatic information exchange system—and the cooperation of emerging countries in that system—in order to address their domestic concerns with offshore tax evasion. To date, however, the G20's substantive commitments to provide technical assistance in this regard are inadequate, as reflected in the Saint Petersburg Development Outlook and implicitly acknowledged in the G20's September 2013 Leader's Declaration and the 2014 "roadmap" provided to the G20 Development Working Group regarding developing country participation in AIE (G20 Leaders, 2013; Global Forum, 2014). Resources available for training developing world tax administrators and IT overhauls must be increased.

For some less developed countries the technical capacity to engage fully in AIE will not be in place for many years. Countries in this category likely include many of those recognized as least developed countries (LDCs) by the UN (including substantial parts of Africa), and many smaller developing states, as well as countries emerging from conflict. However, compliance benefits from automatic exchange can accrue even for some countries that lack automatic matching capability. Searchable electronic information can be used as a basic risk assessment tool to reveal taxpayers that may be appropriate for audit. G20 countries should support LDCs by creating meaningful technical assistance programs intended to facilitate some level of usage of a multilateral information-reporting architecture through IT support, training, and policy advice.[7] The OECD/United Nations joint Tax Inspectors Without Borders program—officially launched in July 2015—could eventually provide a useful platform from which the developed economies could make this significant investment.

[7] The IMF, OECD, United Nations, and the World Bank all recommend that G20 countries act in concert with or on behalf of developing countries in parallel to their own actions to address offshore tax evasion. Separately, the Global Forum has repeatedly affirmed its commitment to serve as a platform to facilitate the coordination of technical assistance with respect to information exchange.

Finally, developed jurisdictions and asset management centers will not readily send information to a country that cannot ensure that exchanged information will not be misused or left unprotected from misuse. Thankfully, the extant Global Forum peer review process regarding the protection of taxpayer information, as well as associated technical assistance, is helping to bring many developing countries up to international standards. Countries that fail the Global Forum's standards for preventing misuse of information should continue to receive technical assistance to meet the standards. However, civil society advocates of automatic information exchange should recognize that if information obtained through a multilateral system were misused to facilitate extortion or kidnapping, it could destroy the system despite widespread benefits. Thus, the entire global community should firmly commit to the idea that for countries without adequate protections against misuse of information, unfettered access to automatic information exchange is inappropriate.

1.3.5 Privacy Concerns and their Limits

A few commentators extrapolate from the specter of possible misuse of information to argue from a human rights perspective that governments should not cooperate to collect tax on offshore accounts. They argue that bank secrecy vis-à-vis tax administrations is part and parcel of a basic right to privacy. However, if one believed that privacy extends to keeping bank information hidden from the government of the country in which a taxpayer resides, then one would have to conclude that the basic information reporting/ information availability architecture for collecting tax domestically in most major developed economies is unjust. To the contrary, long-standing legal and policy notions in every major developed economy suggest that tax administration access to resident taxpayer financial information is consistent with a taxpayer's reasonable expectations of privacy. Offshore bank secrecy advocates have thus lost the moral and legal argument domestically in almost every developed country.

Some bank secrecy advocates may claim that cross-border bank secrecy is different, and needs to be preserved because of the existence of authoritarian and corrupt regimes. This argument conflates the idea that the benefits of a multilateral information exchange system should not be extended to all governments with the proposition that any individual, regardless of whether they reside in a just or unjust, democratic or undemocratic, or morally legitimate or illegitimate state, should have the option to individually elect to securely evade their taxes. What the argument underscores is merely the need for safeguards to ensure that information made available for tax purposes is used only for taxing purposes. And given the existence of illegitimate states, some allowance for governments to decide that their financial institutions will not give information to certain other governments is both inevitable and appropriate.[8] These safeguards and prudential judgments must be balanced against the right of governments to enforce their law and raise revenue from elites evading tax—wherever they may bank—in order to fairly distribute the cost of government. Effectuating that balance through an international regime will be the greatest challenge in this area of international law in the coming decade.

1.3.6 Technical Architecture

The first task of the new international governance structure is to endorse and formalize the technical features of a multilateral AIE system. The key technical features of a multilateral AIE system on which international agreement is required are (1) what information financial institutions are required to report cross-border (reporting), (2) how information travels from financial institutions to the government where a taxpayer resides (routing), (3) which financial institutions are included in the system (scope), and (4) how the system identifies taxpayers and their country of residence (identification). The incentives to ensure that countries and financial institutions join the system and that safeguards against misuse of information are abided by also have technical dimensions that must be addressed. The CRS has created a strong foundation to answer these questions, but a standard-setting body of the sort described in section 1.3.1 of this essay is still advisable to make sure the international consensus on these issues addresses emerging country concerns, and a monitoring body is needed to evaluate whether an agreed consensus is put into action.

As suggested above, the FATCA negotiations between the United States and the G5, and the subsequent process of developing the CRS, produced tenable proposed solutions for most of the key technical issues raised by automatic information exchange. The CRS generally adopts FATCA's reporting rules and scope (importantly treating hedge funds, private equity funds, and certain insurance products as financial institutions in addition to traditional banks). It

[8] Advocating for a system of automatic information exchange does not imply that every country must provide information to every other country. For example, the United States is very unlikely to require its financial institutions to provide information about Iranians' or Venezuelans' financial deposits in the United States to the governments of those countries so long as their present regimes remain in power, nor, in the view of this author, should it do otherwise. Like the United States, other governments will make the decision to deny another specific sovereign information regarding its residents based on a conclusion that the receiving sovereign is illegitimate, fundamentally unjust, or an enemy of their state. That result is unavoidable. But saying sovereigns should and will retain the capacity to deny information to certain jurisdictions is very different from saying that the wealthy and sophisticated should be able to individually elect to evade paying tax to their state of residence simply by taking their wealth offshore.

largely bows to commercial reality to address identification problems by relying on information already in a financial institution's possession through anti-money laundering and know-your-customer (AML/KYC) rules for existing accounts, while tightening identification processes with respect to new accounts. It also provides for direct government-to-government routing of information initially gathered by local financial institutions in a manner modeled on the system piloted by the European Union in its Savings Directive.[9]

The necessity of complying with FATCA in order to avoid FATCA withholding has already prompted financial institutions, accounting firms, and other relevant private actors to massively mobilize to implement a similar technical architecture for automatic information exchange embodied in the United States' bilateral FATCA IGAs. However, even faster progress would be possible if all of the leading governmental actors cooperated more extensively. Moreover, achieving the uniform compliance architecture that provides the greatest prospect of providing benefits to developing and emerging economies will eventually require the United States to bring FATCA further into convergence with the CRS.

The CRS has already addressed many of the questions associated with how FATCA-style rules must differ from US FATCA rules if a multilateral automatic information exchange system is to function. For example, the first and most obvious distinction between the CRS and FATCA is that the CRS focuses on residence rather than citizenship in identifying beneficial owners, since outside the United States no major country taxes its citizens worldwide on a citizenship basis. Compliance exceptions from FATCA for "local FFIs"—very generally, institutions based in one country that do not have US citizen account-holders—are appropriately abandoned, as they should be in the context of a multilateral system. In a system that reports on all offshore accounts and forms an important part of the basis for tax information reporting in every country, carve-outs based on small numbers of non-resident account-holders become nonsensical. Other issues remain to be addressed. For example, one emerging trend that may be particularly damaging for emerging countries involves certain jurisdictions in effect selling "alternative" residency certificates to wealthy tax evaders; such certificates may facilitate avoiding reporting under the CRS. The operation of exceptions in the short- to medium-term for local financial institutions in less developed

[9] The EUSD is an early example of a program implementing automatic exchange of bank information. The directive, which became effective in 2005, requires financial institutions in a specific subset of jurisdictions to report information on certain interest income, and only interest income, paid to EU residents who reside in a jurisdiction other than the one in which the financial institution is located. The financial institutions report the information to the tax administration where the financial institution is resident, and the relevant information is then routed to the tax administration of the state in which the account holder is resident.

countries, where as of now neither the financial institutions nor the tax administration has the technical sophistication to participate fully in AIE, also needs to be further developed if these jurisdictions are to be encouraged to participate in the CRS. These are just two examples of the many technical issues that remain to be resolved, in particular in considering how emerging and developing countries should interact with a multilateral AIE system. Further guidance under the CRS should address these questions in collaboration with the Coordinating Body of the Multilateral Convention and the Global Forum.

1.4 CONCLUSION

In just a few short years, the world has gone from assuming that financial institutions generally do not support residence country taxation cross-border to arguing about how they should act as tax agents for residence countries. This is a remarkable shift in international norms.

Nevertheless, a great deal is at stake in the choices that remain to be made regarding the details of implementation of FATCA and the CRS in the developing world context. If the international community successfully converts FATCA into a uniform, implemented multilateral system, it has the potential to substantially improve the ability of countries around the world to tax portfolio income from capital and much domestic business income. However, the tendency for institutional structures in this area to become embedded suggests that decisions made in the next few years by a small number of powerful actors could dictate sub-optimal outcomes for both those actors and the rest of the world for a prolonged period.

Emerging-economy governments and other stakeholders, including civil society, have many reasons beyond sheer revenue to weigh in on the choices being made in the context of the CRS and FATCA implementation by the major actors in this evolutionary moment. Automatic information reporting could help sustain tax morale in a financially integrated world. Information reporting could also allow capital income taxation to play an expressive role in building liberal democracies that are accepted as legitimate by their people, and encourage taxpayers to engage with the polity and demand government accountability.

A multilateral automatic information exchange system that provides benefits to the tax administrations of developing, emerging, and developed economies alike will require both an efficacious institutional architecture and a standardized technical architecture. With international financial law as the model, and the G20 as an agenda setter, the institutional architecture for such a system is within reach. Emerging and developing country governments should make their voices heard—alongside interested developed economy governments, civil society, and financial institutions concerned about duplicative compliance costs—to encourage the emergence of the requisite institutional architecture. The most socially meaningful ongoing task of the new international governance structure in AIE is to endorse, implement, and refine the technical features of a uniform multilateral system the details of which take the interests and concerns of emerging and developing countries into account.

As Thomas Pogge and Krishen Mehta rightly point out in the introduction to this volume, the first-line responsibility for poverty-related human rights deficits lies with the governments of the countries in which severe, truly abject poverty persists. But these countries need policy tools to address this dire problem. Moreover, the underlying policy reasons for taxing capital income at the individual level may be distinct and particularly compelling in smaller developing countries (Grinberg, 2013). Especially for governments and practitioners who, like me, believe that many of the substantive international tax policy proposals described in later chapters of this volume could be counterproductive to growth and prosperity in the developing world, creating an international tax environment where the decision as to whether and how to tax capital income at the individual level is returned to developing countries should garner strong support.

REFERENCES

Bates, Robert H. and Da-Hsiang Donald Lien, 1985. "A Note on Taxation, Development, and Representative Government," *Policy and Society* 14: 53.

Bennett, Mary C., 2013. Letter to Achim Pross, Head of Division, International Co-operation and Tax Administration Division, Organization for International Co-operation and Development. http://www.theagc.com/2013-07-26%20AGC%20letter%20to%20OECD%20on%20TRACE.pdf, accessed 15 July 2015.

Bird, Richard M. and Eric M. Zolt, 2005. "Redistribution via Taxation: The Limited Role of the Personal Income Tax in Developing Countries," *UCLA Law Review* 52: 1627.

Brummer, Chris, 2012. *Soft Law and the Global Financial System: Rule Making in the 21st Century*. Cambridge: Cambridge University Press.

Cavanaugh, Maureen B., 2003. "Democracy, Equality, and Taxes," *Alabama Law Review* 54: 415.

Ferguson, Niall, 2002. *The Cash Nexus: Money and Politics in Modern History, 1700–2000*. London: Penguin.

Franco, Oscar, 2010. "The Use of Technology: Information Systems and Databases," *CIAT Thematic Tax Series* 5: 94.

G20 Finance Ministers, 2013. "Communiqué, Meeting of Finance Ministers and Central Bank Governors." http://www.google.com/url?sa=t&rct=j&q=&esrc=s&source=web&cd=2&ved=0CCQQFjABahUKEwjH0aOC8_3GAhXGiw0KHdSyAE4&url=http%3A%2F%2Fen.g20russia.ru%2Fload%2F781659263&ei=LH-3VceLL8aXNt-TlgvAE&usg=AFQjCNFHHwDi-rzsKAAru3h_wuYXXKpLxg, accessed 28 July 2015.

G20 Leaders, 2009. "Declaration on Strengthening the Financial System." http://www.g20.utoronto.ca/2009/2009ifi.pdf, accessed 15 July 2015.

G20 Leaders, 2013. "G20 Leaders' Declaration." https://g20.org/wp-content/uploads/2014/12/Saint_Petersburg_Declaration_ENG_0.pdf, accessed 6 August 2015.

Global Forum on Transparency and Exchange of Information for Tax Purposes, 2014. "Automatic Exchange of Information: A Roadmap for Developing Country Participation, Final Report to the G20 Development Working Group." http://www.oecd.org/tax/transparency/global-forum-AEOI-roadmap-for-developing-countries.pdf, accessed 6 August 2015.

Grinberg, Itai, 2013. "Taxing Capital Income in Emerging Countries: Will FATCA Open the Door?" *World Tax Journal* 5: 342–44.

Grinberg, Itai, 2012. "The Battle Over Taxing Offshore Accounts," *UCLA Law Review* 60: 304.

Hathaway, Oona and Scott Shapiro, 2011. "Outcasting: Enforcement in Domestic and International Law," *Yale Law Journal* 12: 252.

Lawson, Keith, 2013. Letter to Robert Stack, Deputy Assistant Secretary (International Tax Affairs), United States Department of the Treasury. http://www.ici.org/pdf/27379.pdf, accessed 15 July 2015.

Levi, Margaret, 1988. *Of Rule and Revenue*. Berkeley and Los Angeles: University of California Press.

Levin, Carl, 2010. "United States Congressional Record, 18 March," daily edition. United States Government Printing Office.

Moore, Mick, 2007. "How Does Taxation Affect the Quality of Governance?" *Institute of Development Studies, Working Paper No. 280.*

Organization for Economic Cooperation and Development, 2011. "Tax and Development Programme: Work Plan 2011/12." http://www.oecd.org/ctp/tax-global/48438767.pdf, accessed 15 July 2015.

Polayes, Faye M., 2011. Letter to Manal Corwin, International Tax Counsel, United States Department of the Treasury. http://www.bsmlegal.com/pdfs/fatca_hsbc.pdf, accessed 28 July 2015.

Prichard, Wilson, 2010. "Taxation and State Building: Towards a Governance Focused Tax Reform Agenda," *Institute of Development Studies, Working Paper No. 341.*

Scheve, Kenneth M. and Matthew J. Slaughter, 2007. "A New Deal for Globalization," *Foreign Affairs* 86: 34.

The Boston Consulting Group, 2013. "Global Wealth 2013: Maintaining Momentum in a Complex World," *The Boston Consulting Group*. May. https://www.bcgperspectives.com/Images/Maintaining_Momentum_Complex_World_May_2013_tcm80-135355.pdf, accessed 28 July 2015.

Further reading

Backhaus, Michael and Angelika Hellemann, 2011. "Sigmar Gabriel: 'Und wir sollten die Bürger darüber abstimmen lassen,' Teil 2 [Sigmar Gabriel: 'And We Should Let the Citizens Vote on It,' Part 2]," Bild. http://www.bild.de/politik/inland/sigmar-gabriel/wir-muessen-die-eu-reformieren-die-buerger-abstimmen-lassen-teil-2-20134564.bild.html, accessed 28 July 2015.

Der Spiegel. "Liechtenstein Tax Evasion Scandal: Informant in Investigation 'Fears' for His Life," Spiegel Online International, 3 March. http://www.spiegel.de/international/business/liechtenstein-tax-evasion-scandal-informant-in-german-investigation-fears-for-his-life-a-540283.html, accessed 28 July 2015.

2

Let's Tax Anonymous Wealth!

A Modest Proposal to Reduce Inequality, Attack Organized Crime, Aid Developing Countries, and Raise Badly Needed Revenue from the World's Wealthiest Tax Dodgers, Kleptocrats, and Felons

James S. Henry

Law? What do I care about the law? Ain't I got the power?

Cornelius Vanderbilt

2.1 INTRODUCTION

At the height of the First Gilded Age in the early 1900s, a conservative advisor to King Edward VII responded to His Majesty's concerns about supporting liberal political reform with the following brief apology: "Yes, Sire, it is true, we have made changes. But we have made them at the *right time*. And the *right time* is, *when there is no other choice*!"

This essay makes a similar case for a potentially lucrative and distinctively equitable new global withholding tax on $trillions of anonymous private financial wealth that is now parked in the world's eighty-odd financial secrecy jurisdictions.

As we'll see, most of this wealth, secreted by way of an opaque network of shell companies, trusts, foundations, and nominee owners, belongs to at most the *top 0.1 percent* of people on the planet. Much of it is derived from tax dodging, kleptocracy, money laundering, bribery, and other criminal enterprises. It has been carefully recruited, hidden away, and tenderly cared for by the mercenary army of more than 200,000 well-paid professionals—private bankers, asset managers, accountants, lawyers, trustees, hedge fund managers, high-end real estate brokers, and corporate registrars—that constitutes *the global haven industry.*

As a result of this highly efficient industry's diligent efforts on behalf of its worthy clientele, all this anonymous loot is simply not paying its fair share of the essential costs of government, especially in developing countries. At a time of soaring global wealth inequality, tolerating such behavior is simply unacceptable.

Our proposed new transnational Anonymous Wealth Tax ("AWT," pronounced "ought") would be levied at a modest 0.5 percent annual rate. If implemented carefully by a determined coalition of rich countries and key developing countries, even this modest rate could generate tens of $billions per year of badly needed revenue—either directly, or by providing an incentive for anonymous wealth to return to the surface and come back home, where it can be invested and taxed by local authorities.

Nor would any new revenue generated by the AWT simply disappear into the boundless ocean of generic government spending. Under our plan, reflecting the truly global origins of anonymous wealth, any incremental revenue would be dedicated to the global community's most pressing needs—helping poor countries to pay for the costs of adapting to climate change; recover from "natural" disasters; manage epidemics; supply clean water and safe food; and backstop the First World's shrinking foreign aid budget. A new international trust fund would be created to channel AWT revenue to critical projects and keep them free from corruption.

It is also important to note that AWT is not intended to be a substitute for other badly needed reforms to the international tax and financial systems. Since 2012, the OECD and the G20 have been working on a series of such reforms that are designed to increase transparency and reduce tax dodging.

These include (1) the automatic exchange of information on cross-border income and assets among tax authorities; (2) public registration of the true beneficial owners of companies and trusts; (3) country-by-country reporting of corporate profits, assets, sales, employment, and business units; (4) tougher anti-money laundering regulations; (5) apportioning corporate tax revenues according to the location of real economic activities rather than of artificial haven-based shell companies; (6) tougher regulation of cross-border private banking, money laundering, and financial secrecy jurisdictions; and (7) curbing the tax incentives that individual and corporate investors now have to become "citizens of nowhere" for tax purposes.

These are all worthy structural reforms. But most of these reforms have been on the table *since at least the 1970s.*[1] They may take a long time to be

[1] For example, an explicit demand for "country-by-country reporting" on financial results and offshore entities by multinational companies was reportedly first proposed by US consumer advocate Ralph Nader in 1977. See Nader, Green, and Seligman (1977: 173–6):

implemented, and even longer to pay off. This is partly because they have to be implemented by dozens of countries, including many that cannot even make effective use of enforcement data they already have.

It is also because such structural reforms inevitably kick up stiff resistance from the global haven industry, especially the banks and secrecy jurisdictions that earn a handsome living by helping the world's less deserving rich to become even richer and less deserving.

In short: if the global tax justice movement limits itself to pursuing such OECD/G20 –type structural reforms, it may well be many years before they generate any significant additional revenue. But developing countries, in particular, don't have that kind of time. While we wait for the structural reforms to pay off, a modest collective AWT would help to insure that the world's wealthiest citizens, leading MNCs, and its most avaricious kleptocrats and criminals at least contribute *something* toward the unavoidable costs of preserving the planet.

Of course all such global tax schemes, including carbon taxes, transportation taxes, financial transactions tax (FTT), and our own AWT, are highly imperfect. But so are *all the other* available alternatives for financing development and climate adaptation. By now we have tried them all—debt, foreign aid, charity, the privatization of state assets, public–private ventures, and inflationary finance. The real issue is, "Compared to what?" I will argue here that the AWT would be *comparatively* easy to implement and to sell politically.

Perhaps the best argument, however, is that we simply have to *try something soon,* because we are running out of time to tackle the dire problems noted above. To face up to our responsibility, we can no longer afford *not* to experiment with creative new global finance solutions. In the words of Edward VII's advisor, "*There is no other choice.*"

The arguments for this proposal will be developed in more detail below. To help us assess its merits, however, it will be helpful to step back and understand the roots of the problems that it is meant to address. The tale is complicated, with many twists and turns, and quite a few puzzles that remain

> "Consolidated" financial statements should represent the full operations of the firm instead of, as at present, often only partial segments, with subsidiary or affiliated corporations reporting as separate corporations. In multinational firms, statements should be broken down on a "U.S." and "all foreign" basis, in addition, there should be foreign financial reports furnished on a country-by-country basis.

This proposal actually had earlier roots in work by the UN's international group of account experts ("GEISAR"), convened in 1976. See Matti Ylonen (2015, in press). From 2002 on, the proposal was rediscovered and elaborated on by other authors, including the British chartered accountant Richard Murphy. (Automatic information exchange among tax authorities was enabled by Article 6 of the 1988 OECD/Council of Europe "Multinational Convention on Mutual Administrative Assistance in Tax Matters," and a significant expansion of this system was proposed by the noted US tax attorney David E. Spencer in 1992. See Spencer (1992).

to be solved. As usual, however, some things may be said, even now.[2] And we feel obliged to say them.

2.2 GLOBALIZATION AND THE TAX JUSTICE MOVEMENT

Only a decade ago, the impact of the prevailing international system for taxing the world's richest citizens and MNCs was grossly under-estimated by all but a tiny band of tax justice advocates and fringe economists.

Since then, however, we have begun to understand that this system's influence on growth, investment, inequality, and overall economic and political development is truly pervasive—and that the current system is *riddled* with inefficiency and injustice.

As former US Treasury Secretary William Simon once put it, "It would be really nice to have a tax system that looked as if someone had actually designed it *on purpose*." However, constructing an international tax system that makes sense for rich and poor alike is no simple matter. And recent experience has clearly demonstrated that this task cannot simply be left to up to *the multilateral establishment*—institutions like the OECD, the IMF, and the World Bank, First World governments like the United States and the United Kingdom, and the handful of larger developing economies that are G20 members. Nor can it be left up to the many other much less well-organized developing countries, most of which believe—quite correctly—that, on their own, they have little choice but to go along with the powers that be.

To address the need for fundamental reform, in the last decade a new *global grass-roots movement for tax justice* has taken root in dozens of countries. Naturally tax justice activists like me would like to take all the credit for it. But in fact the real driver has been the hasty, rather *devil-may-care* character of the world's most recent experiment with globalization, the numerous short-term crises and systemic pathologies that this experiment has produced, and the multilateral establishment's abject incompetence at handling these crises.

2.2.1 Corporate Globalization

In the long run, the complex market-based economic system that we usually refer to as "capitalism" may or may not turn out to have been an essential engine of growth and innovation on the one hand, and an intrinsic source of

[2] After J. K. Galbraith, The Great Crash 1929. (1955, 2009).

instability and conflict on the other. After centuries of debate, the jury is still out.

But by now it should be clear to everyone that *our own particular version of capitalism* still leaves much to be desired.

It remains prone to all sorts of nasty shocks and surprises, including acute financial crises, extreme inequality and economic injustice, environmental calamities, and the proliferation of financial crimes. For want of a better term, we might call this actual system "*crapitalism*," reflecting its recurrent tendency to soil itself and then toss the consequences out onto the commons for the rest of us to clean up.

Ever since capitalism's earliest days, on the other hand, some of its most fervent advocates have been infatuated with a rather more utopian vision. This is the u-topia ("no where" in Greek) of an anything-goes, laissez-faire economy, supposedly a kind of beautiful autonomous self-winding clock, once liberated from all ham-handed state intervention.

Of course by now we have accumulated abundant real-world experience with the original concept of "central planning" that was briefly adopted by numerous self-described "socialist" regimes in the twentieth century. While a form of central planning (with artificial transfer prices) is surprisingly common within giant multi-divisional corporations like GE and GM, most observers outside Zimbabwe and North Korea have long since concluded that on an economy-wide scale, there are serious limits to that system's practical ability to deliver material goods as well as political and economic freedom.

By comparison, the so-called "free-market" vision continues to exert profound influence on our imagination, and on economic policy. This is not only because of the elite interests that it serves, but also because on an economy-wide level, except in a handful of very poor countries, it has never really been tried—its actual incarnation on this Earth seems to lie perpetually just around the corner.[3] Indeed, this may be its greatest virtue.

It may be possible, however, for us to glean something about the pragmatics of the "free market" vision by examining recent "neoliberal" experiments with implementing bits and pieces of it. These experiments had deep intellectual roots in nineteenth-century laissez-faire economics, roots that never died out completely even in the depths of the Great Depression and the peak years of Keynesian welfare statism during the 1950s and 1960s. But the neoliberal counter-revolution really took off during the 1970s and early 1980s in just a handful of market economies, especially the United States, the United Kingdom, and satellite laboratories like Chile.

[3] We have several approximations of real-world stateless "free market economies" in certain crisis-ridden developing countries, such as Haiti and Somalia. But these are subject to too many other exceptional conditions to be able to regard them as test cases.

Since the early 1990s, this neoliberal experiment has acquired global influence. The result was a brave new era of corporate globalization, especially after the demise of the Soviet Union. During this period, the worldwide mobility of capital, labor, technology, energy, information, and trade in products and services has increased dramatically. Government barriers to cross-border trade and investment have been slashed. There has been a dramatic increase in competition among countries, states, provinces, and localities with respect to tax rates and other forms of regulation. Furthermore, all of these deregulatory trends in market structure have been reinforced by big power realignments and the impact of pervasive new global technologies like computing, the Internet, and mobile telephony.

This was not the world's first wave of globalization; there were earlier ones in the seventeenth and nineteenth centuries. But it has been by far the most far-reaching. The world's first two waves of globalization were spearheaded by rising nation states and empires. The most recent wave has been heavily influenced, if not quite orchestrated, by private interests, especially MNCs, big banks, and the world's largest accounting firms and law firms. They have been supported in these efforts by numerous civil-society true believers in the neoliberal paradigm—not only fund-seeking politicians, but also think-tanksters, neoliberal journalists, academics, religious leaders, and senior government regulators, many of which had either arrived through the revolving door or intended to use it on their way back to lucrative positions in the private sector.[4] For surprisingly modest sums, these civil society interests were available to provide a thin veneer of respectability to what C. Wright Mills might have called the "higher immorality" of the neoliberal agenda. From the early 1990s right up until the 2008 financial crisis, the result was an absolute torrent of triumphalist rhetorical neoliberal nonsense about "deregulation," "the Third Way," "the end of ideology," "Celtic Tigers," and the limitless potential of unbridled free-range capitalism.

[4] Influential neoliberals in US politics during the 1990s included President Bill Clinton and US Vice President Al Gore (1993–2001), US Republican Senator Phil Gramm, Chair of the US Senate Banking, Housing, and Urban Affairs Committee (1999–2001), and Rep. Newt Gingerich, Speaker of the US House of Representatives (1995–9). Key neoliberal think tanks in the 1990s included The Institute for International Economics, the Institute for International Finance, the Center for Strategic and International Studies, the American Enterprise Institute, CATO, and, only slightly to the left, the Brookings Institution. Key neoliberal journalists in the 1990s included Thomas Friedman, *New York Times* editorial writer, Robert Barnett, editor of the *Wall Street Journal*, and George Will, ABC News. Among the key neoliberals in academia during the 1990s and early 2000s were Prof. Francis Fukuyama (Johns Hopkins); Prof Glenn Hubbard (Columbia U); Prof Lawrence Summers (Harvard), who also served as US Treasury Secretary; and Prof. Michael Porter (Harvard Business School.) Key neoliberal regulatory advocates in the 1990s and early 2000s included US Treasury Secretary Robert Rubin; US Federal Reserve Chairman Alan Greenspan; NY Federal Reserve head and future US Treasury Secretary Timothy Geithner.

2.2.2 The Neoliberal Consensus

Consistent with this, in the early 1990s, leading political parties and business interests in most OECD countries, joined by multilateral institutions like the OECD, the IMF, and the World Bank, converged on a neoliberal policy agenda that came to be known as "the Washington Consensus." Actually the agenda had stronger intellectual ties to institutions like the University of Chicago, Harvard, LSE, and Catholic University in Santiago than to Washington DC. Up close, the "consensus" also turned out to be a dog's breakfast of contradictory "reform" policies. For example, it supported deregulating capital markets—unless and until it came to challenging the interests and prerogatives of large, increasingly global incumbent banks, or, say, the rampant insider deal-doing engaged in by Russia's new oligarchy. The "consensus" supported eliminating trade barriers and monopoly positions—except for drug companies, corporate farmers, software companies, and giant international brands. It favored the privatization of state assets—except for lousy foreign bank loans, many of which were either nationalized outright or "Brady-fied" by government-backed private bonds,[5] and except for important state-owned companies that were dominated by local elites, like Codelco in Chile.[6] As Auden says, "When there was peace, he was for peace. When there was war he went."

2.2.2.1 Tax Competition and Secrecy Jurisdictions

For our purposes here, with respect to tax justice, the single most important contribution of the neoliberal consensus was its implicit endorsement of "tax competition." This is the (peculiar) notion that in order to attract investment and talent, nation states—and indeed all other levels of government—ought to compete aggressively with each other with respect to tax rates, regulations, and government standards—rather than, say, use their *unique powers* to *collaborate* among themselves on such matters without violating antitrust laws.[7]

[5] This is a reference to US Secretary of the Treasury Nicholas F. Brady (1988–93), who promoted a plan to swap developing country loans for new country bonds backed in part by US Treasury securities. This helped leading First World banks, but not necessarily the countries, to quickly put the "Third World debt crisis" of the 1980s and early 1990s behind them, and turn their full attention to First World deregulation and securitization.

[6] For example, the case of the Suharto family's control over state-run banks in Indonesia, one World Bank field auditor discovered accounted for about a third of the country's entire loan portfolio in the late 1990s. According to my source, the Bank decided that restructuring that portion of the portfolio was off limits. "World Bank Auditor," interview with the author, June 2007.

[7] For example, unique, given the anti-trust laws that pertain to cooperation among private enterprises.

A direct corollary of tax competition was the tacit support for the proliferation of so-called "offshore financial centers" ("OFCs," in IMF jargon)—otherwise more commonly known as "tax havens," "treasure islands," or "secrecy jurisdictions." As discussed later, from the late 1960s on, the number of these sovereign bolt-holes rose dramatically. By June 2000 their behavior had become so flagrant that even the OECD had temporarily blacklisted thirty-five of them as tax havens. More than a dozen countries followed suit, adopting "national blacklists" that penalized domestic investors for doing business or booking taxable revenue in such places.[8]

But this soon produced a firestorm of protest from the global haven industry and its apologists in civil society.[9] Under fierce attack from the US Treasury, in particular, by 2005 the OECD had retreated to describing just a handful of unimportant havens as "uncooperative"—Andorra, Liberia, Liechtenstein, the Marshall Islands, and Monaco. All the others had suddenly become "participating partners." By 2009 the OECD had dropped out of the haven blacklisting business completely, placing every single jurisdiction on a toothless white list. The laborious, thankless, but essential job of assessing the behavior of individual "secrecy jurisdictions" rigorously was turned over to NGOs like Tax Justice Network.[10]

Meanwhile, the multilateral establishment's basic support for the *overall global haven industry* has continued to be unbroken right through the 2008 financial crisis and beyond—notwithstanding occasional fits of critical rhetoric from G8 and G20 leaders about "bank secrecy" and "tax havens,"[11] plus the agonizingly slow structural reform efforts that were noted above.

For example, one searches the literature in vain for any serious empirical work or critical assessments of the haven industry by the IMF, the World Bank, or any regional development banks. Instead, the cadres of unreconstructed neoliberal economists employed by these institutions actually welcomed the offshore industry as a useful way of encouraging still more tax cutting and financial deregulation. As one former Deputy IMF Director explained to the author in 2013, when questioned about the paucity of in-depth IMF/World Bank research on these matters, "It's really pretty simple: More than 80 of our members are tax havens."[12]

[8] See, for example, Jason Sharman and Gregory Rawlings (2005), "Deconstructing National Tax Blacklists."

[9] Sharman and Rawlings (2005), "Deconstructing National Tax Blacklists."

[10] See, for example, Tax Justice Network's "Financial Secrecy Index" (2009, 2011, 2013), a detailed assessment and ranking of more than eighty secrecy jurisdictions.

[11] See, for example, the strong denunciations of "bank secrecy" and "havens" at the April 2009 G-8 by British PM Gordon Brown and French President Nicholas Sarkozy (*The Guardian*, 2009; *The Telegraph*, 2009) included a clear blacklist for tax havens. Essentially this tough talk led to nothing; Sarkozy, of course, is a former tax haven lawyer whose clients included several extremely wealthy French investors.

[12] "Former IMF Deputy Director," interview with the author, May 2013.

2.2.2.2 Political Liberty

As for political liberty, in the early 1990s, during the brief hey-day of post-Berlin Wall triumphalism, at first the neoliberal consensus produced quite a bit of heady rhetoric about promoting "democracy" as well as "economic reform" around the world.[13] By the late 1990s, however, this meme had largely disappeared. Eventually this has set the stage for the erosion of elite enthusiasm about democracy at home as well—and rationalized the use of secrecy jurisdictions to conceal private wealth from public taxes.

Neoliberalism's initial passion for democratic reform in the early 1990s cooled for several reasons. First, Russia's experience with "democratic capitalism" soon turned out to be a kleptocratic nightmare. And the multilateral establishment was not just an innocent bystander. It was heavily involved in designing and financing Russia's entire post-Soviet restructuring, including one of the largest transfers and *reconcentrations* of state-owned wealth in the hands of a tiny private elite in world history.[14]

Second, after China's brutal Tiananmen crackdown in June 1989, the West proved to be quite willing to acquiesce in its faster-growing, not to say immensely more lucrative, if autocratic, form of state capitalism.[15]

Indeed, compared to Russia, there was even a preference on the part of Western neoliberals for China's combination of "free" markets, astute technocratic economic policy, and political authoritarianism. This was not a question of influence. If anything, back then, the multilateral establishment's influence in Russia was much greater. At the end of the day, naked economic interests proofed decisive. Chinese workers were simply available in much larger numbers, at a fraction of the cost of Russian workers. And China also offered a much larger potential market in the medium run.

So the brief post-Berlin Wall neoliberal flirtation with democracy quickly cooled. Since then the "democracy meme" has been wheeled out by the West mainly for very special occasions—periodic denunciations of Venezuela's populist regime, Cuba's tiny island dictatorship, Assad's brutal dictatorship in Syria, North Korea's dictatorship, and Putin's maneuvers in the Ukraine

[13] "Democracy" is rarely defined very precisely even by its best-funded official advocates—for example, the partially US-government-sponsored "National Endowment for Democracy," founded in 1983. Usually "democracy" is identified simply with voting—the holding of periodic, at least minimally representative and freely contested elections. By this definition, of course, Venezuela, Egypt, and Iran might argue that they are more "democratic" than some states in the US South.

[14] The story of profound re-concentration of wealth during the 1990s in Russia underscores the crucial role that political decisions have played in recent increases in global wealth inequality. To cite just one example from the Russian case: the rapid transfer of more than 350 "crown jewel" formerly state-owned companies in Russia to the private sector—about 20 key future oligarchs—for a grand total of $12.5 billion in 1994–6.

[15] The author happened to be in Tiananmen Square during May 1989, as a journalist writing for a magazine covering that year's Asian Development Bank meetings.

and Crimea in 2014–15. "Building democracy" also served as part of the official explanation for US military interventions in Nicaragua (1982–92), Granada (1983), Panama (1989–90), Afghanistan (2001–15), and Iraq (2003–11).[16] Elsewhere, however, the democratic sails have been trimmed to fit other priorities. Overall, it is very hard to predict neoliberal attitudes toward any given regime on the basis of whether it is run by elected leaders, dictators, kleptocrats, kings, one-party state bureaucrats, or religious clerics.

Indeed, some noted neoliberals have even joined in a series of recent, rather disturbing attempts by conservative economists to distinguish "democracy" and "political freedom" from "economic liberty," and to support the latter while distancing support from the former. In their view, "economic liberty" can be narrowly defined to include private property rights, personal security, and other market rights, even against the will of elected governments. This is a striking contrast to the 1989–92 pro-democratic rhetoric, as well as to the "small-r republican" philosophical tradition that sees political freedom and economic liberty as *empirically* joined at the hip.[17]

In any case, since the early 1990s, the multilateral establishment's neoliberal agenda has increasingly become an economic one. It focuses on the globalization of *corporate economic rights* like patent protection, the right to sue governments for compensation for regulations or the nationalization of private investment, and market entry rights, including the unfettered right to offer all kinds of financial services across borders. Conspicuously absent are global civil rights, political rights, labor rights, environmental rights, respect for tax justice, or any enforceable corporate *duties*—let alone the rights of other species.[18]

[16] In Iraq's case, this was especially true after the failure to find any WMDs or very many Al Qaeda members who had not arrived after the invasion. The pro-democracy rhetoric has continued to be invoked though the Iraqi governments established since 2003 have hardly been very "democratic," and even though one key by-product of the war may have been to entrench dictatorial regimes in neighboring countries like Saudi Arabia, Kuwait, Yemen, Syria, Egypt, and Iran. In Iraq's case, democracy rhetoric was only really deployed after the invasion, after the number of ISIL militants proved to have soared *in response*. Ironically, in Iraq's case, the pro-democracy by the US right through 2014, was clearly too illiberal.

[17] In liberal republicanism, "liberty" is defined to include freedom from private as well as public tyranny—for example, private monopolies. It also emphasizes the fact that, empirically, there are almost no historical cases where economic and political freedom have been able to survive apart for very long. This is quite distinct from the standard neoliberal/libertarian view of "liberty," which views it primarily as a negative defense against "government." This begs the question of where the arbitrary power of "government" leaves off and arbitrary "private" power begins. In feudal times, of course, all "government" power was in a sense "private" and a matter of contract. Similarly, libertarian theory also has no coherent view of why so-called voluntary slavery is wrong and should be prohibited. See the illuminating discussion of republican conceptions of freedom in Skinner (1998) and Pettit (2012).

[18] These new corporate rights, for example, included the right to sue governments for enacting environmental laws or trade restrictions, and to the resulting legal disputes mediated by the World Trade Organization and its appointees.

In the process, neoliberalism has appropriated, contorted, and debased the whole rich philosophical tradition and language of "rights." Whereas "rights" once stood for the defenses of private individuals and enterprises against arbitrary state power, they now stand mainly for the defense of the prerogatives of private corporate power against individuals and states—and the enforcement of corporate rights by captive states. So the polity has come full circle, and, indeed, returns to its feudal roots. Only the serfs pay taxes and do most of the fighting; the lords decide how to spend the taxes and who to make war on next. And this time around the lords and their wealth are safe behind virtual walls.

2.3 TAKING STOCK—THE PATHOLOGIES OF CORPORATE GLOBALIZATION

Two decades after this corporate neoliberal revolution began, we have weathered the Great Recession of 2008 and the painful recovery since then. This recovery has been agonizingly slow even in the United States, let alone Europe—the slowest on record since the 1930s. There have also been numerous local and regional financial crises, including Mexico (1995–6), Thailand (1997–9), Indonesia (1998), Russia (1998–9), Korea (1999), Brazil (1999), Argentina (2001–2), Cyprus (2013), and Greece (2015).

In light of this track record, many analysts now realize that the original corporatist version of globalization was oversold, to say the least. The main elements of the indictment of the corporate neoliberal form of globalization are clear.

First, apart from exceptions like China's "vast surplus labor/huge domestic market," and except for the very top of the world's wealth distribution, corporate neoliberal globalization has failed to deliver sustained higher income growth and prosperity for most people in most countries.

Second, the hasty financial deregulation of the 1990s and 2000s and the subsequent economic crisis, ultimately saddled many countries with monstrous public and private debts. In the first instance, deregulation, based on neoliberal naiveté about banker behavior, permitted the world's largest banks to take on much more leverage than they knew how to handle, in the pursuit of higher profits and record-setting levels of pay for their senior managers (see Figure 2.1). As we will see, to sustain their growth, leading banks—including all the top leaders in global private banking—engaged in massive amounts of financial crime, especially mortgage securities fraud.

When the game of musical chairs finally stopped in 2008, the resulting economic downturn and the bailouts of leading banks and corporations that followed led to soaring public deficits and unemployment, stagnant real

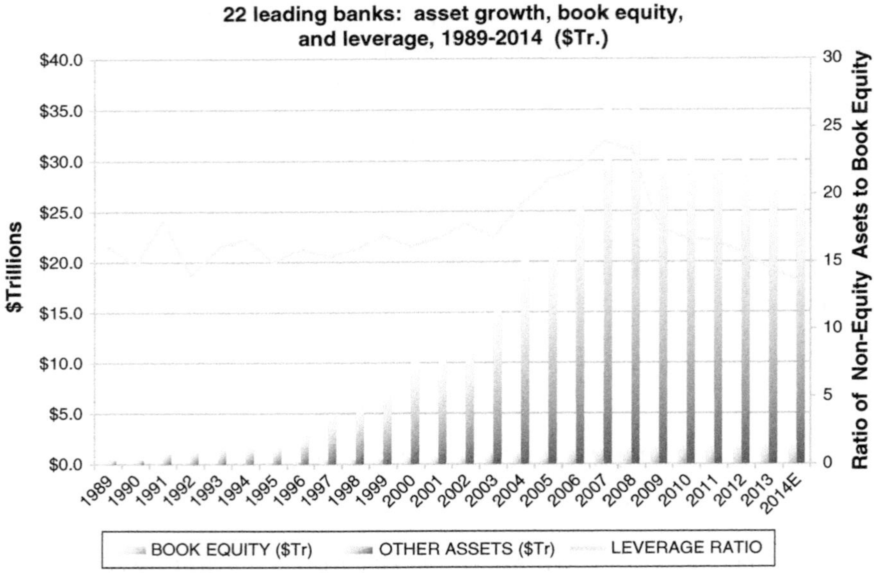

Figure 2.1 Roots of the 2008 global banking crisis

Source: SEC reports, financial data by bank, 1998–2014; author's database on fines and settlements; author's analysis

incomes for all but top wage-earners, under-funded public investment, and sharp increases in inequality. Given that global capital markets are now more integrated than ever before, government after government felt compelled to curtail spending and slash taxes on capital and high-income labor, even while bailing out big banks and corporations that were deemed "too big to fail or jail." The result has been severe cutbacks in fiscal stimulus, even in the midst of the recession—a bizarre repetition of the pre-Keynesian policies that prolonged the Great Depression.[19] Despite this austerity, especially in southern Europe, unemployment soared to record levels, and the public sectors of many countries remain close to bankruptcy even a half decade later, particularly after projections for long-term public sector obligations like pensions and health care are taken into account.

[19] Given the weakness of fiscal policy, to avoid an economic collapse, from 2008 through 2014 the US Federal Reserve loaned trillions to private capital markets at zero or even negative real interest rates. In the EU, delays in agreeing on looser monetary policies, combined with stiff tax competition and budget austerity, have delayed the recovery and made the costs of unemployment even higher. Overall, exclusive reliance on loose lending, reinforced by tax competition, has only exacerbated wealth inequality, since it is the wealthy who have benefitted most from the resulting stock market boom produced by cheap money.

Third, from the standpoint of tax justice, kleptocracy, and organized crime, corporate globalization has also led to the rise of a vast new grey zone of quasi-legal economic activity that is either completely off the books, entirely stateless, or resident only in secrecy jurisdictions where tax authorities and other regulators have trouble finding it. It has also produced an international tax system that is characterized by soaring tax competition, an *accelerating race to the bottom* and the new, highly efficient *global haven industry* (see section 2.3.2).

Of course the "underground economy" is a long-standing phenomenon that is present in every economy, including Vatican City. But historically it has consisted almost entirely of low-income, off-the-books activity by unorganized workers and small domestic business. The worrisome thing about the new grey-zone enabled by the global haven industry is that it concerns the economic elite. It has expanded rapidly with the help of a powerful network of allies in secrecy jurisdictions—including the more than eighty that are now official members of the OECD's Global Forum as well as of the IMF.[20]

The resulting alliance not only threatens rich countries with progressive tax systems and stronger regulation. It also threatens developing countries by undermining their abilities to tax, regulate, and control kleptocracy—and, indirectly, by undermining the ability of richer countries to afford to aid them. Furthermore, increased tax competition and globalized capital markets have made it much more painful to recover quickly from economic instability, shifting the costs of economic downturns to the middle class and the poor.

2.3.1 The Race to the Bottom

As noted, one key byproduct of globalized markets has been much fiercer tax and regulatory competition among countries (and companies) than ever

[20] For the 2011 "Financial Secrecy Index" list of the top 71 havens, most of which are not First World countries, see http://www.financialsecrecyindex.com/Archive2011/FSI-2011/FSI%20-%20Rankings%20-%202011.pdf. The 2013 FSI index provided evaluations of more than 80 jurisdictions http://www.financialsecrecyindex.com/introduction/fsi-2013-results. Compared with the early 1970s, when there were only about than 15 havens, many more are now official members of the IMF and OECD's Global Forum. They include sultry tropical paradises like Panama, Belize, the Bahamas, Aruba, Anguilla, Barbados, Bermuda, the Cayman Islands, and the British Virgin Islands. They also include stuffier European havens like Andorra, Jersey, the Isle of Man, Guernsey, Gibraltar, Liechtenstein, Malta, and Monaco. There are even more remote "treasure islands," like the Cook Islands, the Marshall Islands, Mauritius, Nauru, the Seychelles, and Vanuatu. But not all such secrecy jurisdictions are "offshore" and far away. Leading "onshore" secrecy jurisdictions include Switzerland, the City of London, Delaware, Nevada, Luxembourg, and the Netherlands, especially for corporate tax dodging.

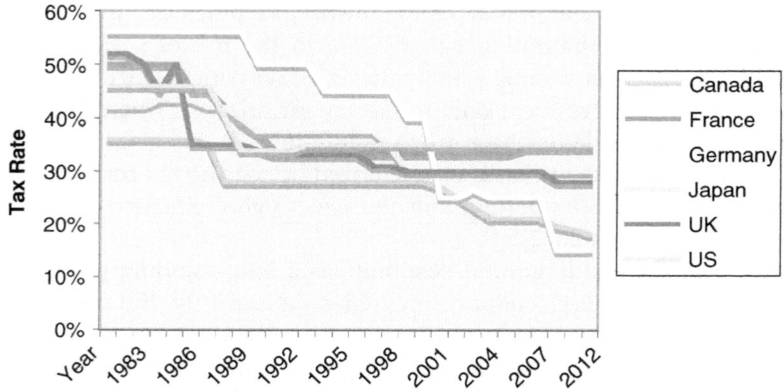

Figure 2.2 Top corporate income tax rates by country, 1981–2012
Source: Tax Policy Center (2013), author's analysis

before. On the corporate side, ever since the 1990s we have seen a dramatic expansion of abusive tax dodging, with many of the world's largest, most prominent companies using separate corporate shell entities in multiple countries to park profits and assets beyond the reach of tax authorities, slashing their tax bills to record lows.

As more and more countries have adopted this easily reproducible, beggar-thy-neighbor policy—a copycat tactic that is really not a sustainable "strategy" at all—the result has been race to the bottom. From the late 1980s on, average effective corporate tax rates across OECD and developing countries have fallen significantly. The share of total tax revenue raised by corporate income taxes, as well as the tax rates paid by top income recipients, have also declined in most countries (see Figures 2.2–2.4). Indeed, for many developing countries, potential investors can now expect to pay *negative* marginal tax rates on their investments because of all the special subsidies and tax holidays.

2.3.2 The Global Haven Industry

Globalization's other key longer-term pathology has been the rise of *the global haven industry.* As noted, this industry has made a fine art out of the dubious business of helping the world's wealthiest tycoons, kleptocrats, and organized criminals move their money offshore, invest it secretly and tax-free, conceal it from law enforcement and tax authorities as well as hostile business partners, and family members, and access it from anywhere on the planet.

This author first began to explore the curious relationship between global private banking and high-end tax dodging in the 1980s, after stumbling on the

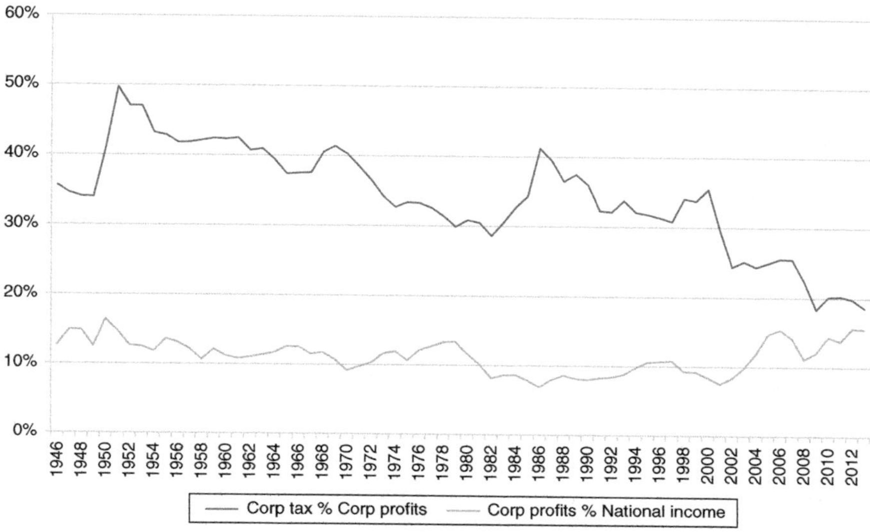

Figure 2.3 US corporate profits as a percentage of GDP vs US corporate taxes as a percentage of reported corporate profits 1946–2013

fact that leading so-called "lenders" to developing countries—Citigroup, Bank America, JP Morgan, UBS/SBC, Credit Suisse, and Deutsche Bank, among others—had quietly set up lucrative "international private banking" departments that were actually taking more money out of developing countries than their parent banks were lending to them (see Figure 2.5).

Of course "tax havens" and "secrecy jurisdictions" have existed for centuries. But the global haven industry's real takeoff has only occurred since the 1970s. At first it was fueled by petrodollars and loose lending to developing countries in the late 1970s and early 1980s, and, to a lesser extent, by the growth of the international underground economy, especially drug traffic. After the fall of the Soviet Union, the re-crapitalization of Russia, China, and Eastern Europe, and the fall of apartheid in South Africa, the haven industry's growth was propelled by huge net capital outflows from all these areas, as well as by the "Asian crisis" of 1998–9.

As discussed below, the sheer scale of these reverse outflows was such that by the late 1990s, leading developing countries like Argentina, Brazil, China, Mexico, Nigeria, the Philippines, Russia, and Venezuela had all become *net creditors* of rich countries like the United States, the United Kingdom, Switzerland, and Germany.

The key drivers behind the haven industry's growth were not only tax dodging but also organized crime and kleptocracy—the massive outright diversion of public assets and foreign loans by government officials.

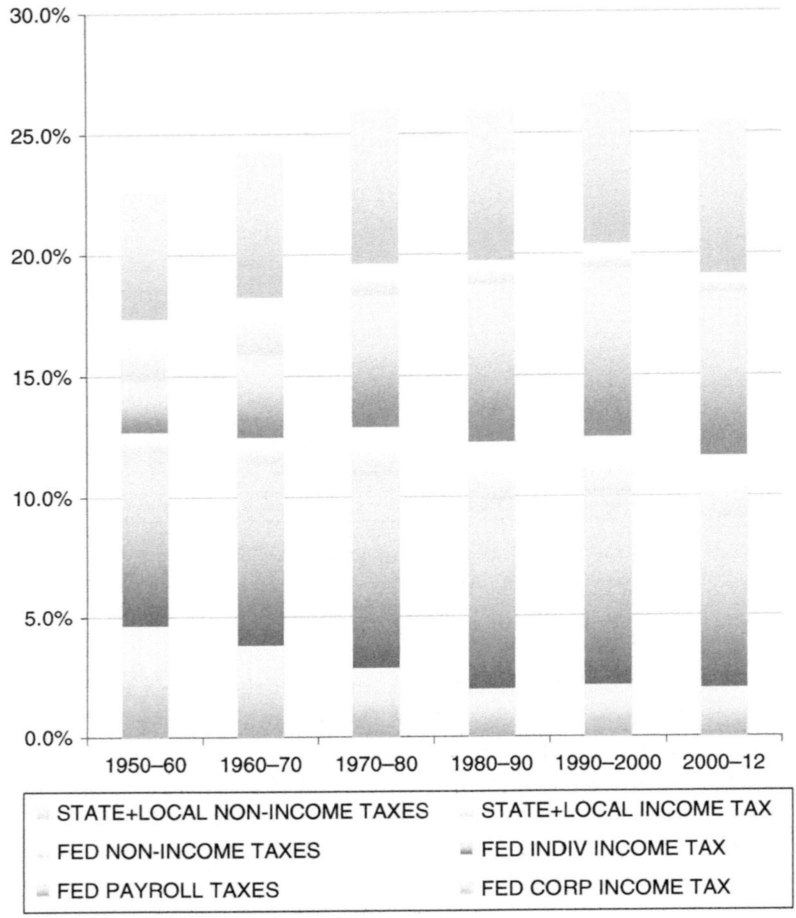

Figure 2.4 Total US tax receipts/GDP (%) period medians, 1950–2012
Source: US Bureau of Economic Analysis (2013) data, author's analysis

Indeed, ironically, this expansion took place even as marginal income tax rates on high-income earners were falling in most countries—alongside the cuts in corporate tax rates just noted above. To compete for human capital, the global haven industry encouraged countries to slash their tax rates on capital gains, stock options, executive compensation, and retirement accounts. Over time, this kind of upper-class tax reduction has shifted the costs of government services to the so-called "immobile factors"—middle-income taxpayers, labor, and the poor.[21] Far

[21] A striking example of tax regressivity is Brazil, where the top 10 percent of the population now pays a lower share of government costs than the bottom half.

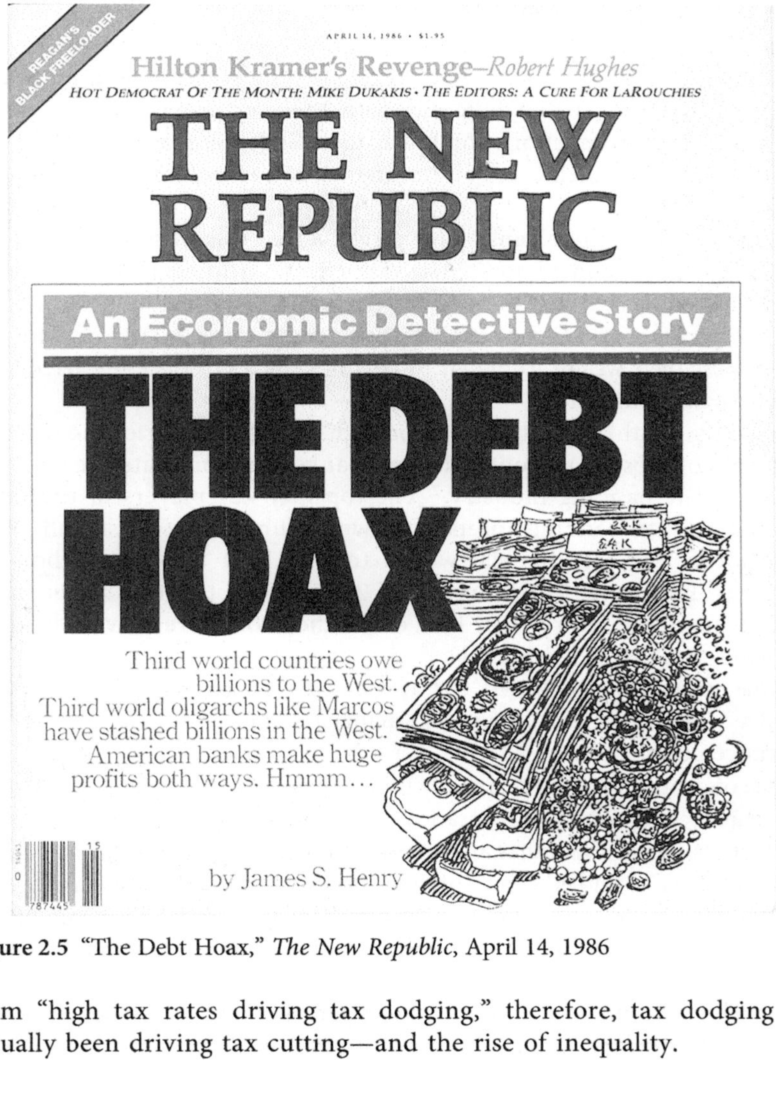

Figure 2.5 "The Debt Hoax," *The New Republic*, April 14, 1986

from "high tax rates driving tax dodging," therefore, tax dodging has actually been driving tax cutting—and the rise of inequality.

2.3.3 The Rise of Pirate Banking

The system architects and "network traffic controllers" for this rise of the global haven industry have been the world's largest private banks—giant brand-name institutions like HSBC, UBS, Credit Suisse, Citigroup, BankAmerica, RBS, Barclays, Lloyds, Standard Chartered, JPMorganChase, Wells Fargo, Santander, Credit Agricole, ING, Deutsche Bank, BNP Paribas, Morgan Stanley, and Goldman Sachs.

Most of these names will be familiar to anyone who knows the history of the 2008 financial crisis, or for that matter, the 1980s Third World debt crisis before it. As discussed below, these banks also accounted for a huge share of the bailouts that followed both these crises, as well as for the lion's share of prosecutions for mortgage fraud, tax fraud, money laundering, sanctions busting, illegal trading, and innumerable other financial crimes.

Since the 1970s, these banks have played a lead role in secretly recruiting wealthy investors and senior officials as clients, helping them move their wealth abroad secretly and invest it tax-free under the cover of offshore trusts and companies, providing portfolio management services, and also helping them access their wealth from afar by way of vehicles like back-to-back loans and pre-paid credit cards.

Not only are this handful of major high-income countries the ultimate recipients of most flight loot, but their banks also dominate the so-called "global pirate banking industry." The top fifty key players in the international private banking industry now account for at least half of all cross-border private financial wealth (e.g. at least $12–$14 trillion out of $24 trillion to $35 trillion, as of 2015). And the top *dozen banks alone* account for more than half of all these offshore private banking financial assets (see Table 2.1).[22] An even larger fraction of private offshore assets is accounted for if we expand the list to include the world's 100 largest banks, wealth managers, hedge funds, and private insurance companies.

The concentration of all this shady money in a comparative handful of blue-chip banks, hedge funds, insurance companies, and their affiliated asset managers is ironic. Of course these institutions will tell you that this simply reflects the quality and efficiency of their services. But the real reasons are even more basic. The offshore world abounds in *shady players*—no-name banks, bent lawyers, and fraudsters.[23] Furthermore, the evidence is that many wealthy offshore investors are surprisingly "risk averse" when it comes to managing their offshore wealth, which they tend to regard as a nest egg, to be relied on if their base businesses go bust. To be cautious, therefore, they tend to favor

[22] This data includes cross-border "assets under management" and non-managed cross border assets like deposits, custody assets, and assets managed by "pseudo-independent" asset managers who are formally outside these institutions.

[23] The 2008–09 multi-billion dollar frauds by Bernard L. Madoff and "Sir" R. Allen Stanford are just two recent examples. See, for example, *Business Insider* (2014), "5 Years Ago Bernie Madoff Was Sentenced to 150 Years in Prison—Here's How His Scheme Worked"; CNBC (2014) "Five Years After Stanford Scandal, Many Victims Penniless"; *The Telegraph*, (2012) "From King of the Caribbean to Penniless in Prison."

Table 2.1 Top 50 global private banks, 2005–10 (assets under management, $bn)

Rank 2005	Rank 2010		Jun-05	Mkt %	Dec-09	Mkt %	Dec-10	Mkt % / AAGR% 2005–10
		Top 10—Total	$2,272.8	42.2%	$3,660.8	45.5%	$5,551	
		Next 10—Total	$1,412.4	26.2%	$2,319.9	28.8%		
		Next 30—Total	$1,706.0	31.6%	$2,069.4	25.7%		
		Top 50—Total	$5,391.3	100%	$8,050.1	100%	$12,066.4	
1	1	UBS	$1,349.2		$1,627.6		$1,789.0	5.8%
2	2	Credit Suisse	$469.2		$770.1		$932.9	14.7%
6	3	Deutsche Bank	$180.9		$464.2		$367.5	15.2%
19	4	Bank America	$108.5		$433.8		$643.9	42.8%
8	5	Morgan Stanley/ SSB*	$165.0		$365.0		$297.0	12.5%
9	6	BNP Paribas	$158.0		$293.0		$338.0	16.4%
4	7	JPMorganChase	$187.0		$266.0		$284.0	8.7%
5	8	HSBC	$183.0		$250.0		$390.0	16.3%
11	9	Pictet	$150.0		$236.6		$270.0	12.5%
13	10	Barclays	$135.3		$230.0		$238.3	12.0%
7	11	Goldman Sachs	$166.0		$220.5		$840.0	38.3%
16	12	Credit Agricole	$114.1		$215.2		$171.0	8.4%
38	13	Commerzbank	$30.2		$207.1			
12	14	Bank Leumi	$138.0		$202.5		$251.0	12.7%
10	15	ABN Amro	$150.8		$199.1		$218.4	7.7%
24	16	Wells Fargo	$78.0		$187.3			
34	17	Banque Julius Baer	$46.8		$160.2		$181.0	31.1%
17	18	Northern Trust	$111.5		$141.5		$154.0	6.7%
18	19	Banco Santander	$111.4		$131.8			
14	20	Lombard Odier	$123.0		$130.1		$153.9	4.6%
27	21	Societe General	$66.3		$109.1		$112.5	11.1%
42	22	EFG Intl	$26.0		$93.3		$91.7	28.7%
31	23	LGT	$52.8		$91.2		$92.0	11.7%
33	24	BP Edmund de Rothchild	$47.1		$88.9		$99.1	16.0%
25	25	Bk of Montreal	$71.3		$87.7		$103.8	7.8%
30	26	ING Group	$56.8		$86.5			
23	27	Bk of New York	$82.6		$84.0		$166.0	15.0%
37	28	BSI Bank	$39.7		$82.8		$84.5	16.3%
29	29	UBP	$61.0		$82.4		$69.3	2.6%
22	30	KBC/KBL	$83.2		$69.0		$48.6	−10.2%
35	31	Raiffesen Banking Group	$46.4		$68.2			
32	32	TD Canada	$49.4		$65.0		$183.0	29.9%
36	33	RBS/Coutts	$41.3		$51.0		$44.7	1.6%
41	34	Bank Sarasin	$27.3		$46.4		$49.6	12.7%
40	35	MM Warburg	$27.4		$43.6		$48.2	12.0%
43	36	RBC	$22.2		$42.9			
3	37	Citigroup*	$293.7		$35.0			
45	38	Standard Chartered	$21.8		$30.8		$46.0	16.1%
46	39	Berenburg Bank	$19.1		$30.6		$34.1	12.2%
47	40	Lloyds TSB	$17.9		$30.1			

(*continued*)

Table 2.1 Continued

			Jun-05	Mkt %	Dec-09	Mkt %	Dec-10	Mkt %
39	41	SEB	**$28.3**		$26.2			
51	42	Vontobel AG	**$15.8**		$24.6		**$31.6**	14.9%
49	43	**Wegelin**	**$16.0**		$24.1			
50	44	**Luzerner Cantonal**	**$15.9**		$23.3		**$27.8**	11.9%
54	45	OCBC (Sing)	**$6.0**		$23.0		**$22.4**	30.1%
44	46	**Schroders**	**$22.0**		$22.9		**$25.1**	2.7%
48	47	**VP Bank**	**$16.1**		$18.5			
52	48	Bankhause Lampe	**$10.0**		$15.0		**$20.0**	14.8%
53	49	Reuscheul & Co	**$8.0**		$10.0			
55	50	DZ Privatebank	**$5.3**		$6.7			

Source: Banks' financial statements, private banking industry interviews, author's analysis

larger, more established financial institutions that can usually—not always—be counted on to safeguard their wealth even at long distances.[24]

Especially since numerous banking crises of the last two decades, most offshore investors also realize that they need to place their funds with institutions that are able to withstand the ups and downs of world economy—and in particular, with banks that are indeed "too big to fail." Indeed, during the 2008 financial crisis, the United States, the United Kingdom, and other governments effectively subsidized the global private banking industry by bailing out many of its largest players, including Citibank, BankAmerica, RBS, Lloyds, and UBS.

Together, these two factors help to explain the relatively high level of asset concentration in a handful of established pirate banks. An important corollary, examined in more detail below, is that the handful of key rich OECD countries where most of these giant banks hail from—the United States, the United Kingdom, Switzerland, France, Germany, the Netherlands, and Belgium—are actually the true *ultimate* havens, when it comes to where most of the capital flight from developing countries ends up.

This concentration of offshore wealth in a comparative handful of leading financial institutions, and a handful of rich countries, is of course rather embarrassing for the OECD, when it comes to the question of the role that its members play in global tax justice. But we'll see that we can also put these

[24] Of course beyond a certain level—say $50 to $100 million of net worth—ultra-high-net-worth investors may be able to afford to set up their own "family wealth" offices, diversify their wealth among multiple institutions, and even hire their own portfolio managers. There is some evidence that offering private banking services to the ultra-high-net-worth segment has become much more competitive.

embarrassing facts to good use, when it comes to developing this paper's proposal.

2.3.4 The Role of Treasure Islands

These leading financial institutions have also played a decisive role in the proliferation of offshore havens. As noted, by now the world is dotted with more than eighty "financial secrecy jurisdictions," compared with just a dozen or so in the early 1970s. In order of appearance, the ranks include sultry tropical paradises like Panama, the Bahamas, Anguilla, Aruba, Barbados, Belize, Bermuda, BVI, the Cayman Islands, St. Lucia, St. Kitts and St. Vincent. They also include much older traditional European havens, like Andorra, the Channel Islands, Cyprus, Gibraltar, the Isle of Man, Jersey, Guernsey, Liechtenstein, Malta, and Monaco. There are also many other newer, even more remote, havens, including the Cook Islands, Mauritius, the Marshall Islands, Nauru, the Seychelles, and Vanuatu.[25] For certain purposes, several reputable "onshore" secrecy jurisdictions like the City of London, Switzerland, Delaware, Nevada, Luxembourg, Dubai, Singapore, Malaysia, and Hong Kong have also become important members of the pack.

The basic role of such "treasure islands" is to rent their sovereignty to wealthy foreigners. They provide anonymity for their financial and corporate capital, intellectual property, and non-financial assets, helping to put their offshore private wealth beyond the reach of taxes, regulations, and law enforcement.

But most of this wealth is not actually invested in these treasure islands themselves. While most of the smaller so-called "conduit havens" do offer banking services, shell companies, trusts, and low-tax residency, they may also have tiny capital markets and loose financial regulations. They also may have regulators, police, and judges who are not quite as impervious to back-door influences as First World enforcers. So just as they distrust fly-by-night banks, offshore investors are also generally unwilling to trust such places with large amounts of their financial wealth. Like ordinary domestic investors, tax-dodgers, kleptocrats, and crime bosses all like to be able to count on reliable legal frameworks and the rule of law when it comes to protecting their investments. They also prefer to invest in places with liquid markets, access to top-flight investment managers, and financial and political stability.

Most of these attributes are only readily available in the world's most advanced capital markets. This helps to explain why most offshore wealth

[25] For the 2011 "Financial Secrecy Index" list of the top 71 havens, most of which are not First World countries, see Tax Justice Network (2011). The 2013 FSI index provided evaluations of more than 80 jurisdictions.

winds being routed by way of secrecy jurisdictions to the *penultimate havens*—First World financial centers like New York, London, Zurich, Geneva, Frankfurt, and to a lesser extent, Singapore, Hong Kong, and Dubai. It is these ultimate havens, and not the archipelago of offshore conduits or treasure islands, that is the final resting place for the vast bulk of so-called "offshore" private wealth.

Accordingly, to accommodate the world's wealthy, all of these ultimate havens have tailored their tax laws and their specially negotiated arrangements on taxation, banking, securities, and financial secrecy to cater to the needs of ultra-wealthy non-resident elites.[26] Of all the marketplaces where tax competition works its will, the market for ultra-high-net-worth investors—those whose net worth is at least $30 million—is probably the most efficient. In the limiting case, the marginal tax rate on the interest, capital gains, and dividends earned by the most liquid forms of offshore financial wealth invested in these ultimate havens—bank deposits, bonds, and publicly traded stocks—is virtually zero.

The end result is that the global haven industry basically enables the world's happy few to become *citizens of nowhere* for purposes of tax law, as well as for purposes of most other regulations. If you are, say, the wealthy son of a billionaire Hong Kong real estate promoter, or an Argentine cattle breeder, or the daughter of an Angolan dictator, or the world-famous lead singers in an Irish rock band, or the sole inheritor of an Italian auto magnate, or an Israeli-Ukrainian arms dealer, you can be free to wander the globe from golden pond to golden pond, carefully dividing your time between your residences in New York, London, Geneva, Zug, Paris, Sanya China, Costa del Sol, and your own Panama or Caribbean island so as to remain virtually tax free, even after death, as a UK "non-dom" ("non-domiciled"), a US "NRA" ("non-resident alien"), or, if your net worth is at least €100 million, a low-flat-tax "forfait" in Switzerland.[27]

Of course few wealthy investors are interested in arranging all this on their own, any more than they want to fly their own Gulfstream G650s, drive their own armored limousines, or provide for their own personal security. They all depend very heavily on legal advisors, private bankers, asset managers, accounting firms, and other *professional enablers* for all these sophisticated arrangements—the best talent that money can buy. The industry's 200,000 professionals specialize in arcane subjects like dynasty trusts, back-to-back

[26] For example, for wealthy "non-resident aliens," the United States exempted interest income and capital gains from taxation, even while allowing them to live in the United States up to half a year at a time, while the United Kingdom did even more for so-called "non-domiciled" residents.

[27] One recent example of a Swiss "forfeit" is the former American rock star Anna Mae Bullock, aka "Tina Turner," originally from Nutbush, Tennessee. She reportedly has been living in the elite Zurich suburb of Kuesnacht since the mid-1990s, and in 2013 she announced plans to forfeit her US citizenship. See Fisher (2013).

loans, LLC partnership agreements, protected cell companies, structured finance, captive insurance for yachts, aircrafts, and polo ponies, intellectual property, and intra-company transfer pricing.[28] With their help, big-ticket investors gain access to sophisticated wealth management services that typically cut across multiple individual havens.

As a result, the leading pirate banks listed above have been the most important single contributor to the proliferation of "treasure islands" since the 1970s, not only by helping to design them and keep them competitive with each other, but also by implementing complicated cross-haven wealth holding structures for their clients, and by facilitating complex global money laundering schemes to conceal recurrent payments.

From this angle, it is interesting to rank secrecy jurisdictions against each other, on the basis of their individual characteristics, but it is also somewhat misleading. In fact all truly sophisticated legal arrangements for holding and managing the wealth of high-end private clients—and for enabling MNC tax dodging as well—always rely on *several* shell companies, trusts, bank accounts, foundations, and other entities that are not only located in *multiple* haven jurisdictions, but can be "redomiciled"—shifted from one to another—at a moment's notice. The only true "central servers" in such financial networks are the private clients themselves, and their most trusted advisors—usually their private bankers.

2.3.5 Political Representation without Taxation

The other key value provided by the global haven industry to its wealthy clients involves political representation. The industry, its lobbyists, accountants, lawyers, and political action committees, essentially works hard to lobby for financial secrecy and favorable tax laws, and lenient tax enforcement. In effect, this helps the happy few to become *super-citizens of everywhere*, from the standpoint of being able to enjoy extraordinary *political representation without taxation*—or, in Albert Hirschman's terms, "Voice *plus* Exit *minus* Loyalty."[29]

Indeed, in the case of OECD countries, despite the rather miserable economic performance of the neoliberal agenda for most OECD country residents since the 1990s, the alchemy of big money into power has recently become more direct than ever. Since the 1990s, especially in the United States, but also

[28] For a description and analysis of "protected cell companies," see Republic of South Africa, FSB (2013). PCCs now exist in Guernsey, Jersey, Ireland, Bermuda, and the Cayman Islands, and several US states like Delaware and Vermont have also gotten into the "captive insurance company" game, which is easily manipulated for tax dodging. See Zolkos (2013).

[29] Compare Hirschman (1970).

in several other OECD countries, the political influence of contributions and lobbying by major corporations and private investors has expanded even as taxation and regulation have become less progressive. Indeed, for elite interests, there has been a worldwide trend toward *over-representation without taxation.*

By supporting the proliferation of extreme forms of private "economic liberty," therefore, the neoliberal agenda may well have ended up not just being indifferent to democracy, but actually undermining it.

2.3.6 Alternative Explanations

Other analysts have offered slightly different explanations for the dramatic rise of the global haven network since the 1970s. For example, one former Senate investigator has attributed it in part to capital controls imposed by the United States during the Vietnam War.[30] Supposedly these encouraged US companies to retain dollar earnings abroad in financial centers like London rather than repatriate them to the United States. The British journalist Nicholas Shaxson has emphasized the crucial role of the United Kingdom and the City of London in the proliferation of havens, as part of Britain's post-World War II strategy to maintain its role as a financial center.[31]

These alternative explanations have some merit, but they really don't account for the actual pattern of capital flight and offshore financial wealth from developing countries and the developed world since the 1970s. They understate the key role played by Third World lending, neglect the importance of non-British-related havens, and understate the role of "ultimate havens" like the United States, the United Kingdom, Switzerland, and a relative handful of other key European and Asian havens where most offshore investment actually winds up.

Most important, they neglect the essential role played by the global haven industry, especially major banks, law firms, and accounting firms.

Consistent with this perspective, the main source of Eurodollar deposits and loans in the 1970s was not MNC profits stashed abroad, but capital flight and bank deposits from developing countries, not only from the Middle East, but also from new oil producers like Mexico, Nigeria, and Venezuela after the oil price spikes of 1973 and 1979. Most of the capital flight from Latin America—by far the largest source of flight capital for the global haven industry from the 1970s to the 1990s—did not end up in British banks or havens, but in US banks like Citibank, Chase, JPMorgan, BankAmerica, and Bank of Boston. In

[30] See the comments by US attorney Jack Blum in the 2012 Sundance documentary "We're Not Broke," available on Netflix, and at http://werenotbrokemovie.com, accessed 15 July 2015.

[31] See Shaxson (2012) *passim.*

the case of Argentina and Brazil, Swiss, Dutch, German, French, and Spanish banks were also very important. While members of the British haven archipelago, like the Bahamas, BVI, the Cayman Islands, and the Channel Islands, Cyprus, Gibraltar, Hong Kong, Malta, and Singapore have served as key conduits, so have non-British conduit havens like Panama, the Netherlands Antilles, Dubai, Lebanon, Martinique, Mauritius, the Seychelles, St. Lucia, and Uruguay. And *onshore* conduits like Switzerland, Delaware, Nevada, the Netherlands, and Luxembourg have also been crucial.

Most important, whatever the roots of the global haven industry, by now it is indeed a truly global industry, with most big-ticket investors able to rely on global banks and other enablers to manage their investments across multiple havens. These clients could care less whether any particular treasure island, or even the entire UK-, US-, Dutch- or Swiss-centered subnets of havens, lives or dies, so long as there are other havens and secrecy structures—either onshore or offshore—to take their place. Given the fact that financial secrecy services have become something of a commodity, and that global regulation has usually lagged far behind state-of-the-art private banking, so far there always have been.

2.3.7 The High Crimes of Pirate Bankers

As we've argued, the global haven industry did not simply arise out of the misguided policies, strategies, and laws of tax havens, developing countries, or even First World governments. Nor will it suddenly be curtailed merely because we tighten up on financial secrecy and improve information exchange and tax enforcement among countries. Such measures will help over time, but they don't address the core problems—the lucrative global haven industry, the powerful interests that it serves, and the influential neoliberal (pro-tax competition and financial secrecy) ideology that it propagates.

To a newcomer to international finance, it may come as a shock to learn that world's largest, best-known banks—with the help of other enablers—have been up to their eyeballs in facilitating massive amounts of tax evasion, capital flight, and kleptocracy, from rich and poor countries alike. In financial secrecy jurisdictions, these activities were greeted with understanding, tolerated, and even encouraged. Back in the home countries, they are serious crimes.

Indeed, when we examine the whole spectrum of financial crimes routinely committed by major banks, turns out that for decades most of these giant "too big to fail" institutions have behaved as if they are nothing less than *transnational quasi-criminal enterprises*. This is especially true of the global leaders in private banking, all of which are based, not in dodgy Third World backwaters, but in "well-regulated" First World banking markets.

Furthermore, since the 1990s, under the influence of the neoliberal agenda, corporate globalization and deregulation, *organized* criminal misbehavior by the world's largest financial institutions appears to have worsened significantly. This period unleashed a torrent of outright fraud, price fixing, illegal trading, sanctions busting, and other financial crimes, which contributed significantly to the 2008 financial crisis as well as to the slow pace of the recovery since then. We are only now beginning to appreciate the sheer magnitude of this corporate financial crime wave.

2.3.7.1 Key Findings—The Financial Crimes Data Base

Data on *the aggregate* illegal activities of major banks as an industry group over time are hard to come by. Most financial journalists and stock analysts tend to focus only on the latest juicy tales about individual banks, partly because that is what investors care about.

For purposes of this chapter, we have assembled a "Financial Infractions Data Base" that is based on a comprehensive survey of all published penalties and assessments by financial institutions of all kinds on a global basis, for the period 1998–2014. This database includes all such penalties and assessments by public and private industry regulators, courts, prosecutorial plea bargains, and settlements entered into with private or public litigants.

The value of the fines and settlements reported include all publicly announced fines and penalties, provisions for restitution required to be paid to customers or investors for their losses, all mandatory payments of back interest and disgorgements of profit, and the declared amounts of all publicly announced settlements. This data has been compiled from our own comprehensive survey of press releases and official publications by fifty-one regulatory agencies and prosecutors in thirty-five countries, as well as from an extensive survey of press reports and company financial filings. To our knowledge, it is the most comprehensive summary to date of such financial penalties, assessments, and settlements.

When we examine the cumulative misbehavior of the global banking industry, the results are striking. As Tables 2.3–2.7 and Figure 2.6 show, our new "Financial Infractions Data Base" reveals that our leading global banks have recently been engaged in nothing less than a *bacchanal* of financial misdeeds, including many corporate felonies.

For the period 1998–2014, we have identified a total of 845 cases where individual financial institutions have received specific declared penalties and assessments for infractions. We found eight other cases where private settlements were reached but the amounts involved were kept secret, fifty-three cases where private lawsuits involving allegations of financial misconduct are

Table 2.2 Top 22 global private banks: Incidence of corporate crime, 1998–2014

	Assets ($bn) 2000	Assets ($bn) 2014	2000–14 % rise	Lehman under-writer	Aiding tax cheating	LIBOR rigging	Money laun-dering	Mort. fraud: RMBS/ CDOs	"Rogue" trading	Sanction busting	Wrongful foreclosure	FX rigging	MUNY fraud	Securities fraud	Energy/ metals rigging	Bribery	Lending bias	Card/ PPI fraud	Offense categories	No. of offenses
HSBC	$674	$2,729	405%	•	✔	✔	✔	✔	Sander	✔	✔	✔		✔	✔			✔	11	28
Deutsche Bank	$875	$2,168	248%		✔	✔	✔	✔	Bittar/ Adoph	✔		✔				✔			8	40
JPMorgan Chase	$715	$2,527	353%		✔	✔	✔	✔	Iksil	✔	✔	✔	✔	✔	✔	✔		✔	13	68
BNP Paribas	$640	$2,624	410%	•	✔	✔	✔		Crassier	✔		✔		✔					7	9
Barclays	$473	$2,218	469%		✔	✔	✔	✔	Diamond, etc.	✔		✔		✔	✔			✔	10	22
Credit Agricole	$477	$2,196	460%		✔	✔	✔	✔	Zrihen	✔		✔		✔	✔	✔			9	9
Bank America	$642	$2,124	331%	•	✔	✔	✔	✔	✔		✔	✔	✔	✔	✔	✔	✔	✔	12	97
Citicorp	$902	$1,883	209%	•	✔	✔	✔	✔	Eurbd Team	✔	✔	✔	✔	✔	✔	✔	✔	✔	13	69
RBS/ABN Amro	$480	$1,699	354%	•	✔	✔	✔	✔	Tsang	✔		✔		✔	✔	✔		✔	10	41
Soc Gen	$429	$1,638	382%	•	✔	✔	✔	✔	Kerviel	✔		✔				✔			8	8
Santander	$154	$1,574	1022%	•	✔	✔	✔	✔	✔	✔									5	5
ING	$580	$1,257	217%	•	✔	✔	✔	✔		✔				✔	✔				5	5
Wells Fargo	$272	$1,637	601%	•	✔	✔	✔	✔	✔	✔	✔		✔	✔	✔		✔		10	46
Lloyds	$338	$1,391	412%		✔	✔	✔	✔		✔		✔						✔	7	8
UBS	$674	$1,103	164%	•	✔	✔	✔	✔	Kweku/ Hayes	✔	✔	✔	✔	✔	✔	✔			12	50
Credit Suisse	$399	$999	250%		✔	✔	✔	✔	Serageldin	✔		✔	✔	✔	✔				10	35
Goldman Sachs	$290	$869	300%		✔	✔		✔	Tourre etc.		✔	✔	✔	✔	✔	✔			10	33
Rabobank	$340	$858	252%		✔	✔	✔		✔			✔							5	6

(continued)

Table 2.2 Continued

	Assets ($bn) 2000	Assets ($bn) 2014	2000–14 % rise	Lehman under-writer	Aiding tax cheating	LIBOR rigging	Money laun-dering	Mort. fraud: RMBS/ CDOs	"Rogue" trading	Sanction busting	Wrongful foreclosure	FX rigging	MUNY fraud	Securities fraud	Energy/ metals rigging	Bribery	Lending bias	Card/ PPI fraud	Offense categories	No. of offenses
Morgan Stanley	$427	$815	191%	•	✔	✔	✔	✔	Moryoussef		✔		✔	✔	✔	✔	✔		11	60
SCB	$103	$690	671%		✔	✔	✔		✔	✔		✔							6	6
BNY/ Mellon	$100	$386	386%	•	✔	✔	✔	✔	✔	✔		✔		✔	✔		✔		8	8
Julius Baer	$12	$83	699%		✔		✔												2	2
Total	**$9,996**	**$33,467**	**335%**																**Total**	**655**
AAGR%			*9.7%*																	
			Incidence		22	21	19	18	13	11	10	9	7	5	4	5	3	1	148	
					22	22	22	22	22	22	22	22	22	22	22	22	22	22	286	
					100%	95%	86%	82%	59%	50%	45%	41%	32%	23%	18%	23%	14%	5%	52%	

Source: Internet/literature search, author's analysis

Table 2.3 Penalties and settlement costs, global banks, 2014 (a)

Date	($m)	Offense	Financial institution	Plaintiff
18/12/14	$1.50	Money laundering	Wells Fargo	US FINRA
16/12/14	$2.44	Securities mispricing	BAC/ML	US FINRA
14/12/14	$31.30	Overcharging - credit cards	ANZ	Suit - customers
12/12/14	$4.00	Conflicts of interest - analysts	BAC/ML	US FINRA
12/12/14	$5.00	Conflicts of interest - analysts	Barclays	US FINRA
12/12/14	$5.00	Conflicts of interest - analysts	Citigroup	US FINRA
12/12/14	$5.00	Conflicts of interest - analysts	Credit Suisse	US FINRA
12/12/14	$4.00	Conflicts of interest - analysts	Deutsche Bank	US FINRA
12/12/14	$5.00	Conflicts of interest - analysts	Goldman Sachs	US FINRA
12/12/14	$5.00	Conflicts of interest - analysts	JPMorganChase	US FINRA
12/12/14	$4.00	Conflicts of interest - analysts	Morgan Stanley	US FINRA
12/12/14	$2.50	Conflicts of interest - analysts	Needham	US FINRA
12/12/14	$4.00	Conflicts of interest - analysts	Wells Fargo	US FINRA
11/12/14	$409.77	Invalid mortgages	Northern Rock	UK Cts
03/12/14	$14.90	Mis-sale of interest rate swaps - rural customers	ANZ	NZ Comp Cmm
01/12/14	$5.48	IT systems failure - world's largest	RBS/ Ulster Bank	IRE - CBnk
25/11/14	$15.00	Improper analyst comms w corp clients	Citigroup	US FINRA
25/11/14	$12.50	Tax dodging/ improper advice to US clients	HSBC	US SEC
21/11/14	$88.00	IT systems failure	RBS	UK FCA/ PRA
18/11/14	$315.00	Sanctions - Sudan/Iran - pressured PWC cover up	Bank of Tokyo	US NY-DFS
13/11/14	$250.00	Price fixing - FX market	Bank of America	US - OCC
13/11/14	$310.00	Price fixing - FX market	Citigroup	US - CFTC
13/11/14	$349.44	Price fixing - FX market	Citigroup	UK FCA
13/11/14	$350.00	Price fixing - FX market	Citigroup	US - OCC
13/11/14	$0.73	Illegal incentives for loans	Franklin Loan	US - CFPB
13/11/14	$275.00	Price fixing - FX market	HSBC	US - CFTC
13/11/14	$339.69	Price fixing - FX market	HSBC	UK FCA
13/11/14	$310.00	Price fixing - FX market	JPMorganChase	US - CFTC
13/11/14	$348.79	Price fixing - FX market	JPMorganChase	UK FCA
13/11/14	$350.00	Price fixing - FX market	JPMorganChase	US - OCC
13/11/14	$290.00	Price fixing - FX market	RBS	US - CFTC
13/11/14	$340.69	Price fixing - FX market	RBS	UK FCA
13/11/14	$4.40	IT mismanagement	RBS/Ulster Bank	IRE - CBnk
13/11/14	$290.00	Price fixing - FX market	UBS	US - CFTC

Source: Author's survey of 51 regulatory agencies and comprehensive literature search

Table 2.4 Penalties and settlement costs, global banks, 2014 (b)

Date	($m)	Offense	Financial institution	Plaintiff
13/11/14	$367.07	Price fixing - FX market	UBS	UK FCA
12/11/14	$139.00	Price fixing - FX market	UBS	SW - FINMA
11/11/14	$34.74	Overcharges - late payment fees	NAB	Suit - customers
31/10/14	$35.00	Selling insur to MNCs w/o a license	AIG	NY DFS
29/10/14	$1,066.00	Price fixing - LIBOR	Rabobank	UK FCA/ Dutch/ DOJ
24/10/14	$1,300.00	Price fixing - LIBOR	Deutsche Bank	US - DOJ
21/10/14	$11.65	Price fixing - Swiss Fr Deriv	Credit Suisse	EU Comm
21/10/14	$13.38	Price fixing - Swiss Fr Deriv	JPMorganChase	EU Comm
21/10/14	$78.23	Price fixing - Swiss Fr Deriv	JPMorganChase	EU Comm
21/10/14	$16.07	Price fixing - Swiss Fr Deriv	UBS	EU Comm
06/10/14	$2.00	Unfair billing practices - identity protection	PNC	US - OCC
03/10/14	$6,200.00	Tax dodging - faciltation	UBS	FRANC
02/10/14	$4.74	Tax dodging - VAT - France - deposit	Julius Baer	FRANCE
01/10/14	$0.04	Misleading ads	NAB	Australia ASIC
29/09/14	$7.65	Reg capital overstatements	Bank of America	US SEC
29/09/14	$37.50	Illegal foreclosures	Flagstar Bank	US - CFPB
26/09/14	$12.70	Misuse of client data	Barclays	Suit - customers
25/09/14	$48.00	Unfair billing practices - identity protection	US Bancorp	US - CFPB
24/09/14	$4.00	Unfair billing practices - identity protection	US Bancorp	US - OCC
23/09/14	$61.70	Failing to protect L16.5b of custody assets	Barclays	UK FCA
23/09/14	$15.00	Systemic compliance failures	Barclays	US SEC
22/09/14	$5.00	Fraud - altered docs	Wells Fargo	US SEC
15/09/14	$0.28	Money laundering	Morgan Stanley	US - CFTC
12/09/14	$550.00	Fraud - RMBS	HSBC	US FHFA
11/09/14	$18.50	Improper accounting	Wilmington Trust	US SEC
09/09/14	$7.50	Discrimination - sex	Goldman Sachs	Suit - employee
03/09/14	$0.22	Sanctions - Iran	Citigroup	US OFAC/DOJ
27/08/14	$24.03	Poor advice - mort biz	RBS	UK FCA
26/08/14	$1.20	Failure to supervise	Bank of America	US - CFTC
22/08/14	$3,150.00	Fraud - RMBS	Goldman Sachs	US FHFA
21/08/14	$245.04	Fraud - RMBS	Bank of America	US SEC
21/08/14	$16,405.00	Fraud - RMBS	Bank of America	US - DOJ
21/08/14	$7.83	Failure to accurate report CFD equity swaps	Deutsche Bank	UK FCA
20/08/14	$23.00	Improper margin calls	Barclays	Suit - trustee

Source: Author's survey of 51 regulatory agencies and comprehensive literature search

Table 2.5 Penalties and settlement costs, global banks, 2014 (c)

Date	($m)	Offense	Financial institution	Plaintiff
19/08/14	$25.00	PWC consultants hid data on BOT sanctions busting	PWC	US NY-DFS
19/08/14	$300.00	Sanctions - violating def. pros. agreement	Standard Chartered	US NY-DFS
12/08/14	$20.80	Fraud - mortgages - bait and switch	Amerisave	US - CFPB
04/08/14	$0.50	Fraud - securities	Citigroup (x Dir)	US - CFTC
30/07/14	$1,270.00	Fraud - RMBS	Bank of America	US - DOJ/ US Att NY
30/07/14	$402.00	Tax dodging - facilitation	UBS	GER
29/07/14	$0.65	Illegal trading - FTF	JPMorganChase	US - CFTC
28/07/14	$86.00	Price fixing - LIBOR	Lloyds	US - DOJ
28/07/14	$105.00	Price fixing - LIBOR	Lloyds	US - CFTC
28/07/14	$178.50	Price fixing - LIBOR	Lloyds	UK FCA
25/07/14	$5.00	Failing to protect customer data	Citigroup	US SEC
24/07/14	$16.56	Sanctions - narcotics	Bank of America	US OFAC/DOJ
24/07/14	$80.00	Fraud - Dept of Agr supplier credits	BNP Paribas	US - DOJ
24/07/14	$275.00	Fraud - RMBS	Morgan Stanley	US SEC
14/07/14	$7,000.00	Fraud - RMBS	Citigroup	US - DOJ
10/07/14	$667.00	Sanctions - Iran	Commerzbank	US - DOJ/US Att NY / OFAC
03/07/14	$49.00	Fraud – fin. planning products	Commonwealth Bank	Suit - customers
03/07/14	$225.00	Fraud - mortgages - HAMP program	Suntrust	US - DOJ
01/07/14	$10.00	Overcharges - FHA mort. service fees	HSBC	US - DOJ
30/06/14	$8,963.60	Sanctions busting - Sudan, Iran, Cuba	BNP Paribas	US OFAC/ DOJ/ FINMA
30/06/14	$200.00	Violating FHA req	US Bancorp	US - DOJ
25/06/14	$51.00	Misreporting non-accrual loans	Regions Bank	US FED/ SEC/AG-Ala
19/06/14	$172.50	Discrimination – race - mortgages	GE Credit	US - CFPB/DOJ
19/06/14	$99.50	Fraud - RMBS	RBS	US FHFA
17/06/14	$968.00	Fraud - mortgage origination	SunTrust	US DOJ/CFPB/ 49 States
16/06/14	$4.08	Fraud - misleading sales pitches	Credit Suisse	UK FCA
29/05/14	$0.89	Excess exposure to one account	BMO	IRE - CBnk
23/05/14	$43.81	Conflicts of interest - gold fixings	Barclays	UK FCA
22/05/14	$0.21	Internal controls	Deutsche Bank	HK SFO

(*continued*)

Table 2.5 Continued

Date	($m)	Offense	Financial institution	Plaintiff
19/05/14	$2,403.50	Tax dodging - facilitation	Credit Suisse	US DOJ/ FED/ NYS DFS
08/05/14	$0.28	Sanctions - Cuba	AIG	US Treas/OFAC
24/04/14	$280.00	Fraud - RMBS	Barclays	US FHFA
22/04/14	$0.21	Internal controls – unauth. trading	RBS	HK SFO
16/04/14	$950.00	Fraud - RMBS	Bank of America	Suit - insurer
16/04/14	$99.00	Fraud - RMBS	Ernst & Young	Suit - investors

Source: Author's survey of 51 regulatory agencies and comprehensive literature search

still in process, and twenty-one cases where public prosecutions are still in process, for a grand total of 927 cases (see Table 2.2).

Among the most widespread infractions were the following: (1) defrauding pension funds and other investors in mortgage-backed securities and mortgage CDOs; (2) defrauding investors in corporate securities; (3) money laundering for drug cartels, arms dealers, fraudsters, and other criminals; (4) illegal securities trading, including insider trading and market manipulation; (5) rigging interest rates (especially LIBOR and credit-card charges); (6) rigging foreign exchange and derivatives markets; (7) rigging the US municipal bond market; (8) rigging commodity markets—gold, other precious metals, electricity, and food; (9) the systematic evasion of US and UN trade sanctions with respect to Burma, Cuba, Iran, Libya, North Korea, Serbia, the Sudan, and Zimbabwe; (10) illegal mortgage foreclosures; (11) retail credit card or "payment insurance" fraud; (12) bribery of public officials, municipal bond issuers, and pension fund managers; (13) racial discrimination in lending; and, the most widespread of all, (14) helping wealthy clients and corporations engage in tax fraud (see Table 2.2; see also Tables 2.3–2.6).

Out of these fourteen types of corporate misdeeds, each of the top twenty-two global banks in our sample have been involved, on average, in at least ten during the period 1998–2014. But they did not commit these infractions only once. As a whole, these banks were penalized for these fourteen financial misdeeds *655 times*.[32] The top ten offenders—Bank of America (97), Citicorp (69), JPMorganChase (68), Morgan Stanley (60), UBS (50), Wells Fargo (46), RBS (41), Deutsche Bank (40), Credit Suisse (35), and Goldman Sachs

[32] For the period 1998–2014, of the 845 completed instances where specific penalties, assessments, or settlement amounts have been announced, the top 22 global banks in our sample accounted for 655. They also accounted for all 8 of the undisclosed settlements, and 70 out of 74 of the cases that are still in process. All told, therefore, out of the 927 cases either in process or concluded, the top 22 banks in our sample account for 700, or 79.1 percent of the total.

Table 2.6 Penalties and settlement costs, global banks, 2014 (d)

Date	($m)	Offense	Financial institution	Plaintiff
09/04/14	$727.00	Overcharges - credit cards	Bank of America	US - CFPB
07/04/14	$25.00	Unfair billing practices - identity protection	Bank of America	US - OCC
07/04/14	$1,130.00	Fraud - RMBS	Citigroup	Suit - investors
31/03/14	$60.00	Soliciting insurance biz in NY w/o a license	MetLife	NY DFS/ Manhattan DA
27/03/14	$0.49	Failure to protect customers' data	Morgan Stanley	US - CFTC
26/03/14	$9,300.00	Fraud - RMBS	Bank of America	US FHFA
26/03/14	$20.42	Misleading advice to investors	Santander	UK FCA
24/03/14	$0.20	Illegal trading - Pos limits	Morgan Stanley	US - CFTC
21/03/14	$885.00	Fraud - RMBS	Credit Suisse	US FHFA
18/03/14	$0.44	Breach of risk controls	Unicredit	IRE - CBnk
12/03/14	$0.83	Fraud - CDOs	Goldman Sachs	US SEC
27/02/14	$122.00	Fraud - RMBS	Societe General	US FHFA
26/02/14	$275.00	Fraud - RMBS	Morgan Stanley	US SEC
21/02/14	$196.50	Unreg. invest. services	Credit Suisse	US SEC
20/02/14	$1,060.00	Retaliation vs outside investor	Deutsche Bank	Suit - victims
19/02/14	$275.00	Fraud - RMBS	RBS	Suit - investors
18/02/14	$7.90	Overdraft fee pumping	Citigroup	Suit - customers
07/02/14	$1,250.00	Fraud - RMBS	Morgan Stanley	US FHFA
04/02/14	$614.00	Fraud – mortgages - false claims	JPMorganChase	US - DOJ
31/01/14	$8,500.00	Fraud - RMBS	BAC/ Countrywide	Suit - investors
31/01/14	$37.56	Overcharging customers	State Street Bank	UK FCA
29/01/14	$64.42	Overcharges - personal loans	ANZ	Australia ASIC
28/01/14	$25.00	Fraud - RMBS	Jeffries LLC	US SEC
27/01/14	$69.10	Overcharges - credit cards	Amex Bank	US - CFPB
27/01/14	$9.50	Sanctions - Iran	Bank of Moscow	US OFAC
23/01/14	$151.90	Sanctions - Iran	Clearstream	US OFAC
23/01/14	$12.62	Money laundering - PEPs	Standard Chartered	UK FCA
07/01/14	$537.00	Fraud - Madoff	JPMorganChase	Suit - trustee
07/01/14	$1,700.00	Money laundering - Madoff fraud	JPMorganChase	US - DOJ
06/01/14	$350.00	Money laundering - Madoff fraud	JPMorganChase	US - OCC
02/01/14	$0.25	False statements	SMP (Russia)	US - CFTC

Source: Author's survey of 51 regulatory agencies and comprehensive literature search

(33)—accounted for more than half of these 655 offenses. Furthermore, this list is incomplete—as of 2015, at least seventy public charges and private lawsuits involving these top twenty-two giants are still in process (see Table 2.3).

These are not marginal institutions. As of 2014, for example, HSBC was the world's largest bank by total assets, and the top *four* US banks—JPMorganChase, Wells Fargo, Citibank, and BankAmerica—accounted for $8.3 trillion of total assets, more than half the assets of all 6,656 US financial institutions.[33] All told, the total assets of these twenty-two global institutions were worth more than twice those of the entire US banking system.

2.3.7.2 What Penalties Did Big Banks Receive?

What penalties did these top-tier banks receive for all this misbehavior? The international judicial system works very slowly, especially where such large institutions are concerned. As of 2009, less than $35 billion in fines, settlements, and other legal costs had been imposed, even though most of this misbehavior had already occurred (see Figures 2.6 and 2.7).[34]

After that, partly because of public pressure, regulatory authorities in the United States and Europe became somewhat less lenient. As a result, the *average yearly* penalties, settlements, and other legal costs incurred by these major banks for financial misdeeds increased nearly fifteen times in 2009–2014, compared with the prior decade (see Figure 2.7).[35] For 1998–2014, the cumulative total reached $246 billion.[36] In 2014 alone, the

[33] See the FDIC's June 2014 Statistics on Depository Institutions; quarterly 10-Q reports for individual financial institutions for the quarter ending in June 2014.

[34] These slides are based on my Financial Infractions Data Base, as discussed above. Other analysts have arrived at similar conclusions. For example, a December 2014 survey of "litigation costs for leading European and U.S. banks for 2009–September 2014" by the Boston Consulting Group found a cumulative total of $188 billion for the period 2009–2014. See Boston Consulting Group (2014). Similarly, a British NGO, CCP Research Foundation, estimated "total conduct cost" for this group of £173.22 billion for 2009–13. See CCP Research Foundation (2014). See also Arnold (2014), and Comfort (2013) which estimated that "18 European banks" had incurred "$77 billion in legal costs since Sept 2008." Note that our estimates employ actual reported settlements, fines, disgorgement, restitution, and interest, in preference to forward-looking company provisions, which are often highly inaccurate.

[35] As Figure 2.7 shows, about 80 percent of the assessments in the 2009–14 period were due to public regulators, compared with 39 percent for the 1998–2008 period. This was partly due to a belated increase in enforcement activity by US, UK, and continental European bank regulators during this period.

[36] In real $2014 this cumulative 1998–2014 total was least $236 billion to $245 billion, depending on the deflator. There is no simple global price index that measures the equivalent real burden of these assessments to the corporations involved. Since the largest banks in our sample are based in the US, we have used, alternatively, the most recent BLS CPI deflator, which

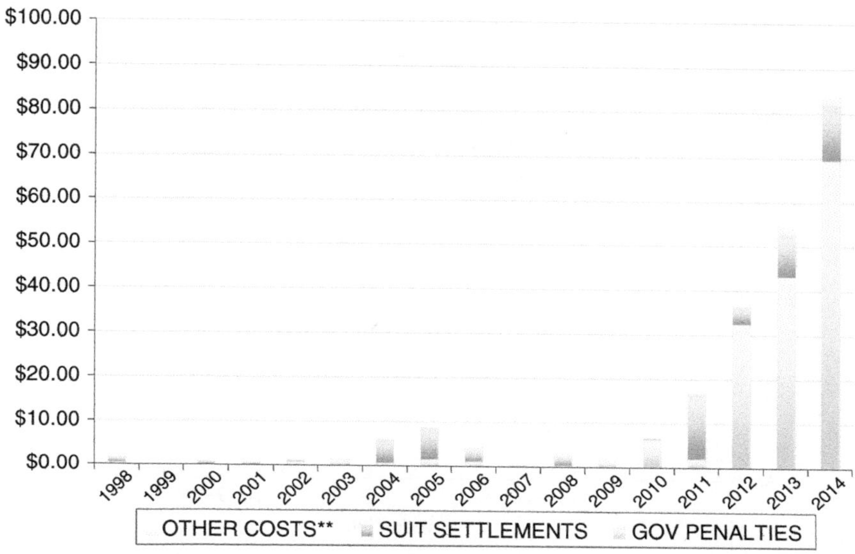

Figure 2.6 Total fines, settlements, and other legal costs, global financial services industry 1998–2014 ($bn)

Note: ** restitution, back interest, and disgorgement
Source: Author's survey of 51 regulatory agencies plus author's comprehensive literature search

twenty-two industry leaders reported 134 separate fines and settlements totaling $87 billion. In real terms, this accounted for 37 percent of all assessments during this 16-year period.

For the sake of comparison, the total revenue collected from all US federal corporate income taxes in 2013 was $274 billion,[37] and the total federal corporate income taxes paid by *all US banks and insurance companies* totaled $97 billion.[38] Evidently we have arrived at the point where *prosecuting illegal activity by big banks is more lucrative to the government than taxing their legal activities.*

Classifying these penalties by type of crime, more than half of the $246 billion in penalties and assessments was accounted for by mortgage fraud alone, which totaled $127 billion. Corporate securities fraud—for example,

gives a real total of $236.3 billion for all penalties and assessments from 1998–2014, and the US GDP deflator, which gives $244.8 billion. For our purposes the order of magnitude is the same. See Figures 2.6 and 2.7.

[37] See Office of Management and Budget (2015).
[38] See US Bureau of Economic Analysis, Department of Commerce (2014).

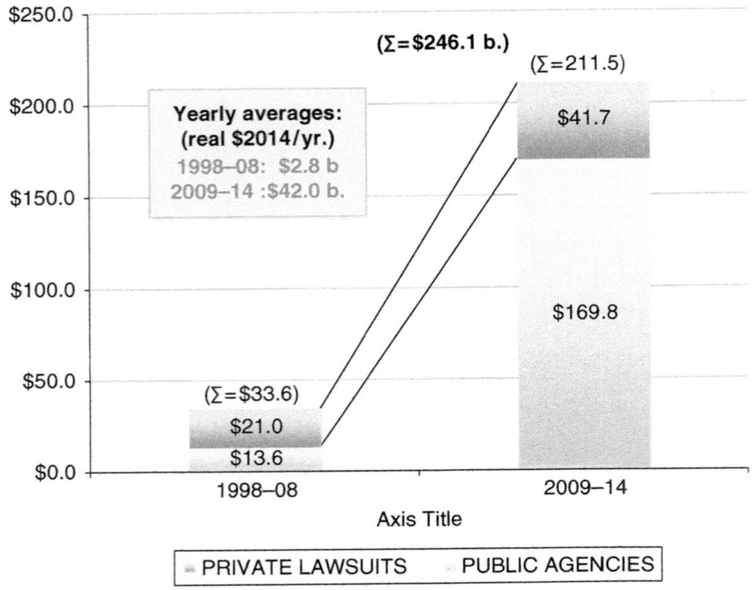

Figure 2.7 Regulatory penalties vs legal settlements, global financial services industry, 1998–2014 ($bn)

Source: Author's survey of 51 regulatory agencies plus author's comprehensive literature search

helping Enron and Parmalat to mislead investors—came in second, at $33 billion (see Figure 2.8). In third place, at $14.1 billion, was helping clients to evade sanctions against countries on the US "trading with the enemy" sanctions list. Most of this was accounted by fines against European banks, notably BNP, HSBC, and Credit Suisse. Finally, facilitating international tax dodging took fourth place, at $11 billion. This relatively low rank is partly because the fines imposed for this offense have been lenient, and also because banks have only been prosecuted by the United States, France, and Germany for facilitating tax dodging by their own wealthy residents, not for helping the wealthy residents of developing countries like Argentina, Mexico, China, or Russia to dodge taxes.[39]

[39] A good example of such leniency is the plea bargain entered into with the US Department of Justice by Credit Suisse in May 2014. Under its terms, no senior CS executives were jailed, bank secrecy was preserved, the $2.6 billion assessment imposed remained tax-deductible under Swiss law, and the bank secured waivers from US government agencies like the Federal Reserve and the US Department of Labor that allowed it to continue to serve as an advisor to US pension funds and as a "prime dealer" for US Treasury and Federal Reserve securities, despite having pled guilty to a corporate felony.

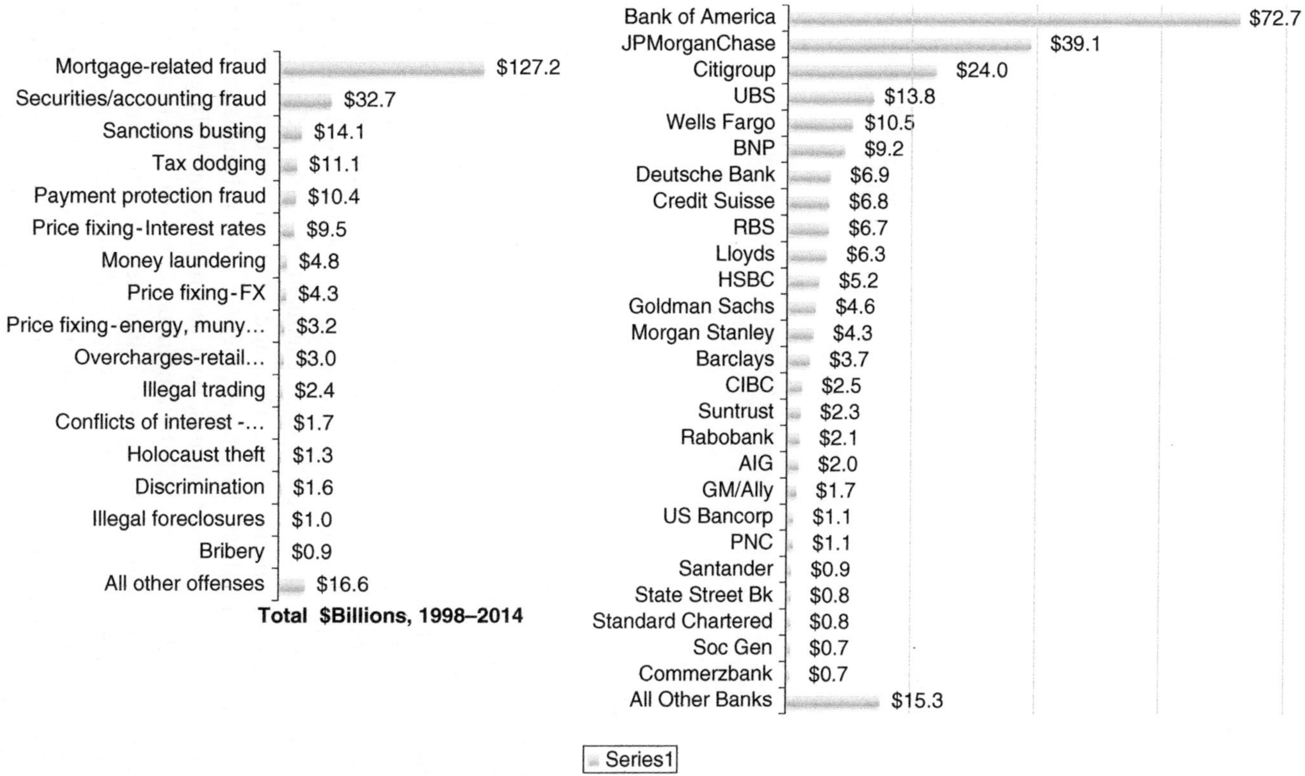

Figure 2.8 Total assessments for corporate crimes by offense and bank, 1998–2014 ($bn)

Source: Author's survey of 51 regulatory agencies plus author's comprehensive literature search

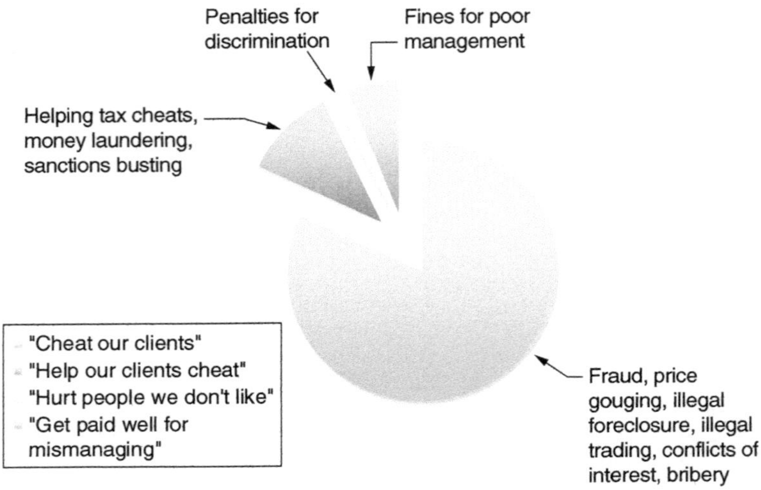

Figure 2.9 In the *present*, we will . . .

Note: ** After HSBC's well-known ad campaign
Source: Author's survey of 51 regulatory agencies plus author's comprehensive literature search

As noted, a handful of these global financial institutions accounted for most of these offenses and a disproportionate share of the assessments. For example, Bank of America alone, the world leader in mortgage securities fraud, accounted for nearly $73 billion of the 1998–2014 total (see Figure 2.8). It was followed by JPMorganChase ($39.1 billion), Citigroup ($24.0 billion), UBS ($13.8 billion), BNP Paribas ($9.1 billion), Deutsche Bank ($6.9 billion), and Credit Suisse ($6.8 billion). All told, the top "dirty dozen" banks accounted for $205.4 billion in fines and settlements, 84 percent of the total.

The misdeeds underlying these record fines and settlements can also be grouped into several "activity" categories. About $30 billion, or 11 percent, derived from crimes that involved "helping clients of the bank to cheat"—tax fraud, accounting fraud, money laundering, and sanctions busting. Another $20 billion, or 7 percent, derived from penalties for sheer mismanagement—information technology systems failures, poor record-keeping, billing errors, and losing client data. Another $3 billion in penalties, or 1 percent, was awarded for illegal discrimination against minorities, women, and the disabled. Finally, fully 82 percent of the $247 billion total derived from misdeeds that involved "cheating the bank's own clients"—for example, price fixing, CDO and mortgage-backed securities fraud, bribery, illegal trading, and biased market analysis (see Figure 2.9). Perhaps the world's top private banks are not so trustworthy after all.

2.3.7.3 How Severe Were the Penalties?

All this is consistent with the behavior of an industry whose senior executives, in addition to whatever pure banking skills they may possess, have also acquired extraordinary skills in "regulatory mining"—behavior that the American social critic Thorstein Veblen would have labeled "clever chicanery or the thwarting thereof." Some of their misbehavior might be attributed to "a few bad apples," or to the past misbehavior of smaller failing institutions that larger ones were compelled to acquire. But there are simply too many incidents of misconduct by leading institutions that were never compelled to acquire failing ones for this explanation to have much cash value.

In short, here we have many of the world's largest and most profitable financial institutions systematically violating all sorts of laws over and over again, in multiple countries, especially during the period of financial globalization since the 1980s. What accounts for this crescendo in bank criminality?

Running this question to ground would require a far more extensive analysis than we are able to provide here—for example, we would need to look closely at executive compensation incentives at these banks. However, a few patterns do stand out.

First, while the industry's record penalties appear to be very large numbers, in most cases they have really been only a modest share of the banks' total assets, asset growth, shareholder equity, and market value. For example, for our sample of twenty-two major banks, the cumulative real value of all financial penalties and settlements from 1998–2014 was just 6.2 percent of total real cash flow (see Table 2.7). For all but the top four offenders, it was less than 5 percent (see Figure 2.10).

Second, these corporate penalties and other legal costs only arrived years down the road, long after any profits from misconduct had been booked and the worst miscreants among senior executives had moved on to other jobs or retired.

In the case of the rampant mortgage banking fraud that underwrote the 2008 financial crisis, for example, the preliminary period of concentrated perfidy in 2000–7 generated temporary, *spurious* above-average rates of return (see Figure 2.14).

This, in turn, led directly to huge spurious increases in executive compensation for senior bank managers, especially in the value of their (tax-deductible) corporate stock options. It also underwrote large increases in the financial services industry's spending on lobbyists and contributions to political campaigns, especially in the US and the UK.[40] From 1998 to 2007 the

[40] The author has estimated that from 1990 to 2006, spending by the US financial services industry on federal political contributions and lobbying totaled about $2,600 per Congressperson and Senator per day, day in, day out.

Table 2.7 Global private banking industry: Does crime pay?

	Total assets ($bn) YE 2000	Total assets ($bn) QIII 2014	Penalties** corporate crimes 1998–2014 ($bn)	% of 2014 assets	% of 2014 SH Equity	% of QIII 2014 PBT	% of Yearend Mkt cap
HSBC	$674	**$2,729**	$5.17	0.19%	2.7%	1.12	2.9%
Deutsche Bank	$875	**$2,168**	$6.93	0.32%	8.2%	19.65	16.7%
JPMorgan Chase	$715	**$2,527**	$39.09	1.55%	16.9%	5.08	16.7%
BNP Paribas	$640	**$2,624**	$9.20	0.35%	7.9%	3.01	12.6%
Barclays	$473	**$2,218**	$3.69	0.17%	3.8%	1.81	6.0%
Credit Agricole	$477	**$2,196**	$0.21	0.01%	0.2%	0.07	0.6%
Bank America	$642	**$2,124**	$72.70	3.42%	30.4%	168.69	38.6%
Citicorp	$902	**$1,883**	$24.01	1.28%	11.3%	4.90	14.6%
RBS/ ABN Amro	$480	**$1,699**	$6.70	0.40%	6.6%	3.16	9.7%
Soc Gen	$429	**$1,638**	$0.74	0.05%	1.0%	0.16	2.3%
Santander	$154	**$1,574**	$0.88	0.06%	0.9%	0.26	0.9%
ING	$580	**$1,257**	$0.66	0.05%	1.1%	0.34	1.3%
Wells Fargo	$272	**$1,637**	$10.46	0.64%	5.7%	1.22	3.7%
Lloyds	$338	**$1,391**	$6.35	0.46%	8.4%	5.06	7.7%
UBS	$674	**$1,103**	$13.82	1.27%	25.9%	na	21.6%
Credit Suisse	$399	**$999**	$6.76	0.68%	14.7%	4.61	16.8%
Goldman Sachs	$290	**$869**	$4.64	0.53%	5.6%	1.41	5.5%
Rabobank	$340	$858	$2.13	0.25%	na	na	na
Morgan Stanley	$427	**$815**	$4.26	0.52%	5.8%	1.92	5.3%
Standard Chartered	$103	**$690**	$0.77	0.07%	1.6%	0.24	2.1%
BNY/Mellon	$100	**$386**	$0.38	0.10%	1.0%	0.23	0.9%
Julius Baer	$12	**$83**	$0.08	0.10%	1.3%	0.29	0.8%

** Regulatory fines, disgorgement, interest, restitution, and publicly announced lawsuit settlements, all "financial misbehavior"

Source: Company 10-Ks, author's database on corporate financial sanctions, compiled from survey of 51 regulatory agencies in 35 countries

result was a strong temporary surge in these big banks' overall *measured* cash flows and returns on equity. (See Figures 2.11–2.15 for alternative measures of the top twenty-two global banks' economic performance in 1998–2014, relative to the penalties that it paid).

In contrast, during this initial period of maximum criminality, the penalties paid per dollar of cash flow and shareholder equity for bank crimes were close to zero. This was followed by several years of economic contraction, during which bank lobbyists protested that it would be counterproductive to penalize the banks during recovery, much less to hold their senior managers criminally liable. Only after several years was it deemed appropriate to seek even civil penalties.

Furthermore, when it comes to playing defense, these big banks are able to incur hundreds of $millions in (tax-deductible) legal and accounting expenses,

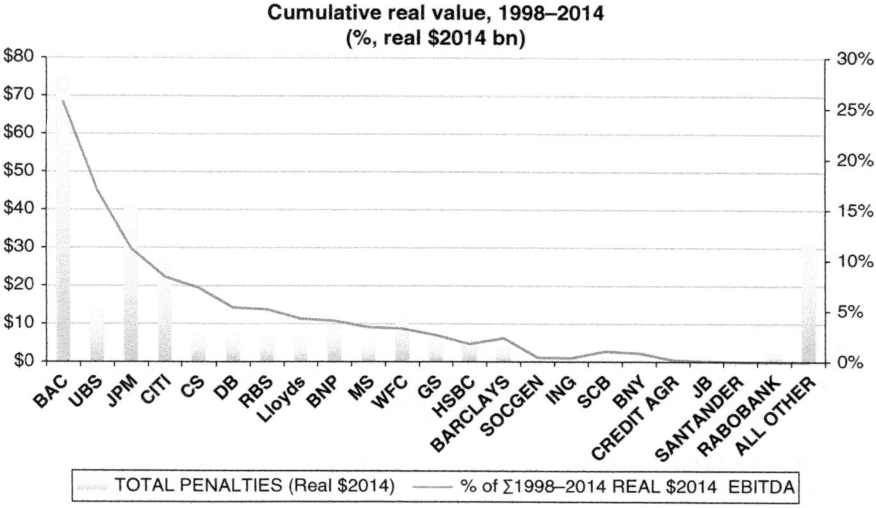

Figure 2.10 Top 22 global banks: penalties vs cash flow

Source: SEC and company reports for EBITDA; author's database on bank financial penalties (fines, disgorgement, back interest, restitution, and settlements); author's analysis

and leverage their long-standing relationships with the world's most expensive, influential law firms, accounting firms, and lobbyists. Attorneys general, IRS chief counsels, and SEC chairmen come and go, but key "enablers" like Covington & Burling, Wilmer Hale, and Shearman & Sterling have been part of the corporate establishment's backbone for generations. Not surprisingly, their involvement does not shorten litigation.

All told, therefore, this "*ex post* litigation" approach to regulating financial services has taken bank regulators more than eight years to catch up with the hundreds of corporate crimes that led to the *last* financial crisis. Among other things, this means that statutes of limitation on many types of financial crimes have already run.

For senior managers at big banks the message is clear. (See Figures 2.12, 2.13, and 2.15 for graphical illustrations of the reward-penalty ratios over time for individual banks.) In "net present value" terms, taking risks with the law may be risky in the long run, but by the time the long run arrives, the stock options have already vested.

Third, the fact is that *no* senior bankers from any top-tier institutions, either in the United States or abroad, have done *any* jail time for any of these 1998–2014 offenses. To date, only one top-22 bank, Credit Suisse, has even been required to plead guilty to a corporate felony for abetting tax dodging.[41]

[41] See Smythe (2014).

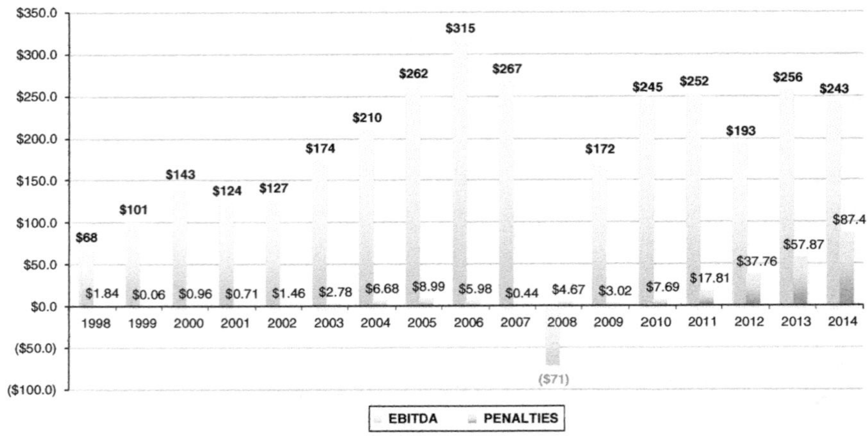

Figure 2.11 Global haven industry: cash flow vs penalties, 1998–2014 (22 global haven banks, current $bn)

Note: EBITDA = earnings before interest, taxes, and depreciation; penalties = total fines, restitution, back interest, disgorgement, and reported private settlements, as of the date reported
Source: SEC financial data and company reports by bank, 1998–2014; database on all reported penalties from regulatory agencies; press releases and press reports, compiled by the author 1998–2014; author's analysis

And that plea—in November 2014, to one count of a federal felony of "conspiring to aid US citizens in filing false tax returns"—was pre-arranged on condition that the bank would not lose its US banking license, nor its right to serve as a "prime dealer" for US Treasury debt—the need for which has only been aggravated by the kind of big-ticket tax dodging that it promoted to at least 20,000 wealthy US taxpayers. Nor will Credit Suisse lose its right to offer investment advice and specialty products to US public pension funds—many of which depend on taxpayer funding.[42]

It is important to note that while this policy of *zero-jail-time-for-big-bankers* is quite common in Europe, it is actually rather novel in the US. In particular, it is a striking contrast to the policy pursued by the first Bush Administration during the 1988–92 US "savings-and-loan" (S&L) crisis. Back then, more than 3,000 bankers were charged with felony offenses, and 880 actually did jail time.[43]

This time around, however, in the wake of the 2008 financial crisis, the US Justice Department, the SEC, and other federal regulators focused mainly on small-scale Ponzi schemes and a myriad of tiny mortgage fraud cases that

[42] See Lynch (2015).
[43] See Breslow (2013).

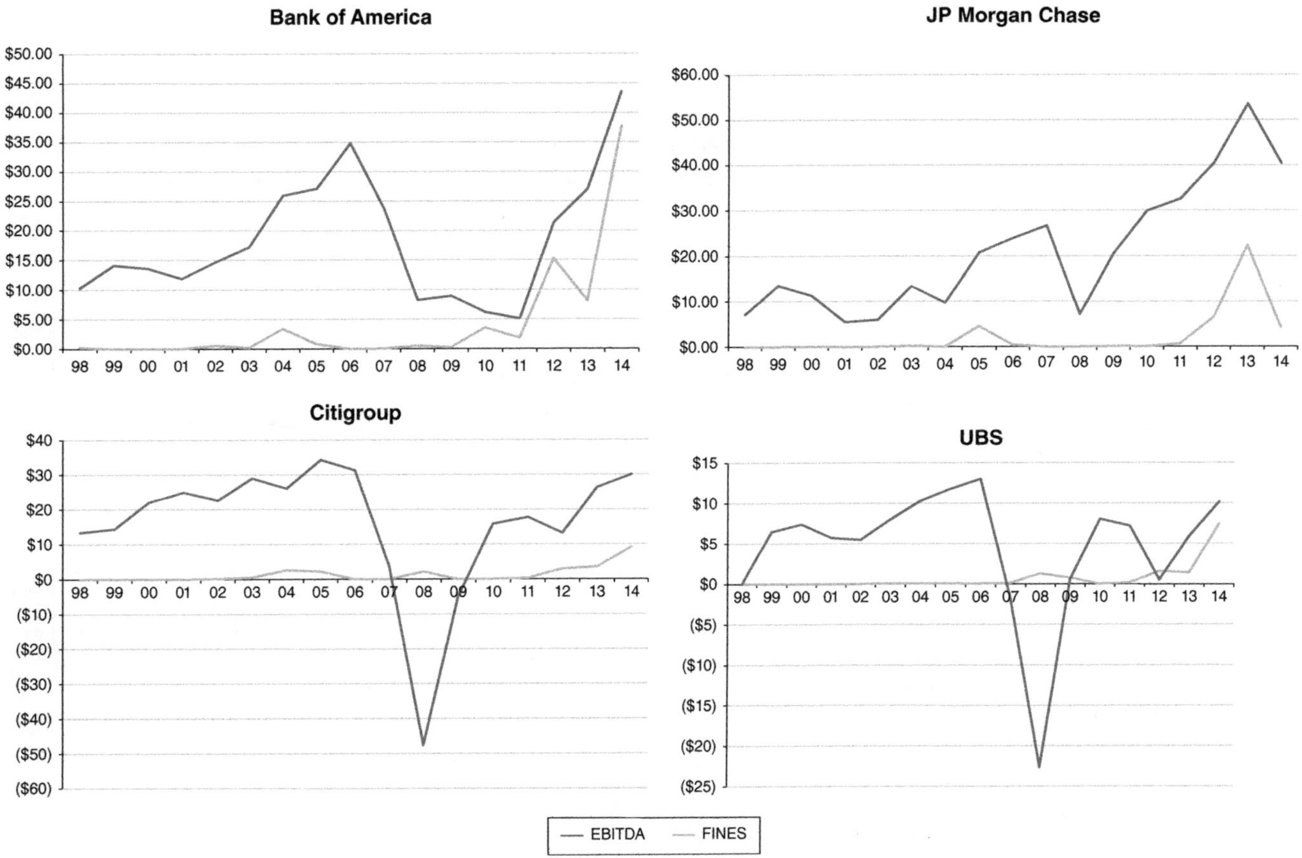

Figure 2.12 Cash flow ($bn) vs penalties ($bn), major banks 1998–2014

Source: SEC reports, financial data by bank 1998–2014; author's database on fines and settlements; author's analysis

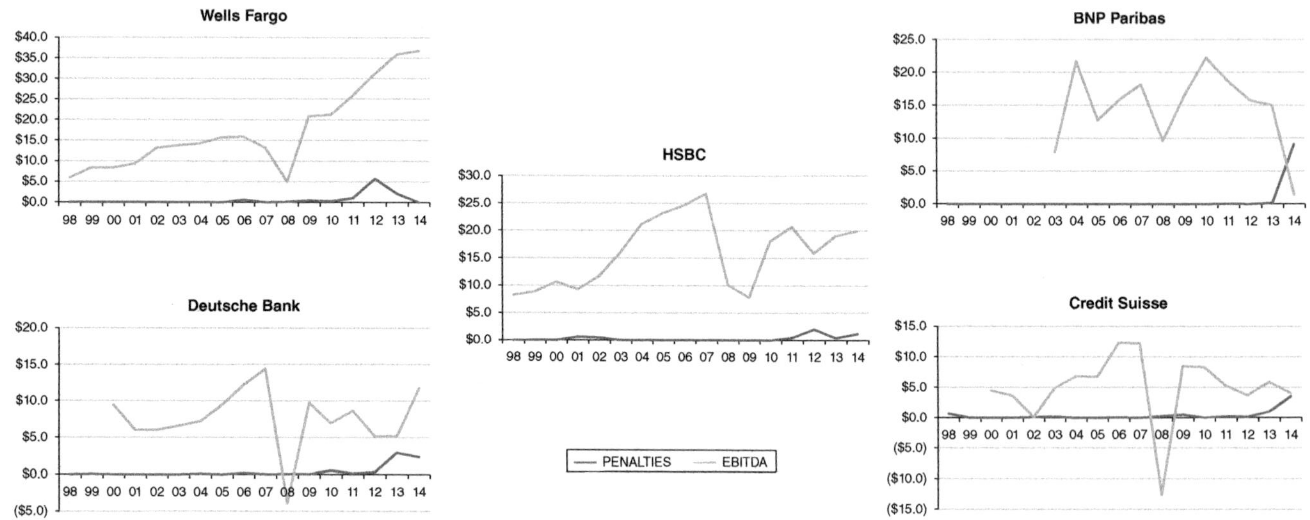

Figure 2.13 Cash flow ($bn) vs penalties ($bn), major banks 1998–2014

Source: SEC reports, financial data by bank 1998–2014; author's database on fines and settlements; author's analysis

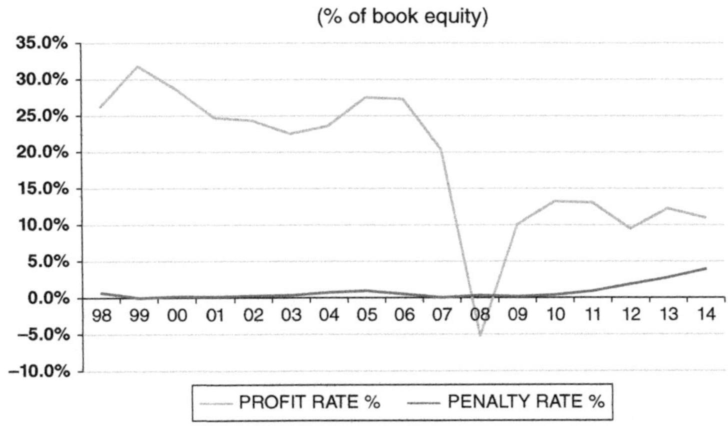

Figure 2.14 Profit rate vs penalty rate, 22 global banks, 1998–2014

Notes: Profit rate % = EBITDA/book equity, 22 global banks, 1998–2014E; penalty rate % = fines, other penalties, and settlements reported, divided by book equity

Source: SEC and company financial reports, financial data by bank, 1998–2014; author's database on fines and settlements; author's analysis

involved small-scale brokers, not on the major frauds that were committed by the largest banks.[44, 45]

In this corner of the white-collar crime world, then, "too-big-to-fail-or-jail" is firmly in place. Given the rise of corporate neoliberalism since the 1990s and its profound increase in political and ideological influence, the global pirate banking industry has not only dramatically expanded its economic clout. It also appears to have acquired effective impunity from all serious *criminal* prosecutions. The fines it pays sound huge on paper, but as we've seen, they are a tiny fraction of profits, and are easily digested or passed along to customers—especially in rigged markets.

We urgently need to find other, more effective ways to regulate these major banks' involvement in financial crime, money laundering, and tax evasion.

2.3.7.4 The Costs of the Crisis

Even allowing for the financial penalties paid by these big banks since 2010, the cardinal sin is that these only amounted to a tiny fraction of the total cost of the financial crisis that these banks helped to produce. The 2008 financial

[44] See the Wikipedia article on Operation Broken Trust, which describes the rather limited efforts of Obama's "Financial Fraud Tax Force," established in November 2008. For the US DOJ's roundup of its financial fraud cases, see http://www.stopfraud.gov/news-index.html, accessed 15 July 2015.

[45] See Sidel (2012). As of November 2012, 17 bankers had been jailed for fraud pertaining to the 2008 crisis, mainly at small failed banks.

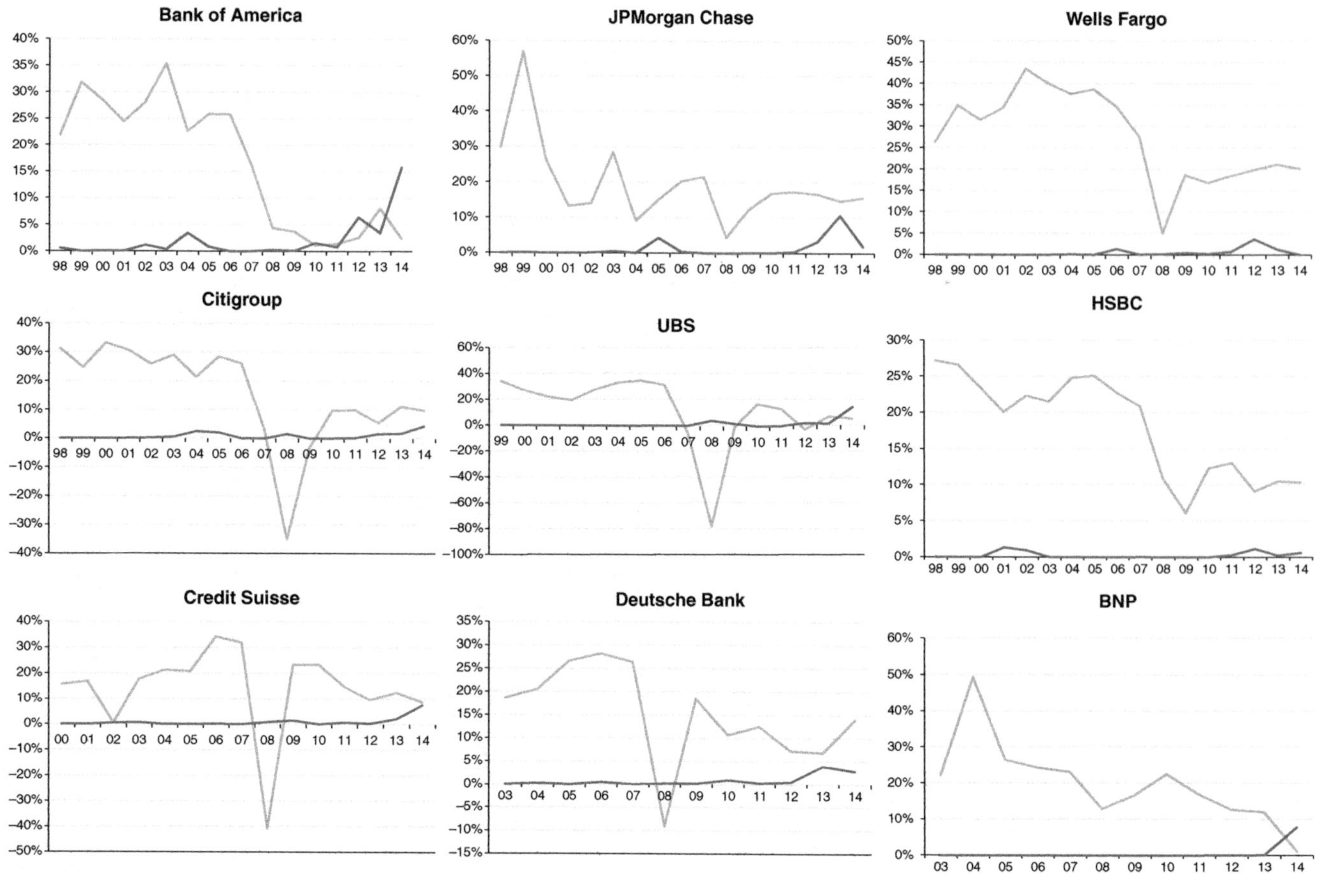

Figure 2.15 Profit rates vs penalty rates, 1998–2014

Source: SEC and company financial reports, financial data by bank, 1998–2014; author's database on fines and settlements; author's analysis

crisis was at least seventy times as large as the 1980s S&L crisis. In the US alone, 22 million people were laid off, experienced long-term unemployment, or dropped out of the labor force entirely.[46] There were 14.2 million foreclosure filings against US residential homeowners, and 7.3 million families lost their homes to foreclosures.[47] At least 323,000 small businesses, 5.4 percent of the total, disappeared from 2007 to 2012. Big banks reduced lending to small businesses even as many smaller banks were failing.[48] Societal rates of suicide, poor health, depression, domestic violence, racial and ethnic conflict, and anti-immigrant violence tension also escalated.[49] By 2013, 22 percent of all children in the US, the highest rate since the 1960s, were living in poverty.[50] Taking into account the effects of the 2008 crisis, overall real per capita household incomes have stagnated since the 1990s;[51] *all* of the increased income generated by the so-called "economic recovery" since 2009 was consumed by the top 1 percent, which happened to own stocks and bonds. Indeed, from 2008 to 2011 there was a *$10.7 trillion* reduction in US household wealth—except for the top 1 percent.[52] Meanwhile, government assistance programs for the poor and the unemployed, as well as funding for public investments in education, roads, hospitals, and schools was starved for funding. We didn't need fancy theories about technical change or "r>g" to account for rising inequality—it was a policy-made phenomenon.

[46] Civilian employment in the US economy fell by 8.58 million from November 2007 to December 2009, and only recovered the 2007 level by September 2014. The number of US workers experiencing more than 27 months of unemployment increased by 5.1 million, or 381 percent, from November 2007 to December 2010. This understates the total increase in the number of workers who experienced long-term unemployment because many gave up looking for work and dropped out of the labor force. As of January 2015, it was 2.8 million, or more than twice the November 2007 level. The US labor force participation rate—the number available and willing to work as a percentage of the total civilian non-institutional labor force—declined from 66.0% in November 2007 to 62.9% in January 2015, a departure of 7.7 million workers. BLS (2015) data; my analysis.

[47] See RealityTrac (2015a), and (2015b).

[48] Data from Bureau of the Census (2007, 2012, 2015), "Statistics on Small Businesses," available at http://www.census.gov/econ/susb/, accessed 15 July 2015; author's analysis. "Small business" is defined as employing less than 500 employees. As of 2012, by this definition, there were 5.71 million small businesses in the US, employing an average of 9.8 employees each, for a grand total of 56.1 million employees. In 2007 the figure was 6.03 million, employing a total of 59.82 million. See also Cole (2012).

[49] See Reeves, McKee, and Stucker (2014). See also Feldman (2014) and Cylus, Glymour, and Avendano (2015).

[50] See National Center for Children in Poverty (2013).

[51] See Johnston (2015).

[52] Real aggregate net worth per household wealth in the US only recovered its 2007 level by 2013, after several years of decline. By far the greatest recovery occurred among the top 1.2 million households, the top 1 percent that participated in the strong stock market recovery from 2011 to 2015. For all other segments of the wealth distribution, given the continued stagnation of the housing market, the middle class's stock market's median household net worth continued to be below 2007 levels.

This was just the American experience. In many European countries—Greece, Spain, Italy, Ireland, Iceland, Hungary, and France—the social and economic costs of the 2008 Great Recession were even more severe.

Furthermore, the leading banks received hundreds of $billions of taxpayer-supplied capital and zero-interest central bank loans to keep them afloat and help them recover from the crisis they had engineered. In the US alone, the US Treasury provided $608 billion of federal "TARP" bailout capital to 936 banks and other financial institutions in 2008–10, at least $237 billion of which will never be paid back.[53]

Back in the 1980s, almost all of the top 22 financial institutions were also deeply implicated in the Third World debt crisis, which cost developing countries an entire decade of growth. Back then, these very same big banks—or their ancestors—had also digested hundreds of $billions of bailouts, tax breaks, and write-downs from the US Treasury, the World Bank, the IMF, and other development banks and governments, in order to avoid paying the costs of *that* crisis.

Finally, since the 2008 crisis, around the globe, these very same big banks, their lawyers and lobbyists, have been working overtime not only to avoid penalties and prosecutions for their past crimes, but also to lobby *against* the tougher new financial regulations and penalties that are needed to prevent the *next* financial crisis. And, as we will see shortly, in addition to shifting the costs of the financial crisis to the middle class and the poor, these same taxpayer-dependent banks have also been helping the world's wealthiest people hide $trillions of wealth from taxation and the rule of law.

As Bertold Brecht once remarked, "For what is the crime of robbing a bank, compared with crime of *owning* one?"

But what is perhaps most surprising, in light of what we've just seen, is that in order to crack down on all this serial chicanery by the global haven industry, the world community—as represented by the G20 and the OECD—have decided to rely on *information reporting measures* that essentially depend heavily on the assumption that banks, accounting firms, law firms, and other professional enablers are really willing to suddenly give up regulatory mining and become tax collectors. A wiser course of action would be to examine

[53] See the "Bailout Tracker" at http://projects.propublica.org/bailout/ (2013) (accessed 15 July 2015) for the gross and net US Treasury aid to the banking system. As of November 2013, of $608 billion of US Treasury TARP and other direct aid to 936 institutions, including FHFA (Fannie and Freddie), $371 of capital had been returned to the federal government. In addition, interest and warrants on this aid yielded the US Treasury $198 billion of income. All told, an "NPV" basis, even at a modest 2 percent discount rate, and allowing for the earnings on the $608 billion, the US Treasury registered a $62 billion net loss on this "investment." All of the largest banks paid back the initial capital that was provided to them, with interest and warrants, but of course they also played a major role in the uncompensated $billions of losses on fraudulent mortgaged-backed securities and CDOs that were purchased by Fannie Mae, Freddie Mac, and many other institutions, as well as the far greater losses suffered by the larger society, as discussed above.

their overall track records, as we have just done, and consider precisely what tougher incentives are needed to fundamentally alter their behavior. The good news is that all this sordid behavior, especially rampant tax avoidance, may at least have created one opportunity for near-term tax justice—the AWT.

2.3.8 The Size and Growth of Hidden Offshore Wealth

While there are obviously no public estimates of the value of all the offshore private wealth stashed in havens, it is possible to estimate it indirectly. Our estimation methods, described in detail elsewhere,[54] approach this like the challenge of estimating the size of a black hole, and triangulate on the estimates indirectly, using a combination of several different, independent data sources. These include (1) data from the Bank for International Settlements on cross-border bank deposits by "non-banks," most of which are from shell companies, trusts, and individuals; (2) discrepancies in "sources and uses" data on foreign capital flows from the IMF, the World Bank, and central banks; (3) direct estimates of cross-border assets under management, unmanaged deposits, and custodial brokerage assets for the top fifty international private banks, drawn from the these banks' own publications, and supplemented by private banking industry sources; (4) data on the volume of large-denomination currency outstanding for major currencies, including the US dollar, the Swiss franc, and the Euro; (5) direct estimates of the value of international investment portfolios, from the IMF's so-called "IIP" data; and (6) estimates of the value of cross-border non-financial assets, including offshore-registered real estate, gold, art, yachts, planes and other collectibles, drawn from a variety of market-specific sources.

According to our estimates, the global stock of *unrecorded private financial net assets—including currency, bank deposits, stocks and bonds, and other tradable securities*—invested in or through offshore havens already totaled $21 to $32 trillion by the end of 2010, about 10 to 15 percent of global financial wealth (see Table 2.8).[55] And this "missing" wealth stock has continued to grow since then. Indeed, from 2004 to 2015, right through the financial crisis, it grew at a nominal annual average rate of nearly 16 percent a year.[56] As of 2015, this "missing" stock of offshore private financial wealth is worth at least $24 to $36 trillion.

[54] For more details, see Henry (2012); Henry (2016).

[55] Henry (2012), supra. See also PRNewswire (2012). For an alternative $7 trillion estimate of total offshore financial wealth, which is implausibly low—about the same as our estimate for the developing world alone—see Zucman (2015.) Zucman's estimates are based largely on IMF's IIP data, which has well-known holes. These become clearest at the level of individual countries. For further analysis, see Henry (2016).

[56] Based on our data for offshore private banking assets under management, these assets grew at an average rate of 15.8 percent per year from 2005 through 2010, and have continued to grow

Table 2.8 Offshore financial assets, high-net-worth individuals (December, $trn)

	2002	2003	2004	2005	2006	2007	2008	2009	2010
Offshore Deposits[1]	$3.11	$3.8936	$4.566	$4.681	$5.946	$7.46	$6.9999	$6.5899	$6.9892
External deposits – non-banks							$6.9999	$6.5899	$7.0030
									$6.8983
Unallocated liabilites to non-banks	$0.08	$0.26	$0.07	$0.063	$0.08	$0.09	$0.1060	$0.1096	$0.1103
Intl organizations – non-bank deposits	$0.06	$0.08	$0.08	$0.09	$0.11	$0.13	$0.0992	$0.0559	$0.06
TOTAL	3.186	4.159	4.633	4.744	6.029	7.417	7.007	6.644	7.052
	0.208	0.369	0.428	0.462	0.608	0.853	0.707	0.692	0.265
	3.394	4.528	5.061	5.206	6.637	8.270	7.713	7.335	7.317
Liquidity Ratio[2]									
>Minimum[3]	3.0	3.0	3.0	3.0	3.0	3.0	3.0	3.0	3.0
>Max (ML/CG Ave)[4]	4.5	4.5	4.5	4.5	4.5	4.5	4.5	4.5	4.5
Liquid Assets									
>Minimum	$9.3	$11.7	$13.7	$14.0	$17.8	$22.4	$21.0	$19.9	$21.2
>Max (ML/CG Ave)	$14.0	$17.5	$20.5	$21.1	$26.8	$33.6	$31.5	$29.9	$31.7
Est Average	$11.7	$14.6	$17.1	$17.6	$22.3	$28.0	$26.2	$24.9	$26.4

[1] BIS Table 1: external deposit liabilities to non-banks

[2] Yearly average portfolio ration, deposits to total liquid financial assets (including tradable equities and fixed income)

[3] Using TJN's very conservative assumption for liquidity ratio, based on the 2004 McKinsey study

[4] Using ML/CapGemini's average portfolio allocation for HNWIs, 2004–10

Source: BIS data (2004–10), ML/CapGemini (2004–10) HNWI asset allocations, author's analysis

In addition, the value *of private non-financial net cross-border wealth*—real estate, gold, other precious metals, precious gems, art, rare books, cars, religious icons, photos, stamps, yachts, ships, submarines, jets, real estate, farms, mines, forests, oil fields, copyrights, brands, patents, and other intellectual property—that is owned through anonymous haven companies, trusts, foundations, and private vaults—is now worth at least another \$8–\$10 trillion.[57]

From a tax justice angle, the key fact about all this underreported offshore private wealth is that its ownership is very concentrated. More than 90 percent of it belongs to less than 10 million people, just 0.014 percent of the world's population. And the top 100,000 families on the planet, each of which has a net worth of at least \$30 million, own a third to half of it (see Table 2.9).

For purposes of economic and political development, another crucial fact is that at least a third of all this offshore private wealth—at least \$7–\$9 trillion—derives from unrecorded capital flows that originated in low- and middle-income developing countries. In many cases the resulting unrecorded capital outflows and stocks have been large enough to more than offset net foreign direct investment entirely (see Figure 2.16).

The top twenty source countries alone account for about 80 percent of developing country flight wealth (see Figure 2.17). In particular, key source regions like Latin America have contributed more than \$1.4 trillion of unrecorded real net outflows (see Figure 2.18). Since more than half of these unrecorded flows has been reinvested offshore at untaxed yields, the accumulated *stock* of Latin American financial wealth resulting from these outflows is now worth more than \$2 trillion. And at least \$1.2 trillion to \$1.6 trillion this belongs to the wealthy residents of just four countries: Argentina, Brazil, Mexico, and Venezuela (see Table 2.10).

Up to now, published estimates of "illicit flows" and "capital flight" have failed to take account of these *reinvested*, untaxed, and unreported earnings. But "illicit flows" are not all consumed, and the investments they generate, in turn, yield income that tends to be reinvested offshore. This highlights the importance of the global haven industry, which plays a huge role in tending to such investments.

These offshore reinvestments have been especially important for regions like Latin America, Africa, and some Asian countries where capital flight has been

at double-digit rates since then, driven by surging capital flight from key source countries like Russia and China.

[57] Indeed, anonymous high-net-worth offshore investors—including not a few crooks and kleptocrats—have become significant investors in many of the world's cultural and financial capitals, including the City of London, New York City, Tokyo, Los Angeles, Paris, Miami, San Francisco, Boston, Chicago, Singapore, Shanghai, Sydney, Hong Kong, Monoco, Panama, Malta, Cyprus, Vienna, Swiss cantons like Geneva, Zug, and Zurich, and a surprisingly large number of private islands. For a recent investigation of the role of secretive offshore investors in the New York City real estate market, see Story and Saul (2015).

Table 2.9 Global distribution, net financial assets 2010

		Total number	Ave. net financial worth per capita ($m)	Total liquid net worth ($trn)	Of which: 'offshore' ($trn)	% of all global net financial wealth	% of All People
"Happy Few"	> $30m	91,186	$183.1	$16.7	$9.8	30.3%	0.001%
"Just Rich"	>$5–$30m	839,020	$12.8	$10.7	$5.1	19.4%	0.01%
"Barely Rich"	>$1–$5m	8,419,794	$2.1	$17.4	$4.7	31.6%	0.13%
GLOBAL ELITE	All > $1m	9,350,000	$4.4	$44.8	$19.6	81.3%	0.14%
EVERYONE ELSE		6,643,863,592	$0.0016	$10.3`	$1.0**		99.86%
TOTAL		6,653,213,592	$0.01	$55.1	$20.6	100%	100%

Note: ** Foreign currency (mainly dollars and euros)
Source: ML/Cap Gemini (2001–9); World Bank data; UN Wider (07); US Treasury (09); our analysis© JSH 2010, 2014

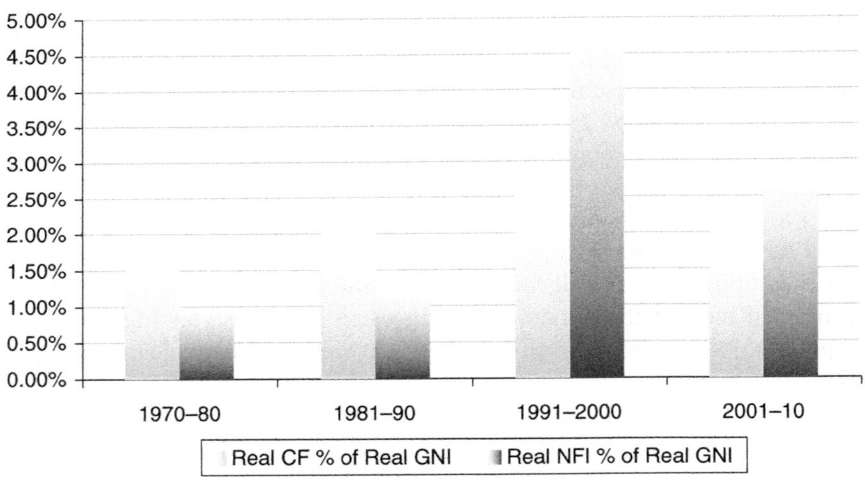

Figure 2.16 Top 8 Latin American source countries

going on for decades. Indeed, for such regions, the amount of reinvested offshore earnings is now substantial enough so *that even if all new unrecorded capital outflows dried up completely*, the total stock of missing offshore wealth would continue to grow, tax free, for decades (see Figure 2.19 and Table 2.11). This is an important amendment to the traditional concepts of "capital flight" and "illicit flows," which ignore such reinvestments, and don't really answer the question—where do all those flows wind up?

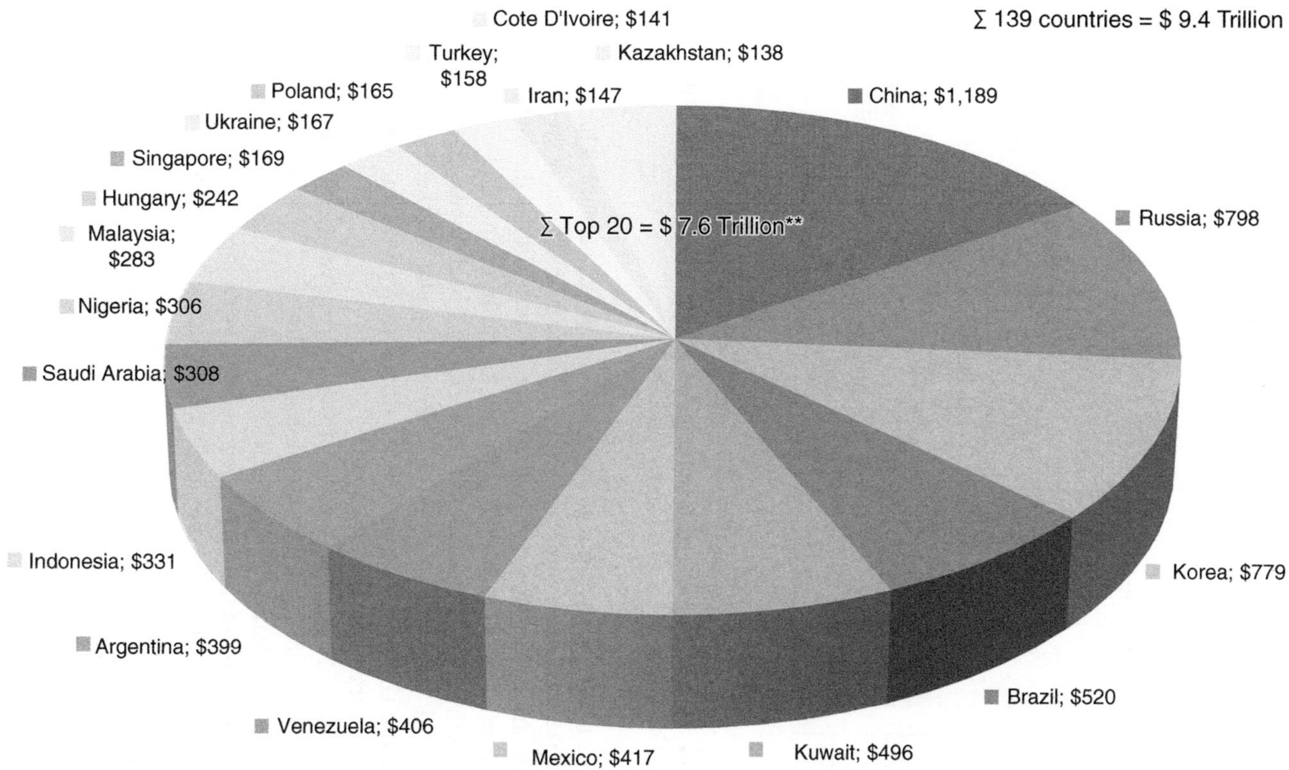

Figure 2.17 Global flight wealth—key source countries, including China (2010, $bn)

Note: Of these, 13 low- to middle-income countries account for $5.4trn

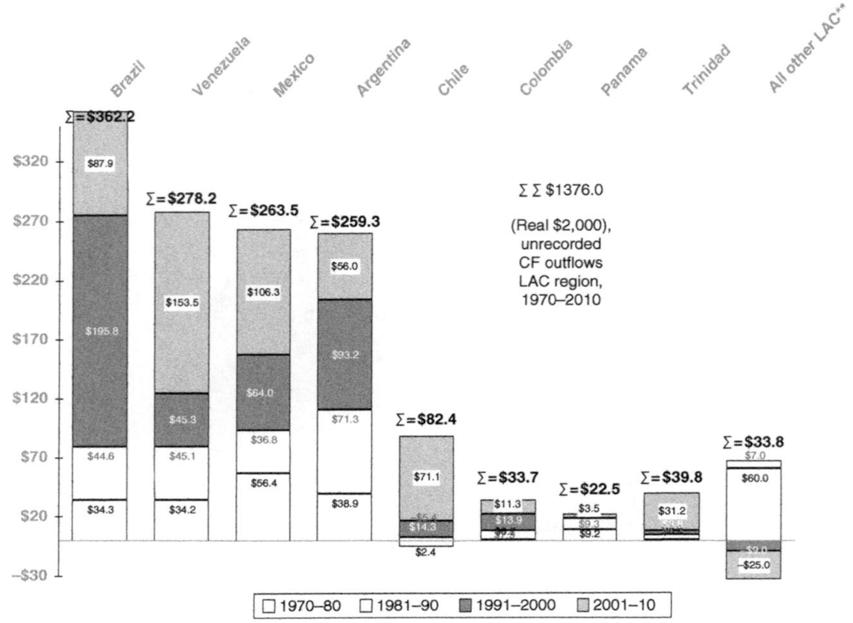

Figure 2.18 Unrecorded net capital outflows from Latin America, 1970–2010

Source: World Bank (WDI 2015 raw data); author's analysis

Once we take all this accumulated offshore wealth into account, it turns out that developing countries as a whole, and, indeed, each and every one of the top twenty source countries, have not really been "debtor countries" since the mid-1990s.

First, most of the $7 to $9 trillion of missing offshore financial wealth owned by the wealthy elites of developing countries has been invested, not in other Third World countries, but in First World capital markets and banks—especially the United States, the United Kingdom, Switzerland, Germany, and a handful of other European markets.

Second, as of 2014, $7.0 trillion of official reserves (including gold) was owned by low-middle-income developing countries.[58] Most of this is also invested in First World assets, especially US Treasury bills. Third, we can net out about $5 trillion of the gross external debt of developing countries, most of which was owed to First World creditors, including the World Bank and the IMF.[59]

All told, therfore, as of 2014, developing countries as a whole were *net creditors* to the First World and the multilateral establishment to the tune of

[58] World Bank (2014) data, our analysis.

[59] Projected from the latest World Bank (2014) figures for gross external debt stocks of all low-middle-income developing countries (WDI).

Table 2.10 Unrecorded capital flows, offshore assets, and offshore earnings, 1970–2010

Latin American and Caribbean Region
FOREIGN DEBT ADJUSTED FOR CURRENCY CHANGES, RESCHEDULINGS, AND ARREARS
(Nominal and Real 2000 $bn)
(40 countries in region - 34 with data)

Periods	Country	Original unrecorded outflows	Original unrecorded outflows	Offshore earnings (Σ$bn)	CF/ GNI	CF/ Sources	Flight Stock	External Debt	CF Stock/	Real Offshore Earnings/
		Σ Nom $bn	Σ Real #bn		Period medians		($B 2010)	($B 2010)	Ext. Debt	Real Original Outflows
Periods	Country		($2,000)	($2,000)	%	%	(Nominal)	(Nominal)	%	%
1970–2010	Brazil	$345.00	$362.60	$247.30	1.70%	43%	$519.50	$324.50	160%	68%
1970–2010	Argentina	$213.90	$259.30	$272.80	3.40%	68%	$399.10	$129.60	308%	105%
1970–2010	Mexico	$221.70	$263.50	$299.10	1.80%	36%	$417.50	$186.40	224%	113%
1970–2010	Venezuela	$269.10	$278.20	$202.00	5.70%	82%	$405.80	$55.70	728%	73%
	Big Four	$1,049.70	$1,163.60	$1,021.20			$1,741.90	$696.10	250%	88%
1975–2010	Chile	$94.50	$82.40	$14.40	0.90%	43.40%	$105.00	$86.40	122%	17%
1970–2010	Colombia	$32.40	$33.70	$21.40	0.90%	29.70%	$47.90	$63.00	76%	63%
1970–2010	Panama	$14.30	$23.30	$37.60	9.90%	73.00%	$37.60	$11.40	330%	161%
1970–2010	Trinidad	$44.30	$39.80	$11.60	5.40%	80.30%	$53.00	$4.00	1314%	29%
1970–2010	Uruguay	$9.60	$9.40	$5.20	1.00%	41.50%	$13.30	$12.90	103%	55%
1970–2010	Dom Rep	$7.90	$7.90	$3.10	1.40%	34.80%	$10.20	$13.10	78%	39%
1970–2010	Ecuador	$6.30	$11.50	$23.60	2.10%	57.10%	$21.60	$14.80	146%	205%
1970–2010	Peru	$1.70	$3.30	$11.70	1.68%	37.20%	$8.10	$36.10	22%	353%
1970–2010	El Salvador	$8.10	$8.50	$5.50	1.90%	39.40%	$11.20	$10.10	110%	64%
1970–2010	Bolivia	$9.50	$11.70	$14.30	5.20%	63.60%	$18.40	$5.30	349%	122%
	Next 10	$228.60	$231.60	$148.30		$326.30	$257.00	$0.00	127%	64%
	All Other LAC (n=24)	($23.50)	($19.70)	$20.80	-0.60%	9.10%	($9.90)	$60.20	−17%	
	LAC TOTAL	$1,255	$1,376	$1,190	2.50%	51%	$2,058	$1,013	203%	87%

Source: World Bank/IMF/UN/central bank/CIA (data); author's analysis. Adjusted for currency composition of debt; 75% reinvestment rate; average yield = US$ 6 mos CD rate

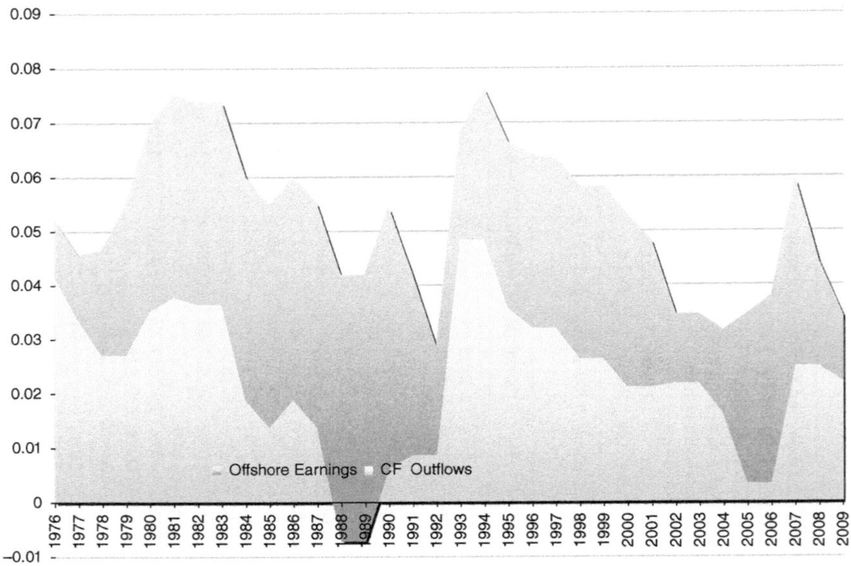

Figure 2.19 New unrecorded capital outflows and imputed offshore earnings as a percentage of GNI, 1976–2009 (real value of cumulative net outflows by period, 2000 $bn)

Note: ** Thirty other Latin American and Caribbean countries
Source: Data from World Bank/IMF (1979–2008); author's analysis

Table 2.11 Real cumulative offshore earnings vs real cumulative capital outflows, by region 1970–2010 (Σ real 2000 $bn)

	Offshore earnings	Capital outflows	Ratio
LA	$1,190.30	$1,375.50	86.5%
FSU/Casia	$354.10	$1,509.90	23.5%
SSA	$354.70	$361.70	98.1%
Mena	$1,072.60	$963.20	111.4%
E Asia	$685.30	$1,881.70	36.4%
S Asia	$72.70	$60.70	119.7%
All regions	**$3,729.70**	**$6,152.80**	**60.6%**

at least $10.1 trillion.[60] Of this, China alone accounted for $4.4 trillion. This reflects not only its leading role as a source of capital flight, but also the accumulation of more than $3.8 trillion of official reserves, compared with an external debt of just $800 million. The story of China's enormous role in financing US deficits is of course well known. But this other side of the story is less well known. Apart from China, in the aggregate, other low–middle

[60] World Bank (2014) data, our analysis.

income countries are *even larger* net creditors of OECD countries, to the tune of nearly $6 trillion.

In this sense, therefore, the so-called "Third World debt problem" is not really a "*debt problem*" after all, nor has it been a debt problem for more than a decade.[61] It is really a *tax problem*—reflecting the inability of developing countries to tax their own high-net-worth citizens on their offshore wealth, once they move it abroad.

They are not able to do so for many reasons—including poorly trained local tax administrations, domestic corruption, and the intrinsic complexity of global tax enforcement.

But by far the most important reason for the inability of most developing countries to tax offshore wealth and income is the fact that they are up against an influential transnational elite whose wealth is managed and secured by the most talented professional money launderers and tax dodgers that money can buy—the global haven industry.

These countries need our help. They certainly deserve it. After all, as we have just seen, this is *our* industry.

2.4 WHAT SHOULD WE DO ABOUT IT?

So the grand jury has returned with a pretty damning indictment of our careless, imbalanced approach to neoliberal globalization, bank misbehavior, and international tax dodging. The global tax justice movement's job now is not simply to continue this investigation ad infinitum and uncover even more salacious details forever, or to lobby patiently for technical legal reforms. Undoubtedly that kind of investigative economics will continue, but I submit that by now we already know enough to design some very practical, revenue-generating solutions.

From this angle, it is important to recall the difference between the role of historical agents and detached spectators.[62] Activists have a responsibility to develop pragmatic solutions that stand a chance of gaining international support, in order to address the most pressing problems of development finance: severe public revenue shortfalls, the shifting of tax burdens to the poor, rising debt levels, and cutbacks in essential public

[61] Based on a historical time series of aggregate unrecorded net capital outflows, I estimate that the overall value of the offshore flight wealth owned by the wealthy citizens of developing countries, plus official reserves, eclipsed the *book value* of low- and middle-income developing country foreign debt as early as 1994. Had developing country debt been "marked to market," given the low market-to-book ratio for many developing countries in the early 1990s, the eclipse would have occurred even earlier.

[62] As the philosopher Richard Rorty (1998: 14–15) wrote, "In so far as a Left becomes spectatorial and retrospective, it ceases to be a Left... The academic Left has no projects to propose..., no vision of a country to be achieved by building a consensus on the need for specific reforms."

spending. These are the very problems that created the demand for a global tax justice movement in the first place.

By now it should be clear that neoliberal globalization has created a lengthy list of problems that go considerably beyond the problem of financial transparency. Reigning in these abuses requires many initiatives—not just measures like automatic information exchange and beneficial ownership registration, but also (1) more effective preventive regulation of the global haven industry; (2) tougher penalties for tax dodgers, kleptocrats, and their enablers; (3) mandatory on- and offshore wealth disclosure for public officials; (4) stronger protection for financial whistleblowers; and (5) innovative new taxes that can provide incentives for greater transparency—like the AWT.

Implementing such reforms will take time. But the global tax justice movement should not be content merely with lobbying for technical amendments to the existing international tax system that might succeed in slightly reforming this hodge-podge system some fine day; we need stretch targets.

As we have argued, trillions in anonymous, largely untaxed, in many cases crime-related private wealth is just sitting there, invested in relatively low-yield offshore investments. If we can figure out how to levy a modest global tax on it, or at least encourage it to return to the surface where it can be more productively invested, all this wealth might begin to make a positive contribution while we wait for more comprehensive reforms.

Here are the key elements of our Anonymous Wealth Tax (AWT) proposal, in addition to those noted earlier:

1. As discussed, in the offshore world, wealthy investors and even kleptocrats tend to favor larger, more established private banking, wealth management firms, hedge funds, and insurance companies. The resulting concentration of financial wealth in the hands of a handful of giant financial institutions opens the door to a wealth tax that would be relatively simple to administer.[63]

We are proposing an initial a 0.5 percent per year withholding tax on the average gross asset value of all "anonymous" customer assets under management and non-managed assets (deposits, currency, gold, and custodial/brokerage assets), for all asset-managing hedge funds, trusts or trust-equivalents, insurance companies, and deposit-taking financial institutions with total assets under management greater than a reasonable lower bound—in the first instance, say, $100 million.

Even if the 0.5 percent tax only applied to anonymous cross-border client financial assets under management by in the top fifty global private banks,

[63] For example, despite record levels of financial secrecy, record numbers of secrecy jurisdictions, and record numbers of "enablers."

wealth managers, hedge funds, and insurance firms, it could generate at least $50 to $60 billion a year—at most 10 percent of the annual income earned by these offshore assets.

2. This proposal is for a wealth levy, *not* an income tax. It recognizes that the value of financial assets is often easier to define than income, that income is more volatile than wealth, and that important classes of offshore investors—especially wealthy individuals, corrupt officials, and criminals—are much less concerned with yield than with asset preservation.

3. The levy would be applied on a worldwide assets basis by the national governments of the countries where financial institutions and wealth managers have their corporate headquarters and/or major operations. Much like a value-added-tax or "carbon tax," it could be levied on a pro rata basis on the financial institutions themselves, based on the global aggregates of reported quarterly customer assets under management, non-managed assets, and custodial assets. Financial institutions would then be free to apportion these charges to individual customers or nominee account holders as they see fit—probably in proportion to asset values. One appeal of this approach is that we don't have to know precisely who owns any specific accounts or assets, and that it could be levied even though the 10 million high-net-worth investors who own the anonymous wealth are scattered all over the globe.

4. Since private banking institutions and other asset managers are already required to mark to market the value of customer financial assets, in order to report such aggregate asset values in their own financial statements and regulatory reports every quarter, and also to regularly report these market values to their customers—often on an intra-day basis—the costs of assessing and collecting this tax should be minimal. This is especially true compared with the cost of collecting the Tobin tax on literally billions of capital market or currency market transactions. Financial institutions might be permitted to exempt small account holders from their proportionate share of this levy. AWT will also not try to tax the value of less liquid forms of offshore wealth, which raise trickier valuation questions, and are also already often subject to local property taxes.

5. Our discussion of the protracted quasi-criminal history of leading financial institutions was useful preparation for designing this tax. Based on this experience, we should certainly not expect compliance to be perfect. Indeed, there are notorious cases where the leading banks like HSBC, Credit Suisse, and Wegelin have gone to extraordinary lengths to move assets off the books by using devices like storage vaults, omnibus trust accounts, "independent" trustees, "foundations," and other gambits to avoid new regulations designed to catch tax dodgers.[64]

[64] See, for example, the revelations about HSBC helping the UK clients of its Geneva office to avoid withholding tax in Leigh, Ball, Garside, and Pegg (2015).

To anticipate the serious risk of institutional non-compliance, part of this initiative should include a special monitoring and enforcement arm with adequate resources for investigating bank asset reporting and recommending appropriate penalties—including possible jail time for any senior executives involved.

6. Despite these challenges, this withholding tax should not be any more difficult to enforce against major banks, accounting firms, and law firms than many other laws and regulations. Indeed, since 2014, the US Foreign Account Tax Compliance Act (2010)[65] requires more than 100,000 financial institutions, trusts, and companies that do business in the United States to register, to report the foreign assets of US citizens and any income paid abroad to them or to companies they control, and to withhold up to 30 percent of these payments. AWT's requirements are much less onerous.

7. As noted one possibility is that the revenues raised by this levy would be dedicated to the costs of addressing pressing global problems such as climate change—which may cost upwards of $100 billion per year by 2020. Funds collected would therefore be remitted to a new Earth Trust, jointly established and administered by the G20 and the UN, in order to finance climate change relief, and secondarily, vital development projects.

8. Once formed, the Earth Trust would implement agreements with each key reporting banking center. It is possible that only the BIS' existing - forty-four reporting IFCs would need to be involved in the front-end collection process. Of those, the top five account for more than half of all private banking assets, so the United States, the United Kingdom, Switzerland, Germany, Hong Kong, and Singapore would constitute a critical mass.

9. National authorities may decide to permit taxpayers to reclaim a portion of withheld levies, upon showing that they have paid all domestic income taxes due in their home countries, and that their offshore assets are from lawful sources. This would make this a "tax on anonymity." Even this would help to level the playing field between offshore and onshore taxation.

However, another key objective of this program is to shift part of the cost of climate change to wealthy "citizens of nowhere" who not only can better afford the burden, but may also have been avoiding tax burdens up to now. So the best universal policy might well be to agree that this relatively tiny levy on offshore wealth should not be refundable, but dedicated to climate relief.

10. Of course for all this to happen we have to assume an unprecedented level of multilateral cooperation. So far, most other such multilateral taxing schemes, like the Tobin Tax, have proved to be politically intractable. The difference now may be, not only that we understand that all this criminal

[65] For more details about FATCA's extensive regulations, see IRS (2015).

wealth is escaping taxation, but that over the next two decades, the world really is desparate for global tax revenue to tackle urgent problems like climate change.[66]

Moreover, a uniform global levy on offshore wealth, widely adopted and enforced, wouldn't disadvantage any particular offshore center. So, US, UK, and Swiss banks could continue to compete for the funds of wealthy foreigners. And tax justice activists can continue to press these jurisdictions to adopt more fundamental reforms.

With respect to gaining the support of other tax havens, the key target is not individual jurisdictions but the financial institutions, accounting firms, and law firms behind them. Assuming strong leadership in the world's key capitals, most conduit jurisdictions will fall in place.

In the end, however, no such tax is ever foolproof. The right question is not, "Is this complex and difficult?" Nor is it, "Is this a perfect tax?" The right question is the economist's question: "Compared to what?" From this angle, compared with other alternatives for taxing the world's elite, this one takes advantage of the convenient fact that all this anonymous offshore wealth is not widely distributed all over the planet, but concentrated in a comparative handful of global financial institutions. What have we got to lose?

2.5 CONCLUSION

Will the world's offshore elite scatter to the ends of the earth in response to such a modest wealth tax? Will the world's largest financial institutions—which have benefitted so much from government bailouts, low interest loans, and subsidies, and which also happen to have been heavy lenders to projects and companies that stand to lose from climate change—help them do so? They may try. But hope springs eternal, even among tax justice activists: at some point I think they might well have an epiphany—"Hey, we're talking about $50–100 billion a year out of $22 trillion here. That's 0.5 percent a year. If we can't figure out how to boost investment yields by a half a percent in this great wide world in order to save the planet, maybe we shouldn't be your private bankers."

[66] It is also important to note here, for the sake of gaining US support for this proposal, that US taxpayers have often paid a disproportionate share of the costs of international development initiatives. They need to understand that it might really be in their best interests if the rest of the world—especially tax dodgers and kleptocrats—help to pick up the tab for climate change.

ACKNOWLEDGMENT

Research support for this chapter was provided by the Norwegian Research Council's Norglobal Taxation Capital and Development Programme #212220/H30 ("Systems of Tax Evasion and Laundering"), 2012–15.

REFERENCES

Arnold, Martin, 2014. "Bank Settlements Hit $56bn in Most Expensive Year on Record," *Financial Times.* 26 December. http://www.ft.com/intl/cms/s/0/baa2d2c0-89c2-11e4-9dbf-00144feabdc0.html?siteedition=intl#axzz3NghRZT14, accessed 10 September 2015.

BLS 2015. Online Database on Labor Force Statistics, Available at http://www.bls.gov, accessed 28 August 2015.

Boston Consulting Group 2014. "Global Risk 2014–2015: Building the Transparent Bank." https://www.bcgperspectives.com/content/articles/financial_institutions_growth_building_transparent_bank_global_risk_2014_2015/, accessed 10 September 2015.

Breslow, Jason M., 2013. "Were Bankers Jailed in Past Financial Crises?" *PBS.* 22 January. http://www.pbs.org/wgbh/pages/frontline/business-economy-financial-crisis/untouchables/were-bankers-jailed-in-past-financial-crises/, accessed 15 July 2015.

Business Insider, 2014. "5 Years Ago Bernie Madoff Was Sentenced to 150 Years in Prison—Here's How His Scheme Worked," 1 July, http://www.businessinsider.com/how-bernie-madoffs-ponzi-scheme-worked-2014-7, accessed 28 August 2015.

CCP Research Foundation, n.d. "Conduct Costs Results." http://conductcosts.ccpresearchfoundation.com/conduct-costs-results, accessed 15 July 2015.

CNBC, 2014. "Five Years After Stanford Scandal, Many Victims Penniless," 15 February, http://www.cnbc.com/2014/02/14/-many-victims-penniless.html, accessed 28 August 2015.

Cole, R. A., 2012. "How Did the Financial Crisis Affect Small Business Lending in the US?" Small Business Administration. November. https://www.sba.gov/sites/default/files/files/rs399tot.pdf, accessed 15 July 2015.

Comfort, Nicholas, 2013. "European Banks Legal Tab Tops $77 Billion as Probes Widen," *Bloomberg.* 21 November. http://www.bloomberg.com/news/2013-11-21/european-banks-legal-tab-exceeds-77-billion-amid-probes.html, accessed 15 July 2015.

Cylus, J., M. Maria Glymour, and M. Avendano, 2015. "Health Effects of Unemployment Benefit Program Generosity," *American Journal of Public Health* 105 (2): 317–23. http://ajph.aphapublications.org/doi/abs/10.2105/AJPH.2014.302253

David, Javier E., 2015. "Ayn Rand Is 110 and still in Your Face after all These Years," *CNBC.* 7 February. http://www.cnbc.com/id/102402020, accessed 15 July 2015.

FDIC, 2014. "Statistics on Depository Institutions." https://www5.fdic.gov/sdi/main.asp, accessed 10 September 2015.

Feldman, Justin, 2014. "Suicides during the Great Recession in the United States, Canada and Europe," *Journalist's Resource.* 25 June. http://journalistsresource.org/studies/society/public-health/suicides-during-great-recession-united-states-canada-europe, accessed 15 July 2015.

Fisher, Luchina, 2013. "Tina Turner to Become Swiss Citizen," *ABC News*. 25 January. http://abcnews.go.com/blogs/entertainment/2013/01/tina-turner-to-become-swiss-citizen/, accessed 15 July 2015.

Henry, James S., 1976. "Calling in the Big Bills: A Painless Way to Catch Tax Evaders and Cripple Organized Crime." *The Washington Monthly*, May, 1976, 27–33. (Cover story.)

Henry, James S., 1978. "Why the Underground Economy Is Booming." *Fortune Magazine*, October, 1978 (Study of the demand for cash).

Henry, James S., 1979. Statement, "Hearings on the Underground Economy." US Congress, Joint Economic Committee, November 15, 1979 (pp. 38–55, 70–6 of the Committee report).

Henry, James S., 1980. "How to Make the Mob Miserable: The Cash Connection." *The Washington Monthly*, June, 1980, 54–61.

Henry, James S., 1981. "The Illicit Cocaine Market: Recent Trends in Latin American Production and U.S. Consumption." (Paper presented to Panel on the Underground Economy, Southern Economics Association Meetings, New Orleans, Louisiana, October, 1981.)

Henry, James S., 1983. "Noncompliance with U.S. Tax Law: Evidence on Size, Growth, and Composition" (Washington, DC: Paper presented to American Bar Association Conference on Noncompliance, Reston, Va., March 16–19, 1983.). Published in *The Tax Lawyer*, Vol. 37, No. 1 (Fall, 1983), and in *Income Tax Compliance: A Report of the ABA Section of Taxation* (Washington, DC, ABA, 1983). 15–115.

Henry, James S., 1986. "U.S. Role as an International Tax Haven." Presentation to American Association of Legal Scholars Annual Meeting, New Orleans, Louisiana, January, 1986. (AALS Transcript).

Henry, James S., 1986. "The Debt Hoax: "Where Third World Loans Went." *The New Republic*, April 14, 1986, 20–3. (Cover story.)

Henry, James S., 1987. "Morgan's Fallen Angel," Manhattan Inc, April, 1987, 63–72.

Henry, James S., 1988. "Capital Exodus," *The New Republic*, November 14, 1988, 19–20.

Henry, James S., 1988. "Flight and Debt," *The Washington Post*, Outlook, December 11, 1988.

Henry, James S., 1989. "America the Tax Haven," *The Washington Post*, January 19, 1989.

Henry, James S., 1989. "The Philippines: The More Things Change . . . " Pts 1-4. International Development Review (Beijing: Int'l Media Partners, May 1989). Report from Tiananmen.

Henry, James S., 1989. "Paraguay's Dictator." *IMF Annual Meeting News*, September 28, 1989.

Henry, James S., 1989. "Hot Money Pipeline," *The Washington Post*, November 26, 1989.

Henry, James S., 1990. "Where's the Money?" *Midweek* (Manila), January 24, 1990, 32–4.

Henry, James S., 1996. "Banqueros y Lavadolares." The role of international banks in third world debt, capital flight, corruption, and anti-development" (Bogota: *Tercer Mundo Editores*, May 1996, 564 pages).

Henry, James S., 2003, 2005. *The Blood Bankers. Tales from the Global Underground Economy*. Foreword by Senator Bill Bradley (New York: Basic Books, November 2003, 2005, 427 pp.).

Henry, James S., 2007. "The Mirage of Debt Relief," in Steven Hiatt (ed.), *A Game As Old As Empire* (SF: Barrett Koehler, 2007), 219–60.

Henry, James S., 2008. "The Attack of the Pirate Bankers," *The Nation*, July 22, 2008. http://www.thenation.com/article/attack-global-pirate-bankers/.

Henry, James S., 2009. "Tax Haven Crackdown Could Deliver At Least $120 billion a Year to Fight Poverty," Oxfam GB. Submitted to G20, March 13, 2009. (https://www.oxfam.org/en/pressroom/pressreleases/2009-03-13/tax-haven-crackdown-could-deliver-120bn-year-fight-poverty).

Henry, James S., 2012. "The Price of Offshore Revisited," *Tax Justice Network* (July 2012). http://www.taxjustice.net/cms/upload/pdf/Price_of_Offshore_Revisited_120722.pdf, accessed 15 July 2012.

Henry, James S., 2016. *Pirate Bankers* (NY: Columbia University Press, forthcoming).

Hirschman, Albert, 1970. *Exit, Voice, and Loyalty: Responses to Decline in Firms, Organizations, and States.* Harvard University Press, Cambridge.

IRS, 2015. "Foreign Account Tax Compliance Act." http://www.irs.gov/Businesses/Corporations/Foreign-Account-Tax-Compliance-Act-FATCA, accessed 15 July 2015.

JLL, n.d. "Global Capital Market Research." http://www.joneslanglasallesites.com/gcf/global-capital-markets-research/cities, accessed 15 July 2015.

Johnston, David Cay, 2015. "Economy Grows, Incomes Shrink," Aljazeera America. 30 January. http://america.aljazeera.com/opinions/2015/1/economy-grows-incomes-shrink.html, accessed 15 July 2015.

Leigh, David, James Ball, Juliette Garside, and David Pegg, 2015. "HSBC Files Show How Swiss Bank Helped Clients Dodge Taxes and Hide Millions," *The Guardian*. 8 February. http://www.theguardian.com/business/2015/feb/08/hsbc-files-expose-swiss-bank-clients-dodge-taxes-hide-millions, accessed 15 July 2015.

Lynch, Sarah N., 2015. "U.S. Regulators Question whether Credit Suisse Has Rule-breaking Culture," *Reuters*. 15 January. http://www.reuters.com/article/2015/01/15/us-creditsuisse-exemption-idUSKBN0KO0E120150115, accessed 15 July 2015.

Nader, Ralph, Mark Green, and Joel Seligman, 1977. *Taming the Giant Corporation.* Norton, New York.

National Center for Children in Poverty, n.d. http://www.nccp.org/topics/childpoverty.html, accessed 15 July 2015.

Office of Management and Budget, n.d. http://www.whitehouse.gov/omb/budget/Historicals, accessed 15 July 2015.

Pettit, Philip, 2012. *On the People's Terms: A Republican Theory and Model of Democracy.* Cambridge University Press, Cambridge.

PRNewswire, 2012. "Credit Suisse: Global Household Wealth Falls 5.2% to USD 223 Trillion, with Eurozone Crisis as Backdrop," *PRNewswire*. 10 October. http://www.prnewswire.com/news-releases/credit-suisse-global-household-wealth-falls-52-to-usd-223-trillion-with-eurozone-crisis-as-backdrop-173564661.html, accessed 15 July 2015.

RealityTrac, 2015a. "1.1 Million U.S. Properties with Foreclosure Filings in 2014, down 18 Percent from 2013 to Lowest Level since 2006," *RealityTrac*. 14 January. http://www.realtytrac.com/news/foreclosure-trends/1-1-million-u-s-properties-with-foreclosure-filings-in-2014-down-18-percent-from-2013-to-lowest-level-since-2006/, accessed 15 July 2015.

RealityTrac, 2015b. "7.3 Million Boomerang Buyers Poised to Recover Homeownership in Next 8 Years," *RealityTrac*. 26 January. http://www.realtytrac.com/news/foreclosure-trends/boomerang-buyers/, accessed 15 July 2015.

Reeves, A., M. McKee, and D. Stucker, 2014. "Suicide Rates in the Great Recession in Europe and North America," *British Journal of Psychiatry* 205:246–7.

Republic of South Africa, FSB, 2013. "Review of Third Party Cell Captive Insurance and Similar Arrangements." https://www.fsb.co.za/Departments/insurance/archives/Documents/2013.06.11%20Discussion%20paper.pdf, accessed 10 September 2015.

Rorty, Richard, 1998. *Achieving Our Country*. Harvard University Press, Cambridge.

Sharman, Jason and Gregory Rawlings, 2005. "Deconstructing National Blacklists: Removing Obstacles to Cross Border Trade In Financial Services: A Report Prepared for the Society of Trust and Estate Practitioners." September. https://www.step.org/sites/default/files/Comms/DeconstructingNationalBlacklists.pdf, accessed 15 July 2015.

Shaxson, Nicholas, 2012. *Treasure Islands: Tax Havens and the Men who Stole the World*. Vintage, London.

Sidel, Robin, 2012. "Jailed Banker Is Rare Prize for U.S.," *Wall Street Journal*. 11 November. http://online.wsj.com/news/articles/SB10001424127887324073504578109262775186452, accessed 15 July 2015.

Skinner, Quentin, 1998. *Liberty Before Liberalism*. Cambridge University Press, Cambridge.

Smythe, Christie, 2014. "Credit Suisse Judge Accepts $2.6 Billion Tax Plea Deal," *Bloomberg*. 21 November. http://www.bloomberg.com/news/articles/2014-11-21/credit-suisse-judge-accepts-2-6-billion-tax-plea-deal, accessed 15 July 2015.

Spencer, David E., 1992. "Capital Flight and Bank Secrecy: The End of An Era?" *International Financial Law Review*. May.

Story, Louise and Stephanie Saul, 2015. "Hidden Wealth Flows to Elite New York Condos," *The New York Times*. 8 February. http://www.nytimes.com/images/2015/02/08/nytfrontpage/scan.pdf, 15 July 2015.

Tax Justice Network, 2009, 2011, 2013. "Financial Secrecy Index." http://www.financialsecrecyindex.com, accessed 17 July 2015.

The Guardian, 2009. "G20 Shuts the Door on Tax Havens," 2 April, http://www.theguardian.com/world/2009/apr/02/g20-summit-tax-havens, accessed 28 August 2015.

The Telegraph, 2009. "G20: Nicholas Sarkozy and Angela Merkel Demand Tough Market Regulations," 1 April.

The Telegraph, 2012. "From King of the Caribbean to Penniless in Prison," 9 June, http://www.telegraph.co.uk/finance/financetopics/sir-allen-stanford/9321282/Allen-Stanford-From-king-of-the-Caribbean-to-penniless-in-prison.html, accessed 28 August 2015.

US Bureau of Economic Analysis, Department of Commerce, 2014. "Taxes on Corporate Income by Industry." http://www.bea.gov/iTable, accessed 15 July 2015.

Wikipedia, n.d. "Operation Broken Trust." http://en.wikipedia.org/wiki/Operation_Broken_Trust, accessed 10 September 2015.

World Bank, 2014. *World Development Indicators*, http://databank.worldbank.org/data/home.aspx, accessed 10 September 2015.

Ylonen, Matti, 2015 (in press). "Early Precedents of (sic) Country-by-Country Reporting: Implications for the Analysis of Corporate Power."

Zolkos, Rodd, 2013. "IRS Increases its Scrutiny of Captive Insurance Arrangements," *Business Insurance*. 11 August. http://www.businessinsurance.com/article/20130811/NEWS06/308119974, accessed 15 July 2015.

Zucman, Gabriel, 2015. *The Hidden Wealth of Nations*. (Chicago: University of Chicago Press, 2015).

3

Country-By-Country Reporting

Richard Murphy

3.1 INTRODUCTION

It is now more than a decade since I first proposed the idea of country-by-country reporting by multinational corporations (Murphy, 2003). In essence the idea is a simple one. All that country-by-country reporting demands is that multinational corporations publish a profit and loss account and limited balance sheet and cash flow information for every jurisdiction in which they trade as part of their annual financial statements. Though the idea is simple, it has been the subject of much debate and not a little controversy since I first outlined it in 2003.

That process of debate has not, however, been fruitless. Country-by-country reporting has made enormous strides in the last few years although, as yet, no one is talking about delivery of the key idea of publishing audited separate accounts for each jurisdiction in which a multinational corporation operates. We have instead had statutory requirements in both the United States and European Union (CCFD-Terre Solidaire, 2013) that companies in the extractive industries (relating to oil, gas, mining and in the EU only, forestry) must report the taxes that they pay and limited additional data for each country in which they operate. In addition, the EU has now required (Directive 2013/36/EU, Article 89) that banks publish data on a country-by-country basis for their turnover, number of employees, profit, tax paid, and any subsidies received. Debate is now also taking place in the EU parliament on whether this requirement should be extended to other companies in other sectors. And perhaps most importantly of all, the G8 under the chairmanship of UK Prime Minister David Cameron asked the Organization for Economic Cooperation and Development (OECD) in June 2013 to consider whether multinational corporations should report their profits on a country-by-country basis to all the tax authorities who might consider their affairs (G8 Leaders, 2013, para. 25). This has now been included for consideration by the OECD's Base Erosion and Profit Shifting Program (see Action 13 in OECD, 2013).

As this chapter notes, all these developments under the country-by-country reporting brand name (for that is what it now seems to be) are welcome. However, the core demand has not been achieved. That is why the campaign for full country-by-country reporting is continuing despite progress made to date.

3.2 THE ISSUE AND REFORM PROPOSAL

At the core of the demand for country-by-country reporting is a contention that globalization is not working for the benefit of everyone. Some nation states and large parts of the world's population have lost out as the power of the global corporation has risen, including its power to not pay tax in the right place at the right rate and at the right time. That has been obvious since 2008 and popular agitation since then has highlighted the scale of worldwide tax avoidance by many of the most profitable multinational corporations, leading with Google.[1] What is now also increasingly appreciated is that the model of accounting put forward by the accountancy profession (International Financial Reporting Standards) exacerbated the financial crisis that erupted in that year in a number of ways.[2]

Most obviously, current accounting standards fail by treating multinational corporations as if they operate in a homogenous global ether that floats above the physical and human geography of the world. As a result they report just one profit or loss irrespective of where their money is earned and have only one balance sheet wherever assets may be located. The financial markets focus exclusively on this consolidated balance sheet even though for a great many reasons this is a completely incorrect view of the enterprise. As the events of 2008 clearly indicated, companies are unavoidably tied to real places. They operate within national frameworks of law and regulation. What they do in each place, what they report, and how they spread risks between different locations—these are all of enormous significance to the jurisdictions that host their activities.[3]

Furthermore, all limited companies are granted a license to operate by each and every country in which they trade. It is commonplace (but not universal) for multinational companies to set up subsidiary companies for their operations in each country in which they work. That ring fences their risk in the country in question, makes it easier to differentiate their tax liabilities between territories and, of course, grants them limited liability within that jurisdiction.

[1] See, for example, Drucker (2010). [2] See, for example, UK Parliament (2012a).

[3] This concern is the foundation of the enquiries by the UK parliament's Public Accounts Committee into the activities of Google, Starbucks, and Amazon—see UK Parliament (2012b).

The issue remains relevant even when they do not establish a formally constituted subsidiary in a jurisdiction. In that case, country-by-country reporting has the advantage of revealing trade in a jurisdiction that may otherwise remain hidden from view. That is because it requires disclosure of trades undertaken in jurisdictions through what are called "permanent establishments" that are, in effect branches of companies incorporated in another place but which also enjoy limited liability as a result.

This privilege of limited liability is an extraordinary thing. It is enjoyed by multinational corporations as a whole, but just as importantly it is usually also enjoyed by the subsidiary companies they create in each and every jurisdiction where they operate. This concept of limited liability within limited liability appears to have evolved more by accident than by design, but the result of the grant of that privilege by each of the jurisdictions in which a multinational corporation works affords it enormous financial reward. This benefit arises because a multinational's cost of capital, for the entity as a whole and for each of its subsidiaries, is substantially reduced by the availability of limited liability to it and its subsidiary companies. It needs much less capital to trade than would an individual or organization without limited liability. The enterprise as a whole is not exposed to risks incurred by its subsidiaries. Societies around the world explicitly accept that if for any reason a constituent of a multinational corporation ceases to trade then that company and the owners of its capital will not have to make good the loss they have incurred. The risk of a subsidiary's collapse will instead be transferred to the state in which it traded and the members of the community who traded with it in that place.

Most of the time this risk is ignored and the cost of the resulting failures is contained within the business, banking, and investment communities of each country as a part of the collective risk they take. However, as is very obvious now, that is not always the case. Since 2008 large parts of the world's banking community, almost all of it protected by limited liability, has required massive state bailouts at cost to the communities the world over. That process has yet to end.

There is then a clear dichotomy: global financial accounting ignores international borders because it says that the primary users of general purpose financial reporting are present and potential investors, lenders, and other creditors of the company who use that information to make decisions about buying, selling, or holding equity or debt instruments and providing or settling loans or other forms of credit (Deloitte, 2010). There is no doubt that some of these may primarily view the entity as a single global enterprise for the purposes of their risk assessment at present and existing accounts are designed to facilitate that process. On the other hand, the fact that they say they use accounts in this way is not surprising; this information is the only data that they have. If they had country-by-country data they may well use it; without any experience of having it, the fact that they say they do not use it is not evidence that they would not do so. This potential use is the first reason for providing country-by-country data, and its significance should not be ignored. Existing financial reporting standards help senior management of many companies hide from view much of what they do. Providing a more rounded insight on those activities, which country-by-country reporting is bound to do, has to be of benefit to all those who represent the shareholder community.

Indeed, country-by-country reporting would, by providing data that is not currently available, ensure that the providers of capital to companies enjoy a view of the risks that they face that is currently unavailable. This data will also allow participants in capital markets to better appraise the risks they accept and if risk is better understood then the cost of capital for companies will be reduced. That has an inevitable consequence, which is an increase in investment and so growth. As such, the call for country-by-country reporting is an intensely pro-business demand.

This argument for country-by-country reporting does, however, ignore the fact that there are many other stakeholders of the company, including the authorities and populations of the many jurisdictions in which it trades, who will also wish to appraise the risks that it creates for them locally. Enabling this stakeholder process of financial risk assessment is the second reason for country-by-country reporting because it empowers those exposed to the risks created by the subsidiaries of multinational operations to assess just what those subsidiaries are doing. The various risks to which national jurisdictions are exposed are outlined later in this paper.

One risk that stands out as needing assessment does, of course, relates to tax paid and (as importantly) not paid both within a particular jurisdiction and also within others where one jurisdiction thinks a multinational corporation might be hiding profits that it has the right to assess to tax. Country-by-country reporting is particularly well suited to this task because, by demanding data for each and every jurisdiction in which a multinational corporation trades, it requires reporting for those jurisdictions where it is quite legal for accounts to not be put on public record at present. Colloquially called tax havens, but for the purpose of this analysis more accurately defined as secrecy jurisdictions,[4] these places provide a double veil of secrecy for multinational corporations. If the financial statements of multinational corporations are already deficient in not requiring them to account for their activities locally then secrecy jurisdictions exploit this fact by providing them with a deliberately created environment where no local information is published, meaning

[4] I define secrecy jurisdictions as places that intentionally create regulation for the primary benefit and use of those not resident in their geographical domain with that regulation being designed to undermine the legislation or regulation of another jurisdiction and with the secrecy jurisdictions also creating a deliberate, legally backed veil of secrecy that ensures that those from outside the jurisdiction making use of its regulation cannot be identified to be doing so.

that certain parts of the multinational corporations activities can, at its choice, entirely disappear from view, in the process destroying any form of accountability for its activity. Country-by-country reporting has been deliberately designed to counter this opportunity for corporate secrecy.

All of this supports the reform proposal inherent in country-by-country reporting, which is that multinational corporations publish within those annual financial statements a profit and loss account and limited balance sheet and cash flow data for every jurisdiction in which the company trades, without exception.

3.3 WHAT IS COUNTRY-BY-COUNTRY REPORTING?

3.3.1 Why Do We Need Country-By-Country Reporting?

We need country-by-country reporting for the reasons noted above, but we especially need country-by-country reporting in a world in which there is a crisis in collecting the tax that appears to be due by multinational corporations because of the obvious deficiencies in current accounting practices for tax purposes.

Current accounting practice makes it possible for multinational enterprises to avoid tax due while obeying the letter of the law. This effective exemption from tax enjoyed by a significant chunk of the global economy has contributed to a fiscal crisis. Vast corporate cash piles accumulate offshore as social programs and infrastructure investments onshore are cancelled.

The International Accounting Standards Board (IASB) is responsible for the International Financial Reporting Standard, which are the most widely spread accounting standards now used by multinational corporations. The IASB are aware of this deficiency: they have stated that the financial statements created using its standards are not suitable for tax authority use even if prepared for a single entity on a non consolidated basis (IFRS, n.d.:15). The problems in using group accounts for tax purposes include the following:

1. Those financial statements do not necessarily include all the companies that make up a group for tax purposes.
2. They do not disclose all the companies that are consolidated, or where they are, or what they do.
3. They purposefully exclude from consideration and view all intra-group transactions—which are precisely those that create transfer pricing risk.
4. They do not provide segment data that provides almost any useful indication of the location of transactions for tax purposes.

5. They do not necessarily reflect the transactions undertaken in the underlying accounts disclosed to the individual tax authorities dealing with the affairs of the individual companies that make up the group entity. That is because of the impact of what are called group consolidation journals that remove from account, without it being apparent, those intra-group profits arising, for example, from different accounting standards being used in different group companies. It is precisely this type of transaction about which tax authorities require information.

Country-by-country reporting was designed to address these deficiencies in existing accounting reporting when used for tax purposes. So far there is no alternative proposal that seeks to address these deficiencies in reporting for this purpose.

3.3.2 Country-By-Country Reporting is Designed for Use by All Multinational Corporations

Country-by-country reporting was always designed to be accounting disclosure applying to all multinational corporations, whatever the sector they worked in. That is because the problems it addresses are universal and apply to all sectors. It is stressed that country-by-country reporting is not an initiative for the extractive industries or banking alone. And nor is this an issue relating solely to tax payment or eliminating corruption, important as those issues are. Country-by-country reporting is about an integrated form of financial reporting that should be part of the financial statements of a multinational corporation.

3.3.3 The Questions Country-By-Country Reporting is Designed to Answer

Country-by-country reporting was specifically designed to answer questions on the following issues:

a. In which countries does a multinational company operate?
b. What are the subsidiaries of each multinational corporation called in each jurisdiction in which it operates?
c. What is the scale of a multinational corporation's operations in each country in which it operates?
d. How much does a multinational corporation have invested in each place where it trades?
e. Where does a multinational corporation record its profits?

f. Where does a multinational corporation pay tax and how much does it pay there?
g. What is the extent of intra-group trading within multinational corporations?
h. Where does the company engage staff and how well, on average, do they pay their staff in each jurisdiction in which they work?
i. Where does a multinational corporation exploit natural resources, and to what extent?
j. By implication, and based on analysis of the foregoing data:
What is the risk of there being serious transfer mispricing within the group?
If the level of activity and profit vary widely within the group does this suggest a high risk of tax enquiry at potential cost to future earnings?
Is the multinational corporation a big user of tax havens, and if so what is the likely scale of the risk that results?
What is the geopolitical risk within a multinational corporation and is that exacerbated by low tax payments?
What degree of risk does a company face if its operations in any country were to close?
Is the company's employment policy universally fair and if not what risk does that imply?
Is the company's activity sustainable?

These questions, and many others, cannot be answered on the basis of financial statements prepared under International Financial Reporting Standard. This was the motivation for creating country-by-country reporting. These questions, the answers to which are vital for tax purposes but also for the effective operation of capital markets and for nationally based economic risk assessment, are clearly significant and yet they are ignored by the IASB and the other accounting standards setters.

This omission arises because, according to the IASB, the main purpose for the accounts produced using its International Financial Reporting Standard (IFRS) is to provide potential investors, lenders and other creditors of a company with the information they need to make decisions about buying, selling or holding equity or debt instruments issued by it or on providing or settling loans or other forms of credit with it (Deloitte, 2010).

This is an extraordinarily narrow view of accounting and accountability, which fails even on its own terms. It is made all the narrower by the fact that they are aware that "other parties, including prudential and market regulators, may find general purpose financial reports useful. However, the Board considered that the objectives of general purpose financial reporting and the objectives of financial regulation may not be consistent. Hence, regulators are not considered a primary user and general purpose financial reports are not primarily directed to regulators or other parties."

As a result the IASB notes "that general purpose financial reports cannot provide all the information that users may need to make economic decisions. They will need to consider pertinent information from other sources as well." What they do not go on to say is what that other data that they chose that accounts produced using their standards do not supply might be, or how it might be obtained. Country-by-country reporting explicitly seeks to fill that gap, not least with regard to tax authorities.

3.3.4 The Data Supplied by Country-By-Country Reporting

Country-by-country reporting would require disclosure of the following information by each multinational corporation in its annual financial statements:

1. The name of each country in which it operates; a country for these purposes being defined as any jurisdiction in which it has a permanent establishment for taxation purposes.
2. The names of all its companies trading in each country in which it operates.
3. What its financial performance is in every country in which it operates, without exception, including:
   - 3.1 Its sales, both third party and with other group companies
   - 3.2 Its hedging transactions, both third party and intra-group
   - 3.3 Purchases, split between third parties and intra-group transactions
   - 3.4 Labour costs and employee numbers
   - 3.5 Financing costs split between those paid to third parties and to other group members
   - 3.6 Its pre-tax profit
   - 3.7 The tax charge included in its accounts for the country in question split as noted in more detail below
   - 3.8 Details of the cost and net book value of its physical fixed assets located in each country including the cost of all investments (including those relating to exploration) made in assets related to extractive industries activity by location and the proceeds of sale from disposals of such assets by location
   - 3.9 Details of gross and net assets in total for each country in which the entity operates. Note that if sales data on source and destination bases for a jurisdiction are more than 10 percent different both must be disclosed on both bases for both third parties and intra-group transactions.

4. Tax information would need to be analyzed by country in more depth requiring disclosure of the following for each country in which the corporation operates:
   4.1 The tax charge for the year split between current and deferred tax
   4.2 The actual tax payments made to the government of the country in the period
   4.3 The liabilities (and assets, if relevant) owing for tax and equivalent charges at the beginning and end of each accounting period
   4.4 Deferred taxation liabilities for the country at the start and close of each accounting period.
5. Separate accounting, distinct from the turnover category, for all futures, derivative, and forward contract sales with separate disclosure of purchases of similar financial instruments being disclosed with netting off not allowed.
6. Cumulative disclosure on a year-by-year and country-by-country basis of:
   6.1 Provisions made for taxes from the time that country-by-country reporting commenced
   6.2 Total tax payments made from the time that country-by-country reporting commenced.

There are additional requirements for companies operating in the extractive industries.

Vitally, this data is expected to reconcile with the audited group consolidated accounts and a statement proving that it does so would be a necessary part of country-by-country reporting. As such country-by-country reporting is not an alternative set of accounts for tax or other purposes: it holds the company to account for what it does and requires it to declare where that activity has arisen or is at least recorded (the two not necessarily being the same thing).

3.3.5 The Benefits of Country-By-Country Reporting

The disclosure provided by country-by-country reporting would meet the needs of many users of the financial statement of multinational corporations that accounts prepared under International Financial Reporting Standard, which they currently rely on, cannot. Space available here does not, however, allow many of those benefits to be discussed. Instead we will focus on the issue that first prompted the idea: tackling international transfer mispricing by multinational corporations.

Country-by-country is designed to offer access to new data for tax authorities anxious to ensure that the subsidiary companies of multinational corporations are tax compliant when operating within their jurisdictions. Tax compliance in this context is defined as seeking to pay the right amount of tax (but no more) in the right place at the right time, where right means that the economic substance of the transactions undertaken coincides with the place and form in which they are reported for taxation purposes.

The first, and perhaps most important use of country-by-country reporting by tax authorities would be in undertaking risk assessments on the corporate tax returns they receive to determine which ones they wish to investigate. All tax authorities have limited resources at their command and these have, therefore, to be used to greatest effect if tax abuse is to be tackled effectively.

Country-by-country reporting data lets any tax authority better and more cost- effectively assess the risk that the constituent members of a multinational corporation trading in its jurisdiction are avoiding tax. This could best be done by applying a unitary apportionment formula to the group accounting data reported by country that is disclosed in the multinational corporation's financial statements. This does not require that unitary taxation be in operation; this is a risk assessment tool whether or not it is in use. Such an apportionment approach seeks to locate profit in the places where it is likely to have arisen on the basis of what are called "key allocation drivers," which are discussed in more detail below.

This risk assessment process is not possible at present. The country data that a multinational corporation reports at present need not be prepared consistently from state to state since different accounting standards can be applied in each whilst if a "bottom up" approach is adopted intra-group profits may be apportioned inappropriately whilst group adjustment journals that are used to ensure that the overall group result that is reported is true and fair may be ignored, again distorting any such analysis. Country-by-country reporting has been designed to overcome these problems and to make such apportionment analysis for risk assessment purposes possible. Indeed, for tax authorities this contribution to the cost effectiveness of their risk assessment process is the way in which country-by-country reporting can almost certainly deliver the greatest added value in tackling international tax abuse, by identifying which companies might be undertaking that abuse, and where. This enables tax authorities to direct scarce resources to best effect.

This approach implicitly accepts the principles behind unitary taxation even if that system is not then used to assess the resulting profit. This point is important: using a unitary taxation approach to tax risk assessment does not require using unitary taxation to assess the resulting tax due. It is a tool to assess the appropriateness of profit allocation for tax purposes, just as arm's length pricing is a tool.

The techniques of unitary taxation have been widely used to allocate profits between companies operating in different states within the USA and have therefore been tried and tested. No one pretends they are perfect. But they can provide powerful indicators of likely acceptable or unacceptable profit allocations that can in turn guide the inquiries of national tax authorities.

Unitary apportionment allocates the total group profit earned by a multinational corporation to locations on the basis of a formula. The classic formula is called the Massachusetts apportionment and it allocates profit on the basis of a formula that gives equal weighting to third-party sales, employees and physical fixed assets made from or located in a jurisdiction. This approach is discussed in more detail in Chapter 4 of this book.

There is good reason for choosing these three "allocation keys" for determining whether or not the economic substance of the transactions undertaken coincides with the place and form in which they are reported for taxation purposes: companies cannot make profit without sales and they cannot make sales without employing people and physical assets, many of which will be linked to the production process. Of course the choice is not always going to be perfect and different methods and weights can be chosen if it is considered desirable for different commercial sectors. But the point is that if chosen with care such a method should indicate within reasonable boundaries of probability (which is the appropriate measure for a risk assessment tool) of whether or not profit is being recorded where it is most likely to be earned. It was this thinking that led to the requirement that employee and fixed asset information to be disclosed under country-by-country reporting.

Using such a formula apportionment method has the advantage of meaning that artificial reallocations of activity within a group (through intra-company trading, debt and intellectual property charges, for example) can be largely eliminated from consideration when deciding what the likely real location of the profit arising within a group might be. This is especially so if third party sales are stated net of intra-group purchases to negate their artificial reallocation, which is why data on intra-group transactions within country-by-country reporting is essential in any such accounting system.

Importantly, the issues that this risk assessment method would address are also those activities that are, unsurprisingly, those where the greatest difficulty arises with arm's length transfer pricing (see chapter 9 of this book for more information on this issue). The result is that the objectives of fair profit allocation reflecting underlying economic substance, that the "arms length principle" of transfer pricing that the OECD promotes as the ideal solution to solving transfer pricing disputes, can be replicated and improved upon, using a unitary apportionment calculation based on country-by-country reporting data but with much less effort and so cost than is the case under the OECD's chosen bilateral approach, which can in any event lead to more than or less than the whole of a group's profit being taxed.

Three consequences would follow from this.

First, companies could themselves present this data to all authorities with whom they engage to show that their profit allocations are reasonable. If linked to "safe harbour" provisions suggesting degrees of tolerance on allocation, especially with regard to profit attributed to low-risk states, such an approach could be used to significantly reduce the degree of transfer pricing documentation required in compliant organizations. This would save them and tax authorities considerable cost, while at the same time adding substantial certainty to their tax affairs. It is hard to see why major multinational corporations would not welcome this.

Second, all tax authorities would know that they were all receiving the same data from a multinational corporation at the same time; the doubt that quite reasonably exists at present that tax authorities are themselves subject to arbitrage by multinational corporations would be eliminated. This would also benefit companies because what they could make clear is that they were declaring all their taxable profits once, and once only, to all relevant tax authorities.

Third, it would be easier to resolve disputes since the impact of any adjustment would be more readily apparent if country-by-country reporting data were to be supplied to tax authorities. Again, the risk of double taxation would be reduced as a result.

The consequence of these advantages is obvious: one of business' key objectives with regard to international taxation—the elimination of double taxation—is bound to be easier to achieve if country-by-country reporting is in place, whilst the goal of tax authorities—the elimination of double non-taxation—will also be easier to facilitate. The inevitable consequence is a more equitable and easier-to-resolve tax system. Moreover, given the considerable savings that could be achieved for a multinational corporation that seeks to be compliant in its tax allocation if its obligation to prepare the onerous documentation that arm's length pricing currently requires was waived, the overall burden on business would be reduced as a result. Even ignoring the other benefits for a great many stakeholders,[5] the case for country-by-country reporting for tax purposes is compelling on this basis.

3.4 OBSTACLES TO IMPLEMENTATION AND CREATING A COALITION OF THE WILLING

Whilst the case for country-by-country reporting may be compelling to its advocates, and progress towards delivering it has been extraordinary in the decade since it was first proposed, there are obstacles to its implementation. As Reuters (Bergin, 2013) reported in October 2013 when considering submissions

[5] Elaborated at length in Murphy (2012).

on the subject to the OECD as part of its transfer pricing documentation review that in turn forms part of its Base Erosion and Profits Shifting project:

> Business groups were cool on a proposal tabled in June by the Group of Eight (G8) leading developed economies, that companies should provide information to tax authorities on their earnings and tax payments on a country-by-country basis.
>
> The idea was that greater transparency would help tax authorities—especially those in developing nations which lack the investigative resources of richer nations—to spot when companies were shifting profits out of their countries, and thereby avoiding taxes.
>
> But business groups including Britain's Confederation of British Industry, the United States Council for International Business (USCIB) and French employers' body Medef, expressed concerns that business would face unreasonable administrative burdens and risked having confidential commercial information leak out to competitors.
>
> "Because of these concerns, we suggest that the OECD ought to consider alternatives to country-by-country reporting," wrote William Sample, chairman of the tax committee at USCIB, whose members include Microsoft and Exxon Mobil Corp.

In saying this they reflect the concern expressed by Big Four accountancy firm Ernst & Young who in 2013 wrote in a report entitled "Tax Transparency: Seizing the Initiative" (Ernst & Young, 2013):

> In making the decision in terms of what to disclose, the range of information that can fall under the "tax transparency" banner is broad. One approach is country by country reporting of tax payments, an approach creating concern for some organisations. In its raw form, it is seen by many as complex, burdensome and still not necessarily the panacea to improved transparency. For example, country by country reporting does not directly inform stakeholders about whether an organisation has or has not adopted aggressive tax positions, albeit positions that are within the letter of the tax law.
>
> Still, as a recognised reporting concept, adopted by the Extractive Industry Transparency Initiative, the influence of country by country reporting has begun to extend and it is now supported by the EU and set to become a requirement for banking as well as extractive entities. Country by country reporting has also been proposed at a territory, rather than sector, level by the Australian Treasury.
>
> The floodgates are, however, not yet open. Any further regulatory developments, in the EU at least, will take a number of years. This suggests that the development by organisations of alternative tax transparent reporting approaches such as increased narrative disclosure and more informative rate reconciliations may yet stem the tide on country by country reporting. Alternatively, voluntary adoption of a more refined version of country by country reporting may allow organisations to create a balanced, workable framework that meets the concerns of stakeholders.

The source of the opposition to country-by-country reporting is clear: it comes from big business and its advisers. Their anxiety on the issue is apparent, as is its source. They do not want, at any cost, to disclose what they actually do and where, precisely what country-by-country reporting would require. Global companies fear being held to account locally.

They therefore seek to avoid country-by-country reporting in a number of ways. They say they do not have the data to prepare country-by-country reporting or that it would be too expensive or onerous to prepare the data. Most commonly they argue that the data produced by country-by-country reporting would simply not be useful.

Some of these claims are just nonsense. If, for example, a multinational corporation does not know where its transactions are located it cannot accurately determine its tax liabilities. As such it is failing to both maintain proper books and records of account as required by the law of almost all countries and proper internal control systems as required, for example, by Sarbane Oxley. Similarly the argument that this data will be hard to audit is just wrong: it may increase audit cost because auditors might have to consider the accounts they review in more depth but it is hard to say that this does not provide benefit to shareholders whose risk is reduced as a result.

Perhaps the most absurd argument though is the one most often put forward, that country-by-country reporting data will simply not be useful, which is resorted to by the management of multinational corporations when all other arguments have failed. They seem in the process to be suggesting that:

a. Users of accounts will not understand country-by-country reporting data, despite that fact that it will be presented in similar format to all other financial reporting.
b. There are no civil society users of accounts.
c. Tax authorities, regulators, and others never look at or comprehend accounts.
d. Investors will not use data if it is made available to them but will instead choose to ignore it when making their decisions.

None of these arguments is plausible. However, powerful and wealthy lobby interests back these arguments. The OECD (2014) discussion paper on country-by-country reporting, published in January 2014, was a disappointment to many campaigning for it. It is not clear from the report that the OECD has even understood the basic principles on which country-by-country reporting is based. For example, the OECD have asked whether country-by-country reporting should be supplied by what is, in effect, simple republication of local statutory accounting for the member companies of multinational corporation rather than by attributing the activities recorded in the single, consolidated set of financial statements issued by the group as a whole to individual jurisdictions, which is what country-by-country reporting requires. Some of the data they propose should be published, such as the tax actually paid in a jurisdiction instead of the tax due within it, also makes almost no accounting sense. It is clear as a result that the argument for country-by-country reporting has not yet been won despite the promising noises made in 2013.

That is disappointing; as has been argued here, country-by-country reporting data has considerable potential value in use. It is likely that when live data is available very many more uses will be found. In that case this argument has to be seen for what it is, which is a claim that management should be trusted with the stewardship of assets without consequent accountability.

It is this last idea that offers the prospect for taking this idea forward. Three major concerns have emerged since 2008 that suggest that the demand for full country-by- country reporting could be the basis for a campaign attracting a broad coalition of support.

The first demand is for accountability: the unquestioning relationship of trust with big business based on the assumption that all trade is good has been shattered in the aftermath of the crash.

The second demand is for transparency: the idea that opacity left the world's economy unprepared for what hit it in 2008 is clear. David Cameron made this a theme of his G8 summit in June 2013 (G8 Leaders, 2013).

The third concern is, of course, about tax, which issue was almost unheard of by the public before 2008 but is now well and truly known.

Each of these concerns is manifested in a number of ways. The concern about trade clearly has a focus on banking for some, especially in places like the UK where this has lead to greater austerity than many countries. For others, such as those in countries dominated by the extractive industries, corruption is the concern. For others it is environmental concern that makes them want to hold business to account. Consumers are worried about unaccountable energy companies. A worry about massive social media concerns who appear to be accountable nowhere motivates many. Some just want to know who they are dealing with and that they are good citizens.

In each case there is a coincidence of aims. Politicians feel powerless in the face of these enterprises and those they deal with feel helpless in the face of leviathans. That is why the common aim of all who seek to make corporations accountable is to link the global to the local. This helps ensure that tax is paid in the right place at the right time. But it also means politicians can gauge what they're up against and supply chains can be appraised. This is a major concern already and is likely to loom larger as global logistics are increasingly stressed by climate change.

The reality is that no single lobby with these interests can win this reform by itself and to date it is the tax case that has stimulated demand for country-by-country reporting. That has delivered some results—and got business worried. However, the tipping point will come when this demand reflects a coalition of interests. That means politicians have to see the gains, and not the threats. And that will happen when the three biggest campaign aims in the world coalesce around this demand. They are the development community, who have driven this agenda to date, the environmental campaigning community, and those who demand the resources to meet education and health needs, both of whom are now seriously impacted by increasing private sector involvement worldwide.

One campaign lobby is powerful: three utterly persuasive. That means country-by-country reporting will work when it delivers the accountability and tax that means that trade is seen to be of benefit and trust is restored in global business. This is possible. One lobby has got us a long way. Making this a concern for the environment, education, and health will deliver the desired outcome.

And at that point something else will happen. As Schopenhauer argued, truth goes through three stages. In the first stage, it is ridiculed. In the second stage, it is violently opposed. And in the third stage, it is accepted as self-evident. Country-by-country reporting has got through the ridicule stage. It is now facing serious opposition. With enough being persuaded of its merits the time will come when a fourth lobby will embrace it as self-evidently useful, and that is business itself. That may be a while off yet, but enlightened fund managers may yet help trail a path in that direction.

We have not got country-by-country reporting yet. When we do, global business will never look the same again. Rather than busying itself with tax avoidance and the associated grand corruption it will be free to concentrate on productive activity. The sector will be able to compete in good faith, free from the suspicion that it is exploiting covert monopolies or subverting democratic governments. If we could convince it that the outcome may be in its best interests then real reform will happen, and that's now within the boundaries of possibility.

REFERENCES

Bergin, Tom, 2013. "Big Companies Push back against G20 Tax Avoidance Plan," *Reuters*. 23 October.

CCFD-Terre Solidaire, 2013. "Country by Country Transparency: Dodd Frank Act and EU Directives." http://www.oecd.org/ctp/tax-global/Country_by_country_transparency-DoddFrankAct_and_EUDirectives.pdf, last accessed 8 August 2014.

Deloitte, 2010. "Conceptual Framework for Financial Reporting 2010." IAS*Plus*. http://www.iasplus.com/en/standards/other/framework, accessed 5 August 2015.

Directive 2013/36/EU of the European Parliament and of the Council of 26 June 2013. http://eur-lex.europa.eu/LexUriServ/LexUriServ.do?uri=CELEX:32013L0036:EN:NOT, accessed 5 August 2015.

Drucker, Jesse, 2010. "Google 2.4% Rate Shows How $60 Billion Is Lost to tax Loopholes," *Bloomberg*. 21 October. http://www.bloomberg.com/news/2010-10-21/google-2-4-rate-shows-how-60-billion-u-s-revenue-lost-to-tax-loopholes.html, accessed 27 August 2014.

Ernst & Young, 2013. "Tax Transparency: Seizing the Initiative." http://www.ey.com/Publication/vwLUAssets/Tax_Transparency_-_Seizing_the_initiative/$FILE/EY_Tax_Transparency.pdf, accessed 5 August 2015.

G8 Leaders, 2013. "Lough Erne G8 Leaders' Communiqué." https://www.gov.uk/government/publications/2013-lough-erne-g8-leaders-communique, accessed 5 August 2015.

IFRS, n.d. "Meeting Summaries and Observer Notes." http://www.ifrs.org/IFRS-for-SMEs/histroy/Meeting-Summaries-and-Observer-Notes/Documents/SME0806b02-Aobs.pdf, last accessed March 2013.

Murphy, Richard (on behalf of the Association for Accountancy and Business Affairs), 2003. "A Proposed International Accounting Standard Reporting Turnover and Tax by Location." http://visar.csustan.edu/aaba/ProposedAccstd.pdf, accessed 5 August 2015.

Murphy, Richard, 2012. "Country-by-Country Reporting: Accounting for Globalisation locally." Tax Justice Network. http://www.taxresearch.org.uk/Documents/CBC2012.pdf

OECD, 2013. *Action Plan on Base Erosion and Profit Shifting*. OECD Publishing. http://www.oecd.org/ctp/BEPSActionPlan.pdf, accessed 5 August 2015.

OECD, 2014. "Discussion Draft on Transfer Pricing Documentation and CbC Reporting." 30 January. http://www.oecd.org/ctp/transfer-pricing/discussion-draft-transfer-pricing-documentation.pdf, accessed 5 August 2015.

UK Parliament, 2012a. "Banking Standards: Written Evidence from Timothy Bush." 21 August. http://www.publications.parliament.uk/pa/jt201314/jtselect/jtpcbs/27/27iv30.htm, last accessed 27 August 2014.

UK Parliament, 2012b. "Public Accounts Committee—Nineteenth Report." 3 December. http://www.publications.parliament.uk/pa/cm201213/cmselect/cmpubacc/716/71602.htm, last accessed 27 August 2014.

4

Hanging Together

A Multilateral Approach to Taxing Multinationals

Reuven S. Avi-Yonah

4.1 INTRODUCTION

The recent revelation that many multinational enterprises (MNEs) pay very little tax to the countries they operate in has led to various proposals to change the ways they are taxed. Most of these proposals, however, do not address the fundamental flaws in the international tax regime that allow companies like Apple or Starbucks to legally avoid taxation. In particular, the Organization for Economic Co-operation and Development (OECD) has been working on a Base Erosion and Profit Shifting (BEPS) project and is supposed to make recommendations to the G20, but it is not clear yet whether this will result in a meaningful advance toward preventing BEPS (OECD, 2013). This chapter will advance a simple proposal that will allow OECD member countries to tax MNEs based in those countries without impeding their competitiveness. The key observation is that in the twenty-first century unilateral approaches to tax corporations whose operations span the globe are obsolete, and a multilateral approach is both essential and feasible.

The chapter is divided into five parts. Section 4.3.1 addresses the fundamental question of why corporations should be taxed at all, and what are the implications for taxing MNEs. Section 4.3.2 advances a proposal to tax MNEs at a reduced rate on all of their global profits on a current basis and outlines some of the advantages from such an outcome. Section 4.3.3 responds to some of the common critiques against this proposal and evaluates it in comparison with alternative proposals. Section 4.3.4 addresses the implications of the proposal for developing countries. Section 4.3.5 concludes by evaluating the likelihood that such a proposal may be adopted.

4.2 REFORM PROPOSAL

This chapter proposes that each OECD member country impose tax at its normal corporate rate on the entire profit of multinationals that are managed and controlled from headquarters within it, with a foreign tax credit for taxes imposed by other jurisdictions.

4.3 DISCUSSION

4.3.1 Why Tax Multinationals?

Before we address the issue of *how* to tax multinationals, it is important to address the basic normative issue of *why* corporations should be taxed at all. While the corporate income tax has been a feature of tax regimes around the world for over a century, a prevalent view among tax academics is that there is no good reason to tax corporations at all (Brauner, 2008). The main argument against taxing corporations or other legal entities is that the burden of all taxation ultimately falls on individuals and that because of the uncertainty involved in establishing which individuals bear the burden of the corporate tax, ordinary voters are misled into thinking the tax does not fall on them. This uncertainty makes the corporate tax popular among politicians, because they can benefit from the fiscal illusion that its burden falls on "the corporation" while in reality it is imposed on the voters. It would be better and more transparent not to tax legal entities at all. In addition, the revenue from the existing corporate tax is relatively low in OECD member countries (typically less than 10 percent of total revenue) and it can easily be replaced by raising individual taxes by a small amount. Finally, the corporate tax is very complicated and the transaction costs of trying to avoid it impose significant losses on the economy.

These arguments strike me as facially persuasive, despite the political unlikelihood of the corporate tax being abolished anytime soon (precisely because of the fiscal illusion mentioned above, which renders it politically popular). But there are three reasons why the corporate tax should nevertheless be retained, and they are particularly relevant to taxing multinationals (Avi-Yonah, 2004).

First, while in OECD countries the corporate tax is a relatively unimportant source of revenue, that has generally not been true in developing countries, where it frequently amounts to over 25 percent of total revenues. Because developing countries find it very difficult to collect the individual income tax, taxing multinationals is crucial for them because otherwise they would have to rely entirely on the regressive Value Added Tax (VAT). From the perspective of a developing country the uncertainty regarding the incidence of the corporate tax is less important because some of the likely bearers of the burden (providers of capital and consumers) are residents of other countries. Moreover, even if one presumes that the corporate tax falls on labor in the developing country, taxing the multinational may be a more efficient way of collecting revenues than attempting to tax individual workers. Finally, in the case of multinationals in developing countries a lot of the corporate profit may be rents for the exploitation of country-specific resources and that is an efficient tax for the country to impose. These issues are explored more fully in section 4.3.4 below.

Second, it has long been observed that the corporate tax is an important backstop for the progressivity of individual tax, because in the absence of the corporate tax rich individuals would be able to park their money in corporations and obtain indefinite deferral (i.e., not pay tax until there is a dividend distribution or a sale of the shares). In the case of privately held entities, it is possible to overcome this problem by treating these entities as pass-throughs and currently taxing their owners on the income earned by the entity. But this solution will not work for publicly traded entities like multinationals because of the difficulty of establishing who their shareholders are at any given moment. It may still be possible to tax shareholders of publicly traded entities on the market value of their shares, since in that context there are no valuation issues (the price is established by the trading) and no liquidity issues (it is easy to sell the shares to pay the tax). But there is frequently a discrepancy between the market value and the underlying earnings, and because the stock market fluctuates for reasons unrelated to the performance of any given corporation, taxing share values is not an accurate way of defeating deferral. In addition, mark to market taxation is very unpopular because of the uncertainty inherent in taxing unrealized income (if the shares fall in value, it is unclear whether the taxpayer can use the loss to recover the tax paid). Thus, in the case of publicly traded entities, the corporate tax is still a way to make sure that rich individuals are not able to reduce their effective tax rate by delaying the payment of tax until a dividend is distributed.[1]

Third, corporations are such important actors in any modern economy that the ability to regulate their behavior is crucial to achieving economic goals, and the corporate tax has since its inception been seen as an important vehicle to regulate corporate behavior. The tax can provide disincentives for behavior the legislator deems to be undesirable (e.g., paying bribes or participating in

[1] I do not take a position here on the question of whether shareholders should be given relief from double taxation by adopting some method of integrating the corporate and shareholder tax, because the commonly applied methods of integration do not affect the corporate level tax. See Avi-Yonah and Chenchinski (2011).

boycotts) and incentives for desirable behavior (investments incentives, hiring incentives, clean energy incentives, etc.). A lot of the complexity of the corporate tax stems from these "tax expenditures." Some of these goals can perhaps be accomplished by direct regulation and some by paying subsidies, but there are cases where tax is a more effective vehicle for regulation than either command-and-control regulation or subsidies (e.g., a carbon tax vs. cap and trade to reduce global climate change) (Avi-Yonah, 2013).

These three reasons all support taxation of multinationals. In the case of developing countries, the domestic corporate tax base is usually quite limited and most of the revenue stems from taxing foreign multinationals. The individual deferral argument suggests that multinationals should be taxed because if they are not, rich individuals can invest specifically in multinationals and obtain the same benefit as if there was no corporate tax. And the regulatory argument also supports taxing multinationals because while some regulatory aims can be achieved just by taxing domestic activities, others (e.g., curbing pollution, bribery, or child labor) require a global focus on all the activities of the multinational.

These arguments also support adopting a multilateral approach to taxing multinationals. If a residence country adopts global taxation unilaterally, its rich residents can still defer taxation by investing in multinationals based in other countries, and these multinationals can also escape the residence country's regulatory reach. But if a multilateral approach is adopted, neither of these avenues of avoiding taxation remains open.

4.3.2 Taxing Multinationals on Global Profits: A Multilateral Approach

Having established that multinationals should be subject to tax, the next question is how to tax them. The current approach is for each country to generally only tax the portion of the multinational that is located within it, and to permit exemption or at least deferral for foreign source profits. This approach is widely seen as conducive to massive tax avoidance. In addition, it is inconsistent with the three reasons to tax multinationals outlined above. Taxing multinationals on a country-by-country basis leads to tax competition, which has significantly eroded the ability of developing countries to collect revenues from multinationals. Permitting exemption or deferral allows rich individuals to delay paying tax on the income they earn within those portions of the multinational that are not subject to tax. And taxation on a territorial basis allows multinationals to escape regulation by shifting their regulated activities out of the regulating jurisdiction.

The proposed solution to taxing multinationals on global profits is this: *Each country in which a multinational is resident should tax the profits of the entire multinational on a current basis, with a credit for taxes paid by the multinational to foreign (source) jurisdictions up to the level of tax in the residence jurisdiction.*

This approach requires determining what is the residence jurisdiction of the multinational. In most cases, the residence jurisdiction is both where the multinational is incorporated and where its headquarters are. However, because it is relatively easy to shift the location of incorporation, the residence should be determined by the location of the headquarters.[2]

The proposed approach treats the multinational in the same way it is treated for financial reporting purposes: As a single unified enterprise controlled by the parent. Under twenty-first century conditions this is a much more realistic approach than taxing each entity separately. Multinationals operate as a unitary business in most cases and most decisions are taken at the parent level.

Ignoring the separate incorporation of the multinational's subsidiaries is consistent with the ability of the multinational to operate via subsidiaries or branches. It also leads to significant simplification and eliminates most of the techniques used by multinationals to avoid the corporate tax. For example, the OECD has identified hybrid entities and thin capitalization as two prominent techniques to reduce the corporate effective tax rates. Under the proposed approach hybrid entities (treated as a branch by one jurisdiction and as a subsidiary by another) will not exist because all of the multinational will be treated as a single entity. Thin capitalization (capitalizing subsidiaries with debt rather than equity and deducting the interest) will be eliminated because dividends, interest, and royalty payments within a multinational will be ignored.

The proposed approach will also eliminate outbound transfer pricing because it will ignore transfers of goods and services within a multinational for tax purposes. Inbound transfer pricing will still exist, but the incentive to engage in it will be reduced if the profit has to be shifted to the parent jurisdiction rather than to a tax haven.

Importantly, it is envisaged that the proposed approach will be adopted on a multilateral basis by the OECD (on the likelihood of this happening, see section 4.3.5). The vast majority (over 90 percent) of multinationals are currently resident in OECD member countries. Moreover, the corporate tax rates in most OECD member countries are similar, between 20 percent and 30 percent. The proposed approach will enable outliers like the US to reduce its corporate tax rate below 30 percent without losing revenue. Other OECD members whose taxes are unusually low, such as Ireland (12.5 percent), may be able to raise them for domestic resident corporations without losing

[2] This is a crucial safeguard and therefore countries that currently define corporate residence in formal terms as country of incorporation or where the board of director meets should switch to the UK location of headquarters approach.

investments because they will not benefit multinationals from other OECD countries.

Foreign tax credits will be available for taxes paid to source jurisdictions. In most cases, these taxes will be lower than the tax rate in the country of residence, even when withholding taxes are taken into account. Importantly, the proposed solution will significantly reduce the incentive of developing countries to engage in harmful tax competition, because tax holidays granted to multinationals will only result in a transfer of revenue to the country of residence. Under current conditions, multinationals are able to pit developing countries one against the other and frequently obtain tax benefits from both. Given that the multinational will make the investment absent the tax incentive, this result is an unjustified windfall and the coercion applied to the developing country will disappear if the above proposal is adopted. See section 4.3.4 for further discussion of this issue.

The advantage of the proposal for multinationals is the treatment of losses. Currently, multinationals are frequently not able to use losses from foreign operations to offset profits from domestic operations. Under the proposal all such losses will be currently available.

This proposal is of course not new. It is essentially the approach proposed by the Kennedy Administration in 1961 for United States-resident multinationals, and it is also the approach adopted until recently by Brazil. The Kennedy proposals were met by severe criticism and were not adopted, and the Brazilian Supreme Court has cut back on the reach of the Brazilian tax on subsidiaries. In the next part, I will address these critiques and show that they are invalid for a multilateral approach.

4.3.3 Response to Common Critiques

There are three common critiques of the above approach. First, it is said that it violates certain economic neutrality norms and is therefore less efficient that territoriality (i.e., each country only taxing the income of the multinational earned within it) (Hines, 2009). Second, adopting the proposed global approach is said to harm the competitive position of any given country's multinationals (Kies, 2007). Third, adopting the proposed approach will, it is said, provide an incentive for multinationals to shift their residence to tax havens (Shaviro, 2014).

4.3.3.1 Neutrality

There are three types of neutrality arguments that apply to cross-border investment. The two traditional ones are capital export neutrality (CEN) and capital import neutrality (CIN). CEN requires neutrality in the location of investment between the residence and source jurisdictions, and therefore supports taxing multinationals on a global basis as envisaged above. CIN requires neutrality between two different investors in a third jurisdiction (which is assumed to impose no tax) and therefore requires territoriality if the other jurisdiction taxes on a territorial basis.

It is often said that CEN and CIN are mutually incompatible in a world with different tax rates, and therefore a choice must be made. Traditionally, CEN was regarded as more important than CIN because investment locations were shown to be more sensitive to tax rates than the rate of savings, and CIN was considered to affect the rate of savings in each resident jurisdiction. But in the current environment where the tax rates of most OECD countries have converged, if the above multilateral proposal is adopted it is possible to achieve both CEN and CIN simultaneously.[3]

A new variant of the neutrality argument is capital ownership neutrality (CON), which focuses on the multinational itself and not on its investors. It is said that multinationals exist because of ownership advantages that render them more efficient than their competitors. If one multinational is subject to a higher effective tax rate than a competitor because of global taxation, then it may be forced to forego an investment in a third country even if it is the more efficient one. But if the proposed solution is adopted on a multilateral basis, then all likely competitors will be taxed in the same way and CON can be preserved as well.

4.3.3.2 Competitiveness

Historically, the main argument against adopting the Kennedy proposal and similar unilateral proposals is that they would put US-based multinationals at a competitive disadvantage because multinationals from other countries are not subject to the same type of rule. I have always found this argument less than persuasive for several reasons: (a) it is not clear that competitiveness is a meaningful economic concept, or that the United States as a country should care particularly about the competitiveness of multinationals resident in it (as opposed to the competitiveness of the US economy as a whole or of its population); (b) the same argument was made in 1961, where US-based multinationals clearly dominated the globe, as in more recent years when their position was less dominant; (c) there is no evidence that current US rules, which deviate from the global norm of territoriality and impose tax on some foreign source income of US-based multinationals, have injured those multinationals in any significant way. In fact, empirical studies suggest that EU-based multinationals and US-based multinationals pay similar effective

[3] See Appendix for further elaboration of this point.

tax rates even though the former benefit from territoriality and the latter do not (Avi-Yonah and Lahav, 2012).

But even if competitiveness is a valid argument (and it clearly carries weight among politicians), if a multilateral approach is adopted it loses its force. As stated above, over 90 percent of multinationals are resident in OECD countries, and the others are mostly resident in large developing countries that may also be willing to join a multilateral approach. Under these circumstances, there will be no competitive disadvantage to any residence country that adopts the global approach unless it stems from its domestic corporate tax rate. As suggested above, the United States is an outlier in this regard because its corporate tax rate of 35 percent is significantly above the OECD average. In the context of adopting such a reform the United States can and should reduce its rate on a revenue neutral basis.[4]

4.3.3.3 Corporate Expatriations

The last argument against taxing multinationals on a global basis is that the tax can be avoided by shifting the residence of the multinational to a jurisdiction that does not impose such a tax. In fact, we are currently in the midst of another wave of "inversions," or corporate expatriations, out of the United States because of the high US corporate tax rate.

But this argument assumes that there are other jurisdictions that the multinational can move to. If all OECD countries adopt the proposal, most of the likely destinations disappear (again, assuming this is coupled with a reduction in the US corporate tax rate). There are good business reasons why the headquarters of almost all multinationals are in OECD countries, and those reasons will militate against a move outside the OECD.

A move to a tax haven may be possible if residence is defined as place of incorporation. But as suggested above corporate residence should be defined as location of the corporate headquarters, and those are much less likely to be moveable to tax havens because corporate management are not likely to want to relocate there and other facilities that usually follow the headquarters location, such as research and development, cannot easily be moved there. For the same reasons, it is unlikely that new multinationals can be founded in tax havens outside the OECD and G20 countries.

Thus, it seems that none of the common arguments against taxing multinationals on a current basis is valid if one assumes that this approach can be

[4] In fact, none of the G20 countries that are the main motivator of the BEPS effort have a corporate tax rate below 20% and only a few of them have a tax rate above 30%, so that they could commit to maintain a rate between 20% and 30% with only minimal changes. See Appendix.

adopted on a multilateral basis. The key question is therefore whether a multilateral approach is realistic, which is discussed in section 4.3.5 below.

4.3.4 Implications for Developing Countries

What are the implications of this proposal for developing countries? Specifically, would multilateral action by the OECD to restrict tax competition help or hurt developing countries?

First, it should be pointed out that developing countries need tax revenues at least as much as developed countries do, if not more. A common misperception is that only OECD member countries are confronted by a fiscal crisis as a result of the increasing numbers of elderly people in the population. In fact, the increase in dependency ratios (the ratio of the elderly to the working population) is expected to take place in other geographic areas as well, as fertility rates go down and health care improves. Outside the OECD and the transition economies, the dependency ratio starts in the single digits in the 1990s, but rises to just below 30 percent by 2010. Moreover, while outside the OECD and the transition economies direct spending on social insurance is much lower, other forms of government spending (e.g., government employment) effectively fulfill a social insurance role. In Latin America, for example, direct government spending on social insurance is much lower than indirect spending through government employment and procurement programs.

Moreover, it seems strange to argue that developing countries need tax revenues less than developed countries because they have less developed social insurance programs. If one accepts the normative case for social insurance, it applies to developing countries with even greater force because of widespread poverty, which means that losing a job can have much direr consequences. But the need for revenues in developing countries goes far beyond social insurance. In some developing countries revenues are needed to insure the very survival of organized government, as the Russian experience demonstrates. In other, more stable developing countries revenues are needed primarily to provide for adequate education (investment in human capital), which many regard as the key to promoting development. For example, the UN has estimated that for only an additional $50 billion per year, all people in the world can obtain basic social services (such as elementary education). Given current trends in foreign aid, most of these funds have to come from developing country governments.

Second, the standard advice by economists to small open economies is that they should refrain from taxing foreign investors, because such investors cannot be made to bear the burden of any tax imposed by the capital importing country. Therefore, the tax will necessarily be shifted to less mobile factors in the host country, such as labor and/or land, and it is more efficient to tax those factors directly. But while this argument seems quite valid as applied to portfolio investment, it seems less valid in regard to foreign direct investment (FDI), for two reasons. First, the standard advice does not apply if a foreign tax credit is available in the home country of the investor, which frequently would be the case for FDI. Second, the standard advice assumes that the host country is small. However, an extensive literature on multinationals suggests that typically they exist in order to earn economic rents. In that case, the host country is no longer "small" in the economic sense. That is, there is a reason for the investor to be there and not elsewhere. Therefore, any tax imposed on such rents (as long as it is below 100 percent) will not necessarily drive the investor to leave even if it is unable to shift the burden of the tax to labor or landowners.

This argument clearly holds in the case of rents that are linked to a specific location, such as natural resources or a large market. But what if the rent can be earned in a large number of potential locations? In this case, the host country will not be able to tax the rent if the multinational can credibly threaten to go elsewhere, although once the investment has been made the rent can be taxed. This situation, which is probably the most common, would require coordinated action to enable all host countries to tax the rent earned within their borders. The proposal outlined above addresses this issue directly.

This relates to the final argument, which is that host countries need to offer tax incentives to be competitive. An extensive literature has demonstrated that taxes do in fact play a crucial role in determining investment location decisions. But all of these studies emphasize that the tax incentives are crucial *given the availability of such incentives elsewhere*. Thus, it can be argued that given the need for tax revenues, developing countries would in general prefer to refrain from granting tax incentives, if only they could be assured that no other developing country would be able to grant such incentives.

Thus, restricting the ability of developing countries to compete in granting tax incentives does not truly restrict their autonomy or counter their interests. That is the case whenever they grant the incentive only for fear of competition from other developing countries, and would not have granted it but for such fear. Whenever competition from other countries drives the tax incentive, eliminating the competition does not hurt the developing country, and may aid its revenue-raising efforts (assuming it can attract investment on other grounds, which is typically the case). Moreover, under the proposals described above, developing countries remain free to lower their tax rates generally (as opposed to granting specific tax relief aimed at foreign investors).

Two additional points need to be made from a developing country perspective. The first concerns the question of tax incidence. Since the tax competition that is most relevant to developing countries concerns the corporate income tax, it is important to attempt to assess the incidence of that tax in evaluating the effects of collecting it on the welfare of the developing country. Unfortunately, after decades of analysis, no consensus exists on the incidence of the corporate tax. While the older studies have tended to conclude that the tax is borne by shareholders or by all capital providers, more recent studies have suggested that the tax is borne to a significant extent by consumers or by labor. Another possibility is that the tax on established corporations was borne by those who were shareholders at the time the tax was imposed or increased, because thereafter it is capitalized into the price of the shares. It is unlikely that this debate will be decided any time soon (in fact, the incidence may be shifting over time, especially as globalization may enable corporations to shift more of the tax burden to labor). However, from the perspective of a developing country deciding whether to collect taxes from a multinational, three out of the four possible alternatives for incidence (current shareholders or capital providers, old shareholders, and consumers) are largely the residents of other jurisdictions, and therefore from a national welfare perspective the developing country gains by collecting the tax. And even if some of the tax is shifted to labor in the developing country, it can be argued that as a matter of tax administration it is more efficient (as well as more politically acceptable) to collect the tax from the multinational than to attempt to collect it from the workers.

Finally, it should be noted that a developing country may want to collect taxes from multinationals even if in general it believes that the private sector is more efficient is using the resources than the public sector. That is because in the case of a foreign multinational, the taxes that the developing country fails to collect may indeed be used by the private sector, but in another jurisdiction, and therefore not benefit the developing country. One possible solution, which is in fact employed by developing countries, is to refrain from taxing multinationals while they re-invest domestically, but tax them upon remittance of the profits abroad. However, such taxation of dividends and other forms of remittance is subject to the same tax competition problem discussed above. Thus, it would appear that overcoming the tax competition problem is in most cases in the interest of developing countries, and the proposal developed above would seem to be in their best interest.

4.3.5 Can the Proposal Be Adopted?

By this point, I hope the reader will be convinced that (a) current taxation of all multinationals on a global basis is the preferred approach, (b) *if* such taxation can be adopted on a multilateral basis, then all the usual arguments against its unilateral adoption by any country disappear. This is an unusual situation because in most tax policy debates there are good arguments on either side. In this case, however, the case in favor of multilateral current taxation would seem to be quite convincing, with no significant drawbacks if it can be achieved.

But, the reader is likely to object, this assumes that a multilateral approach is possible on such a sensitive issue as taxation. What is the evidence that this is in fact the case?

In order to assess whether multilateral action is possible, it is first necessary to establish the interests of the parties involved. Tax competition for FDI typically involves a MNE deciding which countries are possible investment locations from a non-tax point of view, that is, taking into account location, infrastructure, education, political stability, and other factors. Once the MNE has established a list of plausible countries, it then approaches these countries and asks what they would be willing to offer it in return for the investment. The countries then engage in a bidding war to grant tax reductions, culminating in the winner receiving the investment. Frequently, more than one country is able to get the investment.

Under these circumstances it is clear that the investment would be made in any case, whether or not the tax incentive is granted. The tax incentives are therefore a pure windfall for the MNE. If the countries could find a way to coordinate their approaches, they would still get the investment but without the tax cost.

Thus, it is in the interest of most countries to coordinate their approaches to prevent this type of tax competition. The same rationale obtains for capital exporting jurisdictions like the large countries in OECD. They would prefer to tax their MNEs on a current basis, but are constrained from doing so because of the competitiveness and expatriation concerns outlined above.

Thus, in my opinion all OECD member countries would benefit from a multilateral approach. Capital exporting countries could obtain revenues from their MNEs without concerns about harming their competitiveness or MNEs migrating to other OECD countries. Capital importing countries could obtain FDI without concern that if they do not grant tax holidays the investment would end up in other countries. In the latter case, if all OECD and G20 countries were on board, the limits on tax competition would apply outside the OECD as well since almost all MNEs are based in these countries. Countries outside the OECD/G20 would have no incentive to grant tax holidays against their own interest if the income were taxed in the residence country of the MNE, since in that case there would be no benefit to the MNE from the tax holiday.

In addition, if the proposal above were adopted, this would also help alleviate the current opposition by MNEs and some countries to country-by-country reporting, which is being considered by OECD as part of the BEPS project. Since MNEs would obtain credit for taxes levied by source countries under the proposal, they should be less hostile to country-by-country reporting, which is designed to aid source countries collect their fair share of taxes.

If the interests of the countries are aligned, what has prevented multilateral action so far? In my opinion, it is primarily because of lobbying by the MNEs themselves. They are the primary beneficiaries from the status quo and they have successfully lobbied both countries and the OECD against meaningful reform.

A useful contrast is to examine a case in which the countries and MNEs were aligned. Prior to 1977, there were no domestic limits on MNEs paying bribes overseas to obtain contracts from corrupt government officials. In 1977, following several scandals, the United States enacted the Foreign Corrupt Practices Act, which imposed criminal sanctions on such bribes by United States-based MNEs and their executives. Predictably, US MNEs complained that this ban put them at a competitive disadvantage, especially when other countries like Germany permitted foreign bribes to be deducted for domestic tax purposes.

Somewhat surprisingly, the outcome was not relaxation of the US law. Instead, the Clinton administration successfully pushed the OECD to adopt the same provisions as part of a binding, multilateral treaty, which eliminated the competitive disadvantage issue.

The key reason for this success is that not only were the interests of the countries aligned; the MNEs did not like paying bribes either and therefore lobbied in favor of the provision. This will not be the case for tax, where the MNEs are already pushing back against the OECD BEPS project. However, there have been instances in the past where resistance by MNEs has been overcome. For example, the US Congress in 2010 adopted the Foreign Account Tax Compliance Act (FATCA) in spite of fierce opposition by the banks because of an outcry by civil society over tax evasion, and this innovative law is now being copied in many countries and has led the OECD to propose a Multilateral Agreement on Administrative Assistance in Tax Matters (MAATM) which has been endorsed by over eighty countries.

At the current juncture there is huge pressure on the OECD governments to do something about corporate tax avoidance, and a broad consensus that more corporate tax revenues are needed at a time of widespread recession and austerity. Thus, lobbying in favor of a multilateral approach is likely to push the OECD in the right direction.

If the reader agrees that the solution proposed above is the right one, now is the time to act. We should not assume that multilateral action is impossible. If academics and NGOs unify behind global taxation and reject attempts to retain the current system, a multilateral binding treaty like the anti-corruption one may be achievable.

APPENDIX

Can Corporate Tax Rates Be Coordinated?

In 1980, Thomas Horst published an extremely influential and widely cited article in which he demonstrated that under certain assumptions it is impossible to simultaneously obtain capital export neutrality (CEN) and capital import neutrality (CIN) (Horst, 1980). CEN refers to neutrality of investment decisions between the country in which an investor resides and the country in which she is considering making an investment. CIN refers to treating all investors in a given country in the same way.

For example, suppose that A is a resident of country X and B is a resident of country Y, and they are both considering making an investment of 1,000 in country Z. Country X has a tax rate of 35, country Y has a tax rate of 25, and country Z has a tax rate of 0.

CEN would require both country X and country Y to impose their tax on any investment A or B make. This would result in A being taxed at 35 percent whether he invests in X or in Z, and B would be taxed at 25 percent whether she invests in Y or in Z. But this results violates CIN because A and B will bear different rates on their investment in Z.

CIN would require both X and Y to exempt foreign source income. This would preserve CIN because they would each bear only the Z rate (zero) on their investment in Z. But both A and B would have an incentive to invest in Z rather than in their home countries, which violates CEN.

Horst pointed out that CEN and CIN can only be attained at the same time on one assumption: that the X and Y rates are the same. In that case, both X and Y can tax their investors on the investment in Z but because the rates are the same neither CEN nor CIN would be violated.

Horst assumed that this result is unrealistic, and he was right in 1980. But is he still right? I am less sure of that, as far as corporate taxes are concerned.

Countries vary tremendously in terms of their individual income tax rates. In the OECD, these range from 16.5 percent (Slovakia) to 56.6 percent (Sweden). This is understandable because the personal income tax is about the degree of progressivity that countries desire and there is tremendous variation of opinion on how much progressivity is desirable.

But there is considerably less variation in corporate tax rates in the OECD. The lowest is Ireland at 12.5 percent and the highest is the United States at 39.1 percent (including state corporate taxes), but out of thirty-seven OECD countries, twenty-five have a corporate rate between 20 percent and 30 percent, and this includes all the large OECD economies except for France, Italy, and the United States.[5]

Why is there such convergence of corporate tax rates? Fundamentally, because of tax competition. Multinationals compete with each other across national borders, and no country wishes to put its multinationals at a competitive disadvantage. Because of this, corporate tax rates tend to move in unison. When the United States reduced its rate from 46 percent to 35 percent in 1986, most countries followed suit, so that the typical corporate tax rate in the 1990s was in the 30s. Then, in the 2000s, most large

[5] While these are nominal (statutory) rates, the empirical evidence indicates the same convergence in effective rates as well. See Avi-Yonah and Lahav (2012).

OECD countries except the United States reduced their rate to the 20s, led by Germany and eventually followed by the UK and Japan. This dynamic can be seen in the current pressure on the United States to reduce its corporate rate below 30 percent, which is supported by the Obama Administration and both Democrats and Republicans in Congress precisely because the United States now has the highest corporate rate in the OECD.

There are, of course, outliers with rates below 20 percent, such as Ireland, but those are typically small countries with a narrow domestic corporate base, so their low rate is primarily a device to attract FDI without running afoul of the OECD and EU limits on harmful tax competition, which preclude granting tax reductions only to foreign MNEs.

In this situation, one could argue that for the vast majority of MNEs, which are overwhelmingly based in the large OECD countries, the counterfactual to Horst's assumption that tax rates cannot be coordinated has already occurred. Therefore, these countries can apply their tax rates to their multinationals' worldwide income without violating CEN or CIN, as proposed above.

But I think the current BEPS project gives us a chance to go further. The EU has never succeeded in coordinating corporate tax rates within it despite various attempts to do so, because EU membership is too diverse. The same can be said even more strongly of the OECD and *a fortiori* the UN. But the G20, which is driving the BEPS effort, is another matter. These are all very large capital exporting economies, and they are home to over 90 percent of the world's multinationals. If the G20 wanted to they could plausibly commit to taxing their MNEs on worldwide income at a rate that is between 20 percent and 30 percent. No G20 member would be required to raise its current rate and only six would have to reduce their rate (Argentina, Brazil, France, Italy, India, and the United States).[6] Thus, Horst's utopian world of coordinated tax rates which enable both CEN and CIN to be achieved simultaneously may be closer to reality than many economists and policymakers have assumed.

REFERENCES

Avi-Yonah, Reuven S., 2004. "Corporations, Society and the State: A Defense of the Corporate Tax," *Va. L. Rev.* 90: 1193.

Avi-Yonah, Reuven S., 2013. "Carbon Tax, Health Care Tax, Bank Tax, and Other Regulatory Taxes," in David A. Brennen, Karen B. Brown, and Darryll K. Jones (eds), *Beyond Economic Efficiency in United States Tax Law*. Alphen aan den Rijn, Netherlands: Wolters Kluwer.

Avi-Yonah, Reuven S. and Amir Chenchiski, 2011. "The Case for Dividend Deduction," *Tax Lawyer* 65: 3.

Avi-Yonah, Reuven S. and Yaron Lahav, 2012. "The Effective Tax Rates of the Largest US and EU Multinationals," *Tax Law Review*, 65: 375.

[6] In fact, it would be sufficient if the G20 were to commit not to reduce rates below 20%, because tax competition would eventually lead the outliers to reduce rates below 30%. This means that no actual rate changes need to be made at all.

Brauner, Yariv, 2008. "The Non-Sense Tax: A Reply to New Corporate Income Tax Advocacy," *2008 Mich. St. L. Rev.* 591.

Hines, Jr, James R., 2009. "Reconsidering the Taxation of Foreign Income," *Tax Law Review* 62 (2): 269–98.

Horst, Thomas, 1980. "A Note on Optimal Taxation of International Investment Income," *Quarterly Journal of Economics* 94: 793.

Kies, Kenneth, 2007. "A Perfect Experiment: 'Deferral' and the U.S. Shipping Industry," *Tax Notes* 116 (11), 10 September.

OECD, 2013. *Addressing Base Erosion and Profit Shifting*. OECD, Paris.

Shaviro, Daniel, 2013. *Fixing the US International Taxation*. New York: Oxford University Press.

5

Stateless Income and its Remedies

Edward D. Kleinbard

5.1 THE STATELESS INCOME PROBLEM

5.1.1 Overview

This chapter considers the tax consequences and policy implications of the phenomenon of "stateless income"—income derived for tax purposes by a multinational group from business activities in a country other than the domicile of the group's ultimate parent company, but which is subject to tax only in a jurisdiction that is neither the source of the factors of production through which the income was derived, nor the domicile of the group's parent company.[1] In other words, the term describes the income of a multinational corporation that, through internal tax planning, first becomes unmoored from the foreign host country where it originally is earned, and then sets sail for the welcoming harbor of the tax haven of choice. The term has been adopted by at least some tax policymakers around the world.[2]

Stateless income planning is practiced by multinational firms domiciled throughout the world, but the evidence suggests that US firms have been global leaders in developing these tax avoidance technologies. The stateless income phenomenon is very large in size, amounting to lost tax revenues undoubtedly exceeding $100 billion each year. By way of one example, a news article in October 2013 reported that Google Inc., relying on its "Double Irish

[1] I originally introduced the term "stateless income" in 2007, and reused it for a series of academic papers published beginning in 2011. See Kleinbard 2011a, 2011b, and 2013. Condensed versions of the first two articles were published in Tax Notes: Kleinbard 2011c and 2012.

[2] Jacob Lew, United States Secretary of the Treasury, as quoted in Charlton (2013) ("We must address the persistent issue of 'stateless income,' which undermines confidence in our tax system at all levels"). See also Bradbury (2013) and Sheppard (2013) (quoting Edwin Visser, deputy director-general of taxation of the Dutch Ministry of Finance: "Stateless income is the big problem now," Visser, who is involved in the OECD project, echoed. "Stateless income distorts investment decisions and undermines voluntary compliance," he added.)

Dutch Sandwich" tax structure, had through this mechanism alone shifted €8.8 billion in profits to its Bermuda subsidiary in 2012.[3] As of late 2013, US multinational firms carried on their financial statements roughly $2 trillion in retained earnings attributable to low-taxed foreign operations (so-called "permanently-reinvested earnings").

The stateless income problem has important economic efficiency consequences for where multinational firms invest, and for the tax revenues thereby derived, which in turn implicate another set of efficiency concerns. The attention brought to bear on the topic by journalists, policy commentators and academics has culminated in the acknowledgment by the Organisation for Economic Co-operation and Development (OECD) that there is indeed a serious problem in need of fixing. At the encouragement of both the G8 and the G20, the OECD has embarked on an ambitious project to address "base erosion and profit shifting" (BEPS).[4] The OECD occupies an outsized role in the design of the international tax system, so its effective reversal of position (although it would never acknowledge such) and newfound zeal for addressing stateless income is a major development.

It had long been recognized that many multinational firms were "stripping" income out of their home countries (that is, the country in which the parent company of the multinational group is domiciled), principally through "transfer pricing" abuses (as explained below). What arguably was misapprehended until more recently was the magnitude of income shifting by multinational enterprises from one "source" country (a foreign country in which the multinational does business and earns economic income) to another, lower-taxed foreign country. In my academic work, I have used the term "stateless income" to include only the second, less studied, phenomenon; the OECD's "BEPS" terminology is broader and appears to include both.

This chapter and research into the stateless income problem are not inquiries into tax evasion. To the contrary, stateless income is an instance of exactly the opposite: the faithful application by multinational firms of tax rules for the purpose of producing perverse results. For purposes of clarity, however, it is worth identifying the two major strands of international tax evasion not considered in this chapter.

At least in the recent past, international tax evasion by individuals most often has meant simply hiding financial assets in financial accounts in Switzerland, Lichtenstein, Vanuatu, or whichever other tax haven was thought at the time to best combine attractive bank secrecy laws, political stability, and zero taxation. Like a firm hand on a tube of toothpaste, the United States has been the leader in squeezing this simple evasion out of the financial system, through the Financial Account Tax Compliance Act (FATCA). The wildly

[3] Houlder (2013). [4] OECD (2013a; 2013b).

unpopular FATCA effectively requires financial institutions all over the world to report to the US Internal Revenue Service the income earned by US persons in respect of their financial accounts held at such institutions; the enforcement mechanism is to preclude noncomplying institutions from doing any meaningful business in US financial assets or with US financial institutions. At its heart, FATCA takes seriously the idea of bank "know your customer" rules, and levers off that principle to forestall tax evasion.

In the long run, FATCA should serve as a model for other countries. In the not very distant future, it should be the norm that every financial institution in the world reports to all jurisdictions the income earned by residents of each such jurisdiction through financial accounts held at such institution. The trick, of course, will be to have a common reporting format, so that compliance is feasible.

The other, slightly greyer, instance of international tax evasion is the long-understood problem of corporate "transfer pricing" abuse. A multinational firm is not in fact one firm as a formal matter, but rather a cluster of hundreds of subsidiaries domiciled and doing business in different jurisdictions, all under the umbrella of the common parent firm, which might be simply a holding company. (The same issue, however, comes up even with one company that does business in many jurisdictions through branches in those places.) In every case, the issue is, how much income is attributable to each subsidiary? For many decades, the answer, insisted upon by the OECD, has been the "arm's-length principle," which contemplates that each operation of a multinational firm, when interfacing with other operations of the same multinational group, should pretend that it is an independent firm, and deal with its affiliates on the same terms it would deal with an unrelated counterparty—that is, at arm's length. To implement this requires setting actual prices on internal transactions that are not in fact shown to the market—wholly internal "transfer prices."

One does not require an advanced degree in tax law or a swindler's disposition to see that every multinational firm faces the temptation to cause its low-taxed affiliates to charge high transfer prices to the group's high-taxed operations, thereby shifting income to low-taxed jurisdictions. And the results show just that: it cannot be simply the luck of the Irish, for example, that explains why Irish subsidiaries of US multinational firms as a whole are consistently far more profitable than their continental European sisters.

There are rules that say that this is wrong, because after all the internal transfer prices are supposed to be rooted in unrelated party exemplars, but often genuine comparables do not exist. If a firm egregiously ignores the learning of the marketplace in setting internal transfer prices, that fairly can be described as corporate tax evasion. But it should be obvious that the problem lies on a continuum, and many intermediate shades of grey stand between a perfect market comparable and clear tax evasion. This paper does not consider in detail how transfer pricing can be made more perfect, because years of experience have taught that this is largely a fool's errand.

5.1.2 The Moral Dimension in Corporate Taxation

Because this is a book on global tax justice, it is useful to consider for a moment on whose shoulders rests the moral obligation to produce international corporate income tax results that correspond with genuine economic activity (which might be taken for our purposes as a convenient norm). This question has attracted a great deal of interest, particularly among Members of Parliament in the United Kingdom, in respect of the tax positions claimed by Google, Starbucks, Amazon, and other US firms, where firms that plainly are doing a great deal of business in the United Kingdom, in an economic sense, turn their empty pockets inside out to Her Majesty's Revenue and Customs. (No issue touching on moral philosophy seems to gain any traction in the United States in any discipline, including this one, so there is no learning to be gleaned on that side of the Atlantic.)

Perhaps idiosyncratically, I respectfully submit that the moral dimension of corporate income taxation is real, but rests almost entirely on the shoulders of the legislature. The reason is simple: there is no natural law or theology undergirding the income tax in general, and certainly not the corporate income tax, which piles artificiality on artificiality, given that it is an arbitrary set of rules applied to a fictional person.

The income tax essentially is a model of all of economic activity; for every real-life action in the commercial sphere, one finds a tax description and a tax operator, that together yield a tax consequence. But unlike more common economic models, this model is written in the vernacular, by a legislature. The duty of a taxpayer is fully and faithfully to operationalize the tax model, and thereby remit to the fiscal authorities the money that the model prescribes. Hiding money in Cypriot bank accounts fails this standard, and raises a moral issue. So, too, does extreme corporate transfer pricing abuse. Beyond that, what can one ask?

All sorts of international income tax regimes are plausible; so, too, is a legislative decision not to rely on an income tax at all. A tax model thus is inherently normative, because it does not simply describe economic activity, but ascribes what tax consequences should flow from those activities. If those norms are internally contradictory or poorly operationalized, it is difficult to see how a firm can unilaterally supply the missing focus.

What a deep inquiry into stateless income planning teaches is that the international corporate tax model is itself as flawed as the Ptolemaic astronomical model. Only the legislature can address this failing, and the moral opprobrium here rightly should fall on legislatures all over the world, either for their laziness in investing in the upkeep of their tax models, or more often, for their cynical attempts to engage in a sort of tax mercantilism, in which the goal is to demand tax justice from foreign multinationals doing domestic business, while encouraging domestically domiciled multinational firms to engage in just such base erosion and profit shifting at the expense of other host jurisdictions. In this last regard, the United Kingdom appears to this outsider, at least, to have been in recent years an egregious offender.

5.1.3 International Corporate Taxation in a Nutshell

Men and women devote decades to understanding the details of international corporate income taxation, yet go to bed weeping over their failure to achieve mastery. For our purposes, though, we need only to understand a few basic concepts. (Some of the more arcane principles and practices are described in the papers collected in footnote 1.)

Begin with a world in which all business is conducted directly by individuals, so that there are no firms, and in which jurisdictions rely for revenue at least in part on an income tax. If an individual resident in Freedonia breaks with tradition, by looking beyond her borders, and begins to business in neighboring Sylvania with Sylvanian customers (so as to avoid questions of "runaway plants" and the like), both Freedonia and Sylvania must extend their tax models to answer some novel normative questions. For the Freedonian Fiscal Authority, the question will be, should this Freedonian resident and taxpayer be taxed on her Sylvanian branch in the same manner that she is taxed on her Freedonian home office? And for the Sylvanian Revenue Service, the issue is, should this Freedonian arriviste be taxed on her Sylvanian income in the same manner as any other Sylvanian businessperson? For each jurisdiction, the perfectly rational first intuition is to say, Yes!—which promptly would lead to full double taxation, with obvious serious and adverse economic efficiency consequences.

The resolution, almost since the dawn of modern income taxation, has been to recognize that when it comes to the taxation of net business income, the "source" or "host" country—Sylvania, in this instance—has the primary claim to taxation. The underlying and generally unstated norm is that international income taxation is all about *geographic nexus*—and the nexus of the income arising from doing business in Sylvania is Sylvania. Portfolio income, in particular interest income, generally follows the opposite presumption, so that the residence country typically is the one that taxes cross-border interest income. One can say that this is because the capital in question is controlled from the residence country, but one could just as easily say that the capital bears a positive return because it has been put to work in the source country. The theory of geographic nexus seems to hold less sway here than in the case of net business income; phrased differently, one begins to see the arbitrariness of all income tax models.

Some residence countries (Freedonia, here) honor the geographic nexus principle completely, by agreeing to forgo taxation of their citizens' foreign business income. Others cede primary authority to the source country, but impose residual tax on that income if the residence country's tax rate is greater than the source country's. This rule is implemented through a foreign tax credit—a dollar for dollar (or Freedonian pfennig for pfennig) offset against tax liability for the foreign income taxes paid to the source country.

Now add firms (corporations) to the mix. Even in a purely domestic context, firms pose difficult tax conundrums. After all, they are wholly fictional persons, and both their income and their tax liabilities ultimately are attributable to some individuals, although debating which specific group of individuals bears the economic incidence of corporate income taxation to this day remains great sport among economists. Nonetheless, most countries impose a corporate income tax, for obvious political economy reasons, and because alternative schemes to tax shareholders on their shares of corporate revenues are much more difficult to operationalize than most people suspect.

The best way to understand the corporate income tax is that it is effectively a withholding tax imposed on shareholders (in the first instance—the ultimate economic incidence is a separate question) but collected from the firm, because that is the administratively simpler place to measure the income in question and collect the tax. Nonetheless, the tax is imposed on the firm as a legal entity, and from that follows a natural inclination to think of the firm as having both a full juridical personality for tax purposes and a nationality, just as natural persons do. What also follows is the natural tension over the status of a corporate subsidiary (one corporation owned by a second, parent company): is the parent company just a shareholder in the subsidiary, or is the subsidiary just a pseudopod of the parent? That is, should the subsidiary be treated as a separate legal person?

One can muddle through these issues reasonably well in an entirely domestic context, because one can assign a nationality to the firm that is congruent with the nationality of its shareholders, and because a quasi-withholding tax on local residents is not very different from taxing them directly (so long as one has rules to deal with tiers of corporate subsidiaries, to prevent cascading taxation), but the arrangements begin to fall apart in the international context. A Freedonian firm, like the Freedonian entrepreneur at the beginning of this subsection, can cross borders, but now can do so directly or through a Sylvanian subsidiary. Meanwhile, the owners of the firm themselves can be drawn from many countries. We quickly get hopelessly muddled as to which set of tax principles should apply, and to whom.

To talk about a firm as having a nationality is not completely inaccurate when applied to a US public company, because even today US companies are more than 80-percent owned by US persons, but is quite incomplete when applied to public companies in other jurisdictions, such as the United Kingdom, where local ownership of public firms might be closer to 50 percent of the total. The problem is not with how corporate residence is determined (place of incorporation, for example, or place of "mind and management") but with the idea of firms having a nationality at all. Yet every jurisdiction distinguishes to some extent between resident and nonresident companies. In particular, jurisdictions generally do not tax the business profits of nonresident companies unless some threshold level of activity is breached in the host country. Moreover, nonresident subsidiaries are invariably treated as separate juridical persons, not pseudopods of the corporate parent, which implies not only the full panoply of transfer pricing problems alluded to earlier, but also treatment of the subsidiary as outside the reach of the parent's home country, or vice versa, and treatment of intragroup financing arrangements (e.g., loans from the parent company to the subsidiary) as real.

The result is not simply chaos, but opportunity. Multinational groups sprinkle corporate subsidiaries in different jurisdictions, assigning each different functions. For example, high-value intangible assets invariably are treated as owned by subsidiaries in low-tax jurisdictions, from which those intangibles are licensed out to sister operating subsidiaries in high-tax jurisdictions. Because the separate juridical personality of the intangibles owner must be respected, and because its modest business activities (signing a license agreement, for example) are carried out in its low-tax domicile, neither the intangible itself nor the income paid for the use of the intangible follows the multinational group into the jurisdiction where a separate operating subsidiary puts the intangible to work selling products or service to customers. As another example, low-taxed internal financing subsidiaries advance loans to high-tax affiliates, and the interest paid is taxed only in the low-tax affiliate's home jurisdiction.

To add insult to injury, in each case the low-tax affiliate obtains the necessary capital (to buy the group intangible, or to fund its lending activities) from equity injected by the parent company, but once it has received that equity for free, the subsidiary is treated for tax purposes as if it had a brain of its own, rather than as a creature of the parent, as reality might suggest. So for transfer pricing purposes the subsidiary is permitted to demand royalties for the use of the group's intangible assets that compensate the subsidiary for putting "its" capital at risk. Moreover, the entire purpose of a multinational group is to obtain synergies not available to less integrated operations, but even if transfer pricing principles were otherwise to apply perfectly, to which subsidiary do the profits attributable to those synergies belong? The practical answer has been to sweep those returns into the firm's intangible assets, securely tucked into bed in the most convenient tax haven jurisdiction of the moment.

With the active encouragement of the OECD, most developed countries have subscribed to the themes sketched above—the separate juridical personality of corporate subsidiaries, the notion that companies have nationalities, the treatment of nonresident companies as outside a jurisdiction's tax net unless that specific company (not the group as a whole) has some minimum presence in the host country, the respect accorded "risk taking" by wholly owned corporate subsidiaries, and the differing international treatment of returns on business capital (source country) and on interest on loans (residence country), even where the loan capital is furnished by the corporate parent of the obligor. These are the Ptolemaic postulates on which international corporate taxation rests, and these are the building blocks of stateless income tax planning. With a moment's reflection, the surprise should not be that some multinational companies pay tax at single digit rates on their international operations, but rather that other firms pay more.

5.1.4 Economic Efficiency Implications of Stateless Income

The articles cited in footnote 1 develop in detail the efficiency consequences of rampant stateless income planning, but two points need to be highlighted. First, stateless income planning leads to government budget shortfalls, because a jurisdiction's tax revenues no longer mirror the trend in the business activities therein. In an economic sense, a multinational firm might deliver a marvelous new good or service to Sylvanian customers, thereby adding value from that business relationship in Sylvania, but as a tax matter the firm will have sliced up the different functions required to do business with Sylvanian customers, to hold back from the reach of the Sylvanian tax system key drivers of value (intangible assets, capital, etc.). The result is that only a modest distribution function, if that, is visible to the Sylvanian tax system.

If business income tax revenues fall short of expectations, relative to the business actually done, the difference must be made up by other taxpayers. Assuming that Sylvania believes that it got matters right in the first place, the subsequent shifting of relative burdens must be suboptimal, from the perspective of Sylvanian policymakers.

Second, and less obviously, stateless income planning distorts a multinational firm's incentives as to where to invest as an economic matter. Under plausible assumptions of globally efficient capital markets, risk-adjusted after-tax business returns around the world should converge. Given that tax rates differ, this implies that high-tax foreign countries should offer higher pretax business returns than do low-tax countries. Add to this thought the fact that, in the case of the United States, at least, it generally is easier to move profits from a high-tax foreign subsidiary to a low-tax one than it is to move profits from the US parent to a low-tax subsidiary.

These circumstances create an underappreciated incentive for US firms to invest offshore—not in tax havens, but in real high-tax foreign jurisdictions where their customers are, because the resulting income can form the raw feedstock to fuel the stateless income generation machine. The result is that high pretax profits from high-tax jurisdictions, where local returns are set to reflect the implicit cost of those high tax rates, end up not being subject to significant tax burdens at all.

The US firm thereby succeeds in capturing what I call "tax rents"—abnormally high after-tax returns derived by employing stateless income planning to avoid the implicit tax burden on those high-tax country pretax returns. The United States is the loser, because savvy US firms now have a reason to prefer investing in high-tax foreign countries to investing in the United States. So, too, is the high-tax host country, because its domestic firms cannot so easily escape the high tax burdens that the multinational firm has caused to disappear. Investment decisions and business ownership are distorted accordingly, and economic efficiency losses accrue.

US policymakers and observers sometimes understandably articulate the intuition that the United States should not object if US-based multinational firms successfully game the tax laws of foreign jurisdictions in which they do business, but the points summarized in the preceding paragraph demonstrate why the United States would be the loser if it were to follow that strategy. By generating "tax rents"—low-risk supersized returns—through moving income from high-tax foreign countries in which they actually do business to low-tax jurisdictions, US multinational firms have an incentive to locate investment in high-tax foreign countries. And by leaving their global interest expenses in particular in the United States without significant tax constraints, US-based multinationals in turn can erode the US tax payable on their US domestic operations.[5]

5.2 CASE STUDY: STARBUCKS

5.2.1 Tax Minimization through Stateless Income Planning

The US coffee retailer Starbucks's operations in the United Kingdom offer a useful window into stateless income planning in operation.[6] To put matters

[5] The foreign tax credit interest allocation rules of section 864(e) have almost no bite when firms are able to drive down their foreign effective tax rates to single-digit levels, because even after interest expenses are allocated firms still have capacity to claim whatever foreign taxes they do pay as credits in the United States.

[6] This subsection is drawn from Kleinbard (2013).

bluntly, if Starbucks can organize itself as a successful stateless income generator, any multinational firm can. Starbucks follows a classic bricks and mortar retail business model, with direct customer interactions in thousands of "high street" locations in high-tax countries around the world. Moreover, without meaning to deprecate Starbucks' corporate pride in the "Starbucks experience" afforded by its retail outlets, or in its proprietary coffee roasting formulae, Starbucks is not a firm driven by hugely valuable identifiable intangibles.[7] The "Starbucks experience" is a business model by another name, and all successful firms have business models. Despite these facts, it appears that Starbucks indeed enjoys a much lower effective tax rate on its non-US income than would be predicted by looking at a weighted average of the tax rates in the countries in which it does business.

This subsection uses Starbucks as an example of a widespread problem, but Starbucks is not an outlier in its stateless income generating strategies (to the extent they are visible) or its legislative wish list. Nor do I mean to suggest that any of Starbucks' tax planning runs afoul of the laws of any jurisdiction.

Starbucks has operated in the United Kingdom since 1998. In October 2012, Reuters published a news story describing the fact that Starbucks had reported losses in fourteen of the first fifteen years of its existence there, and of course as a result paid virtually no UK company tax, despite a 31 percent market share and shareholder reports indicating solid profitability for the Starbucks group attributable to its UK operations.[8] In its fiscal year ended 2 October 2011 (the most recent year available), Starbucks Coffee Company (UK) Limited ("Starbucks UK"), the principal Starbucks operating company in the United Kingdom, reported under UK financial accounting principles turnover of nearly £400 million, gross profit of £78.4 million, an operating loss after "administrative expenses" of £28.8 million, and a net pretax loss on ordinary activities of £32.9 million.[9] (Fiscal year 2010 was broadly similar in results.)

In reactions that would surprise American observers, where such reports typically have few repercussions, this story unleashed a political firestorm in the United Kingdom, including threats of boycotts of Starbucks stores. Less

[7] See, e.g., Starbucks Corporation 2012 Form 10-K, Shareholders' Letter, and Starbucks Ways and Means Submission, supra n. 3.

[8] Bergin (2012).

At the parliamentary inquiry described below, the M.P.s questioning Starbucks consistently contrasted Starbucks' losses in the United Kingdom to the significant company taxes paid by its largest competitor, Costa, e.g., Public Accounts Committee, House of Commons, Minutes of Hearing HC716, supra n. 7, Q235, Q281.

For the market share figure and "solid profitability" claim, see House of Commons Public Accounts Committee (2012, Item 1, Par. 8). The latter claim is discussed in more detail below.

[9] Audited financial statements of UK companies are available through the website of Companies House, http://www.companieshouse.gov.uk/, accessed 15 July 2015. Starbucks UK's company identification number is 02959325. Its immediate parent is Starbucks Coffee Holdings (UK) Limited; that company's identification number is 03346087.

than a month after the story's publication, the Committee of Public Accounts of the House of Commons convened a hearing to review the UK corporate tax planning of Starbucks, Amazon, and Google. Its report was published two weeks later; it concluded "We found it difficult to believe that a commercial company with a 31% market share by turnover, with a responsibility to its shareholders and investors to make a decent return, was trading with apparent losses for nearly every year of its operation in the UK."[10]

The Reuters news report and subsequent House of Commons hearing focused on three intragroup charges through which Starbucks UK paid substantial amounts to other group companies: (i) royalties and license fees paid to a Dutch affiliate; (ii) markups on coffee purchased via another Dutch affiliate and a Swiss affiliate; and (iii) interest paid on a loan from the US parent company. It was argued that these charges explain Starbucks UK's near-continuous losses for corporation tax purposes. At the same time, it was argued, Starbucks reported a much rosier picture of its UK subsidiary's performance to analysts and shareholders. Finally, the argument went, the royalties and coffee markups in particular were subject to tax at very low rates.

In the interests of brevity, this subsection focuses on the first and third claims, although the second in fact probably has more money associated with it. All three are discussed in more detail in a technical analysis published elsewhere.[11] So too is the murky intersection of tax reporting and financial accounting (in the United States, GAAP) accounts.

Starbucks UK pays a 6 percent royalty to what Starbucks in its parliamentary testimony described only as an "Amsterdam structure,"[12] but as a result of an agreement with the UK tax authorities reduced the deduction it claimed for tax years 2003–9 to a 4.7 percent rate. (Years from 2010 forward were under examination as of the time of the parliamentary inquiry.) The royalty payment covers rights to the Starbucks brand and trademark, rights to "the highest quality and ethically sourced Arabica coffee," expertise in store operations, use of the Starbucks proprietary business model, and store design concepts.[13] Starbuck UK's intragroup royalty payments are in the neighborhood of £20 to £25 million/year.

The royalty payments represent a classic stateless income strategy of stripping out income from a relatively high tax country to a low-tax one through royalties on the intangible assets that form the core of the firm's business. This strategy raises traditional transfer pricing issues; in this regard, the fact that Starbucks UK agreed to reduce its tax deduction for its royalties from 6 percent to

[10] House of Commons Public Accounts Committee (2012, Item 1, Par. 8).

[11] Kleinbard (2013).

[12] Starbucks UK supplementary statement to House of Commons Public Accounts Committee, supra n. 21, at Q 246.

[13] Starbucks UK supplementary statement to House of Commons Public Accounts Committee, supra n. 21, at Q 246.

4.7 percent, from 2003 at least through 2009, might be viewed as an admission that the 6 percent charge was not irrefutably justifiable in this particular case.

But more fundamentally, how is it that a business model has become an intangible asset, and one whose ownership can be both separated from the customer business and situated in a low-tax jurisdiction? The tax policy question is not, what royalties should be charged to third party licensees who take on the risks and benefits of developing local markets, but rather, given that the Starbucks group was responsible for developing the UK market from a standing start in 1998, and that it was Starbucks that took on those risks and benefits, is the resulting income fairly taxed in the United Kingdom? That is, what substance is there to the ownership of the marketing intangibles required to operate the Starbucks business in the United Kingdom neither in the United States nor in the United Kingdom? Starbucks is free to pursue its core business model—pushing out the same "Starbucks Experience" to every high street, mall, and airport in the world—without any commercial exigency requiring it to hold the abstract experience in a low-tax country, whence it is made available to actual customers only through the payment of intragroup royalties that strip income away from the host country where those customers actually sip their lattes.

In an unintended admission against interest, Starbucks submitted a lobbying brief to the US House Ways and Means Committee explains that the brain center of the Starbucks Experience is its Support Center in Seattle; as presented in that letter, foreign operations appear to be reduced to the "localization" of this centrally conceived "experience." Then why does Starbucks UK pay any significant royalties for the rights to the Starbucks Experience playbook to a low-taxed Netherlands affiliates rather than the United States? What is Amsterdam adding for the one-half of UK royalties that stick there? Neither the brains of the operation nor the location-specific tweaks (more umbrella stands?) to reflect British tastes logically should be located there.

Here we see the central role of intangibles—more specifically, the central role of intangible "ownership" divorced from the actual business or customers that the intangibles serve—in stateless income tax planning. (We also see the ease with which multinational firms can turn a simple business model into intangible assets for which royalties must be paid.) This idea—the conceit that a subsidiary can "own" intangibles developed originally by the parent and harness them to commercial use without subjecting the income thereby generated to tax where the business and customers actually are located—is the core reason that base erosion cannot be addressed unless the OECD member states dismantle their traditional institutional acquiescence to such conspicuously non-commercial modes of business organization.[14]

[14] Kleinbard (2011a), supra n. 3: 710.

The other intragroup charge that Reuters identified as eroding Starbucks UK's tax base and that is discussed here is the interest paid by Starbucks UK to the ultimate US parent company (Starbucks Corporation). The loan is a demand loan paying interest at LIBOR plus 400bp.[15] Interest paid on the loan has varied from year to year, both because LIBOR has fluctuated and because (as described below) very substantial amounts of the loan have been capitalized into equity over the years. In fiscal year 2011, intercompany interest payments were around £2 million; in 2010, they were £4.3 million.

Starbucks UK's annual report reveals that the company "is funded by, and meets its day to day working capital requirements through a loan from the ultimate parent company."[16] The company relies on a "commitment of continuing financial support from the ultimate parent company to provide sufficient funding to enable the company to meet its liabilities as they fall due for at least the next 12 months," and it is only the existence of this commitment that enables the firm to prepare its UK financial statements on a going concern basis.[17]

To a US reader, at least, this suggests that Starbucks UK is overleveraged, and indeed it finished its 2011 fiscal year with negative shareholder's equity and a £72 million obligation to Starbucks Corporation. Consistent with this observation, in 2010 Starbucks capitalized £50 million of its intercompany loan into equity.[18] In addition, Starbucks UK has on several occasions sold new equity to its parent companies to fund its annual operating losses (e.g., £4.5 million in 2011, £33 million in 2010, and £14 million in 2009).

All of this suggests that the intercompany demand loan between Starbucks Corporation and Starbucks UK has much of the flavor of a quasi-equity arrangement, at least under US tax norms.[19] And of course the intercompany interest charge (LIBOR + 400) on its face seems quite high.[20] Yet Starbucks UK has relied on this arrangement to strip several million pounds per year from its UK tax base.

When this issue came up before the parliamentary inquiry, Starbucks dismissed the idea that tax avoidance could have played any role in the large intercompany loan: "There is absolutely nothing about the loan that could actually produce tax savings for us, because it is a much higher tax regime in the US than it is in the UK."[21]

This claim was facially plausible, particularly to a UK audience, but is it the entire story? Here again we see the importance of looking at the entirety of the

[15] See e.g. Starbucks UK FY 2011 Annual Report.

[16] Starbucks UK FY 2011 Annual Report: 7.

[17] Starbucks UK FY 2011 Annual Report.

[18] Starbucks UK FY 2010 Annual Report, Financial Statements, note 18.

[19] Cf. *Laidlaw Transportation v. C.I.R.*, 75 T.C.M. (CCH) 2598 (1998).

[20] For this purpose it would be circular to argue that the rate must be so high because the firm is so overleveraged: that would simply rely on one non-arm's-length fact to justify another.

[21] Pollack (2012), quoting testimony of Troy Alstead, chief financial officer of Starbucks.

global picture when considering the claims of any multinational firm. In fact, Starbucks for many years had substantial foreign tax credit carryovers for US tax purposes; the last of those carryovers was absorbed in fiscal year 2012.[22] It is quite likely that the interest income from these intercompany loans could be sheltered from tax by these foreign tax credit carryovers.

The ultimate point is not that this necessarily must be what happened, but rather that the UK parliamentary inquiry did not necessarily have a complete picture, just as source country tax authorities in general also do not have a complete picture of the pressure points that should be of interest to them when trying to piece together why multinational firms organize their internal structures as they do. As the next subsection, Section 5.2.2, elaborates, transnational transparency must be radically rethought, and critically important components of a firm's global stateless income tax planning must be made automatically transparent to each affected jurisdiction. The game of Twenty Tax Questions has grown tiresome. At the same time, the game is fundamentally unfair to source country citizens, who are asked to make up the revenue shortfalls that stateless income planning creates.

5.2.2 Tax Opacity

The Starbucks story—in particular, its UK experience—demonstrates the opacity of international tax planning, in which neither investors in a public firm nor the tax authorities in any particular jurisdiction have a clear picture of what the firm is up to. This murkiness stands in contrast to the frequent calls by multinational firms for tax "transparency" and certainty in their dealings with tax authorities around the world, by which they mean in general that tax rules should be clear in how they apply to a firm's particular situation, authorities as well as taxpayers should follow those rules, and audits should be resolved promptly.[23]

In this case, the exact tax burden imposed on the "Amsterdam structure" is unusually difficult to fathom, for reasons developed at length in the article noted earlier. Why should the presumption be that the basic international tax structure of a multinational firm—particularly one that chooses to divide its integrated business into watertight compartments located in different jurisdictions, with the apparent purpose of minimizing UK tax—should not be transparent to the UK House of Commons or HMRC, or the IRS, or any other tax authority with an interest in the matter? It is not appropriate to expect source country tax authorities to engage in elaborate games of Twenty Tax

[22] Starbucks Corporation 2012 Form 10-K, financial statements n. 13 (p. 83); 2011 Form 10-K, financial statements n. 13: 71.

[23] See, e.g., Bennett (2013).

Questions, in turn requiring detailed knowledge of the tax laws and financial accounting rules of many other jurisdictions, in order simply to evaluate the probative value of a taxpayer's claim that its intragroup dealings necessarily are at arm's length by virtue of alleged symmetries in tax treatment for expense and income across the group's affiliates.

The game is tedious and frustrating, tax authorities have limited time and resources, and the real consequences of these elaborate structures often require analyzing the tax and financial accounting rules of multiple jurisdictions. (The stealth role of the US check-the-box regulations is one obvious example whereby a foreign tax authority might easily be misled as to the tax consequences of intragroup payments.) Yet multinational firms continue to rely on requiring tax authorities to play the game in order to shield their stateless income planning from the harsh glare of direct scrutiny—all the while asking for more tax transparency in how those tax authorities deal with the firms.

The tension is visible in the record of the testimony of Troy Alstead, Chief Financial Officer of Starbucks Corporation, at the inquiry held by the Public Accounts Committee of the UK House of Commons, when he stated "We believe very strongly in transparency—with the Committee, with tax authorities around the world and with consumers—recognising that one of the challenges that we often face is that the global tax structure is very complex. It is very difficult to explain it, and that is without having anything to do with avoidance. It is just a difficult challenge."

The Starbucks UK story demonstrates just how great a challenge it is for taxing authorities to have a transparent view of the consequences of the stateless income planning of multinational firms—or, phrased conversely, what a poor job multinational firms have done in "explaining it." Source country tax authorities in particular have a legitimate interest in a complete and transparent presentation of a multinational firm's *global* tax planning relevant to that firm's source country base erosion strategies. Without such an understanding, a source country's authorities are not able to evaluate, for example, claims made by a multinational firm that there is a natural tax tension between deductions claimed in that jurisdiction (here, the United Kingdom) and income inclusions elsewhere (the United States). That claim cannot be assessed without considering the totality of a multinational group's tax planning surrounding the income side of the equation.

Similarly, without understanding the global tax structure of a firm, it is difficult for source countries to evaluate the economic efficiency consequences of "double dips," or to consider the competitiveness burdens faced by local companies not able to rely on international stateless income tax planning. Source countries typically are in much weaker positions than are tax authorities and policymakers in the parent company's domicile to obtain a clear holistic picture of a firm's global tax planning. And of course when it comes to US multinational firms, source countries are doubly nonplussed by "check-the-box" entities, whose US tax status as disregarded entities stands at complete odds to their apparent status as companies for all other purposes.

It is not appropriate to expect source country tax authorities to engage in elaborate games of Twenty Tax Questions, in turn requiring detailed knowledge of the tax laws and financial accounting rules of many other jurisdictions, in order simply to evaluate the probative value of a taxpayer's claim that its intragroup dealings necessarily are at arm's length by virtue of alleged symmetries in tax treatment for expense and income across the group's affiliates.

The Organization for Economic Co-operation and Development (OECD) has recently focused on this problem in the context of its BEPS project, and it has called for greater transparency in the effective tax rates of multinational enterprises.[24] Similarly, the most recent Annual Report of the UK House of Commons Public Accounts Committee, drawing on the lessons of the Starbucks inquiry, concluded that there was "a complete lack of transparency" concerning the amount of tax paid by multinational firms, and called for the development of best practice standards governing the information that such firms should publicly release about their tax practices.[25]

National governments should respond to these calls by recognizing their common interest and requiring their tax, financial accounting, and securities agencies to promulgate consistent rules providing a uniform worldwide disclosure matrix for actual tax burdens by jurisdiction. A complete and transparent presentation of firms' global tax structures would greatly assist tax authorities everywhere in designing international tax regimes that avoid double taxation while remaining robust to stateless income tax planning.

5.3 RESPONDING TO STATELESS INCOME PLANNING

This chapter has argued to this point that longstanding and fundamental international tax norms, like the separate juridical personality of a wholly owned subsidiary and the tax differences between debt and equity finance, have made stateless income tax planning endemic in the wild. Moreover, multinational firms have a huge informational advantage over source countries, because the latter see only a small sliver of the global functions that in the aggregate comprise the actual economic activity attributable to business earnings in a particular source country.

Until recently, the response of the OECD and many tax authorities has been that transfer pricing practices should be tightened, as if the problem were

[24] OECD (2013a: 6, 47).
[25] House of Commons Committee of Public Accounts (2012: 3–5).

simply one of misestimating the value of arm's-length transactions that happened to be undertaken between affiliates. But this is like the Ptolemaic astronomers revising their theories to explain the precession of Mars in light of data from a new telescope; it should be clear by this point that the problem is not one simply of measurement, but rather of a system whose core premises are inherently noncommercial and noneconomic.

What then should one do? To answer this requires returning to the beginning. The essence of international business income taxation is geographic nexus. Were we able to convince ourselves that a multinational firm's income was demonstrably attributable to Freedonia and Sylvania in specified amounts, we would be done. Imagine that Freedonia has a 30 percent tax rate, and Sylvania a 20 percent tax rate. As applied to a Freedonian firm doing business in Sylvania, Sylvania should tax the income with a Sylvanian nexus, and Freedonia should not. The reason is the implicit tax point already made in Section 5.1. Sylvanian risk-adjusted pretax returns will reflect the lower Sylvanian tax rate, and for Freedonia to tax a Freedonian firm on the 10-percent rate differential on top of the Sylvanian tax would be to overtax the business, partly through explicit taxation and partly through implicit taxation (the lower Sylvanian pretax return in the first place).

Perhaps for this reason (although I suspect more simplistic explanations), the overwhelming global norm is to follow the so-called "territorial" tax model just outlined, under which only source countries tax business profits arising in those source countries. The problem is not with this abstract logic, but rather with our complete inability in practice to determine the genuine geographic nexus of much business income, as the example of the wholly owned subsidiary holding a group's worldwide intangible assets implies. Our existing foundational postulates plainly make things almost impossible here.

There are several possible responses to the overwhelming failure of current tax models to moor a multinational firm's taxable income firmly to where it derives economic income, with the sad consequence that firms today often pay tax on large swaths of their economic income essentially nowhere. Indeed, the entire purpose of the OECD's BEPS Action Plan[26] is to launch a series of coordinated responses—fifteen, to be precise.[27]

Rather than go through the OECD's list, I think it more productive to describe some of the conceptual directions that responses to the stateless income problem could take. In doing so, I write with a particular focus on the United States, where the issue already has been joined, in the context of corporate tax reform.

One response is to develop much more robust rules that specify the geographic nexus of business income more completely in every case, and

[26] Supra note 4.
[27] Many summaries have been published. One recent one is Boidman and Kandev (2013).

that do so by reference to groupwide activities, rather than proceeding on an affiliate by affiliate basis. To succeed in this in practice runs smack into the problem of how to apportion returns to intangibles, which are the drivers of so much value in many new economy multinational firms. The practical answers essentially are all variations on the theme of "formulary apportionment": the idea is that some relevant measurable factors can be specified (and weighted, if desired), and group income apportioned accordingly. These days, the location of the customer (the "sales function") is held in high esteem as a metric, so a formula might simply be, apportion your worldwide profits in proportion to the location of your worldwide sales, and pay tax to the residence country only on profits allocable to the residence country—a "destination based" tax system.[28]

The states of the United States follow formulary apportionment principles to allocate corporate income among themselves; to my knowledge, though, no legal or accounting professional with a conscience who actually works in that field has recommended that it serve as the template for international taxation.[29] The problems are exactly what one might expect. First, not every state uses the same formula. Second, simple-sounding principles (where are your sales?) are not always easy to apply in practice; as a result, some observers have suggested that such formulae are more gameable than might be expected by optimists.[30] Third, by definition the formulae are wrong; they are rough-and-ready approximations of nexus, not fact-specific determinations of nexus, and as applied to different cases those rough-and-ready approximations may be too approximate even for government work.

US multinational firms, the OECD, and most sovereigns all appear to remain skeptical of formulary apportionment solutions. But *faut de mieux*, such solutions may yet have their day, notwithstanding concerns expressed by some that the identical formula must be adopted by many countries if double taxation is to be avoided, and the problem that even if this is accomplished, formulary apportionment at its best produces only rough justice.

A second response to the problem of defining geographic nexus is to limit the availability of the corporate income "territorial" tax model (where the residence country asserts no taxing claim) only to those cases where geographic nexus can be convincingly demonstrated as a factual matter. To my knowledge, there is one real-life example where this has been done, and very successfully to boot, but its complexity serves as a warning to those who

[28] For the case for a destination-based income tax, see Auerbach (2010).
A true destination-based income tax system, as contemplated by Auerbach, would exempt export sales made from the residence country and tax imports, as in the case of a typical value added tax. As such, it creates a taxing nexus over sales into a country that goes far beyond what current tax practice and treaties permit.

[29] The state tax experience is reviewed in Clausing (2014).

[30] Compare Altshuler and Grubert (2010) with Avi-Yonah, Clausing, and Durst (2009).

believe that geographic nexus is a soluble problem, with only the application of a little hard work.

The successful example is section 954(h) of the US tax code, a provision so obscure that even academics who specialize in international taxation are not always familiar with its mechanics. Basically, section 954(h) deals with the taxation of banking-type income earned by a foreign subsidiary of a US parent; if its criteria are satisfied, the foreign banking income is treated as bona fide, and the United States does not assert an immediate taxation claim on the income. A quick look at section 954(h)'s operation demonstrates what is involved in getting serious about defining geographic nexus by relationship to actual activity.

Section 954(h)'s rules are spectacularly complex, and operate like a set of nesting matryoshka dolls. But for this purpose, the core lesson is the requirement that the banking income, in addition to being earned by a licensed bank (or certain other specialized companies), satisfy a "substantial activity" test. Under this test, a foreign subsidiary is required to conduct, *by itself through its own employees*, substantially all of the activities necessary for the generation of income with respect to its business. The point is then hammered home with a laundry list of twelve business functions that must be taken into account in determining whether the foreign subsidiary performed substantially all the business activities by itself, from first flirtation with a customer, through credit analysis and deal negotiations, to collecting the income and holding any collateral.

Then, even if this "super-activity" test (my term, not the statute's) is satisfied, the income gets a free pass only if three more conditions are met: "(1) the income is derived from transactions with customers not located in the United States, (2) substantially all of the activities in connection with such transactions are conducted directly by the [controlled foreign] corporation *in its home country*, and (3) *the income is treated as earned by such corporation . . . in its home country for purposes of such country's tax laws*."[31] An additional set of criteria is imposed on cross-border lending income.

In my experience, section 954(h) actually works to accomplish its intended purpose of specifying how the geographic nexus of one narrow sliver of economic activity is to be determined. But its rules are so complex, and generally are held to be so draconian, that it is doubtful that anyone believes that it can serve as the model for a more general solution to the problem of stateless income.

[31] Staff of the Joint Committee on Taxation (1998: 251) (emphasis supplied). The legislative history is the *only* source for the actual meaning of the statute; a reader of the tax code alone would have no inkling, for example, of the twelve-step elaboration of the meaning of "substantial activity."

The US corporate tax system today is unquestionably broken. The statutory rate is too high relative to world norms, and effective tax rates are much lower (always a sign of a poorly specified tax base). Moreover, the United States is now essentially alone in its insistence on imposing a residual US corporate tax on "repatriated" foreign profits, but that tax can be deferred essentially indefinitely, thereby leading to the worst of all outcomes—a highly distortive tax that collects very little revenue. (It is the design of this repatriation tax that leads US firms to carry $2 trillion or so of low-taxed "permanently reinvested earnings" on their financial accounts.)

Yet at the same time, stateless income strategies are everywhere, and many US firms enjoy single-digit effective tax rates on their international income. US firms remain regarded by the rest of the world as the global leaders in tax avoidance strategies, and no progress will be made in the OECD's BEPS initiative unless the United States demonstrates a commitment to curbing the worst abuses that its own rules have fostered, through exotica like "check-the-box" regulations and the "CFC look-through rules."

US multinational firms originally approached international tax reform with great enthusiasm, because they thought that they would surf the wave of "competitiveness" arguments to a new "territorial" tax system, but they did not seem fully to grasp what a well-ordered territorial tax system would entail. They understood a territorial tax system to be exactly like then-current US law, but without any residual repatriation tax—that is, a system that, through all of its exotica, actively aided and abetted stateless income generation.

The result would have been catastrophic, not just in economic efficiency terms or with respect to the depredations of foreign treasuries, but to US corporate tax collections as well. The stateless income generation machines would have been sent to work overtime, and meanwhile US operations would be leveraged up, in an irresistible arbitrage operation, in which worldwide expenses would offset US tax bills, while foreign low-taxed "tax rents" would cascade in.

These hopes have been dampened somewhat by subsequent developments, both within the OECD and in terms of internal US politics. The OECD continues to push forward aggressively on its BEPS project, with the largest clusters of "deliverables" due in September of 2014 and 2015.[32] US negotiators have found themselves caught between a rock and a hard place, in that US firms now complain that foreign jurisdictions are using the cover of BEPS and the notoriety of those firms' stateless income planning to make novel and far-reaching demands for tax revenues, while at the same time it is difficult not to acknowledge that US firms have been world leaders in tax

[32] The history and status of the BEPS initiative through early 2014 is summarized in Brauner (2014).

avoidance technologies.[33] The BEPS project might yet founder or be substantially diluted to accommodate US ambivalence, but one possible outcome as of mid 2014 would seem to be a relatively strong set of recommendations, premised on the arm's-length principle and the false foundation of the separateness of corporate subsidiaries, which the United States in turn might be slower than other nations to adopt into its internal law.

Within the United States, the quest for a simple "repatriation holiday" along the lines of the temporary provision adopted in 2004 (section 965 of the Internal Revenue Code) appears to have foundered (rightly) on the tax revenues that would be hemorrhaged over the succeeding ten-year budget window, estimated by the nonpartisan staff of the Joint Committee on Taxation to amount to about $96 billion in lower tax collections.[34] At the same time, a wave of completed and proposed "inversion transactions" (in which a US firm merges with a smaller firm in a more congenial taxing jurisdiction, with the foreign minnow becoming the nominal parent company of the US whale) is seen as exposing the US corporate tax base to a substantial risk of being vitiated over time, as well as giving participating US firms a new avenue for extracting their offshore cash without current US tax liability. (Very simply, following such a combination, an offshore tax haven subsidiary holding the former US group's excess cash can lend the cash to the new non-US parent company, whence it can be used to repay the acquisition debt incurred in the inversion transaction itself, or for any other purpose.)

As of mid 2014 Congressional reaction to inversion transactions and to BEPS-type concerns largely has been to invoke such developments as evidence of the urgent need to proceed with comprehensive corporate tax reform, although some legislators have proposed legislation that would impose temporary higher bars to inversion transactions, so as to staunch the revenue bleeding long enough to preserve a revenue base to reform. Although not obvious to outsiders, a great deal of work has been done in the recent past on the contours of such reform, and there is a bipartisan interest in finding a way to enact corporate (or business more generally) tax reform. That reform would have as its centerpiece a much lower headline US corporate tax rate (in the range of 25 to 28 percent) and the curtailing of many domestic business subsidies delivered as tax expenditures.

In this connection, the specific international tax reform proposals floated by Dave Camp in 2011 and Max Baucus in 2013 have not ripened into law, but they nonetheless deserve close scrutiny, because they reflect countless hours of staff deliberation, as well as input from Members. Any legislation in this area is likely to draw on one or both of these models.

[33] Stewart (2014). [34] Rubin (2014).

In October 2011 Chairman Dave Camp of the House Ways and Means Committee circulated a discussion draft for international tax reform. While embracing a territorial tax system in general, the draft coupled that with new anti-abuse rules designed to curb at least some stateless income planning. The Ways and Means Committee approach, then, was to take the first steps down the path of what I have termed "territoriality with teeth"—that is, to acknowledge that, since geographic nexus can never be specified with sufficient precision in practice (*pace* section 954(h))—although we certainly can do better—territorial tax systems must be coupled with anti-abuse rules that set outer limits on acceptable stateless income planning.

In 2013 Chairman Max Baucus of the Senate Finance Committee released his own discussion draft. This again followed the "territoriality with teeth" model, except that the teeth had by now become larger, sharper, and better specified. The direction that seems most likely to prevail at the time of this writing is for the United States to couple its transition to a territorial tax model with (i) improved definitions of what constitutes "active" business income of the sort eligible for the territorial model, and (ii) one of a variety of minimum tax ideas that have been floated, under which active income of a foreign subsidiary of a US firm that nonetheless is very low taxed would be subject to an immediate US soak-up tax, to bring the total tax bill up to the amount of the minimum tax rate. Income that was not "active" income would be taxed immediately in the United States at the US rate.

For example, the Baucus proposal would determine what constitutes active business income as under current law, but would reverse the notorious "check the box" and "CFC look-through rules," prevent arbitrage of global expenses against US income, and treat all income derived from dealings with US persons as ineligible for the territorial regime. Under one minimum tax proposal, the resulting active income nonetheless would be subject to a US minimum tax if necessary to bring the total tax rate, determined on an item-by-item basis, up to 80 percent of the US rate. The other proposal, which I believe to be simpler and more robust to gaming, is presented as an alternative formulation of a minimum tax, but I see it as a form of worldwide tax consolidation, under which US multinational firms would pay current tax on their worldwide profits, subject to a special deduction of 40 percent of certain foreign business income (thereby bringing the effective rate on such foreign income down to 60 percent of the US rate). The catch would be that income eligible for the special deduction would be defined more restrictively than under current law's definitions of active foreign business income through a sort of "super-activity" principle, but not quite so narrowly as section 954(h) of the tax code.

The irony here is that these territorial tax proposals in fact are uneasy combinations of territorial and worldwide residence systems, with the minimum tax operating as a worldwide floor tax rate. Of course, unless the BEPS initiative is extraordinarily successful, the floor will also become a ceiling, with US firms managing their foreign tax rates down just to the level where the minimum tax would bite. But if that is so (and I believe it to be a highly likely outcome of such a system), why not just call it what it is, which is a split rate worldwide system? And then in turn, why exactly would the United States find it desirable to countenance lower taxes on the foreign activities of domestic firms than on domestic activities of domestic or foreign firms? The "competitiveness" argument falls away once the US rate is comparable to that imposed by foreign countries on their domestic firms, and the BEPS project hopefully will quench the majority of stateless income planning employed by multinational firms of whatever nominal residence.

Nonetheless, the ideas embodied in the Camp and Baucus drafts would be far more constructive and conducive to good economic order than is current US law, or, ironically, what Starbucks and others of its point of view had in mind when they first lobbied to put international corporate tax reform front and center in the tax legislative calendar. It is early in the process, but here might be a rare instance where the Pandora's box, once opened, releases tax angels rather than demons into our midst.

REFERENCES

Altshuler, Rosanne and Harry Grubert, 2010. "Formula Apportionment: Is it Better than the Current System and Are There Better Alternatives?" *National Tax Journal* 63: 1145.

Auerbach, Alan J., 2010. "A Modern Corporate Tax," *The Hamilton Project*. December. http://www.hamiltonproject.org/files/downloads_and_links/FINAL_AuerbachPaper.pdf, accessed 4 September 2015.

Avi-Yonah, Reuven S., Kimberly A. Clausing, and Michael C. Durst, 2009. "Allocating Business Profits for Tax Purposes: A Proposal to Adopt a Formulary Profit Split," *Florida Tax Review* 9: 497.

Bennett, Allison, 2013. "Multinational Firms Seeking Transparency, Certainty as Audits Increase, Panelists Say," 85 *BNA Daily Tax Report* G-6. 2 May.

Bergin, Tom, 2012. "How Starbucks Avoids UK Taxes," *Reuters*. 15 October. http://www.reuters.com/article/2012/10/15/us-britain-starbucks-tax-idUSBRE89E0EX20121015, accessed 4 September 2015.

Boidman, Nathan and Michael N. Kandev, 2013. "BEPS: The OECD Discovers America?" *Tax Notes International* 72 (16 December): 1017.

Bradbury, David, 2013. "Stateless Income: A Threat to National Sovereignty," Address to the Tax Institute of Australia. 15 March. http://ministers.treasury.gov.au/DisplayDocs.aspx?doc=speeches/2013/003.htm&pageID=005&min=djba&Year=&DocType=, accessed 5 September 2015.

Brauner, Yariv, 2014. "What the BEPS?" *Florida Tax Review* 16: 55.

Charlton, Angela, 2013. "G-20 to Multinationals: Pay more Taxes," *Bloomberg Business Week*. 19 July.

Clausing, Kimberly A., 2014. "Lessons for International Tax Reform from the U.S. State Experience under Formulary Apportionment," http://ssrn.com/abstract=2359724, accessed 5 September 2015.

Houlder, Vanessa, 2013. "'Dutch Sandwich' Grows as Google Shifts €8.8bn to Bermuda," *Financial Times*. 10 October.

House of Commons, Public Accounts Committee, 2012. "Nineteenth Report." 28 November. http://www.publications.parliament.uk/pa/cm201213/cmselect/cmpubacc/716/71602.htm, accessed 5 September 2015.

Kleinbard, Edward, 2011a. "Stateless Income," *Florida Tax Review* 11: 699.

Kleinbard, Edward, 2011b. "The Lessons of Stateless Income," 65 *Tax Law Review* 65: 99.

Kleinbard, Edward, 2011c. "Stateless Income's Challenge to Tax Policy," *Tax Notes* 132 (5 September): 1021.

Kleinbard, Edward, 2012. "Stateless Income's Challenge to Tax Policy, Part 2," *Tax Notes* 136 (17 September): 1431.

Kleinbard, Edward, 2013. "Through a Latte Darkly: Starbucks's Stateless Income Tax Planning," *Tax Notes* 139: 1515.

Laidlaw Transportation v. C.I.R., 75 T.C.M. (CCH) 2598 (1998).

OECD, 2013a. *Addressing Base Erosion and Profit Shifting*. http://www.oecd.org/tax/beps.htm, accessed 5 September 2015.

OECD, 2013b. *Action Plan on Base Erosion and Profit Shifting*. http://www.oecd-ilibrary.org/taxation/action-plan-on-base-erosion-and-profit-shifting_9789264202719-en, accessed 5 September 2015.

Pollack, Lisa, 2012. "Losing for Tax Purposes: A Diagram," *Financial Times Alphaville blog*. 11 December. http://ftalphaville.ft.com/2012/12/11/1304382/losing-for-tax-purposes-a-diagram/, accessed 5 September 2015.

Rubin, Richard, 2014. "Repatriation Tax Break Costs $96 Billion, Official Estimate Says," *Bloomberg News*. 9 June.

Sheppard, L. A., 2013. *World Investment Report: Global Value Chains: Investment and Trade for Development*. United Nations, Geneva.

Starbucks, 2010. Starbucks UK FY 2010 Annual Report.

Starbucks, 2011. Starbucks UK FY 2011 Annual Report.

Staff of the Joint Committee on Taxation, 1998. *General Explanation of Tax Legislation Enacted in 1998*, JCS-6-98. 24 November. Washington, DC.

Stewart, David D. 2014. "BEPS Failure Is an Option, Says Treasury Official," *Tax Notes Today*, 18 June.

6

The Arm's Length Standard

Making It Work in a 21st-Century World of Multinationals and Nation States

Lorraine Eden

6.1 INTRODUCTION

The twenty-first-century world is dominated by multinational enterprises (MNEs) and nation states, and the role of MNEs in this world is growing ever more important. According to UNCTAD (2011), there are now more than 100,000 multinational enterprises (MNEs) and about 900,000 foreign affiliates, that is, an average of nine foreign affiliates per MNE. Of the world's 100 largest economies, forty-two are MNEs not nation states, if one compares the dollar values of MNE revenues with the gross domestic products of nation states (Eden, 2012). Moreover, UNCTAD (2010) estimates that cross-border transactions that take place within MNEs are now one-third of world exports. Given the dominance of MNEs—and of trade within MNEs—in the twenty-first century's global economy, I see the workability of the arm's length standard as a critically important issue for global tax justice.[1]

The arm's length standard (ALS) is the core norm that underlies the pricing of transactions within multinational enterprises (MNEs) for purposes of determining corporate income tax payments in the home and host countries where the MNE operates.[2] The ALS requires that transfer pricing be based on

[1] An earlier version of this paper was presented at the Global Tax Justice Authors' Workshop, Kings College London, UK, 23–24 November, 2013. I would like to thank Thomas Pogge for inviting me to participate in this project. I also gratefully acknowledge the helpful comments of and discussions with Nathan Boidman, Michael Durst, Krishen Mehta, Thomas Pogge, Lee Sheppard, and two anonymous reviewers. The responsibility for all views and any errors is my own.

[2] The ALS also applies to other government regulations such as customs duties and rules of origin. See, for example, Eden and Rodriguez (2004) and Eden (2012).

the prices that unrelated parties would negotiate if they were engaged in the same or similar transactions under the same or similar circumstances as the related party transactions (Eden, 1998, 2009; OECD, 2010). The pricing of intra-firm transactions is called *transfer pricing* and the price of an intra-firm transaction is called a *transfer price.*

The arm's length standard is almost eighty years old. It dates back to 1935 when Section 45-1(b) of the US Treasury Corporate Income Tax Regulations was published, defining the standard to be used by the IRS Commissioner in allocating corporate income tax among related parties as:

> The purpose of section 45 is to place a controlled taxpayer on a tax parity with an uncontrolled taxpayer, by determining, according to the standard of an uncontrolled taxpayer, the true net income from the property and business of a controlled taxpayer.

The ALS spread rapidly and now more than seventy countries have some form of transfer pricing rules (Ernst & Young, 2013).

However, the criticisms against the arm's length standard have been mounting (see for example, Avi-Yonah, Clausing, and Durst, 2008; Picciotto, 2012, 2015; Sheppard, 2012, 2015). In reading through the enormous literature on the arm's length standard (ALS), the criticisms of the system as an approach to taxing MNEs, appear to fall into two categories: abusive transfer pricing and the lack of comparables.

The first set of criticisms revolves around what I call *abusive transfer pricing.* MNEs use transfer pricing as a method for avoiding paying corporate income taxes (CITs) and mispricing international trade flows. As a result, much of MNE profits escape paying any taxation, lowering the overall CIT rate on MNE profits, especially on large MNEs with sophisticated tax consultants, to close to zero. These activities can drain income out of developing countries and slow their economic development (Reuter, 2012; Christian Aid, 2009; Sheppard, 2012, 2015). Since developing countries now represent more than 50 percent of global inward foreign direct investment (FDI) flows and almost one-third of global outward FDI flows, the impacts of abusive transfer pricing can be of great consequence for developing countries (UNCTAD, 2013: ix). Moreover, certain types of intra-firm transactions, such as business services and intangibles, are critically important for economic development in the twenty-first century, and are especially difficult to price according to the arm's length standard in developing countries (Eden, 2005, 2012).

The economics literature on the problem of *abusive transfer pricing* or *transfer pricing manipulation* (TPM) has been studied by multiple scholars, as far back as Horst (1971) and Rugman and Eden (1985), as a response to differentials in government policies, especially corporate income tax (CIT) policies, across countries. I argue the incentives for TPM have grown much stronger as traditional home country governments over the past ten years have moved from worldwide to territorial CIT systems, encouraging MNEs to use TPM to shift their profits into tax havens. Abusive transfer pricing is one of the key foci of the OECD's current recent BEPS (base erosion and profit shifting) initiative (OECD, 2013a, 2013b; Picciotto, 2013).

The second set of criticisms of the arm's length standard revolves around the *lack of comparables*. The ALS is based on a hypothetical goal—determining the price that would have been set between two unrelated parties engaged in the same or similar transaction under the same or similar facts and circumstances. I refer to the search for comparables as the "What would independent enterprises do (WWIED)?" question. The WWIED question is problematic from both theoretical and practical perspectives. From a theoretical perspective, the ALS compares transactions between related parties to those between unrelated parties. Many authors have argued this comparison makes no sense in theory given the integrated nature of the MNE because the comparison ignores the raison d'être for the MNE: the synergy benefits created by internalizing transactions (Picciotto, 2012, this volume; McIntyre, 2012; Langbein, 1991).

The WWIED question is also problematic in terms of putting the ALS into practice. The question requires that MNEs and governments search for evidence of the same or similar transactions conducted by unrelated firms under the same or similar facts and circumstances as the related party transaction. These can be either *external comparables* (open market transactions between unrelated firms) or, more likely in practice, *internal comparables* (MNE purchases from or sales to an unrelated party that are similar to the related party transaction). The transfer pricing rules require that MNEs prepare extensive contemporaneous documentation of their search for comparable transactions and provide arguments as to why one transfer pricing method should be used in preference to another method. As a result, MNEs have turned to searching databases such as Compustat, Orbis, and ktMINE to find comparable transactions. Finding comparables is difficult, even with these databases, and especially so for transactions involving high-value intangibles (which are not normally traded between unrelated parties) and developing countries (where markets are thinner and there typically are no databases). The search for "WWIED?" has therefore been criticized by many writers as expensive and ultimately impossible (see, for example, Avi-Yonah, 1995; Avi-Yonah, Clausing, and Durst, 2008).[3]

I assume that the ALS will be the predominant method used by national governments for taxing the profits of MNEs for at least the foreseeable future.

[3] Elsewhere, I have referred to this search for comparables, especially for high-value non-routine intangibles, as an example of the 1876 Lewis Carroll poem, "Hunting the Snark (An Agony in 8 Fits)" come to life.

I therefore focus my recommendations for change in terms of possible improvements to the existing system rather than for moving to a formula apportionment (FA) system.

6.2 REFORM PROPOSAL

6.2.1 The International Tax Regime

I have argued elsewhere (Eden, 1998, ch. 2) that MNE–state relations in the tax area are inherently conflictual simply because MNEs are integrated businesses; that is, they are groups of firms under common control that share common goals and resources.

For income tax purposes, MNEs almost always set up their foreign affiliates as legally independent subsidiaries. Profits earned within a host country by a foreign subsidiary are taxable by the host government under the so-called "source and water's edge" rules. Because both home and host country governments claim the right to tax MNE profits, there can be double taxation or under taxation of MNE profits. Transfer pricing comes into play because the pricing of cross-border transactions within the MNE group of affiliated companies affects where the group's profits are allocated for income tax purposes and therefore which government has the right to tax that income.

Because their transactions, income, and assets span many countries, the cross-border activities of MNEs bring them under the jurisdiction of multiple tax authorities. The integrated nature of MNEs makes it difficult for nation states to regulate MNEs at the national level. Vernon (1985: 256), almost thirty years ago, recognized that taxation was one of the few areas where nation states have moved to solve these inter-jurisdictional conflicts through "a rather extraordinary web of bilateral agreements."

Building on international relations theory, I argued that this "extraordinary web" of tax agreements had become strong enough by the 1990s to be characterized as an *international tax regime* with two purposes: to reduce both double taxation and under taxation of MNEs caused by overlapping tax jurisdictions. The regime's norms determine which country has the right to tax (the source and/or the residence country), what the tax base should be (corporate profits, sales), and what should be done about double taxation when both residence and source countries share the right to tax. The regime's rules are the detailed application of these norms or standards in terms of corporate income tax rates, withholding taxes, deferral, exemption, foreign tax credit rules, and so on.

6.2.2 Reducing the Incentives for Abusive Transfer Pricing

I believe that the current criticisms in the public press about transfer pricing are misplaced—an example of "shooting the messenger" instead of focusing on the underlying problem. The problem of abusive transfer pricing is caused by perverse incentives—set in place by national tax authorities—that encourage MNEs to manipulate transfer prices to take advantage of differences in tax rates across jurisdictions. This is not a transfer pricing problem but an international tax regime "design" problem, that is best handled by fixing the source and residence rules in the international tax regime. If governments, NGOs, and the general public do not like the way that multinational firms are allocating their taxable income among countries and the amounts of tax (or lack of tax) they are paying, the problem should be laid at the feet of governments, not the MNEs. A simpler international tax regime—one based on residence taxation of worldwide income as earned with foreign tax credits for source-based taxation—or a regime with stronger anti-abuse (e.g., CFC) rules would eliminate most of the incentives for abusive behavior that riddle the current system. The prescription should be: *Physician heal thyself!*

While there will always be firms that will push the envelope in terms of tax aggressiveness—moving across the "bright line" from tax avoidance into tax abuse and possibly tax evasion—the majority of MNEs pay their taxes and follow the rules laid down for them by national governments. However, the international tax system has gaping holes that provide many legal opportunities for MNEs to engage in regulatory arbitrage. Moreover, the rules are becoming ever more complicated, both in terms of the length and variety of regulations, making it ever more difficult for MNEs to keep up with national regulations.

To end abusive transfer pricing, the first step must be to reduce the incentives for MNEs to engage in these income-shifting activities. Home country governments should tax foreign source income on a worldwide basis as earned, with no deferral provided for income kept offshore. Common residency definitions should be adopted so that MNEs cannot exploit differences in definition (e.g., Ireland versus the United States) so as to become stateless and tax free. MNEs must provide much better information about their activities, both by country and by line of business, in their public reports. Stronger anti-avoidance rules for activities with no business purpose would also provide a backstop against the most egregious activities. Greater transparency in MNE operations on a worldwide basis would also go a long way to reducing opportunities for income shifting. In sum, the first problem associated with transfer pricing—income shifting through abusive transfer pricing—I see as an "income tax design" problem, not a transfer pricing problem. The solution is to re-establish the international tax regime (Eden, 1998, 2009).

The OECD's base erosion and profit-shifting (BEPS) initiative (OECD, 2013a, 2013b) has curtailing abusive transfer pricing as one of its key goals. The OECD's proposals do not change the fundamental division of taxing rights between home and host countries (the separate entity and water's edge principles remain intact); rather, gaps or holes in the tax system that provide opportunities for under taxation of MNE worldwide profits are to be curtailed or eliminated (OECD, 2013a). OECD (2013b: 47–8) identifies several gaps or "pressure areas" that must be addressed (hybrid mismatch arrangements, the digital economy, intragroup financial transactions, transfer pricing, anti-avoidance measures, and harmful tax practices); OECD (2013a) proposes fifteen action items to address these pressure areas. The thrust of the BEPS initiative is towards strengthening the anti-abuse aspects of the international tax regime, rather than engaging in a fundamental overhaul. The success or failure of this enterprise remains to be seen.[4]

6.2.3 Transfer Pricing Regulation: A Regime within a Regime

Within the international tax regime is a sub-regime, which I have called the tax transfer pricing regime (Eden, 1998, 2009); its core norm is the arm's length standard (ALS). The history of the arm's length standard has been well surveyed already (see Eden, 1998; Picciotto, 1992) so I will only briefly highlight the dates here.

At the international level, the draft model tax treaty published by the League of Nations in 1933 was based on the "independent persons" test in IRC Section 45. The arm's length standard was included in article 9 of the draft model tax convention in 1963 and formally adopted in 1977, as follows:

> Where conditions are made or imposed between the two enterprises in their commercial or financial relations which differ from those that would be made between independent enterprises, then any profits which would, but for these conditions, have accrued to one of the enterprises but, by reason of these conditions, have not so accrued, may be included in the profits of that enterprise, and taxed accordingly.

The first set of *Transfer Pricing Guidelines for Multinational Enterprises and Tax Administrations* were issued by the OECD in 1979, building closely on the

[4] Useful commentaries, with different perspectives, on BEPS can be found in Boidman and Kandev (2013) and Picciotto (2013). Boidman and Kandev (2013: 1032) argue that none of the BEPS issues is new or novel, and that "any concerted fundamental changes to international tax law" are "unlikely." Picciotto (2013), on the other hand, sees BEPS as representing a fundamental shift in the OECD's focus, from preventing double taxation to preventing double non-taxation of MNE profits. Picciotto does not expect radical changes either, however, because of political obstacles and flaws inherent in the "separate entity–water's edge" approach to taxing MNE profits.

IRS Regulations. Major updates were published in 1995 and again in 2010 (see OECD, 2010). The OECD is now almost continuously engaged in rewriting and updating the guidelines (see, for example, OECD 2013c).

In US tax law, the ALS dates back almost 100 years. In 1917, the IRS Commissioner in Internal Revenue Code (IRC) Section 41 was authorized to allocate income and deductions among affiliated corporations. The Revenue Act of 1928 in IRC Section 45 added two rationales for reallocating income: the IRS Commissioner was authorized to allocate income and deductions among related corporations so as to prevent tax avoidance and determine the true taxable liability of the related parties. In 1935, the arm's length standard was introduced: the true net income of related parties should be determined so as to place them in tax parity with unrelated parties.

Section 45, renamed in 1954 as Section 482, remained largely unchanged until the US Congress added a one-line sentence in 1986 requiring that the income from a transfer or license of an intangible be "commensurate with the income" (CWI) attributable to the intangible. This change was added to ensure that intangible assets (e.g., patents) transferred by US MNEs to their offshore affiliates received, in return, royalty payments that reflected the income earned offshore by their affiliates.

While the statute has seen little change over the years, the IRS Regulations, on the other hand, have gone through multiple iterations, each edition much larger than the previous one; with the two major versions finalized in 1968 and 1994. The 1968 regulations recommended three methods for determining an arm's length price; the first method, the comparable uncontrolled price (CUP) method, was preferred because it determined the price of the related party transaction based on comparable arm's length transactions. Where there were no external market prices available, the regulations recommended valuing the functions of the simpler of the two related parties: either the distributor/buyer (the resale price method) or the manufacturer/seller (the cost plus method).

In response to addition of the CWI sentence to IRC section 482, new Treasury Regulations were finalized in 1994 that expanded the recommended list of methods to include the Comparable Profit Method (CPM) and (as a last resort) the Profit Split method (PS). The Regulations have continued to grow as IRS has wrestled with applying the CWI standard to intangibles (both transferred and co-developed) and intragroup services. The Regulations now apply the arm's length standard to goods (tangibles), services, intangibles (both transfers and development of intangibles), loans, and other forms of intra-firm transactions.

6.2.4 Current Transfer Pricing Rules

Current transfer pricing regulations and the OECD Transfer Pricing Guidelines require MNEs and tax authorities select the "best method" for pricing intra-firm transactions. The best method is the one that generates the *most reliable measure of an arm's length result.* The basic starting point for determining the best method is a functional analysis of the MNE and the affiliates involved in the related party transactions of interest. Before one can identify comparable transactions involving unrelated parties, it is necessary to construct profiles of the related parties in terms of their functions, businesses, and transactions, and to understand the value chain of the MNE and the industry (so it is clear where the firm sits within the industry). A functional analysis in effect provides a "road map" of the multinational enterprise—its structure, strategies, activities, assets, and flows.

After a functional analysis has been performed, the next step is the identification and analysis of comparables. Comparability takes into account five factors: characteristics of the property or services; contractual terms; functions, assets, and risks performed by the parties; economic conditions of the market; and any special circumstances such as business strategies (e.g., market penetration). Any transactions between the MNE and unrelated parties that are the same or similar to the related party transactions are highlighted as possible internal comparables. To search for external comparables, it is typical to search computerized databases of firms (e.g., Compustat, Amadeus, ktMINE) and/or commodity exchanges (e.g., the London Metal Exchange) to determine whether there are comparable open-market transactions between unrelated parties. Detailed analysis of the comparables is performed, both for the transaction and the firms involved; where there are differences adjustments are made to improve their reliability.

The OECD Transfer Pricing Guidelines and national tax regulations identify a number of methodological approaches for determining arm's length transfer prices. In order to select the "best method," one must consider the economic justification that underlies each method, the conditions where each method applies, and what types of comparability are most important for each method. The three key factors in selecting the best method are (1) comparability, (2) data quality, and (3) reliability of assumptions used in each method; that is, the goal is the most reliable measure of an arm's length result.

The most basic and best known of the transfer pricing methods is the comparable uncontrolled price (CUP), which is directly derived from the definition of the arm's length standard. CUP determines the transfer price by finding an open market price for the same or similar product transacted between unrelated parties under the same or similar facts and circumstances as the related parties. The comparable transaction could be between two unrelated firms (an external comparable) or between one of the two related parties transacting with a third, unrelated party (e.g., affiliate A sells product X to affiliate B and also to unrelated party C, or affiliate B buys X from unrelated party D). In practice, CUP can be very difficult to implement because similar transactions involving similar products trading between unrelated parties can be difficult to identify, especially for new products or intangible assets.

There are two function-based transfer pricing methods, resale price and cost plus, which can be in cases where there are no good CUPs or where a function-based method provides the most reliable measure of an arm's length result. These methods are also referred to as gross margin methods because they compare the gross margin or markup of a related party with those of comparable firms. The tax regulations recommend focusing on the simpler of the two parties, in particular, the party with little or no intangible assets, as the "tested party." The functions, assets, and risks of the tested party are then identified and measured. Through a search for comparables, the gross margins or markups earned by a carefully selected group of firms that are seen as performing comparable functions to the tested party are identified and serve as the basis for determining the gross margin/markup of the tested party. The transfer price can then be determined that is then assigned to the intra-firm transaction.

There are also two profit-based methods. The most commonly used method is the comparable profits method (CPM), which was introduced into the US transfer pricing regulations in 1994. (The OECD Guidelines have a slightly different variant called the transaction net margin method.) CPM is calculated in a manner similar to that for the gross margin methods, but bases its comparison on operating profit margins/markups (after operating costs) rather than gross margins/markups (before operating costs). The key is to compare the operating profits earned by the tested party to "normal" returns earned by comparable firms for comparable activities in the same industry.

The less well known of the two profit-based methods is the profit split method. There are two forms of profit splits; one involving total profits, the other residual profits after returns for routine functions, assets, and risks have been paid to each party. In the residual profit split method (RPSM), the first step is that each party is allocated sufficient profit to provide it with a basic (or routine) return appropriate to the functions it performs and risks it assumes. Normally, the basic return would be determined by the market returns received by similar transactions by independent enterprises under the same facts and circumstances as the related parties. Any remaining profit is considered to be the value associated with intangible assets. In the second step, this residual profit (or loss) is allocated among the parties using an allocation key; the US transfer pricing regulations recommend an allocation key based on relative contributions to intangible property.

In addition to specific guidelines on transfer pricing methods, an important procedural innovation added in the early 1990s has been the advance pricing agreement (APA) as a risk-mitigation strategy for MNEs. An MNE can request an APA with tax authorities and work collaboratively to develop a transfer pricing policy that is mutually agreeable. APAs will cover certain transactions over a specified number of years, including both prior and future years. The APA program "is designed to resolve actual or potential transfer pricing disputes in a principled, cooperative manner, as an alternative to the traditional adversarial process. While the APA process goes on behind closed doors, some governments do release annual statistics on their APA program. The APMA Office within the US Treasury, for example, reports annually to Congress with a summary of the APAs concluded, renewed, or revoked during the previous year, with a summary of the transaction types and methods used.[5] In addition, APAs can be negotiated bilaterally between the two governments and the MNE, although the process typically takes a year longer to negotiate.

6.2.5 The Lack of Comparables

The ALS requires that transfer prices be set based on the prices that independent parties negotiate for the same or similar product under the same or similar facts and circumstances as the related parties. The criterion is: *What would independent enterprises do (WWIED?)*

6.2.5.1 The Lack of Comparables in Theory

A core problem, highlighted by almost all transfer pricing professionals is that MNEs and independent entities are very different organizational forms. It is commonplace now to say that the MNE is an integrated enterprise where "the whole is greater than the sum of the parts." Critics of the arm's length standard regularly point to the integration economies and greater efficiencies of the MNE compared to unrelated parties as the primary reason why the arm's length standard cannot work.

Being a multinational enterprise offers a variety of advantages compared to a domestic firm. These benefits derive partly from *internalization* (Buckley and Casson, 1976), that is, the substitution of intra-firm or related party transactions (the internal market or hierarchy) for arm's length transactions (the external market). The reason why internalization creates benefits that are unavailable (or less available) to open market transactions is that the goals of the trading partners change; this change not only makes a big difference in firm behaviors, but also has different legal implications for MNEs and domestic firms. The goals of parties to an intra-firm transaction are cooperative—their purpose is to maximize joint MNE profit—whereas the goals of arm's length parties when they trade are conflictual—their purpose is to maximize

5 <http://www.irs.gov/pub/irs-drop/a-13-17.pdf> accessed 15 July 2015.

individual profits. In effect, MNE subunits collude rather than compete in the market. Internalization creates opportunities for collusion among MNE subunits, allowing them to take advantage of differences between countries in ways that unrelated parties cannot. Moreover, when unrelated firms collude, they can face legal challenges as cartels, anti-competitive behavior, and/or price fixing since competition laws in most countries outlaw collusive behavior between unrelated firms. Internalization therefore provides both economic and legal opportunities for value creation through intra-firm transactions that are not available in arm's length transactions.

Internalization benefits can be broken down into two broad categories: those that arise from natural market imperfections and those from structural market imperfections (Rugman and Eden, 1985). In terms of natural market imperfections, perhaps the best known are transaction costs in the form of market-making costs, both *ex ante* costs (search, negotiation, monitoring) and *ex post* costs (dispute settlement) due to joint control, better information sharing and higher levels of trust. MNEs also reap greater efficiencies in terms of smoother and easier coordination of flows along the value chain; for example, MNEs can transfer tacit resources such as non-codifiable knowledge more effectively between related parties than between arm's length firms; internalization therefore facilitates cross-border transfer of intangible assets.[6] MNEs also reap economies of scale at the firm level (centralization of functions that offer firm-wide economies of scale through pooling (e.g. accounting, marketing, finance, foreign exchange)), economies of scope where inputs produced for one activity (including R&D) can be used in more than one line of business, and economies of learning (diffusion of best practices throughout the organization, demonstration effects).

MNEs can also reap internalization benefits that arise from *structural market imperfections*; chief among these are the gains that come from cross-border arbitrage. MNEs can arbitrage their activities, taking advantage of differences in factor prices and endowments across countries, putting stages of the production chain such as processing, assembly, and sales where they offer the greatest net value added for the MNE. MNEs can take advantage of differences in product prices by engaging in price discrimination across markets. MNEs also have opportunities for regulatory arbitrage, that is, taking advantage of differences in government policies across countries by, for

[6] These gains are particularly noticeable when one compares an international R&D alliance consisting of arm's-length firms compared with an MNE that has multiple R&D centers. The aim of both organizational forms is knowledge sharing and knowledge creation. However, each international alliance partners must worry about knowledge leakage and appropriation by the other partners, which generates tension between knowledge sharing and fears of knowledge appropriation. As a result, either the amount of knowledge generation will be lower and/or the costs of managing the alliance higher than for related parties within an MNE. Perhaps it is not surprising that knowledge generation is seen as the competitive advantage of MNEs.

example, shifting activities and profits to less taxed or regulated locations (Rugman and Eden, 1985; Eden, 1998). The opportunity to raise global after-tax profits by using transfer pricing to engage in regulatory arbitrage between countries has been a major concern of national tax and other regulatory authorities for many decades, one that prompted the development of the arm's length standard (Picciotto, 1992; Eden, 1998). MNEs can also create structural market imperfections by exercising monopoly/monopsony power in product and factor markets (larger size implies more bargaining power); thus generating higher revenues and/or lower costs compared to arm's length parties.

Thus, integration economies come from several directions, and there have been only limited attempts by policymakers and scholars to try to unbundle these synergies. Perhaps the first approach to understanding these synergies was the identification of the *continuum price problem*, which recognized that the cost plus and resale price methods, the first based on pricing functions, assets and risks of the manufacturer/seller and the second on pricing functions provided by the distributor/buyer, left a pool of residual profits (Eden, 1998). Having given returns to the routine functions, assets, and risks of the two related parties, profits remained to be distributed. These profits were assumed to arise from intangible assets held by one or both parties, but could also be caused by synergies between them.

6.2.5.2 The Lack of Comparables in Practice

I have argued that the real problem with the arm's length standard is the lack of comparables. The ALS suffers both from a theoretical perspective (there cannot be true arm's length comparables because MNEs are integrated businesses) and a practical perspective (finding comparables is time consuming, expensive, and for many types of intra-firm transactions and locations simply impossible).

Particularly difficult are situations where both related parties to the transaction have valuable intangible assets that are not traded on the open market so the CUT (comparable uncontrolled transaction) method using a royalty-rate database such as ktMINE cannot be used. How can one price intellectual property not traded on the open market? What does one do when markets are missing or imperfect? A more complex problem occurs when an MNE has several R&D centers scattered around the world where the R&D centers co-develop technologies that are shared by the group. How should the downstream profits from exploiting these technologies be divided among the MNE group?

From a practical perspective, the comparability problems arising from synergies and intangibles have been addressed in, I believe, four ways.

The US Treasury White Paper (1988) was perhaps the first policy document to suggest how synergies should be handled in the transfer pricing regulations, and therefore in practice. The BALRM (basic arm's length return method) followed a residual profit split method, with the residual being allocated to the parent; thus, BALRM in effect allocated all the synergies to the parent firm. There are good arguments, of course, to allocate synergies to the parent; as the entrepreneurial unit and seat of management of the MNE—the firm that created, oversees, and runs the MNE group—the synergies could rightfully be claimed by the parent.

The co-development of intangibles was recognized early on as a problem; cost sharing and cost contribution arrangements have been allowed under transfer pricing regulations since the 1960s. Typically, the parties engaged in co-development of intangible property allocated the costs among themselves in proportion to their reasonably anticipated benefits from the arrangement. A party expecting, for example, 60 percent of the benefits from the arrangement had to share in 60 percent of the direct and indirect costs. Buy-in and buy-out arrangements were added to cover situations when a related party either was added or dropped from the group.

A third policy example appears in the OECD's Chapter IX on restructuring with its focus on pooling arrangements such as central purchasing (OECD, 2010). These arguments also appear in the 2013 OECD's proposed revision to the intangibles chapter (OECD, 2013c). Where external prices are not available, the OECD recommends dividing the profits among the related parties in the MNE group based on an assessment of (1) the legal and contractual rights and obligations; (2) the economic substance in terms of the parties' functions, assets, and risks; and (3) the relative bargaining power of the parties, taking into account their realistically available options and alternatives (including make-it-yourself, the status quo and the ability to walk away). There is no "right" answer that works all the time; rather, the answer differs for each case because the facts and circumstances matter. Legal title alone is not sufficient to guarantee a related party any share in MNE synergies; the allocation among the group members depends on an analysis of the facts and circumstances.

The last place where the complexities of synergies and intangibles have been addressed in the regulations is the residual profit split method (RPSM). Under RPSM, all parties receive routine returns for their functions, assets, and risks. The remaining profit (or loss) is assumed to flow from non-routine intangible assets. Typically, the residual in fact would include all forms of synergies and intragroup efficiencies that may or may not belong to intangible assets. In RPSM involving co-development of intellectual property by two or more R&D centers, the residual is normally allocated among the parties based on either the capitalized value, or a rolling average, of the parties' R&D spending. While spending on R&D may make some sense as an allocation mechanism for profits from intangible assets, it is well known that income (revenue) derived from intangibles is not directly linked to the costs of R&D development. The allocation key appears to be even less appropriate when the residual profits include all synergies, not just returns to non-routine intangible assets.

6.2.6 Reform Proposal: Fine-tuning the Arm's Length Standard

The problems with implementing the arm's length standard are real problems, ones that have been known for a very long time. Addressing the workability of the current ALS rules in the context of twenty-first century MNEs does require retooling current transfer pricing practices. My recommendations here are directed at reinvigorating—rather than replacing—the arm's length standard. Box 6.1 below provides some suggestions.

The key thrust of my argument is that *facts and circumstances matter*. The best transfer pricing method is the one that most closely fits the facts and circumstances of the particular situation. The economic substance behind the MNE's transactions and activities should matter more than mere legal title. The functions performed, assets provided, and risks assumed—as outlined in a functional analysis—must be the critical foundation for understanding the economics and business aspects of the MNE. Thus, it is critical for tax authorities to have a *holistic* approach to understanding the MNE.

Saying that transfer pricing requires a holistic approach based on a deep understanding of the MNE's activities, however, is different from putting this statement into practice. Moreover, MNEs with their knowledge of the inside workings of their own group will be much better placed to understand their facts and circumstances than will national tax authorities that do not have access to this level of detailed information except in special circumstances such as an Advance Pricing Agreement (APA).

For situations where comparables do exist in the external market, the comparable uncontrolled price (CUP) method (or CUT for intangibles and CUSP for services) has clear advantages over the other methods: it is two-sided and transaction-based. Adjustments can be made for differences in comparability of products, contract terms, and so on.

Where external prices are not available, I am supportive of the approach advocated by the OECD in its 2010 *Transfer Pricing Guidelines* Chapter IX on restructuring, its 2013 draft chapter on intangibles (OECD, 2010, 2013c), and in its 2013 BEPS action plan stating that transfer pricing outcomes should be in line with value creation (OECD, 2013b: 20). Profits should be divided among the related parties in the MNE group based on an assessment of (1) each party's legal and contractual rights and obligations; (2) the economic

Box 6.1 Recommendations: Lack of comparables—focus on the facts and circumstances

Fine-tuning the methods

1 Stress facts and circumstances—economic ownership should matter more than legal title.
2 Emphasize the role of economic substance (the functions, assets, and risks) and the value created or contributed by each related party in the MNE group.
3 Move away from one-sided transfer pricing methods (resale price method, cost plus method, CPM/TNMM) in favor of methods that take all the related parties into account (CUP).
4 Re-establish the commitment to CUP (CUT for intangibles, CUSP for services) as the preferred transfer pricing method when comparables exist and adjustments can be made for non-material differences.
5 Pooling and co-development arrangements are here to stay. MNEs can reap economies of scale, scope, and learning by pooling their resources and costs. We need better methods for allocating the savings from pooling among the group members, and the firm playing the "entrepreneur" and "manager" roles (where one exists). Allocation keys should be based on value creation by the group's members, not on costs spent.

Fine-tuning the process

1 Require more detailed information on the MNE's activities through combined and country-by-country reporting (CaCbCR) and reporting by line of business.
2 Encourage automatic on-request information exchange among tax authorities.
3 Expand and streamline the Advance Pricing Agreement (APA) program, including bilateral and multilateral APAs.
4 Provide more public information on APA outcomes including publication of "best practice" templates based on Advance Pricing Agreement (APA) settlements that can be adopted by other MNEs and tax authorities.
5 Increase opportunities for binding arbitration of international transfer pricing disputes.
6 Encourage joint audits by tax authorities where MNE activities are deeply intertwined across borders.

substance in terms of the parties' functions, assets, and risks; and (3) the relative bargaining power of the parties, taking into account their realistically available options and alternatives (including make-it-yourself, the status quo, and the ability to walk away). There is no "right" answer that works all the time; rather, facts and circumstances matter.

While in general I favor two-sided over one-sided methods, I recognize that any method has great difficulty in allocating the returns to synergies and high-value intangibles among the MNE group. Cost sharing arrangements (CSAs) are difficult, for example, because intragroup transfers must be calculated each time a related party enters into (buy-in) or exits from (buy-out) a CSA, as evidenced by recent changes in US CSA regulations in light of the Veritas and Xilinx transfer pricing court cases.

Profit splits are also difficult because the current keys used to allocate profits among the entities are based on historical cost shares, not on their reasonably anticipated benefits from these activities. Arm's length parties are unlikely to agree to split the profits from their activities based on cost shares, in cases where the distribution of benefits between them is unrelated to their distribution of costs. Finding better metrics for allocating profits among the members of an MNE group is therefore a critical component in transfer pricing reform.

Formulary apportionment methods typically use a three-part formula based on sales, assets, and wages as the allocation key. However, this formulary approach exactly misses the point: the difficulties in dividing up profits among the members of an MNE group are caused by synergies and unique intangibles that have no open market comparisons. Source-based measures (capital and labor) and destination-based measures (sales) are probably preferable to simply using costs, but still do not get at the proper allocation of "beneficial economic ownership" inherent in intangibles and synergies within the MNE group.

Fine-tuning the transfer pricing process can also be a useful reform. I support the provision of more information about the MNEs activities, such as Combined and Country-by-Country Reporting (CaCbCR). I also support more automatic information exchange between tax authorities, and the adoption of international standards in terms of contemporaneous documentation. In situations where the activities of an MNE are deeply intertwined in two or three countries (such as the auto industry in Canada, the USA, and Mexico) joint tax audits could also be considered. The Advance Pricing Agreement (APA) program also needs expansion and streamlining, with more information provided on best practices so that other MNEs and governments can benefit from these "closed door" proceedings.

6.3 DISCUSSION

6.3.1 Other Policy Alternatives: Formulary Apportionment

Many, many pages have been written reviewing the pros and cons of the arm's length standard (ALS) versus formulary apportionment (FA) as methods for taxing multinational enterprises (MNEs). It seems to me that the ALS approach is here to stay, at least for the foreseeable future. In this paper, I therefore chose not to review the pros and cons of the two approaches, nor make arguments for why one should replace the other, but rather have focused on how to improve what we have now.

It does look like the European Union member countries are going to introduce a Common Consolidated Corporate Tax Base (CCCTB). This will provide MNEs, their accounting and legal advisors, policymakers, and academics with the opportunity to watch how a FA system works in a multilateral context. Just as the NAFTA was the first free trade agreement to include both developed and developing countries, and proved that it was possible to establish a north-south free trade agreement, perhaps the EU's introduction of a CCCTB will have a similar demonstration effect.[7] A regional FA system means that the EU member countries must continue to use the ALS for their transactions with non-member countries; how national governments handle these complexities will also be telling.

Our historical experience with FA systems to date has been at the state level within countries, where the federal level of government enforces some consistency in terms of norms, rules and procedures. Moreover, the states within a federal system all operate under a common currency, monetary, fiscal, and international trade policies; a FA system should be more difficult to coordinate where these macro-level policies differ. Hammering out these complexities will provide useful lessons for other countries, both rich countries and developing countries, which contemplate a move from a SA-ALS to FA system.

6.3.2 Obstacles to Reform and Solutions

I believe there are two problems with current transfer pricing regulation: abusive transfer pricing and lack of comparables. I see abusive transfer pricing as a design issue (that is, how to improve the efficiency and effectiveness of the international income tax regime). The lack of comparables, on the other hand, is a problem integral to the theory and practice of the arm's length standard.

There are two key obstacles to reform of the arm's length standard. The first obstacle arises from the parties "at the table" when transfer pricing rules and guidelines are being written. Because the topic is so esoteric, only a few individuals are well-enough informed to participate knowledgeably in the debate. For example, the OECD has multiple working parties involved in overhauling the transfer pricing guidelines and the BEPS initiative; the working parties consist of three groups: tax authorities, MNEs, and tax consultants. The United Nations (2013) has also recently released a *UN Transfer Pricing Manual*, which pays closer attention to the situation of developing countries and their tax authorities; the manual was primarily developed by developing country tax authorities with inputs from MNEs and tax groups. The parties at the table (MNEs, tax authorities, and transfer pricing professionals) have their own vested interests in the outcome.

In terms of solutions, I see NGOs as having an important role to play here in providing a counter-weight to MNEs, particularly through their information dissemination activities. The Tax Justice Network, for example, has been influential in raising public awareness of trade mispricing and its harmful

[7] On the other hand, the experiences of Greece, Portugal, and Spain as members of the euro suggest that the road to integration is not always a smooth one.

impacts on developing countries. While I disagree with those NGOs that see all transfer pricing as abusive, these groups have been instrumental in providing data and case studies supporting the OECD's base erosion and profit shifting initiative (Christian Aid, 2009). Recent work by the World Bank (see Reuter, 2012) has also drawn attention to the problems that can occur if MNEs engage in transfer pricing practices that drain income from developing countries. I argue that academics can also play a useful non-partisan role, particularly in terms of providing an economic analysis of the various proposals.

The second obstacle is a longer-run problem. Transfer pricing problems are inherently puzzles; as such they require puzzle-solving, logic-building skills. They also require understanding the MNE—like an elephant—from multiple perspectives including accounting, business, economics, finance, politics, and law. As a long-run solution to the problem—one that I not surprisingly support as an educator—we need to provide college and university students with training about related party transactions, transfer pricing, and international tax laws.

Very few places in the world offer any kind of training on these topics; most practitioners learn "on the job." As such, they learn practical skills, short cuts, and rules of thumb. While useful, I believe that these tools need to be accompanied by solid training in the fundamentals of international tax law, the economics of international business, and the strategies of multinationals. Transfer pricing reform should be guided by the same principles that guide good international tax reform. To understand the facts and circumstances that underlie the MNE's intra-firm transactions one needs economic analysis. Lastly, a thorough understanding of the twenty-first-century multinational as an organizational form—its strategies and structures, core competencies, and value-adding activities—is required if we really want to understand the "elephant" among us.

6.4 CONCLUSION

The historical approach to taxing intra-firm transactions of multinational enterprises—the arm's length standard—has been criticized as unworkable, out of date, and on death's door. Many academics (including some in this volume) are advocating a shift to formulary apportionment as an alternative. My view is two-fold. First, many of the criticisms of the arm's length standard in terms of abusive transfer pricing are misdirected; the criticisms should be more appropriately aimed at weak international corporate income tax rules that need to be fixed. Second, if the loopholes in the international tax regime can be fixed, the arm's length standard remains the appropriate standard for taxing MNEs. The standard does require fine-tuning—the twenty-first-century multinational is not the same organizational form as the twentieth-century MNE—and I offer a few policy recommendations with that goal in mind.

REFERENCES

Avi-Yonah, R. S., 1995. "The Rise and Fall of Arm's Length: A Study in the Evolution of US International Taxation," *Virginia Tax Review* 15: 89.

Avi-Yonah, R. S., K. A. Clausing, and M. C. Durst, 2008. "Allocating Business Profits for Tax Purposes: A Proposal to Adopt a Formulary Profit Split," The Berkeley Electronic Press, John M. Olin Center for Law and Economics Working Paper Series, Paper 95.

Boidman, N. and M. N. Kandev, 2013. "BEPS: The OECD Discovers America?" *Tax Notes International*, 16, December: 1017–34.

Buckley, P. and M. Casson, 1976. *The Future of the Multinational Enterprise*. Hampshire and London: Macmillan Press.

Christian Aid, 2009. *False Profits: Robbing the Poor to Keep the Rich Tax-free*. A Christian Aid Report. March.

Eden, L., 1998. *Taxing Multinationals: Transfer Pricing and Corporate Income Taxation in North America*. Toronto: University of Toronto Press.

Eden, L., 2005. "Went for Cost, Priced at Cost? An Economic Approach to the Transfer Pricing of Offshored Business Services," *Transnational Corporations* 14 (2): 1–53.

Eden, L., 2009. "Taxes, Transfer Pricing and the Multinational Enterprise," in Alan Rugman (ed.) *Oxford Handbook of International Business*, 2nd edition. Oxford: Oxford University Press, pp. 591–621.

Eden, L., 2012. "Transfer Price Manipulation and Developing Countries," in Peter Reuter (ed.) *Draining Development? The Sources, Consequences and Control of Illicit Funds from Developing Countries*. The World Bank, Washington, DC.

Eden, L. and P. Rodriguez, 2004. "How Weak Are the Signals? International Price Indices and Multinational Enterprises," *Journal of International Business Studies* 35 (1): 61–74.

Ernst & Young, 2013. *Transfer Pricing Global Reference Guide*. Available at: http://www.ey.com/Publication/vwLUAssets/Transfer_pricing_global_reference_guide_2013/$FILE/Transfer_pricing_global_reference_guide_2013.pdf, accessed 5 September 2015.

Horst, T., 1971. "Theory of the Multinational Firm: Optimal Behaviour under Differing Tariff and Tax Rates," *Journal of Political Economy*, 79, September/October: 1059–72.

Langbein, S. I., 1991. "Transfer Pricing and Economies of Integration," in Morrison et al. (eds) *Transfer Pricing: The International Tax Concern of the 1990s*. Englewood Cliffs, NJ: Prentice Hall Law & Business, pp. 27–51.

McIntyre, M., 2012. "Challenging the Status Quo: The Case for Combined Reporting," *Tax Management Transfer Pricing Report* 20 (22), 22 March.

OECD, 2010. *OECD Transfer Pricing Guidelines for Multinational Enterprises and Tax Administrations.* Paris: OECD Publishing.

OECD, 2013a. *Action Plan on Base Erosion and Profit Shifting.* Paris: OECD Publishing, 19 July.

OECD, 2013b. *Addressing Base Erosion and Profit Shifting.* Paris: OECD Publishing, 12 February.

OECD, 2013c. *Revised Discussion Draft on Transfer Pricing Aspects of Intangibles.* Paris: OECD Publishing, July.

Picciotto, S., 1992. "International Taxation and Intrafirm Pricing in Transnational Corporate Groups," *Accounting, Organizations and Society* 17 (8): 759–92.

Picciotto, S., 2012. *Towards Unitary Taxation of Transnational Corporations.* Tax Justice Network.

Picciotto, S., 2013. "Can the OECD Mend the International Tax System?" *Tax Notes International* 71: 1105–15.

Reuter, P. (ed.), 2012. *Draining Development? The Sources, Consequences and Control of Illicit Funds from Developing Countries.* The World Bank, Washington, DC.

Rugman, A. M. and L. Eden (eds.), 1985. *Multinationals and Transfer Pricing.* Croom Helm, London and St. Martin's Press, New York.

Sheppard, L. A., 2012. "Is Transfer Pricing Worth Salvaging?" *Tax Notes,* 30 July: 467–76.

UNCTAD, 2010. *World Investment Report 2010: Investing in a Low-Carbon Economy.* United Nations, Geneva.

UNCTAD, 2011. *World Investment Report 2011: Non-Equity Modes of International Production and Development.* United Nations, Geneva.

UNCTAD, 2013. *World Investment Report 2013: Global Value Chains: Investment and Trade for Development.* United Nations, Geneva.

United Nations, 2013. *Practical Manual on Transfer Pricing for Developing Countries.* United Nations, New York.

US Treasury, 1988. *A Study of Intercompany Pricing under Section 482 of the Code (1988 White Paper).* US Government Printing Office, Washington, DC.

Vernon, R., 1985. "Sovereignty at Bay: Ten Years After." In Theodore Moran (ed.) *Multinational Corporations: The Political Economy of Foreign Direct Investment.* Lexington, MA: Lexington Books.

7

The Taxation of Multinational Enterprises

Lee Corrick

7.1 BASE EROSION AND PROFIT SHIFTING

7.1.1 Introduction

Multinational enterprises (MNEs) now represent a large proportion of global GDP. MNEs sales as a share of world GDP have increased from 27 percent in 1990 to 58 percent in 2007 (UNCTAD, 2009). Also, intra-firm trade represents a growing proportion of overall trade. The United Nations estimates that approximately 60 percent of international trade happens within MNE companies (African Economic Outlook, n.d.). Globalization has resulted in a shift from country-specific operating models to global models based on matrix management organizations (organizations that manage across functions and across business groups, e.g. sales and production functions) and integrated supply chains that centralize several functions at a regional or global level. Moreover, the growing importance of the service component of the economy, and of digital products that often can be delivered over the Internet, has made it much easier for businesses to locate many productive activities in geographic locations that are distant from the physical location of their customers. These developments have been exacerbated by the increasing sophistication of tax planning, which focuses on identifying and exploiting arbitrage opportunities that result in income being taxed nowhere.

These developments have opened up opportunities for MNEs to greatly minimize their tax burden and this has led to a tense situation in which citizens have become more sensitive to tax fairness issues. It has become a critical issue for all parties:

- *Governments are harmed.* Many governments have to cope with less revenue and higher costs to ensure compliance. Moreover, base erosion and profit shifting (BEPS) undermines the integrity of the tax system, as the public, the media, and some taxpayers deem reported low corporate taxes to be unfair. In developing countries, the lack of tax revenue leads to critical under-funding of public investment that could help promote economic growth. Overall resource allocation, affected by tax-motivated behavior, is sub-optimal.

- *Individual taxpayers are harmed.* When tax rules permit businesses to reduce their tax burden by shifting their income away from jurisdictions where income-producing activities are conducted, other taxpayers in that jurisdiction bear a greater share of the burden.
- *Businesses are harmed.* MNEs may face significant reputational risk if their effective tax rate is viewed as being too low. At the same time, different businesses may assess such risk differently, and failing to take advantage of legal opportunities to reduce an enterprise's tax burden can put it at a competitive disadvantage. Similarly, corporations that operate only in domestic markets, including family-owned businesses or new innovative companies, have difficulty competing with MNEs that have the ability to shift their profits across borders to avoid or reduce tax. Fair competition is harmed by the distortions induced by BEPS.

7.2 THE OECD/G20 BEPS PROJECT

Taxation is at the core of countries' sovereignty, but the interaction of domestic tax rules in some cases leads to gaps and frictions. When designing their domestic tax rules, sovereign states may not sufficiently take into account the effect of other countries' rules. The interaction of independent sets of rules enforced by sovereign countries creates frictions, including potential double taxation for corporations operating in several countries. It also creates gaps, in cases where corporate income is not taxed at all, either by the country of source or the country of residence, or is only taxed at nominal rates. In the domestic context, coherence is usually achieved through a principle of matching—a payment that is deductible by the payer is generally taxable in the hands of the recipient, unless explicitly exempted. There is no similar principle of coherence at the international level, which leaves plenty of room for arbitrage by taxpayers, though sovereign states have cooperated to ensure coherence in a narrow field, namely to prevent double taxation.

The international standards have sought to address these frictions in a way that respects tax sovereignty, but gaps remain. Since at least the 1920s, it has been recognized that the interaction of domestic tax systems can lead to overlaps in the exercise of taxing rights that in turn can result in double taxation (League of Nations, 1928). Countries have long worked and are strongly committed to eliminate such double taxation in order to minimize trade distortions and impediments to sustainable economic growth, while affirming their sovereign right to establish their own tax rules. However, gaps and conflicts among different countries' tax systems have emerged that were not taken into account in designing the existing standards and which are not dealt with by bilateral tax treaties. The global economy requires countries to collaborate on tax matters in order to be able to protect their tax sovereignty.

In many circumstances, the existing domestic law and treaty rules governing the taxation of cross-border profits produce the correct results and do not give rise to BEPS. International cooperation has resulted in shared principles and a network of thousands of bilateral tax treaties that are based on common standards and that therefore generally result in the prevention of double taxation on profits from cross-border activities. Clarity and predictability are fundamental building blocks of economic growth. It is important to retain such clarity and predictability by building on this experience. At the same time, instances where the current rules give rise to results that generate concerns from a policy perspective should be tackled.

Over time, the current rules have also revealed weaknesses that create opportunities for BEPS. BEPS relates chiefly to instances where the interaction of different tax rules leads to double non-taxation or less than single taxation. It also relates to arrangements that achieve no or low taxation by shifting profits away from the jurisdictions where the activities creating those profits take place. No or low taxation is not per se a cause of concern, but it becomes so when it is associated with practices that artificially segregate taxable income from the activities that generate it. In other words, what creates tax policy concerns is that, due to gaps in the interaction of different tax systems, and in some cases because of the application of bilateral tax treaties, income from cross-border activities may go untaxed anywhere, or be only unduly lowly taxed.

The spread of the digital economy also poses challenges for international taxation. The digital economy is characterized by an unparalleled reliance on intangible assets, the massive use of data (notably personal data), the widespread adoption of multi-sided business models capturing value from externalities generated by free products, and the difficulty of determining the jurisdiction in which value creation occurs. This raises fundamental questions as to how enterprises in the digital economy add value and make their profits, and how the digital economy relates to the concepts of source and residence or the characterization of income for tax purposes. At the same time, the fact that new ways of doing business may result in a relocation of core business functions and, consequently, a different distribution of taxing rights which may lead to low taxation is not per se an indicator of defects in the existing system. It is important to examine closely how enterprises of the digital economy add value and make their profits in order to determine whether and to what extent it may be necessary to adapt the current rules to take into account the specific features of that industry and to prevent BEPS.

7.2.1 Time to Modernize the Rules for the Taxation of MNEs

BEPS is not primarily an issue of compliance. While there are certainly companies that do not pay the taxes they legally owe, there is a more fundamental policy issue, which is that the international tax rules have not kept pace with the changing business environment.

The OECD published its report *Addressing Base Erosion and Profit Shifting* in February 2013.[1] The report analyzes the root causes of BEPS and identifies six key pressure areas: (1) hybrids and mismatches which generate arbitrage opportunities; (2) the residence-source tax balance, in particular in the context of the digital economy; (3) intra-group financing, with companies in high-tax countries being loaded with debt; (4) transfer pricing issues, such as the treatment of group synergies and location savings; (5) the effectiveness of anti-avoidance rules, which are often watered down because of heavy lobbying and competitive pressure; (6) the existence of preferential regimes.

The report was sent to and discussed at the G20 Finance Ministers meeting in Moscow on 15–16 February 2013: The G20 stated "We welcome the OECD report on addressing base erosion and profit shifting and acknowledge that an important part of fiscal sustainability is securing our revenue bases. We are determined to develop measures to address base erosion and profit shifting, take necessary collective actions and look forward to the comprehensive action plan the OECD will present to us in July" (G20, 2013: §20).

In Saint Petersburg in September 2013 the G20 leaders endorsed an Action Plan[2] to address BEPS. In response to this call, the OECD/G20 BEPS Project was launched to develop the measures envisaged in the fifteen-point Action Plan.

7.2.2 Fifteen Actions to Put an End to BEPS

The digital economy provides a good illustration of the types of challenges facing the international tax system, including novel and ever-changing business models, the importance and mobility of intangible assets, and the ability to provide goods and services without a physical presence. While the actions in the BEPS Action Plan will clearly have an impact on BEPS in the digital economy, there is also a need for a thorough analysis of this sector.

Action 1: Address the Tax Challenges of the Digital Economy

A dedicated task force has been established that will identify the issues raised by the digital economy and possible actions to address them. The work of the

[1] See OECD (2013a). [2] See OECD (2013b).

Task Force on the digital economy will cut across the work done on the other fourteen actions, which are organized according to three main principles: preventing double non-taxation due to gaps in countries' tax rules; aligning taxation with substance; and improving transparency.

7.2.2.1 Preventing Double Non-taxation Due to the Gaps that Exist between Countries' Tax Rules

Tax policy is at the core of countries' sovereignty, and each country has the right to design its tax system in the way it considers most appropriate. Domestic tax systems are coherent—tax deductible payments by one person results in income inclusions by the recipient. At the same time, the increasing interconnectedness of domestic economies has highlighted the gaps that can be created by interactions between domestic tax laws. Currently, there are no international standards to address these gaps and prevent the double non-taxation that can arise as a result. International coherence in corporate income taxation is needed to complement the standards that prevent double taxation with a new set of standards designed to avoid double non-taxation. Four actions in the BEPS Action Plan (Actions 2, 3, 4, and 5) focus on establishing this coherence:

Action 2: Neutralize the Effects of Hybrid Mismatch Arrangements

Mismatches in the way countries' tax laws treat entities and instruments can allow companies to claim multiple deductions for the same economic expense or cause taxable income to disappear (so-called hybrid mismatch arrangements). This Action will result in treaty and domestic law provisions to neutralise these schemes.

Action 3: Strengthen Controlled Foreign Companies (CFC) Rules

One of the sources of BEPS concerns is the use of offshore subsidiaries to stash income in low or no tax jurisdictions through creating offshore entities in those jurisdictions and routing income through them to escape taxation. Strong CFC rules can address this issue by including the income of these offshore entities in the parent entity's income on a current taxable basis.

Action 4: Limit Base Erosion via Interest Deductions and Other Financial Payments

Current rules often allow the use of excessive interest deductions to erode their taxable profits, or use of debt (which generates interest expense deductions) to finance the production of tax-exempt income. This Action will result in recommendations regarding best practices in the design of rules to prevent BEPS through the use of interest expense and other financial payments.

Action 5: Counter Harmful Tax Practices more Effectively

Countries have long recognized that a "race to the bottom" would ultimately drive applicable tax rates on certain mobile sources of income to zero for all countries, whether or not this was the tax policy a country wished to pursue. Agreeing to a set of common rules will help countries make their sovereign tax policy choices, and this Action will result in revamping the work on harmful tax practices to that end.

7.2.2.2 Aligning Taxation with Substance

Existing tax treaty and transfer pricing rules are generally effective, and prevent double taxation of profits, but may in some cases facilitate the separation of taxable profits from the value-creating activities that give rise to those profits. The Action Plan will restore the intended effects of these standards by aligning taxation with substance, while at the same time continuing to prevent double taxation.

The involvement of third countries in the bilateral framework established by treaty partners puts a strain on the existing rules, in particular when done via shell companies that have little or no economic substance: e.g. office space, tangible assets and employees. The Action Plan will ensure that shell companies cannot be used to achieve double non-taxation by inappropriately claiming treaty benefits.

In addition the current interpretation of the arm's length principle used in transfer pricing rules is challenged by the ability of MNEs to artificially shift profits by transferring easily movable assets (such as intangibles and capital). In some cases, MNEs have been able to use and/or misapply the existing rules to separate income from the economic activities that produce that income. This most often involves transfers of intangibles or other mobile assets, overcapitalisation of group companies, and contractual allocations of risk. The Actions in the Action Plan will result in rules to prevent BEPS through transfers of intangibles, through transfers of risk or excessive allocations of capital, or through transactions which would not, or would only very rarely, occur between third parties.

The Action Plan will fix these issues with measures, either within or beyond the arm's length principle, to ensure that taxable profits can no longer be artificially shifted away from the countries where value is created.

Five Actions in the BEPS Action Plan focus on aligning taxing rights with substance (Actions 6, 7, 8, 9, and 10):

Action 6: Prevent Treaty Abuse

While tax treaties are designed to prevent double taxation, in some cases they are used to create double non-taxation, in particular through the use of conduit companies. This Action will result in model treaty provisions and recommendations regarding the design of domestic rules to prevent the granting of treaty benefits in inappropriate circumstances.

Action 7: Prevent the Artificial Avoidance of Permanent Establishment (PE) Status

Under the international standard, a country may not tax the business profits of a foreign company unless the company has a permanent establishment (PE) in that country. For the purposes of the OECD Model Tax Convention a Permanent Establishment means a fixed place of business through which the business of an enterprise is wholly or partly carried on. If the company is not taxed on those profits in its jurisdiction of residence the result is double non-taxation. This Action will result in changes to the definition of PE to prevent the artificial avoidance of PE status in relation to BEPS.

Actions 8 to 10: Assure that Transfer Pricing Outcomes Are in Line with Value Creation

(Action 8) Intangibles—This Action will result in rules that prevent BEPS via the transfer of intangibles.

(Action 9) Risks and Capital—This Action will result in rules that prevent BEPS via transfers of risk or excessive allocations of capital.

(Action 10) Other High Risk Transactions—This Action will result in rules that prevent BEPS through transactions which would not, or would only very rarely, occur between third parties.

7.2.2.3 Improving Transparency

Addressing BEPS will also require greater transparency between taxpayers and tax administrations, and among tax administrations. The Action Plan will level the playing field between companies and tax administrators by creating a common template for MNEs to report to all relevant governments their global allocation of profits, economic activity, and taxes paid among countries. At the same time, work will be done to provide the necessary certainty to encourage global investment and make sure that disputes are resolved quickly. Four Actions in the BEPS Action Plan focus on improving transparency (Actions 11, 12, 13, and 14):

Action 11: Establish Methodologies to Collect and Analyze Data on BEPS and the Actions to Address It

Further work needs to be done to measure the scale and effects of BEPS, and to monitor the impact of the actions taken to address it. This Action will identify tools to monitor and evaluate the effectiveness and economic impact of the actions taken to address BEPS, including its spill-over effects.

Action 12: Require Taxpayers to Disclose their Aggressive Tax-planning Arrangements

Improved disclosure measures can help tax administrations and tax policy makers identify emerging risk areas, and can also serve as a deterrent against aggressive planning. This Action will result in mandatory disclosure rules targeting these kinds of arrangements.

Action 13: Re-examine Transfer Pricing Documentation

This Action will result in rules regarding transfer pricing documentation that enhances transparency for tax administrations while taking into account compliance costs for businesses, and will include a requirement that MNEs provide all relevant governments with the required information on their global allocation of income, economic activity, and taxes paid among countries.

The rules aim to simplify transfer pricing documentation rules and make them more uniform across different tax jurisdictions.[3]

Action 14: Make Dispute Resolution Mechanisms more Effective

The actions to counter BEPS must be complemented with actions to ensure the certainty and predictability needed to promote investment in today's environment. This Action will ensure such certainty by developing solutions to address obstacles that prevent countries from solving treaty-related disputes.

Action 15: Develop a Multilateral Instrument

The delivery of certain actions will result in changes to the OECD Model Tax Convention, which are not directly effective without amendments to bilateral tax treaties. If undertaken on a purely treaty-by-treaty basis, the sheer number of treaties in effect may make such a process very lengthy, the more so where countries embark on comprehensive renegotiations of their bilateral tax treaties. A multilateral instrument, which is innovative in the area of international taxation, will greatly speed up this process.

[3] See OECD (2014a).

7.2.3 How Will the Actions Be Implemented? How Long Will It Take?

The BEPS Action Plan calls for the development of tools that countries can use to shape fair, effective and efficient tax systems. Because BEPS strategies often rely on the interaction of countries' different systems, these tools will have to address the gaps and frictions that arise from the interface of these systems. Some Actions, for example work on the OECD Transfer Pricing Guidelines[4] and the Commentary to the OECD Model Tax Convention[5], will result in changes that are directly effective. Others will be implemented by countries through their domestic law, bilateral treaties, or a multilateral instrument.

Addressing BEPS is critical for most countries and must be done in a timely manner so that concrete actions can be delivered quickly before the existing consensus-based framework unravels. At the same time, governments need time to complete the necessary technical work and achieve widespread consensus. Against this background, it is expected that the Action Plan will largely be completed in 2 years.

7.2.4 Deliverables and Milestones

The BEPS work will result in a number of outputs, scheduled to be finalized in three phases (see Tables 7.1, 7.2, and 7.3):

Table 7.1 Timeline: September 2014

	Action	Expected Output
Action 1	Address the tax challenges of the digital economy	Report identifying issues raised by the digital economy and possible actions to address them
Action 2	Neutralize the effects of hybrid mismatch arrangements	i) Changes to the Model Tax Convention ii) Recommendations regarding the design of domestic rules
Action 5	Counter harmful tax practices more effectively, taking into account transparency and substance—phase 1	Finalize review of member country regimes
Action 6	Prevent treaty abuse	i) Changes to the Model Tax Convention ii) Recommendations regarding the design of domestic rules

(continued)

[4] See OECD (2010). [5] See OECD (2012a).

Table 7.1 Continued

	Action	Expected Output
Action 8	Assure that transfer pricing outcomes are in line with value creation/intangibles—phase 1	Changes to the Transfer Pricing Guidelines and possibly to the Model Tax Convention
Action 13	Re-examine transfer pricing documentation	Changes to Transfer Pricing Guidelines and Recommendations regarding the design of domestic rules
Action 15	Develop a multilateral instrument—phase 1	Report identifying relevant public international law and tax issues

Table 7.2 Timeline: September 2015

	Action	Expected Output
Action 3	Strengthen CFC Rules	Recommendations regarding the design of domestic rules
Action 4	Limit base erosion via interest deductions and other financial payments	Recommendations regarding the design of domestic rules
Action 5	Counter harmful tax practices more effectively, taking into account transparency and substance—phase 2	Strategy to expand participation to non-OECD members
Action 7	Prevent the artificial avoidance of PE status	Changes to the Model Tax Convention
Action 8	Assure that transfer pricing outcomes are in line with value creation/intangibles—phase 2	Changes to the Transfer Pricing Guidelines and possibly to the Model Tax Convention
Action 9	Assure that transfer pricing outcomes are in line with value creation/risks and capital	Changes to the Transfer Pricing Guidelines and possibly to the Model Tax Convention
Action 10	Assure that transfer pricing outcomes are in line with value creation/other high-risk transactions	Changes to the Transfer Pricing Guidelines and possibly to the Model Tax Convention
Action 11	Establish methodologies to collect and analyze data on BEPS and the actions to address it	Recommendations regarding data to be collected and methodologies to analyze them
Action 12	Require taxpayers to disclose their aggressive tax planning arrangements	Recommendations regarding the design of domestic rules
Action 14	Make dispute resolution mechanisms more effective	Changes to the Model Tax Convention

7.2.5 An Inclusive Process: The OECD/G20 Project on BEPS

The work on BEPS is being carried out within the context of the OECD/G20 BEPS Project, to which the eight non-OECD G20 Countries (Argentina, Brazil, China, India, Indonesia, Russia, Saudi Arabia and South Africa) participate as Associates, on an equal footing with OECD countries. Colombia

Table 7.3 Timeline: December 2015

	Action	Expected Output
Action 4	Limit base erosion via interest deductions—phase 2	Changes to the Transfer Pricing Guidelines
Action 5	Counter harmful tax practices more effectively, taking into account transparency and substance—phase 3	Revision of existing criteria to identify harmful tax practices
Action 15	Develop a multilateral instrument—phase 2	Multilateral instrument

and Latvia (who have started the OECD Accession Process) have also joined the OECD/G20 BEPS Project as Associates.

Associates in the OECD/G20 BEPS Project participate in the entire range of the BEPS-related work carried out by the CFA and its subsidiary bodies, including playing a full part in setting the agenda, in the discussions and in the decision-making process. This means that Associates take an active part in establishing the international tax rules and principles provided for in the BEPS Action Plan and in implementing the consensus on all outcomes related to the OECD/G20 BEPS Project.

7.2.6 How Will the OECD Ensure Developing Countries Concerns Are Addressed?

BEPS is a global issue and requires a global solution. The Action Plan marks a turning point in the history of international cooperation on taxation and it is critical that the work include all relevant stakeholders. Developing countries also face issues related to BEPS and the work will take into account the specificities of their national legal and administrative frameworks. In this respect, the Global Fora on Tax Treaties, on Transfer Pricing, on VAT[6] and on Transparency and Exchange of Information for Tax Purposes[7] will be useful platforms for developing countries to provide relevant input as will the OECD's Task Force on Tax and Development.[8] In addition, the CFA will benefit from the input of the United Nations (UN), which has been an observer to the CFA since January 2012.

[6] See OECD (n.d. a). [7] See OECD (n.d. b).

[8] The OECD's Task Force on Tax and Development brings together all major stakeholders on tax and development, including representatives from developed and developing countries, international organizations, business, and NGOs. It is co-chaired by senior officials from an OECD and a non-OECD country, and is supported by a Secretariat—incorporating extensive government transfer pricing experience—managed jointly by the OECD's Center for Tax Policy and Administration and Development Coordination Division, with staffing and other costs met by the OECD and donor contributions.

7.2.7 The Process of Consultation has Already Begun

At the Global Forum on Tax Treaties meeting held in Paris in September 2013 over 300 senior tax officials from more than 100 jurisdictions and international organizations met to discuss solutions to BEPS. Participants discussed the content of the Action Plan and ways through which developing countries can engage and provide input. Discussions with developing countries were also held at the OECD Advisory Group for Co-operation with Non-OECD Partners[9] meeting and the OECD's Task Force on Tax and Development meeting in Seoul, Korea, in October 2013. The Task Force welcomed international action to address BEPS. Four high-level policy events were also held in the first quarter of 2014 in Africa (hosted by the African Tax Administration Forum (ATAF)), Asia, Europe (hosted by Center de rencontre des administrations fiscales (CREDAF)), and Latin America to obtain further input from developing countries and relevant stakeholders. In addition, a special meeting of the Tax Force on Tax and Development on BEPS was held back-to-back to the Global Forum on Transfer Pricing on 26 to 28 March 2014. The meetings considered the views and perspectives of developing countries on the BEPS project and this input informed Part 1 and Part 2 of the OECD report to the G20 Development Working Group titled "A Report to G20 Development Working Group on the Impact of BEPS in Low Income Countries" which the OECD prepared at the request of the G20.[10] In addition to highlighting certain BEPS issues that are of more relevance to developing countries, the report presents several issues, such as tax competition through the use of tax incentives and measures to identify indirect transfers of assets, which are of particular concern to developing countries, but are not included in the BEPS Action Plan. In response, the G20 Finance Ministers have called on the OECD, the International Monetary Fund (IMF), UN, and World Bank Group "to build on its current engagement with developing countries and develop a new structured dialogue process, with clear avenues for developing countries to work together and directly input in the G20/OECD [BEPS] project."[11]

7.2.8 Progress Thus Far

In September and November of 2014, the OECD submitted the first set of deliverables under the BEPS Action Plan to the G20 Finance Ministers and G20 Leaders, respectively. Reports were presented under Action 1 on the Digital Economy and Action 15 on a Multilateral Instrument. Reports were

[9] See OECD (n.d. c). [10] See OECD (2014b) and OECD (2014c).
[11] See G20 (2014).

also presented on hybrid mismatch arrangements, treaty abuse, transfer pricing aspects of intangibles, and transfer pricing documentation and a template for country-by-country reporting. Finally, an interim progress report on the review of country regimes in order to counter harmful tax practices more effectively was presented. The summary of recommendations under each Action Point follows below:

Action 1: Addressing the Tax Challenges of the "Digital Economy"

The Task Force on the Digital Economy has produced a report outlining specific tax challenges of the digital economy. The Task Force has concluded that because the digital economy is increasingly becoming the economy itself, it would be difficult, if not impossible, to ring-fence the digital economy from the rest of the economy. The Task Force has identified certain specific issues generated by the key features of the digital economy that warrant attention from a tax perspective. Work on the actions of the BEPS Action Plan will take these issues into account to ensure that the proposed solutions fully address BEPS in the digital economy. These include: ensuring that core activities cannot inappropriately benefit from the exception from permanent establishment (PE) status, and that artificial arrangements relating to sales of goods and services cannot be used to avoid PE status, the importance of intangibles, the use of data, and the spread of global value chains, and their impact on transfer pricing, the possible need to adapt CFC rules to the digital economy, addressing opportunities for tax planning by businesses engaged in VAT-exempt activities. The Task Force work will also evaluate how outcomes from other BEPS project action points affect the broader tax challenges raised by the digital economy, such as nexus, data, and characterization of transactions. The Task Force recommends a further evaluation of options to address these broader tax challenges in a supplementary report to be delivered in December 2015.

Action 2: Neutralizing the Effects of Hybrid Mismatch Arrangements

The report under Action 2 sets out draft recommendations in two parts. Part 1 provides recommendations for domestic rules to neutralize the effect of hybrid mismatch arrangements. Part 2 sets out recommended changes to the OECD Model Tax Convention to deal with transparent entities, including hybrid entities and addresses the interactions between the recommendations included in Part 1 and the provisions of the OECD Model Tax Convention. Once translated into domestic law and tax treaties, these recommendations and model provisions will neutralize mismatches and put an end to multiple deductions for a single expense, deductions in one country without corresponding taxation in another, or the generation of multiple foreign tax credits for one amount of foreign tax paid.

The work will now turn to developing guidance, in the form of a Commentary which will explain how the rules would operate in practice, including via practical examples. Furthermore there are a number of specific areas where the recommended domestic rules in Part I may need to be further refined. This is the case for certain capital market transactions (such as on-market stock lending and repos) and the rules on imported hybrid mismatches. In addition, concerns were raised by a number of countries and by business in the consultation responses over the application of the rules to hybrid regulatory capital that is issued intra-group. These concerns need to be further explored in order to clarify whether a special treatment under the hybrid mismatch rules is justified. Finally, the report will need to clarify whether or not income taxed under a controlled foreign company (CFC) regime should be treated as included in ordinary income for the purposes of this report and the related language is in brackets. No consensus has yet been reached on these issues but discussion will continue with a view to reaching agreement and to publishing the outcome together with the Commentary no later than September 2015.

Part I of the report recommends specific changes to domestic law to achieve a better alignment between domestic and cross-border tax outcomes. In particular, this report recommends:

- denial of a dividend exemption for the relief of economic double taxation in respect of deductible payments made under financial instruments
- the introduction of measures to prevent hybrid transfers being used to duplicate credits for taxes withheld at source
- improvements to controlled foreign company and other offshore investment regimes to bring the income of hybrid entities within the charge to taxation under the investor jurisdiction and the imposition of information reporting requirements on such intermediaries to facilitate the ability of offshore investors and tax administrations to apply such rules
- rules restricting the tax transparency of reverse hybrids that are members of a controlled group.

In addition to these specific recommendations on the tax treatment of entities and instruments, which are designed to prevent mismatches from arising, Action 2 calls for hybrid mismatch rules that adjust the tax outcomes in one jurisdiction to align them with the tax consequences in another. Action 2 states that these rules may include domestic law provisions that:

- deny a deduction for a payment that is also deductible in another jurisdiction
- prevent exemption or non-recognition for payments that are deductible by the payer
- deny a deduction for a payment that is not includible in ordinary income by the recipient (and is not subject to taxation under CFC or similar rules).

Action 2 therefore calls for domestic rules targeting two types of payment:

- payments under a hybrid mismatch arrangement that are deductible under the rules of the payer jurisdiction and not included in the ordinary income of the payee or a related investor (deduction/no inclusion or D/NI outcomes)
- payments under a hybrid mismatch arrangements that give rise to duplicate deductions for the same payment (double deduction or DD outcomes).

In order to avoid the risk of double taxation, Action 2 also calls for "guidance on the coordination or tie breaker rules where more than one country seeks to apply such rules to a transaction or structure." For this reason the rules recommended in this report are organized in a hierarchy so that a jurisdiction does not need to apply the hybrid mismatch rule where there is another rule operating in the counterparty jurisdiction that is sufficient to neutralize the mismatch. The Report recommends that every jurisdiction introduce all the recommended rules so that the effect of hybrid mismatch arrangement is neutralized even if the counterparty jurisdiction does not have effective hybrid mismatch rules.

Action 5: Countering Harmful Tax Practices more Effectively, Taking into Account Transparency and Substance

Under Action item 5, the Forum on Harmful Tax Practices (FHTP) is to deliver three outputs: first, finalization of the review of member country preferential regimes; second, a strategy to expand participation to non-OECD member countries; and, third, consideration of revisions or additions to the existing framework.

The report outlines the progress made on the delivery of these outputs under Action 5. It shows progress made and identifies the next steps towards completion of this work, in particular on the first output. As regards the review of the existing preferential regimes, the emphasis has been put on (i) elaborating a methodology to define a substantial activity requirement in the context of intangible regimes and (ii) improving transparency through compulsory spontaneous exchange on rulings related to preferential regimes. Finally, it provides a progress report on the review of the regimes of OECD member and associate countries in the OECD/G20 Project on BEPS. Further work on defining "substantial activity" and developing a transparency framework, as well as the review of preferential regimes and outreach to non-OECD countries, will take place in 2015.

Action 6: Preventing the Granting of Treaty Benefits in Inappropriate Circumstances

The report under Action 6 includes proposed changes to the OECD Model Tax Convention. Section A of the report includes recommendations intended to prevent the granting of treaty benefits in inappropriate circumstances. For that purpose, a distinction is made between two types of cases:

1. Cases where a person tries to circumvent limitations provided by the treaty itself.
2. Cases where a person tries to circumvent the provisions of domestic tax law using treaty benefits.

Cases where a Person Tries to Circumvent Limitations Provided by the Treaty Itself

The recommendations for new treaty anti-abuse rules included in the report first address treaty shopping strategies through which a person who is not a resident of a Contracting State attempts to obtain benefits that a tax treaty grants to a resident of that State. Additional recommendations address other strategies aimed at satisfying different treaty requirements with a view to obtain inappropriately the benefit of certain provisions of tax treaties.

The report recommends that a three-pronged approach be used to address treaty shopping arrangements:

- First, it is recommended that treaties include, in their title and preamble, a clear statement that the Contracting States, when entering into a treaty, intend to avoid creating opportunities for non-taxation or reduced taxation through tax evasion or avoidance, including through treaty shopping arrangements (this recommendation is included in Section B of the report).
- Second, it is recommended to include in tax treaties a specific anti-abuse rule based on the limitation-on-benefits provisions included in treaties concluded by the United States and a few other countries (the "LOB rule"). Such a specific rule will address a large number of treaty shopping situations based on the legal nature, ownership in, and general activities of, residents of a Contracting State.
- Third, in order to address other forms of treaty abuse, including treaty shopping situations that would not be covered by the LOB rule described above (such as certain conduit financing arrangements), it is recommended to add to tax treaties a more general anti-abuse rule based on the principal purposes of transactions or arrangements (the principal purposes test or "PPT" rule).

The report includes additional recommendations for new specific treaty anti-abuse rules that seek to address strategies, other than treaty shopping, aimed at satisfying treaty requirements with a view to obtain inappropriately the benefit of certain provisions of tax treaties. These targeted rules, which are supplemented by the PPT rule described above, address: (1) certain dividend transfer transactions; (2) transactions that circumvent the application of the treaty rule that allows source taxation of shares of companies that derive their value primarily from immovable property; (3) situations where an entity is resident of two Contracting States; and (4) situations where the State of residence exempts the income of permanent establishments situated in third States and where shares, debt-claims, rights, or property are transferred to permanent establishments set up in countries that do not tax such income or offer preferential treatment to that income.

Cases where a Person Tries to Abuse the Provisions of Domestic Tax Law Using Treaty Benefits

The report refers to the parts of the Commentary of the OECD Model Tax Convention that already deal with this issue. It indicates that further work may be needed to take account of recommendations for the design of new domestic rules that may result from the work on various Action items, in particular Action 2 (Neutralize the effects of hybrid mismatch arrangements), Action 3 (Strengthen CFC rules), Action 4 (Limit base erosion via interest deductions and other financial payments) and Actions 8, 9, and 10 dealing with Transfer Pricing.

The report adds that the recommendation to include a PPT rule in treaties, which will incorporate the principle already included in paragraph 9.5 of the Commentary on Article 1 of the OECD Model Tax Convention, will provide a clear statement that the Contracting States intend to deny the application of the provisions of their treaties when transactions or arrangements are entered into in order to obtain the benefits of these provisions in inappropriate circumstances. The report recommends the inclusion of additional guidance in the Commentary included in the OECD Model Tax Convention in order to clarify that the incorporation of that principle into tax treaties will not affect the existing conclusions concerning the interaction between treaties and domestic anti-abuse rules.

The report also addresses two specific issues related to the interaction between treaties and specific domestic anti-abuse rules. The first issue relates to the application of tax treaties to restrict a Contracting State's right to tax its own residents. The report recommends that the principle that treaties do not restrict a State's right to tax its own residents (subject to certain exceptions) should be expressly recognized through the addition of a new treaty provision based on the so-called "saving clause" already found in US tax treaties. The second issue deals with so-called "departure" or "exit" taxes, under which liability to tax on some types of income that has accrued for the benefit of a resident (whether an individual or a legal person) is triggered in the event that the resident ceases to be a resident of that State. The report recommends changes to the Commentary included in the Model Tax Convention in order to clarify that treaties do not prevent the application of these taxes.

Section B of the report addresses the second part of Action 6, which required that work be done in order to "clarify that tax treaties are not intended to be used to generate double non-taxation." This clarification is provided through a reformulation of the title and preamble of the Model Tax Convention that will clearly state that the joint intention of the parties to a tax treaty is to eliminate double taxation without creating opportunities for tax evasion and avoidance. Given the particular concerns arising from treaty shopping arrangements, such arrangements are expressly mentioned as one example of tax avoidance that should not result from tax treaties. Under applicable rules of international public law, this clear statement of the intention of the signatories to a tax treaty will be relevant for the interpretation and application of the provisions of that treaty.

Section C of the report addresses the third part of the work mandated by Action 6, which was "to identify the tax policy considerations that, in general, countries should consider before deciding to enter into a tax treaty with another country." The policy considerations that are described in Section C should help countries explain their decisions not to enter into tax treaties with certain low- or no-tax jurisdictions; these policy considerations will also be relevant for countries that need to consider whether they should modify (or, ultimately, terminate) a treaty previously concluded in the event that a change of circumstances (such as changes to the domestic law of a treaty partner) raises BEPS concerns related to that treaty. It is recognized, however, that there are many non-tax factors that can lead to the conclusion, amendment, or termination of a tax treaty and that each country has a sovereign right to decide whether it should do so.

Action 8: Guidance on Transfer Pricing Aspects of Intangibles

The Report contains final revisions to Chapters I, II, and VI of OECD *Transfer Pricing Guidelines for Multinational Enterprises and Tax Administrations* (Guidelines). These changes to the Guidelines clarify the definition of intangibles under the Guidelines, provide guidance on identifying transactions involving intangibles, and provide supplemental guidance for determining arm's length conditions for transactions involving intangibles. These final modifications to the Guidelines also contain guidance on the transfer pricing treatment of local market features and corporate synergies. The guidance is supplemented with numerous examples illustrating the application of the principles contained in the revised text of the Guidelines.

The final guidance contained in this document represents the first installment of the transfer pricing work mandated by the BEPS Action Plan. Because the interactions between work on ownership of intangibles, hard to value intangibles, risk and recharacterization are particularly pronounced, a decision has been made not to finalize the work on some sections of this document at this time. Accordingly, bracketed and shaded portions of this document should be viewed as interim drafts of guidance, not yet fully agreed by delegates, that will be finalized in 2015 in connection with other related BEPS work. It is the intention of the countries involved in the BEPS project to complete these sections of the revised intangibles guidance during 2015 in conjunction with the BEPS work on risk, recharacterization, and hard-to-value intangibles.

Action 13: Guidance on Transfer Pricing Documentation and Country-By-Country Reporting

This report under Action 13 contains revised standards for transfer pricing documentation and a template for country-by-country reporting of income, earnings, taxes paid, and certain measures of economic activity. The revised standards require a three-tiered transfer pricing documentation structure, consisting of: a country-by-country report (CBCR), a master file, and a local file. The CBCR requires multinational enterprises (MNEs) to report annually and for each tax jurisdiction in which they do business the amount of revenue, profit before income tax, and income tax paid and accrued. It also requires MNEs to report their total employment, capital, retained earnings, and tangible assets in each tax jurisdiction. Finally, it requires MNEs to identify each entity within the group doing business in a particular tax jurisdiction and to provide an indication of the business activities each entity engages in.

The guidance on transfer pricing documentation requires MNEs to provide tax administrations high-level global information regarding their global business operations and transfer pricing policies in a "master file" that would be available to all relevant country tax administrations. It also requires that more transactional transfer pricing documentation be provided in a local file in each country, identifying relevant related party transactions, the amounts involved in those transactions, and the company's analysis of the transfer pricing determinations they have made with regard to those transactions.

Action 15: Developing a Multilateral Instrument to Modify Bilateral Tax Treaties

Drawing on the expertise of public international law and tax experts, the report explores the technical feasibility of a multilateral hard law approach and its consequences on the current tax treaty system. The report identifies the issues arising from the development of such an instrument and provides an analysis of the international tax, public international law, and political issues that arise from such an approach. It concludes that a multilateral instrument is desirable and feasible, and that negotiations for such an instrument should be convened quickly.

7.2.9 What are the Next Steps?

In order to facilitate active involvement of all stakeholders, including developing countries in the BEPS project:

- Regular briefs will be delivered through webcasts and will be accessible for free by all interested parties.
- Requests for input are published on the OECD website to inform the work at an early stage.
- Discussion drafts are published on the OECD website on the Center for Tax Policy and administration page for comments.
- Public consultations are organized to discuss the comments received.

The BEPS Project has brought together forty-four countries working on an equal footing: all OECD members and the BEPS Associates. In addition, during the first phase of the Project, more than eighty developing countries and other non-OECD/non-G20 economies have been consulted, and their input has been fed directly into the BEPS process, through four in-depth regional consultations organized in cooperation with regional tax organizations such as the African Tax Administration Forum (ATAF) and the Inter-American Center for Tax Administration (CIAT), five thematic global fora on topics such as tax treaties, transfer pricing, and value-added taxation, as well as targeted seminars at our regional tax centers in Mexico, Korea, and Turkey. This engagement has also been critical to identifying the specific challenges and priorities of low-income countries faced with BEPS issues. These priorities, and how the G20 can provide support to address them, was the subject of the two-part report prepared by the OECD under a mandate from the G20 Development Working Group mentioned earlier in this paper.

Based on the results of that report and at the request of finance ministers, the OECD is now expanding the engagement of developing countries. A number of interested countries, along with key regional tax organizations, will be directly involved in the standard-setting process, while we are institutionalizing a broader, structured dialogue.

Developing countries, drawn from a cross-section of regions and per capita income-levels, will immediately be invited to take part in the meetings where key decisions on BEPS issues are made—the Committee on Fiscal Affairs (CFA)—as well as in its technical working groups. Interaction with countries not able to participate directly will be ensured through regional networks.

Leading regional tax administrations have also been invited to participate in the CFA and all technical working groups, in line with the role the IMF, the WBG, and the UN already have. The OECD will draw on their unique expertise and benefit from their input in the standard-setting process while working with them to ensure that developing countries reap the benefits of this work. This move will ensure developing countries' views are reflected throughout the development of the technical work and standard-setting process.

The report also makes clear that developing countries often face specific policy and other conditions that impact on their abilities to address BEPS. It notes that the interests of developing countries have been addressed in some key areas of the BEPS Action Plan, including for example proposals for country-by-country reporting (Action 13) and the multilateral instrument (Action 15). Drawing on these findings, the OECD, working with other international organizations and regional tax organizations, has been mandated to develop tools to translate the BEPS Action Plan into practical support for lower capacity developing countries, to be delivered over the next two to three years.

7.3 THE OECD TAX AND DEVELOPMENT PROGRAM

The *OECD's Task Force on Tax and Development* was created in January 2010 following the Joint Meeting on Tax and Development between the Committee on Fiscal Affairs (CFA) and the Development Assistance Committee (DAC). Its members include OECD and developing countries, international and regional organizations, civil society, and business and is co-chaired by South Africa and the Netherlands. The role of the Task Force is to advise the OECD Committees in delivering a Tax and Development Program to improve the capacity for developing countries to collect taxes fairly and effectively.

The Task Force has developed a coherent program focusing on key areas of importance to developing countries. The program has four key pillars:[12]

- *Statebuilding, taxation, and aid*—which includes transparency initiatives in respect of tax incentives and taxpayer morale, taxpayer education, and guidance for donors. Work is also underway on a feasibility study on "Tax Inspectors Without Borders," a new initiative to deliver tax audit experts to developing countries on a demand-led basis.
- *Effective transfer pricing in developing countries*—a program of capacity building in specific countries and support to regional organizations in this field.

[12] See OECD (n.d. d).

- *Increased transparency in the reporting of relevant financial data by MNEs*—by identifying best practices in enabling public access to local statutory accounts and tracking ongoing transparency initiatives.
- Supporting the work of the *Global Forum on Transparency and Exchange of Information.*

What will be the impact of a tax and development program in developing countries?

- A closer relationship between state and taxpayers, including both citizens and MNEs in the tax area
- More effective aid for building strong tax systems
- Strengthened tax capacity, particularly in transfer pricing
- Improved tax transparency and increased accountability
- In the long term this will lead to tax systems which are better able to finance government expenditures in a fair and efficient manner
- Reduced cross-border tax evasion through effective exchange of information.

7.3.1 Transfer Pricing (TP) Program

In terms of strengthening tax capacity, particularly in transfer pricing, most OECD and many non-OECD countries have introduced transfer pricing rules into their tax legislation. They have done this in order to ensure that the profits reported by MNEs in their jurisdictions are computed in line with internationally accepted principles, and to counter any inappropriate or abusive transfer pricing by MNEs. In most countries that have transfer pricing rules, the benchmark adopted is the "arm's length principle."

Relatively few developing countries have fully effective transfer pricing regimes in place. Many developing countries that have legislation in place often lack the administrative, technical, and auditing capacity to conduct effective and efficient audits.

In 2011, the OECD's Task Force on Tax and Development began a program of support for developing countries seeking to implement or strengthen their transfer pricing rules (the "TP Program"). The work is being carried out in partnership with the World Bank Group and European Commission to assist developing countries build their capacity to implement effective tax regimes to address issues relating to BEPS, in particular in the area of transfer pricing.

The work helps countries put in place measures designed to protect their tax bases, but also supports efforts towards a transparent and predictable investment climate through the introduction of rules that create certainty and consistency for business. A program of intensive support in the area of transfer pricing is currently underway in five pilot countries: Colombia, Ghana, Kenya, Rwanda, and Vietnam. Other country and regional projects are in the formative stages.

A key feature of these demand-led transfer pricing programs is cooperation between the international agencies involved in their delivery. The OECD, European Commission and World Bank/IFC are working together on each of the country projects providing coherent and coordinated support. The program also works closely with other partners such as German Federal Enterprise for International Cooperation (GIZ), Economic Cooperation and Development Division of the Swiss Secretariat for Economic Affairs (SECO), United States Agency for International Development (USAID) and the Presidential Agency for Social Action and International Co-operation of Colombia. This ensures that work in this area supports wider financial governance reform and country-owned approaches to development.

This work is also closely aligned with existing country tax reform programs.[13] Additional World Bank/IFC projects also benefit, as required, from technical input by the OECD's Tax and Development Program, particularly by the development of tools, guidance, and training materials to assist countries in the practical application of their transfer pricing rules.

The TP Program has already had a significant impact:

Colombia—In Colombia, where the three-year Program worked closely with the EU, the Presidential Agency for Social Action and International Co-operation of Colombia, and World Bank Group, transfer pricing adjustments made as a result of audits of multinational enterprises have increased revenues ten-fold from US$3.3m in 2011 to over US$30m in 2014. The Colombian administration states this has been possible because of the practical advice provided by the Tax and Development Program.

In December 2012, Congress in Colombia passed revised and improved transfer pricing legislation which is aligned with international standards and in December 2013 passed a new Transfer Pricing Decree. The Tax and Development Program has provided significant input and advice to Colombia on the drafting of the new legislation and Decree.

Ghana—New transfer pricing regulations, aligned with international standards, were introduced in Ghana in September 2012. The TP Program has worked closely with Ghana from July 2011, which saw the beginning of Ghana's current initiative to build an effective transfer pricing regime. The TP Program has provided significant input and advice on the drafting of the new legislation, as well as the drafting and design of a Transfer Pricing Practice Note for the guidance of taxpayers and tax officers.

The TP Program has also assisted Ghana in the design of a Transfer Pricing Annual Return Form and in setting up a team of specialist auditors to

[13] In Ghana, for example, the transfer pricing work is closely integrated into Ghana/GIZ's Good Financial Governance program.

enable it to effectively identify and address transfer pricing risk in Ghana. It has also undertaken a comprehensive skills-building program with the newly established team of specialist auditors.

Kenya—In Kenya, where the Program is working closely with World Bank Group, the tax administration in 2012 embarked on a significant training program for its staff on advanced transfer pricing issues. This initiative followed advice from the Tax and Development Program, which is providing support in developing and delivering the training program. The capacity-building program is specifically tailored to Kenya's needs and auditors' level of knowledge.

This skills-building program has resulted in more efficient work by the Kenyan Revenue Authority (KRA) resulting in an increase in the number of audit cases completed, revenue collected, and number of cases going to dispute resolution. Revenue collection from transfer pricing audits has doubled from US$52m for year ended 30 June 2012 to US$107m for year ended 30 June 2014. More specifically, in three recent cases, the KRA successfully negotiated transfer pricing adjustments based on the advice given by the Program, which resulted in additional tax revenue of US$47.3m.

Rwanda—A full assessment of the risk of profit shifting has been carried out with the Rwandan Revenue Authority as the basis on which a new transfer pricing regime is being planned. New transfer pricing guidelines that align with international standards are expected to be implemented in 2015.

Vietnam—In Vietnam, where the Program is working closely with the EU and World Bank Group, the tax administration has significantly increased its capacity to enforce its transfer pricing rules, resulting in an increase in the number of audits conducted by the tax administration from one audit in 2012 to forty audits in 2013, giving rise to transfer pricing adjustments of US$110m by the end of 2013. Vietnam tax administration records the completion of twenty-five audits between 2013 and the first six months of 2014 that resulted in revenue collection of close to US$19m.

The Program has also provided support on organizational changes in the tax administration and policy issues relating to legislation, advance pricing arrangements, safe harbours, and thin capitalization.

7.3.2 Development of Tools and Materials

The TP Program has also developed extensive support and training materials for use by developing countries and by specialists working with developing countries on capacity-building initiatives. This has included:

- A transfer pricing "Needs Assessment" tool to assist developing countries to assess the potential risk to their tax base from transfer pricing

- A "Results Measurement" tool to assist the TP program to assess its impact in each country it is working in
- Training material on APA rules, thin capitalization rules, administrative simplification, safe harbours, secondary adjustments, and return-filing schedules
- Numerous training exercises based on practical examples.

7.3.3 Lessons Learned from the TP Program

The lessons learned through working intensively on transfer pricing in the developing country context are being fed back into the OECD's processes to ensure that a developing country perspective is consistently considered in the development of standards and guidance on transfer pricing. In this context, the TP Program has close links with the OECD's Global Forum on Transfer Pricing, and with the ongoing OECD work on BEPS.

7.3.3.1 Obtaining Relevant Information

The work done with developing countries has highlighted that one of the major challenges tax administrations in developing countries face in effectively implementing their transfer pricing regimes is obtaining all of the relevant information regarding the non-resident members of the MNE which are parties to transactions with their taxpayer. This issue has been fed back into the work that OECD Working Party 6 is currently undertaking on transfer pricing documentation and into the debates held and the work done on country-by-country reporting by the Task Force. This has helped to raise awareness of the importance of increasing transparency in financial reporting by MNEs for tax compliance, particularly for developing countries.

This work fed into the G8 Lough Erne Summit in June 2013 which called on the OECD to develop a common template for country-by-country reporting to tax authorities by MNEs.[14] The objective is to improve the flow of information between MNEs and tax authorities in the countries in which the MNEs operate, enhancing transparency and improving risk assessment. The OECD has responded to that request by taking this work forward through the BEPS Action Plan (Action 13) which will develop rules regarding transfer pricing documentation to enhance transparency for tax administrations, taking into consideration the compliance costs for business. The rules to be developed may include a requirement that MNEs provide all relevant governments with

[14] See G8 (2013).

the required information on their global allocation of income, economic activity, and taxes paid among countries.

Another area of concern expressed by developing countries is the availability and quality of financial data on transactions between unrelated parties that can be used for comparability purposes, which is critical to implementing an effective transfer pricing regime. In response to those concerns the OECD is now exploring, in cooperation with other stakeholders, approaches it might adopt to respond to those concerns.

7.3.3.2 Other Pricing Methodologies

In an attempt to prevent base erosion through reduced sales prices for mineral and commodity products in related party transactions, a number of resource rich countries, in particular in Latin America, have developed what is sometimes referred to as a "sixth method." Certain African countries have now either adopted similar measures or are considering their adoption.

The sixth method requires pricing of commodity transactions in accordance with publicly available data from commodity exchanges as of the date of shipment under certain circumstances. This has the effect of preventing the shifting of commodity product-related income to low-substance trading companies, and the practice of shifting income ostensibly attributable to forward price discounts to such companies. Depending on the country, a variety of exceptions and let-out clauses exist which are intended to have the effect of limiting the method to cases that are deemed potentially abusive. Consideration is currently being given to this issue under the BEPS project.

7.3.3.3 Industry Knowledge

A critical skills gap in building capacity to address transfer pricing risks for many tax administrations is a lack of knowledge of the key industries in the country, in particular, understanding the global value chain and where the resident taxpayer fits into that value chain. The TP Program has received support from certain businesses which have provided industry experts to facilitate training for tax administrations on the global value chains of certain key business sectors in their country. For example Rio Tinto provided a mining expert for a skills-building workshop for the Colombian tax administration's (DIAN) transfer pricing auditor in Bogota on the global value chain in the gold and coal mining industries.

7.3.3.4 Cooperation between Organizations

In October 2012, the TP Program conducted a "Train the Trainers" event at the Vienna Multilateral Tax Center. The event formed the centerpiece of an initiative designed to provide relevant specialists from developing countries with skills and materials to conduct internal and regional training on transfer pricing. Since 2013 the specialists have delivered basic transfer pricing training in their own country/region. This work demonstrates the significant capacity in some developing countries to deliver South-South assistance.

The TP Program has also identified that developing countries often find that the work the tax administrations undertake on transfer pricing issues is closely related to the issues that arise in terms of import duties on goods brought into the country by the MNE. The issue of the interaction of Customs Valuation rules and transfer pricing is therefore an issue of particular importance to developing countries. In response to this the OECD has commenced a collaborative project between the OECD and World Customs Organization (WCO) on the issue of the interaction of customs valuation rules and transfer pricing.

7.4 ADDRESSING THE GOVERNANCE AND MANAGEMENT OF TAX INCENTIVES

The Task Force has produced *Principles to Enhance the Transparency and Governance of Tax Incentives for Investment in Developing Countries.*[15] Consequently, several developing countries have requested OECD support to analyze their tax incentives based on these principles. At the request of developing countries, reviews of tax incentives for investment have been undertaken, applying these principles as a standard diagnostic framework. Key findings of the country reviews include:

- *Ghana.* The analysis revealed an alarming level of revenue loss attributable to special tax provisions and exemptions—6.13 percent of GDP in 2011. This sent shock waves through the government and is triggering a political debate about the rationalization of the tax incentives regime. GIZ and the World Bank are considering follow-up support.
- *Tunisia.* OECD analysis fed directly into recommendations in the new Investment Incentive Code, supporting the efforts of the post-revolution Tunisian government in designing a more effective and transparent framework for tax incentives for investment.
- *Zambia.* The review examined the current level of transparency in the tax incentives regime, which fed a new reform process aimed at streamlining tax incentives and making the tax system more equitable. For example,

[15] See OECD (n.d. e).

tax incentives in the mining sector have been curtailed and those offered to Special Economic Zones and industrial parks have been rationalized. GIZ is following-up.

- *Myanmar.* The Tax and Development Program conducted a Tax Policy review of Myanmar under the Policy Framework for Investment (PFI). The key recommendations concerning streamlining tax incentives for investment and simplifying tax rates have reinforced the ongoing efforts of the International Monetary Fund (IMF) and the Asian Development Bank (ADB) in the implementation of a comprehensive tax reform.
- *Costa Rica.* The Tax and Development Program conducted a review of Costa Rica's investment incentives system under the PFI. The review concluded that a highly targeted, transparent, and well-managed tax incentives regime has been essential in attracting technology-intensive investors.

In 2013, the Tax and Development Program revised the Tax Chapter (Chapter 5) of the OECD's Policy Framework for Investment[16]—a key element of the OECD's Development Strategy.[17]

The *Principles to Enhance the Transparency and Governance of Tax Incentives for Investment in Developing Countries* have become an international "good practice" reference point and an essential tool for undertaking reviews in developing countries.

The Tax and Development Program completed further country reviews in 2014, on a demand-led basis to address the needs of developing countries in improving the governance of tax incentives. In conducting these reviews, close cooperation will have been fostered with other agencies at the country level (including the World Bank, GIZ, IMF, and USAID).

The Program supported regional/global engagements on tax incentives and provided specific and practical tax incentives policy guidance for the Southern African Development Community (SADC), building on the experience of the member countries while integrating the latest methodologies and research in the tax incentives area. In close cooperation with the World Bank and IFC, it supported the Myanmar's Chairmanship of ASEAN in harmonization of tax incentives regimes across ASEAN and safeguarding tax bases of the member countries.

A knowledge-sharing event was organized on tax incentives in 2014 to gather and share the latest thinking and research, integrating findings from the country case studies. The event served as a multi-lateral forum for exchange of experience among countries and institutions active in this area.

[16] See OECD (2006). [17] See OECD (2012b).

The Tax and Development Program has also identified that resource-rich developing countries face challenges to ensure they reap the developmental benefits from the exploitation of their natural resource endowments and promote more inclusive growth. Within the framework of the OECD Development Strategy adopted at ministerial level in May 2012, the OECD Development Center is leading efforts for establishing a multi-year structured Policy Dialogue on Natural Resource-based Development among OECD and partner producing countries to identify and address common challenges in this area.

7.5 TAX INSPECTORS WITHOUT BORDERS (TIWB)

The Tax and Development Program is also leading an initiative to expand the reach of practical assistance to tax administrations in developing countries, focusing on tax audit activities. The Tax Inspectors Without Borders (TIWB) initiative[18] aims to improve tax audit skills in practice, by facilitating the deployment of experts to work on real audit cases. Under TIWB, experts, who are either currently serving or recently retired tax audit officials, will be deployed to apply a "learning-by-doing" approach. Experts work alongside local tax officials to progress current audits, expanding the range and depth of audit techniques and skills as they do so. TIWB focuses on international tax issues, but also general audit skills—for example, cases involving transfer pricing, thin capitalization, exchange of information, or advancing pricing agreements, as well as pre-audit risk assessment, case selection, and audit investigatory techniques.

Deployments are flexible depending on need as well as expert availability and funding; they can be for as little as one-week duration or up to six months or more. The assistance is also flexible in how it is provided. For example, in some cases the expert will reside full-time in the country, in others, they will be periodic deployments, for example where the expert is in-country for a period of ten weeks over a minimum of three visits in a six-month period. For such periodic deployments, when the expert is not in-country, often they will be available to provide assistance over the phone or by email to the local officials, subject to confidentiality requirements.

By focusing on peer-to-peer assistance on real audit cases, TIWB targets a niche area of demand, helping officials shift from a theoretical understanding of international tax issues, to applying that understanding on a daily basis in their audit work. Housed within the OECD, TIWB can also draw on its network of tax administrations and development agencies, to put in place a

[18] See OECD (n.d. f).

database of experts and make links to funding to support deployments under the initiative. By helping developing countries to acquire appropriate expertise and overcome the potential conflict of interest and tax confidentiality issues which can arise, TIWB aims to make this type of practical assistance more broadly accessible. The first review of the TIWB initiative took place at the end of its first eighteen-month mandate, in December 2014.

7.6 CONCLUSION

The very low effective tax rates that multinationals can achieve through international tax planning continue to raise serious concerns. Leaders, civil society, and everyday taxpayers have renewed demands for changes to the international tax rules to restore the fairness and integrity of their tax systems. The above initiatives support governments' efforts to ensure the integrity of tax systems, restore trust in their tax systems by setting the standards, and providing the instruments to combat tax evasion. The OECD's work on Base Erosion and Profit Shifting (BEPS) aims to bring the international tax rules into the twenty-first century. It will provide a level playing field for both companies and countries. The additional revenues collected will give governments greater flexibility in supporting economic recovery. The OECD Tax and Development Program will complement that work by assisting developing countries to build their capacity to address issues relating to BEPS.

REFERENCES

African Economic Outlook, n.d. "Tax base issues." http://www.africaneconomicoutlook.org/en/theme/public-resource-mobilisation-and-aid/challenges-for-african-policy-makers/tax-base-issues/, accessed 7 August 2015.

G8, 2013. Communiqué, G8 Leaders, Lough Erne, June 2013. https://www.gov.uk/government/uploads/system/uploads/attachment_data/file/207771/Lough_Erne_2013_G8_Leaders_Communique.pdf, accessed 7 August 2015.

G20, 2013. Communiqué, Meeting of Finance Ministers and Central Bank Governors, Moscow, 15–16 February 2013. https://g20.org/wp-content/uploads/2014/12/Final_Communique_of_FM_and_CBG_Meeting_Moscow.pdf, accessed 7 August 2015.

G20, 2014. Communiqué, Meeting of G20 Finance Ministers and Central Bank Governors, Cairns, 20–21 September 2014. http://www.bloomberg.com/news/2014-09-21/g-20-communique-following-sept-20-21-meetings-in-cairns-text-.html, accessed 7 August 2015.

League of Nations, 1928. *Double Taxation and Tax Evasion*, II. Economic and Financial 1928.II.49.

OECD, 2006. *Policy Framework for Investment.* http://www.oecd.org/investment/pfi.htm, accessed 7 August 2015.

OECD, 2010. *Transfer Pricing Guidelines for Multinational Enterprises and Tax Administrations.* OECD Publishing.

OECD, 2012a. *Model Tax Convention on Income and on Capital 2010* (updated 2010). OECD Publishing. http://www.oecd-ilibrary.org/taxation/model-tax-convention-on-income-and-on-capital-2010_9789264175181-en, accessed 5 September 2015.

OECD, 2012b. *OECD Week 2012: OECD Strategy on Development.* http://www.oecd.org/belgium/50452316.pdf, accessed 7 August 2015.

OECD, 2013a. *Addressing Base Erosion and Profit Shifting.* OECD Publishing.

OECD, 2013b. *Action Plan on Base Erosion and Profit Shifting.* OECD Publishing.

OECD, 2014a. *Discussion Draft on Transfer Pricing Documentation and CbC Reporting.* OECD Publishing.

OECD, 2014b. *Part 1 of a Report To G20 Development Working Group on the Impact of BEPS in Low Income Countries.* July. OECD Publishing.

OECD, 2014c. *Part 2 of a Report To G20 Development Working Group on the Impact of BEPS in Low Income Countries.* August. OECD Publishing.

OECD, n.d. a. "First Meeting of the OECD Global Forum on VAT." http://www.oecd.org/tax/consumption/first-meeting-vat-global-forum.htm, accessed 7 August 2015.

OECD, n.d. b. "Global Forum on Transparency and Exchange of Information for Tax Purposes." http://www.oecd.org/tax/transparency/, accessed 7 August 2015.

OECD, n.d. c. "Global Relations in Taxation: Setting the Tax Agenda." http://www.oecd.org/ctp/tax-global/settingthetaxagenda.htm, accessed 7 August 2015.

OECD, n.d. d. "Global Relations in Taxation: Tax and Development." http://www.oecd.org/tax/tax-global/taxanddevelopment.htm, accessed 7 August 2015.

OECD, n.d. e. "Principles to Enhance the Transparency and Governance of Tax Incentives for Investment in Developing Countries." http://www.oecd.org/ctp/tax-global/transparency-and-governance-principles.pdf, accessed 7 August 2015.

OECD, n.d. f. "Tax Inspectors without Borders." http://www.oecd.org/tax/taxinspectors.htm, accessed 7 August 2015.

UNCTAD, 2009. *World Investment Report.* http://unctad.org/en/Docs/wir2009_en.pdf, accessed 7 August 2015.

8

More Than Just Another Tax

The Thrilling Battle over the Financial Transaction Tax: Background, Progress, and Challenges

Peter Wahl

8.1 THE THRILLING AND INSTRUCTIVE HISTORY OF THE FTT

In February 2013, eleven EU Member States—among them the four largest economies of the continent, Germany, France, Italy, and Spain—started formal negotiations over establishing a *Financial Transaction Tax* (*FTT*). Civil society had been campaigning for such a tax since the 1990s. With the EU decision, one of the rare success stories regarding civil society campaigns over tax issues could be achieved. Although the tax is not yet implemented, and although the watering down of some details cannot be ruled out, it is very unlikely that the project as such will be stopped completely. The commitment of the eleven governments has gone so far that a "point of no return" has probably been reached.

It is one of the largest successes of neoliberal ideology that taxes are defined as a "negative externality" to the markets, and particularly to financial markets. This means that taxes are generally discredited in public opinion and considered to be an evil per se. But a civilized society cannot exist without an appropriate tax system. Taxes are an essential and indispensable pillar of modern statehood. If they are well designed and democratically legitimized, and if the distribution of the burden is just and fair, taxes promote social well-being, public common goods, and sustainable development. With their double capacity to generate revenues and to regulate economic and social processes, they can be a tool for social emancipation. Under the right conditions, taxes are good.

The history of the FTT demonstrates that success is possible regarding tax issues on progressive grounds. But it also shows the difficulties and political risks. It confirms that tax issues are more than just one parameter in the economy and society. They can have tremendous impact on more general issues. It should be recalled here that American independence was triggered by a tax issue: the Boston Tea Party, protesting a tax imposed by England. The tax issue was also a very important motive for the French Revolution, as the aristocracy and the clergy were exempt from taxation in the *Ancien Régime*. It is therefore not surprising that two articles of the famous *General Declaration of Human and Civic Rights* from August 1789 deal with taxation. One establishes the principle of "No taxation without representation" (Article 14) and the other stipulates the principle of tax justice, as taxes "must be distributed evenly among all citizens considering their property situation" (Article 13).

Today there are no revolutions over taxes, but elections are lost or won over taxation. The issue is highly controversial and stirs up violent passions in the struggle between different social interests.

Over the past decades, the triumph of neoliberalism, liberalization, deregulation and globalization of capital flows has lead to a strong trend towards re-feudalization of the tax system. As in the *Ancien Régime*, the relative share of taxes paid by rich and economically strong actors is continuously shrinking, while the tax burden for the middle class and the poor has increased through a variety of mechanisms—from legal tax evasion through the privileging of big business, finance capital, and rich individuals to the shift from direct to indirect taxation. The financial sector benefits most from this trend and is totally undertaxed.

However, more and more people recognize that these developments have to be reversed. The history of the FTT is an impressive illustration of this and can be regarded as a model case—from which other tax projects, which might not yet have reached the stage of a draft law, can draw lessons. A general pattern is visible under the surface of the history of the FTT.

8.1.1 A Long History

The EU project has a long history, which can be divided into two main periods: the pre-crisis period from 1998 to 2008, and the post crisis-phase from 2008 onwards.

The initial impulse to go for a financial transaction tax did not come from civil society but from UNDP circles. Behind the background of shrinking resources for development after the end of the Cold War, UNDP published a book on innovative financing for development in 1996 in which they presented, among others, the Tobin Tax (Haq, Kaul, and Grunberg, 1996).

The tax was proposed by Nobel Prize-winner James Tobin when the Bretton Woods System perished (Tobin, 1974). Tobin realized that the end of fixed exchange rates would lead to an increase of transactions, more volatility, and the risk of speculative bubbles. From there, his idea (which had already been suggested by Keynes in the 1930s) was to throw "sand in the wheels" in order to calm down currency transactions. Tobin's focus was on the regulatory dimension of taxation, his interest was to preserve financial stability. But as taxes normally generate revenues, he suggested using tax income for development purposes.

The UNDP proposal met harsh resistance from the beginning, in particular from the United States. The UNDP was threatened with financial sanctions if the book was published under its own name. Therefore, the authors released it on their personal behalf.

From the UNDP, the idea of the Tobin Tax spread to some development NGOs. But there was a certain reluctance to deal with it in depth, as development NGOs were not very familiar with taxation and financial markets. However, the Asian financial crisis of 1997–8 gave new impulse to the issue, and the regulatory dimension of the tax drew the attention of those NGOs interested in macroeconomic issues.

A breakthrough came in December 1998 when the French monthly *Le Monde Diplomatique* launched an appeal to "disarm the markets." It suggested the establishment of an organization that would carry the idea of taxing financial transactions. Attac was first established in France and then in other countries. Attac already carries the tax idea in its name: Association pour la taxation de transactions financières et pour l'action citoyenne (Association for the Taxation of Financial Transactions and for Citizens' Actions).

From this moment on, the idea of taxing financial transactions became a kind of spearhead of civil society internationally and also received some media attention. During this period, European political parties of the left, Social Democrats, and the Greens took up the tax issue in their programs. Many trade unions also joined the cause, and not only in Europe.

For instance, the AFL-CIO became a supporter of the tax as well. Even leading politicians such as the French President Chirac and the German Chancellor Schröder showed some sympathy for the idea, though without taking concrete steps towards its implementation.

Here and there, civil society scored some elements of partial progress. For instance, the Belgian parliament adopted a law for a currency transaction tax in 2004—with the clause, however, that it would only enter into effect if other European countries followed suit. Several parliaments, including those in France, Finland, and Canada, also adopted resolutions in favor of the tax. But these declarations were not legally binding and had no practical effect.

All in all, there was a loss of momentum after the initial push. The issue was confined very much to the development community. Some malicious commentators compared the tax with the Loch Ness Monster: from time to time, it arises but leaves no trace behind.

8.1.2 Financial Crash 2008—A Game Changer

The financial crisis, which broke out in 2008, changed the entire game. Under the vivid impression of the crash, some of the elites began to understand that something had gone wrong. The final declarations of the G20 summits in London (April 2009) and Pittsburgh (September 2009) were relatively (self-) critical. The Pittsburgh Leaders' Statement (2009), among others, mandated the IMF to prepare proposals "as to how the financial sector could make a fair and substantial contribution toward paying for any burdens associated with government interventions to repair the banking system."

Civil society immediately seized the window of opportunity and mobilized. When the IMF report was released one year later, the feasibility of the FTT was acknowledged, although priority was given to another instrument, the Financial Activities Tax (FAT) (IMF, 2010).

Given the harsh refusal on the part of the United States for any financial transaction tax, it would have been surprising if the IMF would have had the courage to propose it as its first choice.

Encouraged by the debate, European civil society organized itself, revitalized and expanded the old network, mainly composed of development NGOs. New members joined, including the British TUC, the German DGB and the European Trade Union Congress (ETUC) as well as major NGOs such as Oxfam. New networks also emerged at the national level in some countries, such as the Robin Hood Campaign in the United Kingdom, the German campaign Tax Against Poverty and ZeroZeroCinque in Italy, with a considerably broad membership. A strong campaign with widespread media attention started after the Pittsburgh summit. The campaign also switched from the currency transaction tax to the broader concept of the FTT.

Another key event occurred in Germany during the federal election campaign in September 2009. The Social Democratic Party (the same party whose former finance minister had rejected the tax during eight years in government) put the FTT on the agenda. Some days later, Chancellor Merkel declared that it would be a good idea for her to take over the idea. Although her decision might have been very much based on tactical motives, it was decisive factor for further progress that a big EU country whose government had previously been against the FTT now made a U-turn and even became a forerunner in the project. France also joined the proposal.

The governments of both countries first tried to convince the G20 to participate in the project. But at the Toronto G20 summit in 2010, it became clear that the G20 would not be able to agree on a FTT. As a result, Germany and France took the lead in proposing in the spring of 2011 that the FTT should be implemented in the EU (since global implementation did not seem possible). The European Commission, which had spoken out against the tax several times in the past decade, was charged with working out a proposal.

This move is of significance far beyond the FTT as such: it breaks with the argument that in times of globalization, financial regulation is only possible globally. Given the heterogeneity of vested interests and the competition between nation states, it is practically impossible to reach consensus on financial regulation at a global level. But in the past, this problem had always been used as a pretext for doing nothing.

8.1.3 The EU Roller Coaster

A public consultation process was launched by the European Commission, to which not only the finance industry, but also civil society could make proposals. The occasion was widely used and more than one hundred statements were submitted from civil society.

In the meantime, opinion polls also showed that large majorities in most EU countries were in favor of the FTT. In an official opinion poll conducted by the Commission in the spring of 2011 (Directorate General for Communication, 2011), 61 percent of Europeans supported a tax on financial transactions, while 26 percent were opposed to it and 13 percent expressed no opinion. Among the Member States, Austria was on top, with 80 percent in favor. Supporters numbered 71 percent in Germany, 68 percent in France, 65 percent in the United Kingdom and 61 percent in Italy. Only six countries out of twenty-seven had supporters below the 50 percent threshold. Five of them were in Eastern Europe, among them Poland, and the Baltics. The sixth was Malta.

At the same time, the European Parliament voted on a motion in favor of the FTT. Although this vote is not legally binding, it has a certain political/psychological effect. Also over the following years, the European Parliament supported the process with several motions.

8.1.3.1 A Surprisingly Progressive Draft Law

In September 2011, the Commission presented a draft directive (law), which, to the surprise of civil society,[1] was rather close to the ideas of the proponents of the FTT. Its main elements are:

- a broad tax base including all classes of financial assets—shares, bonds, and all types of derivatives

[1] Only some months before, the Commission had still rejected the tax.

- normal payments and credit business do not fall under the FTT as well as central bank operations, public debt management, and issuing shares and bonds. Currency spot transactions (but not currency derivatives) are also exempted.[2] Nevertheless, the tax basis of the proposal is still broader than in any other existing transaction tax.[3] This is not only relevant with regard to the revenues, but also closes many loopholes for tax evasion. The inclusion of derivatives is especially a breakthrough in this sense
- a relatively high 0.1 percent tax rate for shares and bonds, and a 0.01 percent tax rate for derivatives. Even the civil society proposal of recent years had proposed a tax rate of 0.05 percent, half the rate of the EU proposal. On the other hand, civil society would have preferred a single tax rate that included derivatives
- in return, the underlying of the derivative would be taxed and not the price of the derivative itself. This means, for instance, that for a future which an air company buys to hedge against an increase in kerosene prices, it is the amount of the kerosene that is taxed, and not the price of the derivative, which would only be between 3 percent and 5 percent of the kerosene price
- the buyer and seller would each have to pay the full tax rate. In the event that one of the parties is located outside the territorial scope of the tax, the party within the scope would have to assume the share of its counterpart
- every single transaction is taxed and not the remaining amount after netting-off. This is very relevant for *high frequency trading*, for instance. This business model consists of computer-based automatic transactions, which can take place within nanoseconds, with several thousand transactions per day. The draft directive mentions *expressis verbis* high frequency trading as a target of the tax
- revenues are calculated at 55 billion euros per year, if the EU-27 participates in the project. The Commission's estimate is conservative and there are several studies from both proponents and adversaries of the tax indicating that the potential would be considerably higher
- revenues would go to each national treasury according to the country's share in the overall transactions

[2] The Commission says there would be legal constraints in taxing them, because this would be considered a violation of the principle of the free flow of capital. There are dissident views by legal experts.

[3] There are some 40 countries, most of them in Asia and Latin America, which have taxes on financial transactions. But in all cases, the tax base is small and encompasses only one type of asset (in most cases shares) and with many restrictions, for instance that the tax is only levied from a certain threshold of turnover onwards. In the EU, the UK has the "Stamp Duty," which taxes the purchase of shares of UK corporations.

- as for the tax *incidence*, financial institutions which effectuate the transaction will be liable to pay the tax to the tax authorities, both for their proprietary trade and for trade on behalf of clients. In the latter case, the costs will of course be shifted to the clients.

Looking at who will be most greatly affected by the tax, institutional investors will have to pay the bulk of the FTT. High frequency trade will be hit heavily and might be reduced considerably; the same is true for REPOS (Sale and Repurchase Agreement).[4] Second, individuals involved in speculative activities will be affected as profits shrink. This means that ordinary people are normally not affected. One exception might be pensioners who have invested in private pension funds with aggressive investment strategies. Pension funds with conservative strategies—which should be expected for this type of business—will hardly be hit. If, however, small pensioners were affected, tax experts suggest compensating them through the existing income tax regulations rather than making an exemption for the FTT.

The draft underlines that one aim of the FTT is to make the financial sector contribute to the costs of the crisis. But the regulatory dimension of the FTT is also stressed, particularly with regard to high frequency trade. In the controversy over the tax in the media, there were several statements from EU officials declaring that the purpose of the project was only to raise revenues. Apparently, this was a political reaction to the pressure from the finance industry. As a matter of fact, the tax would have an impact on the behavior of market participants. The draft directive is therefore well balanced between its regulatory and revenue-generating effects.

8.1.3.2 Massive Resistance by the Financial Industry

The financial industry was at least as surprised by the draft as civil society, and immediately started to lobby against the proposal. During the first half of 2012, it became clear that there would be no consensus in the EU-27. In particular, the UK, Sweden, Luxemburg, the Netherlands, Ireland, and the Czech Republic were strongly opposed to the draft. As unanimity is required, it looked for a while as if the whole project would fail.

But then, in the spring of 2012, a new option was envisaged; one that was strongly supported by civil society: the FTT could be implemented via the Enhanced Cooperation Procedure (ECP). This is a procedure that is established in EU regulations. It allows a group of at least nine countries (which must simultaneously represent at least 60 percent of the EU population) to implement a project, even if not all 27 countries participate—a kind of

[4] REPOS are loans between banks, in most cases short term (overnight). Many of them serve speculative purposes.

coalition of the willing. The ECP was meant to prevent blockades on decision-making by a minority of countries. It has only been used twice in the history of the EU, because it is a complicated procedure with many restrictions. The first case in which it was used dealt with patent rights. Negotiations took ten years. For the second case, which was on family law, negotiations took five years. Nevertheless France and Germany were ready to use this procedure for an issue that is politically far hotter than patents and family legislation.

8.1.3.3 Further Improvement

For legal reasons, the Commission had to present a new draft for the ECP negotiations, but the new text is in substance the same as the first draft and contains all the elements described in Chapter 1.5.1. Of course, the revenues in eleven countries will be lower. Still, the Commission estimates that revenues will amount to 32 billion euros per year. On the other hand, there is an astonishing improvement of the provisions against tax evasion. In addition to the *residence principle*,[5] which could already be found in the draft for the EU-27, a second component introduced is the *issuer principle*. The residence principle means that each bank or fund whose legal base is in one of the eleven countries is liable for taxation, even if they trade outside the group of eleven. If, for instance, Deutsche Bank trades in London, the tax also has to be paid even though the United Kingdom is not a member.

Complementary to that, the issuer principle would now also take effect. This means that any share, bond, or derivative issued in one of the eleven countries is taxed, wherever and by whomever it is traded. Hence, Goldman Sachs would have to pay the tax if they sell a financial product that has been issued in one of the eleven participating countries, for instance, to a Hong Kong-based fund, and vice versa. Even if a share of Fiat, Volkswagen, or Renault is traded on the moon, it will be taxed. This is an important step forward to contain tax evasion under conditions of liberalized global financial markets, where capital can be transferred across national borders with a mouse click.

The idea as such is not new. Interestingly, the British Stamp Duty is based on the same principle, taxing the purchase of a share of UK corporations, wherever it takes place. If the tax is not paid, the transaction loses its legal protection ("stamp") from British authorities. The issuer principle might serve as an example for other areas of tax policies. It shows that where there is a political will, there is a way to raise taxes under conditions of globalized financial markets.

[5] Each bank or fund whose legal base is in one of the eleven countries is liable for taxation.

Technically, the tax could be levied electronically through the settlement systems. The financial industry has set up very safe electronic platforms for settlement, such as the Continuous Link Settlement Bank (CLS) or TARGET. As for OTC-derivatives,[6] both the new rules for finance in the United States (Dodd-Frank Act) and in the EU (MIFID—Markets in Financial Instruments Directive) establish central clearinghouses and trade registers, which allow for control through the central banks and supervisors. An additional electronic tag on each transaction would be enough to levy the tax. Thus, almost no administrative costs would occur.

The provisions against tax evasion are one aspect of the draft, which go far beyond a simple tax. The combination of residence principle and issuer principle tackles an arch-evil of globalization: the capability of capital to move via mouse click to any corner of the planet within seconds, giving nation states no possibility to control and tax it. This asymmetry is one of the main reasons that the finance sector has so much power today.

8.1.4 The Risk of Watering Down the Project

The negotiation process among the eleven countries started on 13 February 2013, with continued resistance, both from some governments and the industry. Although non-participating Member States cannot vote under the ECP, they have the right to take part in the meetings and to speak. Opponents used the negotiations to play for time and to block the project as much as possible. According to insiders' reports, Ireland abused its Presidency during the first half of 2013 to slow down negotiations.[7] The United Kingdom even filed a complaint at the European Court of Justice.

Parallel to the obstruction in the negotiations by some Member States, an unprecedented finance industry campaign started up, flooding the media with studies and statements that conjure the ruin of the entire sector. Of course, their arguments are very altruist; they present themselves as noble defenders—not of their profits, but of small investors, small savers, older pensioners, public bonds, and jobs. If one were to believe these studies, the regulatory effect of the FTT would go far beyond what its proponents had hoped for in their boldest dreams. For instance, according to a paper by Goldman Sachs (2013) it would destroy the European repo markets[8] and reduce the profits of the forty biggest European banks by 92 percent. One hedge fund manager even

[6] OTC = Over the Counter. These are transactions that are made bilaterally between financial actors without using a public stock exchange or other trading place.

[7] The EU Presidency rotates every six months.

[8] Sale and Repurchase Agreement. Credits among banks with a highly speculative component.

declared that the FTT had been motivated in its actions by the Sharia (Ungar, 2013).

In September 2013, the legal service of the EU Council presented a paper in which an element of the *residence principle* was declared to be incompatible with international law (Council of the European Union, 2013). The expertise was leaked to the *Financial Times* and some media tried to make believe that the entire project would hence be illegal. However, the expertise only referred to the counterparty issue of the residence principle. As described in section 8.3.1, both seller and buyer have to pay the tax. If one counter-party comes from outside of the countries participating in the FTT, the one from inside would have to pay the share for both. According to the legal service of the Council this would not comply with international law, as it would imply an extraterritorial impact of the tax. In the meantime, the legal service of the Commission has released a counter-expertise, according to which its proposal would comply with international law.[9]

Although the European Commission had publicly rejected that parts of its proposal would not comply with international law, many media channels reported that the FTT was dead. It is obvious that the whole process is being accompanied by a kind of psychological warfare, with disinformation and all the other tricks that spin doctors in PR departments are capable of.

These activities have not been without effect. After the release of the Goldman Sachs paper, the French finance ministry immediately started arguing for an exemption of repos. Only after this was made public by civil society in the media (Plihon and Wahl, 2013) and after pressure from MPs of the Socialist Party did the finance minister release a disclaimer, saying that France would stick to its initial commitment. France also wants to exempt certain categories of derivatives, while Berlin insists on taxing all derivatives. Other governments inside the coalition of the willing are also considering exemptions, such as Belgium for pension funds and Italy for government bonds.

The position pro-FTT was fostered in the German coalition agreement between the Christian Democrats and the Social Democrats for their common government program. In December 2013 they agreed that they "want to implement speedily a financial transaction tax with a broad tax base and a low tax rate in the framework of Enhanced Cooperation in the EU. Such a tax should include all financial instruments, shares, bonds, currency transactions as well as derivatives" (Koalitionsvertrag zwischen CDU, CSU, und SPD, 2013: 64). By including currency transactions the agreement goes even further than the Commission's proposal. Obviously, neither the campaign of the finance

[9] Oral information from German vice minister of finance, Hartmut Koschyk, at the annual meeting of the German FTT campaign, 5 November 2013. The text of the Commission's legal service was not public when finishing this manuscript.

lobby against the FTT nor the legal service of the Council could impress the new government coalition in Berlin.

At the French–German summit in February 2014, both President Hollande and Chancellor Merkel confirmed their commitment to the FTT. Nevertheless negotiations still proved to be difficult both on a technical and on a political level. In particular France preferred a smaller tax basis, excluding derivatives, while Germany insisted on the inclusion of derivatives. Finally a compromise was found: derivatives would be included, but possibly at a lower tax rate than initially proposed.

When this manuscript was finished (March 2014) the FTT was not yet implemented. But there is little probability that the entire project would fail. There will be a tax, but the question is what the details will look like in the end, and hence how efficient it will be in practice, what regulatory impact will be achieved, and how much revenue will be raised. The roller coaster in the EU demonstrates that there will be a fight until the last minute. For civil society, this means that pressure has to be applied until the very final point, which of course leads to some major challenges (see section 8.2 below).

All in all, the thrilling history of the FTT confirms what was said at the very beginning of this text: tax issues represent more than just one parameter in the economy and society.

8.2 CONDITIONS FOR SUCCESS, CHALLENGES, AND OBSTACLES

Looking into the factors responsible for the success up to now, one finds a bundle of determinants, which together enabled a breakthrough.

The first decisive factor was the fact that, as a result of the financial crash, portions of the elites in the industrialized countries were open to reforms. The G20 decision on how the finance sector could contribute to the burden of the crisis, the determination of the German government, and the readiness of France to join changed the balance of power qualitatively. But without the continuity of the grassroots work in previous years, which both prepared the ground and made the FTT popular, these governments would probably not have gone so far.

For civil society commitment it was very important that the FTT was on the way to success. Success delivers encouragement and becomes a source of motivation and attracts people beyond the hard core of activists.

Furthermore the FTT encountered a certain mood or zeitgeist of the period before the crash. One could say, "There was something in the air" and the FTT gave voice to the diffuse feelings of dissatisfaction, which had accumulated over years among many people. It became the flagship demand of the new Global Justice Movement.[10]

Finally, the self-organization of civil society around the FTT worked quite well. From the beginning, the campaign had tried to build broad alliances, including development, environment and social NGOs, trade unions, faith groups, cultural groupings, social movements, and so on. After the crash, the alliances became considerably broader.

In spite of an overall positive balance for the proponents of the FTT, there have also been challenges and risks throughout the process.

The first and most dangerous challenge is the pressure of the financial industry on political decision-makers, who could water down the Commission's proposal. The effect of a mutilated concept would be major, with disappointing revenues and negative side effects. The whole idea would be discredited for a long time and attempts in other countries and regions would be discouraged or discredited.

The lesson is that such a tax project is a long-distance race, where things can change, even in the last few meters. Civil society must monitor the entire process until its very end, with all its legal and technical complexity and its many pitfalls and loopholes, and it must be able to exercise pressure until the very end. This is especially true regarding the EU, with its extremely complicated multi-level governance system and the heterogeneity of interests with so many actors involved.

For civil society, this is a very difficult arena. Their strength lies in mobilizing the support of ordinary citizens on the basis of a clear-cut political and ethical orientation. When it comes to technical and legal details, it is very difficult to keep up the necessary level of attention and mobilization. Even if their headquarters accommodate people who are able to cope with the technocratic discourse, one of their main arms, public pressure from below, is difficult to deploy.

Last but not least, there is a long-lasting contradiction inside the FTT movement, deriving from the double function of the tax: to generate revenues and to regulate markets. One category of civil society actors has concentrated on the revenue side. Most of them are development and environmental NGOs. The regulatory dimension of the tax is not so much a part of their focus. In most cases, they have neither the expertise for this, nor the mandate. Other participants in the campaign are more interested in the regulation of financial markets.

[10] In the mainstream discourse, the movement was called anti-globalist. But most of the activists and organizations did not consider themselves as "anti." Therefore, in French the concept of "altermondialiste" is used and in German-speaking countries "globalisierungskritisch" (critical of globalization) is used.

With the EU crisis in the background, there are now many more actors hoping to gain revenues for purposes such as fiscal consolidation. German Chancellor Merkel has already indicated that a part of the revenues could also be used to combat youth unemployment in the crisis countries of the EU. Of course, using the tax revenues in this way would have some legitimacy and broad public support. But on the other hand, it creates a dilemma for the FTT campaign. It would be very disappointing for many supporters of the tax if the FTT was passed in the end, only to see that revenues were used for purposes which have nothing to do with their initial motivation: funding development and other global public goods. This would also have negative consequences for support from Southern countries (see Chapter 9).

8.3 THE FTT AND DEVELOPMENT

As already mentioned at the beginning, James Tobin's main interest was the regulatory impact of his tax, and he did not give much thought to the use of the revenues. The idea behind his proposal to channel the revenues towards development was simply that income generated trough the taxation of international capital flows might also go to international purposes. Also, in the 1970s, the (geo) political context of development policies was quite different from today. There was a widespread optimism and—unlike today—the development agenda was not dominated by the lack of resources. Typical of the spirit of the time is Robert McNamara (1973)'s declaration as president of the World Bank in 1973: "We should strive to eradicate absolute poverty by the end of this century."[11] The end of the century McNamara is talking about is now one and a half decades behind us, but absolute poverty is far from being eradicated. One reason, though not the only one, is the chronic lack of finance, while additional challenges, such as climate change, have become burning issues and require considerable resources.

With the end of the Cold War an important motivation for development efforts in the North was falling apart. There was no more need to compete with another geo-political block for influence on developing countries. Furthermore, with the hegemony of the neoliberal paradigm, in development politics, too, the belief (crystallizing in the Washington Consensus) that markets and the private sector would do better to solve the problems of development than public money gained ground.

[11] The entire speech, which is highly interesting in the light of our debate on the MDGs is available at: http://juerg-buergi.ch/Archiv/EntwicklungspolitikA/EntwicklungspolitikA/assets/McNamara_Nairobi_speech.pdf, accessed 15 July 2015.

It is therefore not surprising that it was a development organization, the UNDP, which rediscovered in 1996 the taxation of capital flows as an instrument to finance development, nor was it by chance that first development NGOs first took up the issue and are still a driving force in campaigning for the FTT.

In this context a discourse on innovative financing for development emerged, which resulted in the UN Monterrey conference in 2002. In the so-called "Monterrey Consensus" tax issues are considered to be an important issue for development; however, international taxes in general and financial transaction taxes in particular were not mentioned as the United States and some other Western countries were opposing strongly.

Nevertheless, the UN promoted the debate through studies on innovative financing for development, such as the Atkinson (2004) study, in which financial transaction taxes are advocated as one powerful instrument along with taxes on CO_2 emissions, sea transport, air traffic, and even some exotic-sounding proposals such as satellite frequencies (see the overview in Wahl, 2005).

In 2005 a special UN structure was set up, the Leading Group on Innovative Financing for Development. Officials from the development ministries of some forty countries participated here.[12] The Leading Group is quite open to civil society participation and offers citizens the right to speak at meetings and to submit papers. Since its foundation, the Group has kept the FTT on its agenda.

An important impulse came from a study praised by former French President Chirac, which considered a financial transaction tax not only to be feasible, but also desirable (Landau, 2004). Nevertheless, the only real progress in the area was the implementation of an air ticket tax by France in 2005 and other similar, but half-hearted measures in Brazil under president Lula (since cancelled), Chile, and other countries, whose revenues were channelled to the UN Fund on HIV/AIDS, UNITAID.

When France introduced a unilateral financial transaction tax at the end of Sarkozy's presidency, 10 percent of the revenues were earmarked for development—here again for UNITAID, as in the case of the air ticket tax. Also, under the Enhanced Cooperation Procedure the new French President Hollande has announced the use of 10 percent of the French revenues of the FTT for development (Hollande, 2013).

If the estimates on revenues prove to be realistic, this 10 percent would amount to about one billion euro (1.3 bn USD). There is also a discussion in Germany about earmarking a certain proportion of tax revenues to development.

[12] See their homepage: http://leadinggroup.org/rubrique20.html, accessed 15 July 2015.

As the German budget law does not allow for earmarking tax revenues for any purpose there is the idea for a kind of informal political "gentleman's agreement" among all parties in the parliament. But there was no precise figure on the table at the time this manuscript was finished. Given the ongoing fight over exemptions, decisions on allocation can only be expected in the next phase. The German civil society campaign is asking for one third to go to development, one third for environment and one third for social purposes in the EU. But this is quite out of reach, and something like the French ten percent is more realistic.

As for the attitude of governments from emerging and developing countries, the picture is mixed. Some of them, such as Brazil and South Africa, have declared several times their openness for an FTT, while others, such as India, are sceptical. This has partly to do with the fact that the regulatory dimension of the FTT is not that relevant for the southern hemisphere. The financial crisis, which was a decisive catalyst for the breakthrough of the FTT in the EU, is considered to be mainly a problem of industrialized countries. It did not trigger a broad debate on financial reforms in the global south.

But if the FTT is ultimately successful in the EU, interest for such an instrument will pop up in other regions. The Post-MDG-Agenda will also increase pressure for innovative sources of finance and the EU-tax might serve as a blueprint for similar undertakings. International civil society faces the challenge of preparing itself for that moment. They should not wait to discuss with their European colleagues how to seize an opportunity to replicate such a successful project beyond Europe.

8.4 CONCLUSION

The regulatory dimension of the FTT interferes with the function of markets, and consequently considerably affects the interests of the financial industry. Such a market intervention runs both against neo-classical theory, which has been hegemonial over the last three decades, and the dominance of neoliberalism, which wants markets to be the center of society. Therefore, since the end of the Bretton Woods system, financial markets have been liberalized and deregulated all over the world. The free and unfettered flow of capital from and to any corner of the planet has become the "holy cow" of this system, which some describe with the concept of "financialization." Others call it "the big casino" in the tradition of Keynes, while still others speak of a "finance-driven mode of accumulation" or "finance capitalism." However you term it, there has in fact been a fundamental shift over the last thirty years, allowing finance to become the dominant sector of the overall economy in Western countries—with profound consequences for society as a whole.

Against this backdrop, the FTT is a small but paradigmatic contribution in turning the tide. Given this, the enraged opposition of the finance sector comes as no surprise, nor does the ruthless use of resources and every method—including dirty ones—to prevent the success of the tax.

Due to its popular support and as a result of the split among elites into neoliberal hardliners on the one hand, and others open to some reforms on the other, the FTT has become a post-crash spearhead project of emancipatory policies with symbolic character. Its success or failure will have repercussions beyond the tax itself.

The history of the FTT shows that in spite of all the difficulties, it is possible to occupy some discursive and political terrain that pushes finance capitalism onto the defensive. May the lessons learnt with the FTT contribute to progress in other areas of financial reforms as well, forcing finance to serve people before profits.

REFERENCES

Atkinson, A. B. (ed.), 2004. *New Sources of Development Finance, WIDER Studies in Development Economics*. Oxford: Oxford University Press.

Council of the European Union, 2013. Interinstitutional File: 2013/0045 (CNS). OPINION OF THE LEGAL SERVICE. Subject: Proposal for a Council Directive implementing enhanced cooperation in the area of financial transaction tax (FTT)—Legality of the counterparty-based deemed establishment of financial institutions (Article 4(1) point f) of the proposal). 6 September. Brussels.

Directorate General for Communication Directorate C—Relations with Citizens PUBLIC OPINION MONITORING UNIT, 2011. EUROPEANS AND THE CRISIS. 22 June. Brussels.

Goldman Sachs, 2013. "Financial Transaction Tax: How Severe?" Goldman Sachs Research Report.

Haq, Mahbub ul, Inge Kaul, and Isabelle Grunberg (eds), 1996. *The Tobin Tax: Coping with Financial Volatility*. New York/London: Oxford University Press.

Hollande, François, 2013. Discours du Président de la République à l'occasion de la 67ème Assemblée générale des Nations unies. http://www.elysee.fr/declarations/article/discours-du-president-de-la-republique-a-l-occasion-de-la-67eme-assemblee-generale-des-nations-unies/, accessed 29 July 2015.

IMF, 2010. "A Fair and Substantial Contribution by the Financial Sector," Final Report for the G20. Washington, DC.

Koalitionsvertrag zwischen CDU, CSU, und SPD, 2013. Deutschlands Zukunft gestalten. 18. Legislaturperiode. Berlin.

Landau, Jean Pierre, 2004. "Les nouvelles contributions financières internationals," Rapport au Président de la République. Paris. http://www.ladocumentationfrancaise.fr/var/storage/rapports-publics/044000440.pdf, accessed 29 July 2015.

Leaders' Statement, 2009. The Pittsburgh Summit. 24–25 September. https://g20.org/wp-content/uploads/2014/12/Pittsburgh_Declaration_0.pdf, accessed 29 July 2015.

McNamara, Robert S., 1973. The Nairobi speech. Address to the Board of Governors, World Bank Group, 24 September. Nairobi, Kenya.

Plihon, Dominique and Peter Wahl, 2013. "Alerte: la France sabote la taxation des transactions financières!" *Le Monde*. http://www.lemonde.fr/economie/article/2013/07/11/alerte-bercy-sabote-la-taxation-des-transactions-financieres_3446643_3234.html, accessed 29 July 2015.

Tobin, James, 1974. "A Proposal for International Monetary Reform," *Eastern Economic Journal* 4: 153–9.

Ungar, Rick, 2013. "Capitalistpig Hedge Fund Founder Attacks Financial 'Robin Hood Tax' as Motivated by Sharia Law," *Forbes*, 11 August. http://www.forbes.com/sites/rickungar/2013/08/11/capitalistpig-hedge-fund-founder-attacks-financial-robin-hood-tax-as-motivated-by-sharia-law/, accessed 15 July 2015.

Wahl, Peter, 2005. *International Taxation Regulating Globalisation—Financing Development*. Berlin: World Economy, Ecology & Development Association.

9

Towards Unitary Taxation

Combined Reporting and Formulary Apportionment

Sol Picciotto

9.1 INTRODUCTION

9.1.1 The Problem of Taxing TNCs

The evidence recently publicized of widespread and far-reaching tax avoidance by transnational corporations (TNCs) shows that the existing system for assessing the profits of such firms and apportioning those profits between countries is dysfunctional. This is a very serious problem, for a number of reasons. Some were identified by the OECD in its first report on base erosion and profit shifting (OECD, 2013a):

- The direct revenue losses affect all states, undermining the ability to fund public services in richer countries, and the efforts to attain sustainable development in poorer ones;
- Systematic tax avoidance by the richest and most powerful companies in the world also undermines the general legitimacy of taxation;
- It gives the TNCs which exploit these avoidance opportunities very significant competitive advantages over national firms, resulting in inefficient allocation of investment and major distortions to economic activity;
- The problems it causes are particularly great for developing countries, which can ill afford the resources wasted in training officials to master the increasingly complex international tax rules;
- It distorts the decisions of these firms themselves, resulting in some benefits to some countries but overall economic welfare losses (Keuschnigg and Devereux, 2012).

Furthermore, it should also be stressed that international tax avoidance by TNCs exploits the tax haven and "offshore" secrecy system, which was originally devised by and for them (see Palan in this volume). These techniques and facilities cause even more far-reaching damage:

- They are also used for all kinds of evasion, not only of taxes, but of other laws, facilitating money-laundering for public and private corruption, terrorism, and other criminal activities; the measures now being taken to try to deal with all these activities would be easier to enforce if TNCs ceased to use the offshore system;
- The offshore system has particularly distorted the finance sector, as an element in shadow banking and other techniques which contributed to the excessive leverage, helping to feed the bubble which caused the financial crash of 2007–9;
- The system sustains a vast army of professionals engaged in both avoidance and evasion not only of tax but also banking and financial and other forms of regulation, resulting in enormously wasteful expenditures for both firms and governments.

These problems result from a deep structural flaw in the international tax system. This flaw is the failure to treat TNCs according to the economic reality that they operate as integrated firms under central direction (Coase, 1988). Instead, a principle has become gradually entrenched that they should be taxed as if they were separate enterprises in each country dealing independently with each other. This can be referred to as the Separate Enterprise-Arm's Length Principle (SE-ALP) This not merely allows but encourages TNCs to organize their affairs by forming entities in suitable jurisdictions to reduce their overall effective tax rate, by a variety of means.

Hence the problem does not result solely from the immoral and sometimes illegal activities of companies. It is states which are responsible for the rules, and governments should therefore ensure that they are thoroughly reformed. However, it is disingenuous of firms to say that they only obey the rules decided by governments. Business advisers and lobbyists are also heavily involved in designing the rules. Perhaps even more importantly, they are also central to moulding how the system works in practice, through the mutual understandings of business representatives and regulators. These technical specialists form a closed community of interpretation, reinforced by the movement of individuals from government service to working as business advisers (and, less often, in the other direction).

International tax treaty provisions are still based on models drawn up under the League of Nations in 1928, when international investment was mainly loans (see Picciotto, 1992; Picciotto, 2013a). The treaty models gave the state of residence of the investor the primary right to tax the income from investment (interest, dividends, fees, and royalties), while the host country where the business was located could tax its profits. Some TNCs had emerged by the

1920s, and the rules were adapted for them, by requiring branches and affiliates in different countries to be treated as if they were independent entities dealing at arm's length. However, to prevent "diversion" of profits, the treaty models provided that tax authorities could adjust their accounts, and national laws gave them powers generally to ensure that the levels of profit of branches or subsidiaries of foreign firms were similar to those of local competitors, or a fair reflection of their contribution to the firm as a whole.

The TNCs which developed in the last half-century are very different. As business organizations they are highly integrated and centrally directed, but in legal form they consist of often hundreds of different affiliates. In the past few decades tax-driven corporate restructuring has mushroomed, using complex structures designed to take advantage of national tax rules, especially regarding where a company is considered to be resident, and where are the sources of its income. In simplified terms, three stages and types of structure can be identified.

First, and most basic, is a "stepping stone" arrangement (see Picciotto, 2011: 228–33). An operating affiliate in a source country can make payments of fees for services such as headquarters management, of royalties for intellectual property rights, and of interest on loans, all of which are deductible and hence reduce its taxable business profits. These payments flow to one or more affiliated holding companies, in a country with suitable tax treaties (e.g. the Netherlands, Switzerland, or Singapore) so they will be subject to no or low withholding taxes. They can then be passed on, leaving a nominal level of profit for the "conduit" affiliate, to a "base" affiliate in a classical tax haven such as Bermuda or the Cayman Islands which does not tax such profits. This ensures low effective tax rates for the firm's foreign earnings: if they do not need to be repatriated to finance dividends to shareholders, they can be retained for reinvestment by making loans to the firm's affiliates, even to the parent. This ability to finance expansion through lightly taxed retained earnings has long been a major competitive advantage for TNCs.

Next, TNCs began to reorganize their operations to take advantage of tax breaks offered by states (see Christensen and Shaxson in this volume). In the 1990s, competition to attract inward investment led many countries to provide tax holidays, which were attractive especially for mobile business (UNCTAD, 2000; OECD, 2001). For example, computer chip manufacturer Intel opened major manufacturing facilities in Puerto Rico, Malaysia, the Philippines, Ireland, and Israel, all of which offered tax holidays (Avi-Yonah, 2001). This type of avoidance was harder to combat than the basic "stepping stone" arrangement, because these affiliates were not mere letter-box companies receiving only "passive income," which is a key criterion in national laws on "controlled foreign corporations" (CFCs) enacted by the United States and a number of other countries to combat tax avoidance. It is difficult to treat such an affiliate as a CFC so as to deem its income directly taxable as attributable to its parent, because it is engaged in active business.[1] Of course, TNCs have also lobbied to limit the scope of the passive business definitions, so that for example many financial services activities have been excluded. Consequently, the profits of hedge funds and private equity firms can be treated as arising in zero tax countries such as the Cayman Islands, simply because their transactions are booked by an affiliate there, even though the investment decisions are made and trading conducted in major financial centers such as New York and London.

Building further on this strategy, firms began to reorganize their corporate structures by splitting various functions and assigning them to affiliates, organized or located to minimize tax. This became much easier with the shift to the digital economy, which greatly facilitated international communication, enabling firms both to manage their own international value chains, and to deal with customers anywhere in the world. For example, sales to customers can typically be booked to one affiliate, while others deal with activities such as marketing, customer support, delivery, and logistics. The main profit flow of course is attributed to the sales affiliate, located in a suitable jurisdiction where such income can be low-taxed, while the other affiliates are characterized as contractors, making relatively low profits on the specific operations for which they are supposedly responsible. For example, Amazon in Europe separates the functions of sales and website operation (attributed to Amazon SARL Luxembourg) from customer support, warehousing, and order fulfillment, which are done in each country close to its customers. Similarly, Google books its sales of advertising to an affiliate in Ireland, with the income then flowing to another formed in Ireland but considered to be resident in Bermuda; its affiliate in the United Kingdom employs approximately as many people as those in Ireland, many of whom deal directly with customers for advertising, but they are considered to be engaged in "marketing" (Drucker, 2010; Sandell, 2012; Bergin, 2013; UK Parliament, 2013).

These, in outline, are the tax avoidance strategies used to create untaxed "stateless income" (see Kleinbard in this volume), contributing a large slice of the billions of lost government revenues (Henry in this volume). As can be readily understood from this brief analysis, it is the inappropriate nature of the SE-ALP at the heart of the international tax system that provides the perverse incentives for TNCs to devise these elaborate corporate structures.

[1] The US Internal Revenue Service attempted to deal with the problem by treating such affiliates as "contract manufacturers" under transfer pricing rules, but this approach proved hard to sustain.

9.1.2 A Pathway to Reform

The issue now facing us is how to establish international tax rules on a sounder basis. Applying further patches to existing rules seems futile. What is clearly needed is to reorient the rules so as to treat TNCs as single firms, instead of being based on the unrealistic fiction that they are a loose collection of separate and independent entities in each country. A number of proposals with this perspective have indeed been put forward.[2] The most comprehensive is Unitary Taxation with formula apportionment (UT). This is widely accepted as a superior approach in principle, although not without its difficulties.

Such an approach has a long history. It has been used for state taxes in federal systems with unified markets, such as Canada, Switzerland, and the United States. California, for example, developed it to stop Hollywood film studios siphoning profits out by using distribution affiliates in Nevada. Today, all forty-seven US states which have a corporate income tax use formula apportionment, although following a campaign by non-US TNCs in the 1980s, they can choose to have it limited to their US business ("water's edge").

The EU also now has a fully worked out proposal for a Common Consolidated Corporate Tax Base (CCCTB), developed by the European Commission in consultation over several years with business representatives and specialists. It was approved, with some amendments, by the European Parliament in April 2012, and since then it has undergone technical examination by the Council of Ministers, and in June 2015 the Commission announced an Action Plan which includes relaunching the proposal. The proposal could certainly be improved, especially by extending its scope to deal more effectively with avoidance using non-EU tax havens. This could be done by requiring a worldwide combined report (discussed further later). Nevertheless, if adopted it would go a long way towards dealing with many of the avoidance devices, such as the use of dual-resident affiliates in Ireland (the "double-Irish"), and conduit companies in the Netherlands ("Dutch sandwich"), discussed in the previous section. It is not surprising that these member states have opposed the proposal, but it is regrettable that others, including successive UK governments, have been

[2] These include: (i) taxation by the TNC's home country of the consolidated worldwide profits of a TNC, with a credit for foreign taxes paid (i.e. treating all foreign affiliates as CFCs), advocated e.g. by Kleinbard 2011, and Avi-Yonah in this volume; this could have been proposed under Action 3 of the BEPS Action Plan; (ii) changing to a Destination Based Corporate Tax (Devereux and de la Feria 2014); (iii) Michael Durst's proposed Shared Net Margin Method (Durst 2015). All of these treat the TNC as unitary, but do not apply formulary apportionment.

skeptical or hostile, due to an unreasoning Europhobia.[3] A CCCTB would restore national powers of effective taxation of TNCs and hence enhance both the effectiveness and the legitimacy of national taxes.

Proposals have been made for some states to take unilateral measures, moving away from the separate entity principle dominating the current system (e.g. Kleinbard, 2011 for the US; Jarass and Obermair, 2008 for Germany; Avi-Yonah in this volume). Such measures may well be desirable in the short term, although it remains to be seen whether governments' need for revenue and desire to placate public opinion will lead to their actual enactment, in the face of the pressures and threats of disinvestment that will inevitably come from corporate lobbies.

However, we also need to look beyond these, and set our sights on how to achieve greater international coordination, moving towards a UT approach. While this would involve looking at TNCs through a different optic than the SE-ALP, an evolutionary and pragmatic shift towards a unitary approach is both necessary and possible. There are many elements of such an approach within the present system, which can be built upon. What is needed is a road map for such a transition, which this chapter aims to outline.

9.2 ELEMENTS OF A UNITARY APPROACH

Unitary Taxation (UT) is not a panacea, but it would place international corporate taxation on a sounder foundation. It would replace or greatly simplify most of the main complex and problematic areas of international taxation: not only transfer pricing regulations, but also rules on corporate residence and source of income, as well as anti-abuse provisions such as CFCs and limitation of benefits clauses. Compared with those thorny problems, the difficulties to be resolved in making UT workable are relatively minor. It does not involve wholesale replacement of one system by another: a gradual shift to UT is both necessary and possible. As a number of specialists (in particular, Avi-Yonah, Clausing, and Durst, 2009) have pointed out, some elements already exist, which can be built upon. The need is for a road-map and a strategy for transition.

[3] The objection made is that national governments would lose sovereignty by giving up the power to define the corporate tax base; however, the CCCTB would only apply to companies with cross-border activities, and governments generally use their power to define the tax base to compete with each other in offering tax breaks to attract investment.

The time is now right for such a transition, since the G20 world leaders have called for fundamental reforms of the international tax rules. They have proclaimed that "the existing international tax rules on tax treaties, permanent establishment, and transfer pricing will be examined to ensure that profits are taxed where economic activities occur and value is created" (St. Petersburg Declaration of the G20 World Leaders, Tax Annex). Adopting a unitary approach is the only effective way to deliver tax rules which can indeed ensure this.

A workable UT system should have three components: combined reporting, profit apportionment, and a resolution procedure. Each can be introduced to some extent immediately, and could be refined gradually by building on existing provisions.

9.2.1 Combined Reporting

First, any company with a business presence in more than one country should be required to submit a Combined and Country by Country Report (CaCbCR) to each tax authority. This should include: (i) consolidated worldwide accounts for the firm as a whole, taking out all internal transfers; (ii) details of all the entities forming the corporate group and their relationships, as well as of transactions between them; and (iii) data on its physical assets, employees, sales (by destination), and actual taxes paid, in each country where it has a business presence.

An enormous step towards achieving this was taken in 2013, in the calls made by the G8 and G20 world leaders for greater corporate tax transparency: "more transparency will be established, including through a common template for companies to report to tax administrations on their worldwide allocation of profits and tax" (St. Petersburg Declaration of the G20 World Leaders, Tax Annex). The OECD published a template for country-by-country reports in September 2014, followed by two reports on implementation, which were consolidated in the final report, which was one of the outputs of the BEPS project published in October 2015.

This could transform international taxation. At present, tax officials starting from separate affiliate tax returns find it hard to see the big picture, and this is especially difficult for those in poorer countries. This measure will now ensure that for the first time the tax authorities of each country where a firm has a taxable business presence will have access to information on its activities, on both a global and a national basis.

More work remains to be done in designing an effective common template, especially to modify financial accounting standards so that they are appropriate for tax purposes, and to establish an adequate basis for true consolidated accounts for tax purposes (see chapter by Murphy in this volume). Also, the

OECD's proposals for filing and access to these reports are cumbersome and restrictive. They require filing primarily with the country of residence of the ultimate parent entity of the MNE, which should supply them to the tax authorities of other countries where the MNE has an affiliate, under agreements for automatic exchange of information, and subject to conditions. Interestingly, these conditions include an explicit prohibition against using the reports for formulary apportionment; "appropriate use" is defined to mean use only for risk assessment. This creates considerable obstacles, especially for developing countries. To overcome these, countries should use the option envisaged in the scheme of a secondary mechanism for filing directly in each relevant country.

Full transparency of course requires that these global reports should be publicly available. This should be possible in most cases, since the information they will contain should not normally be commercially confidential, unlike the more detailed transfer pricing documentation which the OECD specifies should be provided separately in a Master File and a Local File. Campaigners will fight for this, and it remains to be seen whether business lobbies can muster sufficiently cogent arguments to resist publication. The first and most important step is to ensure that the scope of information made available to tax authorities is adequate for their purposes.

9.2.2 Profit Apportionment

Secondly, states could use the CaCbCR to decide on an appropriate apportionment of the profit. This also can build on existing practice, as there is already considerable experience in applying formulaic apportionment both of fixed and shared costs, and of profits. In particular the profit-split method, which has been one of the five accepted transfer pricing methods in the OECD Guidelines since 1995, apportions aggregated profits of related firms according to appropriate "allocation keys."

Indeed, the profit-split method has in practice become increasingly used, especially with the growing importance of intangibles. This has become an intractable issue because the OECD approach has exacerbated the difficulties created by the SE-ALP, by fetishizing the very concept of "intangibles." The oligopolistic profits of TNCs are to a great extent due to their control of superior know-how, but a firm's knowledge or know-how is very much a result of synergy, and it is very hard to value the different contributions of different parts of the firm to that whole. This is so even (or especially) when such knowledge can take the form of intellectual property, since this concept creates a misleading notion of the nature of innovation or creativity as individualized, episodic, and discrete, instead of collective, continuous, and cumulative.

Recognition of the difficulties led to a reconsideration of Chapter 6 of the OECD Guidelines on Intangibles, begun in 2010, which has now been reinforced by its inclusion as an action point in the BEPS project. The revised chapter of the OECD Guidelines on Intangibles, which was one of the outputs of the BEPS project published in October 2015, provides some long-overdue changes. It moves away from attribution of intangibles profits on the basis of ownership, or provision of finance. This has enabled the likes of Google to accumulate enormous profits in low-tax countries such as Bermuda, due to the foresight of its tax advisers in transferring at an early stage the rights in its search algorithm to an affiliate resident there. Instead, profits would be attributed according to each entity's contribution to "value creation" through its "functions performed, assets used, and risks assumed." The extent to which any of these functions, assets, and risk factors affect value is stated to depend on the facts and circumstances, to be decided ad hoc in each case. The revised chapter is full of equivocation on how this can be done, on the one hand stating that as far as possible the starting point should be "comparables," while also conceding that the identification of reliable comparables in many cases involving intangibles may be difficult or impossible. In fact, attribution of profits based on the contribution to "value creation" should lead to greater use of the profit-split method.

Under the OECD Guidelines, the profit-split method apportions the aggregate profits of related entities using suitable "allocation keys." This approach should be extended, because at present it envisages aggregation at the level of transacting entities, whereas MNEs use more complex cross-linkages among affiliates. The OECD has preferred to limit the scope of profit-split, so that it is used only to apportion the "residual" profit, that which remains after methods based on comparables have been applied as far as possible. It is not surprising that this is regarded as unsatisfactory and arbitrary by many. Treating it as a fallback means that tax officials and advisers must still struggle to try to find "comparables," even though they know that genuine comparables do not exist. Yet when it comes to applying profit-split to the residual, they are left to haggle like traders in the bazaar, since the method has not been systematized. Nevertheless, several tax authorities prefer not to waste time on complex evaluation of comparables, and focus mainly on profit-split. Developing country tax administrations in particular say that suitable comparables are hard to find, and prefer to use profit apportionment methods, which can better take into account the real contribution of affiliates to the global value chain. India and China for example emphasize the role of "location specific advantages," and consider both profit-split and even in some circumstances a "global formulary approach" as a "realistic and appropriate option."[4] Consideration of

[4] See the sections by India and China in Chapter 10 of the UN Practical Manual on Transfer Pricing; the reference to a global formulary approach is in section 10.2.6.3 by China. The

the profit split method was included in the OECD's BEPS Action Plan, but work on it has been postponed, to begin with a scoping paper published as part of the final BEPS package in October 2015.

A broader application of the profit-split method could be developed through Advance Price Agreements (APAs) with individual firms. Many countries offer APA programs, and they can be negotiated with two or more states where appropriate. Indeed, a formula-based apportionment method has been applied for some twenty years in the finance sector, in APAs with banks, to allocate the profits of global trading conducted by offices in different time-zones over 24 hours.[5] If firms such as Apple, Amazon, Google, and Starbucks would really like to pay a fair level of taxes wherever they do business, they too could enter into APAs and agree to an appropriate apportionment.

The experience of using profit-split and APAs could be combined with proper research to determine the most appropriate apportionment formulae. The most balanced approach seems to be a three-factor formula, using physical assets, employees, and sales (see chapter by Durst in this volume). The assets factor should be limited to physical assets (as in the CCCTB), excluding intangibles, which (as discussed above) are elusive to define and value, and can easily be relocated. Some argue that there is no need to include assets, since they are of decreasing importance in the "weightless economy." Nevertheless, in my view a general formula designed to apply as far as possible to all sectors should include an assets factor, provided it is indeed limited to physical assets. As regards employees, US states use employee payroll costs, not headcount, but this would be inappropriate internationally, due to the greater wage differences.[6] The proposed CCCTB would use a 50:50 weighting of payroll and headcount, which seems appropriate. Finally, sales should be quantified according to the location of the customer. Sellers can and do identify the location of their customers for delivery purposes, and for sales of services and digital products at least through their billing address. Although customers may use accounts based in havens for such purchases, they would have no reason to do so in order to reduce the tax liability of the sellers.

Some argue that states would aim to use a weighting which emphasizes the factor which produces the most revenue for them, so would never agree on a formula. In fact, states need also to consider the effects on investment. Hence, in the United States the trend has been towards a greater emphasis on the sales

preference of India's then Competent Authority, Sanjay Mishra, for profit split was revealed by his US counterpart Michael Danilack in forthright remarks at a practitioner meeting in January 2013 (Parillo and Trivedi, 2013); Mishra's subsequent removal was not unconnected to US complaints.

[5] See US Treasury Notice 94-40 (1994 IRB LEXIS 213), which states that the main apportionment factor should be the traders' remuneration.

[6] For this reason also it would be better to convert payroll costs using purchasing power parity rather than ordinary exchange rates.

factor, which does not act as a deterrent on inward investment (Clausing, 2014). A balance between production and consumption factors seems best. This could be locked in by adopting a two-stage apportionment: an initial allocation to each country by production factors, then apportionment of the residual by sales.[7] However, a shift towards a sales factor would not be as detrimental, even for developing countries, as may be thought. Apportionment according to the destination of sales removes the pressure to reduce tax rates, as well as to offer special incentives. Special formulae may be needed for specific sectors. However, it should be remembered that tax on business profits is only one instrument. For extractive industries in particular it must be supplemented by rent taxation, using royalties and/or a rent resource tax, and these may be applied using profit calculations based on sales according to source, and if necessary ring-fenced by project.

It should be stressed that this approach does not seek to *attribute* profit, since it assumes that the profits of an integrated firm result from its overall synergies and economies of scale and scope. It *allocates* profits according to the measurable physical presence of the firm in each country. Some argue that firms could still reorganize themselves to minimize their taxes, which of course is correct. However, if the factors in the allocation formula are based on real physical contacts with a country, such reorganizations would involve actual relocation of such factors. Thus, while competition to attract investment would not be ended, under unitary taxation such competition would become more sharply focused on attracting genuine production. Furthermore, if firms choose to divest to truly independent third parties some operations, for example, retail sales, they would lose the profits of synergy and scale. It is hard to imagine a company such as Apple being willing to transfer to a truly independent wholesaler in a low-tax country a significant slice of its profits. Jurisdiction to tax should be based not on the physical presence concept of Permanent Establishment (PE), but a broad business presence test, to include, for example, sales via a website.[8]

States would remain free to choose their own marginal tax rates. Hence countries could compete to attract genuine investment rather than formation of paper entities aimed at subverting the taxes of other countries. Harmonization of the tax base definition would greatly reduce the existing damaging forms of competition to attract investments by offering special exemptions. UT would therefore eliminate harmful tax competition, while allowing countries to make genuine choices between attracting investment in production and generating revenues from corporate taxation. Such a system would of

[7] As suggested by Avi-Yonah, Clausing, and Durst (2009) who suggest that the first step allocation could be based on operating expenses.

[8] Indeed, the final report on Action 1 of the BEPS project, on the Digital Economy, suggests that states may wish to consider a new PE definition, based on "significant economic presence."

course not be perfect, but aligning tax rules more closely to the economic reality of integrated firms operating in liberalized world markets would make it simpler and more effective.

9.2.3 Resolving Conflicts

The third important element is a procedure for resolution of disagreements and conflicts between states. This also is already provided for in the Mutual Agreement Procedure (MAP) in tax treaties, but it should be improved, and extended to include negotiation of APAs. This could increasingly be done on a multilateral basis, which is favored by some TNCs. Developing countries should strengthen or develop APA negotiation programs, and investment in expertise for these would be much more cost-effective than for transfer pricing adjustments based on comparables.

These procedures could also be considerably improved, and indeed this is one of the OECD's BEPS action points. This proposes to introduce a provision long sought by firms: compulsory and binding arbitration. This has been resisted until now, especially by developing countries, and for good reason. If there is little clarity or agreement on the rules to be applied, referring disputes to arbitrators to decide would be unhelpful, and perhaps dangerous. Further, the secrecy of these procedures undermines their legitimacy and creates public distrust and suspicion of private deals by revenue authorities with big business. The MAP is at present very secretive and decisions often involving hundreds of millions or even billions of dollars are not published. The secrecy of both MAP processes and APAs greatly increases the power of frequent actors in these processes, that is, the international tax and accounting firms, to the great detriment of the system as a whole. Publication of both would be a great step towards a system which could both provide and more importantly be seen to deliver a fair international allocation of tax.

9.3 OBSTACLES TO REFORM AND HOW THEY MAY BE OVERCOME

The main obstacle to reform is the gap between the political concerns about the problems caused by the current system, and the technical knowledge of how it works and could be reformed. It is long been accepted among international tax specialists that UT is a superior approach in principle. The main argument of those opposing it is that political agreement would be impossible.

Indeed, this argument has a long history, going back to when the problem of taxation of TNCs was first considered, by the League of Nations in 1932–3, resulting in the Carroll report (Carroll, 1933). Strong arguments were put forward at that time for adopting a unitary approach, but the view taken by Carroll was that it would be difficult if not impossible to adopt, for political reasons.[9] Such an approach would have to have been based on international agreement on (i) tax accounting principles for assessment, and (ii) a common allocation formula. Nevertheless, the German contribution to the report produced at that time accepted that "fractional apportionment" was a superior approach in principle, and indeed that it would in practice be used in the many cases where separate assessment was not feasible (League of Nations, 1932: 122). It suggested that in practice apportionment of the profits would for a period require close contacts and cooperation between tax authorities, and experience built up in this way could lay the basis for a more systematic approach.

Instead, what has occurred, especially in the past quarter-century, is an increasing technicization of the system. Tax officials, working mainly through the OECD's Committee on Fiscal Affairs (CFA), have elaborated increasingly complex rules, expressed in specialized concepts and language. Together with corporate tax advisers, they form an expert community, reinforced by frequent contact and consultation, movement between the sectors (usually from the public to the private), and meetings and discussions in professional bodies, such as the International Fiscal Association.

Instead of working towards a more economically rational approach by treating TNCs as unitary, the dominant opinion in these expert networks has entrenched the SE-ALP. Notably, they have hardened the requirement for taxation of a foreign company by reaffirming the concept of a Permanent Establishment based on physical presence.[10] Yet it is these same experts who

[9] This is entirely understandable in view of the political weakness of the League of Nations: the United States did not join that body due to a negative vote in the Senate, Russia and Germany were not admitted, and others such as Japan left. In that context international coordination under its auspices of issues such as tax, with the participation of non-member states and indeed in this case with US leadership, was clearly only possible without the involvement of politicians. Since then the technical experts have constructed a system which is now producing outcomes which are equally clearly politically unacceptable.

[10] The CFA by majority first decided that a website could not be a PE (OECD, 2000), and then embodied this interpretation in the model treaty's Commentary on attribution of profits by reports in 2006 and 2008; this culminated in adoption of the so-called "authorized OECD approach," which in effect treats a PE like a separate enterprise; they also removed article 7(4) which allowed fractional apportionment as a method for determining the profits of a PE (OECD, 2006, 2008, 2010; see Kobetsky, 2011). A number of OECD countries expressed reservations about this approach, and it was rejected by developing countries, but domestic courts have followed the Commentary (see e.g. *Income Tax Officer v. Right Florist PVT Ltd*, 2013 in India), enabling internet firms such as Google and Yahoo to rack up large untaxed profits in Ireland and elsewhere. A similar approach was adopted towards taxation of services, reinforcing the restrictions on their taxation by the country where they are actually provided. This reinforcement of residence country taxation encouraged avoidance and the growth of "stateless income,"

have been tasked by the leaders of the G20 states with reform of international tax rules.

Although the focus of this community is on technical matters, it is not value-free. Yet the dominant values have not been a concern to establish an effective system for international coordination of corporate taxation. Rather, the priority has been seen as preventing double taxation in order to facilitate international investment. Although the model tax treaties were devised with the dual aim of preventing both double taxation and "fiscal evasion," in practice the prime aim has been the former. Tax authorities have seen themselves as responding to the concerns of their governments to attract foreign investment, which they have translated into a priority for preventing double taxation. Only relatively recently have they begun, rather timidly, to refer to the need also to prevent "double non-taxation."

This cozy consensus has now been disrupted.[11] The G20 world leaders' St. Petersburg Declaration of September 2013 amounted to a mandate for radical reform of the international tax system. Unfortunately, the approach adopted by the OECD experts has aimed largely at a patch-up of the current system. However, the political pressures which produced this impetus will not easily be dissipated. It seems more likely that reform will be pursued with determination, and not only by the OECD. The strategy adopted by the OECD has been to try to reform and strengthen some of the various parts of the existing system without any reconsideration of the basic structure or principles (Picciotto, 2013b). It also does not include some aspects which concern non-OECD countries, which would reinforce source taxation (such as withholding taxes, and taxation of services). These options may well be pursued by other bodies and groups, such as the UN Tax Committee. Unless these various reforms are adequately coordinated, they will create increasing conflicts (Sheppard, 2013).

These are the forces that should build up a momentum for acceptance of a paradigm shift. We are in the early stages of a reform process that will inevitably take at least five years, maybe ten, perhaps longer.[12] As the momentum builds, conviction of the need for a more rational and comprehensive

especially as rules against controlled foreign corporations (CFCs) were weakened and became ineffective.

[11] Jeffrey Owens, long-standing head of tax at the OECD, was quoted early in 2013 as saying "Governments have made the business tax system more friendly since the mid 1980s . . . Now it is payback time" (Houlder, 2013).

[12] It should be recalled that a similar previous move was initiated in 1996 by the then G7 world leaders, resulting in the OECD report on Harmful Tax Competition in 1998. Following a change of US administration this was greatly weakened, and became a laborious effort to improve exchange of tax information by negotiation of bilateral treaties. Proposals by the tax justice movement for a more ambitious aim of comprehensive multilateral automatic exchange of information were derided as unrealistic. Yet the G8 summit in 2013 adopted the Lough Erne Declaration, which established this as the new global standard, together with a commitment to develop measures for transparency of beneficial ownership.

approach will grow, until a tipping point is reached. What is needed is a continuation of sustained political pressure, combined with careful research and study of feasible and effective alternatives.

9.4 CONCLUSIONS

International taxation is a process of coordination, which is necessary to ensure the effectiveness of national taxation. Hence, far from being a surrender of sovereignty, it is essential to maintaining and restoring the powers of national states. As the patterns of economic globalization have changed, so should the forms of international coordination.

The imperfect rules devised eighty years ago, aimed mainly at portfolio investment, were first adapted then exploited by advisers for transnational corporations. The techniques and strategies they devised for minimizing taxation of retained earnings gave these firms a significant competitive advantage, contributing to their rapid growth in the second half of the last century. They also resulted in the creation of the offshore haven and secrecy system, which came to be used also for a wider range of evasion and facilitation of corruption and crime.

The new wave of economic globalization since the 1980s, and the emergence of the digital economy or post-industrial capitalism, opened up even greater opportunities for reorganization of corporate value chains, often tax-driven. Thus, the inadequate and dysfunctional arrangements for international corporate taxation have greatly distorted competition and international capital allocation. The losses of government revenues are significant, but effects go far wider.

As this chapter has shown, a paradigm shift is both necessary and possible, to place the international corporate tax rules on a sounder foundation. This should abandon the fiction of the separate entity/arm's length principle, and instead recognize the economic reality that a TNC is a unitary entity.

REFERENCES

Avi-Yonah, R., 2001. "World-Class Tax Evasion," *The American Prospect*, 19 December.

Avi-Yonah, R. S., Kimberly A. Clausing, and Michael C. Durst, 2009. "Allocating Business Profits for Tax Purposes: A Proposal to Adopt a Formulary Profit Split," *Florida Tax Review* 9: 497–553.

Bergin, T., 2013. "Special Report: How Big Tech Stays Offline on Tax," *Reuters*, 23 July.

Carroll, M. B., 1933. *Taxation of Foreign and National Enterprises, Volume 4: Methods of Allocating Taxable Income.* League of Nations, Geneva. http://setis.library.usyd.edu.au/pubotbin/toccer-new?id=cartaxa.sgml&tag=law&images=acdp/gifs&data=/usr/ot&part=0, accessed 7 September 2015.

Clausing, K. A., 2014. "Lessons for International Tax Reform from the US State Experience under Formulary Apportionment," ICTD Research Report 2, http://www.ictd.ac/sites/default/files/ICTD%20Research%20Report%202.pdf, accessed 7 September 2015.

Coase, R. H., 1988. *The Firm the Market and the Law.* University of Chicago Press, Chicago/London.

Devereux, M. and de la Feria, R., 2014. "Designing and Implementing a Destination-Based Corporate Tax," OUCBT Working Paper 14/07, http://eureka.sbs.ox.ac.uk/5081/1/WP1407.pdf, accessed 22 October 2015.

Drucker, J., 2010. "Google 2.4% Rate Shows How $60 Billion Lost to Tax Loopholes," *Bloomberg,* 21 October.

Durst, M. C., 2015. "Designing a Hybrid Transfer Pricing Method," *Tax Management Transfer Pricing Report* 23(18): 1.

European Commission, 2015. *A Fairer Corporate Tax System in the European Union: 5 Key Areas for Action.* Doc. COM (2015)302 Final, 17 June. Brussels: European Commission.

Houlder, V., 2013. "Taxation: Unsafe Offshore," *Financial Times,* 13 January.

Income Tax Officer v. Right Florist PVT Ltd, 2013. ITA 1336/Kol./2011. Income Tax Appellate Tribunal, Kolkata B Bench.

Jarass, L. and G. M. Obermair, 2008. "Tax on Earnings before Interest and Taxes instead of Profit—Fair, Simple and Competitive: A Conceivable Initiative of EU Member States for a Common Consolidated Corporate Tax Base," *EC Tax Review* 17: 111–17.

Keuschnigg, C. and M. P. Devereux, 2012. "The Arm's Length Principle and Distortions to Multinational Firm Organization," *Journal of International Economics* 89: 432–40.

Kleinbard, E. D., 2011. "The Lessons of Stateless Income," *Tax Law Review* http://ssrn.com/paper=1791783, accessed 7 September 2015.

Kobetsky, M., 2011. *International Taxation of Permanent Establishments: Principles and Policy.* Cambridge University Press, Cambridge.

League of Nations, 1932. *Taxation of Foreign and National Enterprises: A Study of the Tax Systems and Methods of Allocation of the Profits of Enterprises Operating in more than One Country, Volume I (France, Germany, Spain, the U.K. and the U.S.A.),* No. C.73.M.38, 1932 II A 3. Geneva: League of Nations.

League of Nations, 1933a. *Taxation of Foreign and National Enterprises: Studies of the Tax Systems and Methods of Allocation of the Profits of Enterprises Operating in more than One Country, Volume II (Austria, Belgium, Czechoslovakia, Free City of Danzig, Greece, Hungary, Italy, Latvia, Luxemburg, Netherlands, Roumania and Switzerland).* C.425(b).M.217(b).1933.II.A. Geneva: League of Nations.

League of Nations, 1933b. *Taxation of Foreign and National Enterprises. Studies of the tax systems and methods of allocation of the profits of enterprises operating in more than one country. Vol. III (British India, Canada, Japan, Mexico, Netherlands East Indies, Union of South Africa, States of Massachusetts, of New York, and of Wisconsin),* No. C.425 (a). M.217(a). 1933 II. http://archive.org/details/taxationofforeig031922mbp, accessed 7 September 2015.

OECD, 2000. *Clarification on the Application of the Permanent Establishment Definition in E-Commerce: Changes to the Commentary on the Model Tax Convention on Article 5.* Committee on Fiscal Affairs, OECD, Paris.

OECD, 2001. *Corporate Tax Incentives for Foreign Direct Investment.* OECD Tax Policy Studies No. 4. OECD, Paris.

OECD, 2005. *E-commerce: Transfer Pricing and Business Profits Taxation.* OECD Tax Policy Studies No. 10. OECD, Paris.

OECD, 2006. *Attribution of Profits to Permanent Establishments.* Committee on Fiscal Affairs. OECD, Paris.

OECD, 2008. *Report on the Attribution of Profits to Permanent Establishments.* Committee on Fiscal Affairs. OECD, Paris.

OECD, 2010. *2010 Report on Attribution of Profits to Permanent Establishments.* Committee on Fiscal Affairs. OECD, Paris.

OECD, 2013a. *Addressing Base Erosion and Profit Shifting.* February. OECD, Paris.

OECD, 2013b. *Action Plan on Base Erosion and Profit Shifting.* August. OECD, Paris.

OECD, 2013c. *Revised Discussion Draft on Transfer Pricing Aspects of Intangibles.* OECD, Paris.

Parillo, K. A. and S. Trivedi, 2013. "U.S. Competent Authority Has Harsh Words about India," *Worldwide Tax Daily,* 4 February.

Picciotto, S., 1992. *International Business Taxation.* Weidenfeld & Nicolson, London.

Picciotto, S., 2011 *Regulating Global Corporate Capitalism.* Cambridge: Cambridge University Press.

Picciotto, S., 2013a. *Is the International Tax System Fit for Purpose, especially for Developing Countries?* International Centre for Tax and Development, Working Paper 13.

Picciotto, S., 2013b. "Can the OECD Mend the International Tax System?" *Tax Notes International* 71: 1105–15.

Sandell, J., 2012. "The Double Irish and the Dutch Sandwich: How Some U.S. Companies Are Flummoxing the Tax Code," *Tax Notes International* 67: 867–78.

Sheppard, L. A., 2013. "The Twilight of the International Consensus," *Worldwide Tax Daily,* 7 October.

UK Parliament, 2013. *Tax Avoidance—Google.* House of Commons, Committee of Public Accounts 9th Report 2013–14, HC 112. London.

UNCTAD, 2000. *Tax Incentives and Foreign Direct Investment: A Global Survey.* ASIT Advisory Studies No. 16. United Nations, Geneva.

10

An International Convention on Financial Transparency

Harald Tollan

10.1 INTRODUCTION

Illicit financial flows are often categorized into three types: criminal, corrupt, and commercial. Criminal flows received strong international attention when in 1989 the Financial Action Task Force (FATF) was created to combat money laundering and terrorism financing. Increased transparency and information exchange are part of the FATF Recommendations (see for instance FATF, 2012). Then, in 2000 the United Nations adopted the Convention on Transnational Organized Crime, which included measures to increase financial transparency to aid the prevention of human trafficking and arms smuggling (UNODC, 2004). Measures to address corruption include, for example, the United Nations Convention Against Corruption, adopted in 2003. International attention on illicit commercial flows, such as tax evasion, is more recent.[1]

At the heart of the problem of all illicit flows is the ability to easily move capital through a financial infrastructure designed to maintain secrecy. But the piecemeal approach to combat the different elements of illicit flows just described neglects this commonality between them. Consequently, the international community has so far failed to develop a *comprehensive* response to the problem of illicit financial flows. If, however, international agreement to

[1] The concept and arguments in this paper are based on a recommendation first made by the Independent Norwegian Commission on Tax Havens, and a proposal for an international agreement or convention for transparency was included in a white paper presented to parliament in June 2013. However, while the author works for the Royal Norwegian Ministry of Foreign Affairs the arguments made in the essay do not necessarily represent those of the Norwegian government, but are the author's alone.

Valuable assistance in drafting and researching the paper was provided by Esther Shubert, Yale University.

increase financial transparency could be achieved, illicit money of all kinds would have fewer places to hide. This paper therefore proposes an International Convention on Financial Transparency to combat illicit financial flows in all its forms. Section 10.2 will review the specific problem of secrecy jurisdictions. Section 10.3 makes the case for an International Convention on Financial Transparency that has as its main target the elimination of secrecy jurisdictions to stem the flow of illicit capital. Section 10.4 details what the main body of the Convention could look like, while other priority requirements for the Convention are discussed in Section 10.5. Section 10.6 considers obstacles to implementation and suggests ways that these can be overcome.

10.2 THE PROBLEM WITH SECRECY JURISDICTIONS

Secrecy jurisdictions (or "tax havens," or "offshore financial centers") are major facilitators of illicit financial flows. There is disagreement over exactly what the relevant concept of these jurisdictions is and what features are most important, but there is broad consensus that certain financial structures are particularly harmful—especially when they occur together. This includes low or zero tax rates, favorable regulations for foreigners and companies, and, especially, secrecy regulations such as exemption from the obligations to register and publish beneficial ownership, to preserve accounting documentation and to audit (Norwegian Government Commission, 2009).[2] For our purpose here the term secrecy jurisdictions refers to financial systems that share all or most of these features and so help to facilitate tax evasion, aggressive tax avoidance, and the concealment of ill-gotten gains and criminal profit.[3] Crime, corruption, and illicit enrichment will occur with or without financial secrecy—but ought to be curtailed substantially by making the laundering and cross-border transfer of the proceeds more difficult through increased transparency and improved oversight. Globalization and fairly unrestricted flows of investments, trade, and cash transfers combined with the possibility to conceal real ownership of companies, accounts, and assets, and so on, can be a virtual invitation to engage in illicit transactions.

Secrecy jurisdictions harm both developing and developed countries. Some of the crimes that are facilitated and whose financial reward is secured by opacity include, but are not limited to: money laundering, terrorist financing,

[2] The Commission notes that low tax rates are not necessarily in themselves problematic, but have harmful effects on other countries when combined with these other features.

[3] In addition to commercial tax evasion, secrecy jurisdictions also relate illicit flows more generally; for example, they enable fraud, bribery, illegal gambling, money laundering, and trafficking of contraband goods and services (Henry, 2012).

drug trafficking, human trafficking, illegal arms trading, illegal fishing, corruption and bribery, counterfeiting, insider trading, embezzlement, fleeing of bankruptcy orders, illicit intelligence operations, and all sorts of fraud. There is also a range of more general and less direct, but no less serious, negative consequences. They include a more inequitable distribution of tax resources between countries and within countries, reduced efficiency of resource allocation, encouragement of rent-seeking, the undermining of tax systems and public finances, and impaired institutional quality and growth (especially in developing countries) (Norwegian Government Commission, 2009: 11–13).

Research on the scope of secrecy jurisdictions is limited, and specific estimates on the proportion of global illicit financial flows that goes to tax havens are not publicly available.[4] However, what research there is suggests that most countries lose vast sums of capital via secrecy jurisdictions. The Tax Justice Network estimates that the global total of accumulated offshore financial wealth as of 2010 is between $21 and $32 trillion, which represents a tax revenue loss of $189 billion per year, even with conservative tax rate estimates (Henry, 2012: 5).

Developing countries are generally less equipped to combat illicit financial flows, and the relative size of their loss is greater. It is estimated that more than 25 percent of Latin American and 33 percent of Middle Eastern and African private wealth is invested in secrecy jurisdictions, compared with only about 2 percent of North American private wealth and 8 percent of European wealth (Cohen, 2013: 2). Moreover, Tax Justice Network reports that "Since the 1970s, with assistance from international private banking industry, it appears that private elites [in 139 low- and middle-income countries] had accumulated $7.3–9.3 trillion of unrecorded offshore wealth . . . while public sectors were borrowing themselves into bankruptcy" (Henry, 2012: 5–6). It is also estimated that the capital outflows lost to secrecy jurisdictions (and the future earnings associated with these investments) almost entirely offset ODA and foreign direct investment for some developing countries (Henry, 2012: 7; Norwegian Government Commission, 2009: 13).

However, the damaging consequences of secrecy jurisdictions affect all countries. For example, allowing financial entities to hide the risk or exposure of various assets and instruments threatens the stability of the global financial system and is of global concern. Similarly, secrecy jurisdictions can weaken the effectiveness of global standards on the environment, labour, safety, and so on, affecting developed and developing countries alike. As mentioned above in terms of the efficiency of resource allocations, secrecy jurisdictions can facilitate the hiding or misrepresentation of a company's financial situation, or enable corrupt transfers, or allow for the undercutting of price in tenders,

[4] This data is available at the Bank for International Settlements but Bank rules prohibit the data from being released to researchers in a format that allows for further analysis. Thanks to Tom Cardamone for this point.

potentially leading to sub-optimal investment decisions and a socio-economic loss (not to mention the human cost of a collapsed factory or residential building constructed under corrupt terms). Furthermore, a stronger focus on profit after tax, rather than pre-tax profit, reduces the relative importance of pursuing productivity gains as a means to maximize profits. Fundamentally, financial secrecy undermines free and fair competition. Access to information is the basis for informed and socio-economically optimal investment decisions in any market-based economy.

But beyond all of this, secrecy jurisdictions are problematic because they undermine state sovereignty. States' rights to their own self-determination (sovereignty) is a deeply ingrained principle in international relations. Part of a state's right to self-determination is its ability to impose a tax regime and collect tax revenues. But secrecy jurisdictions have a direct effect on the taxation rights of other countries, with income which should have been taxed locally being concealed in a tax haven, and thus infringing on the state's right to collect its tax revenues (Norwegian Government Commission, 2009: 21).

While it may seem that having secrecy legislation and other regulation favorable to the "offshoring" of wealth from abroad is part of a secrecy jurisdiction's right to self-determination, this is not the case. States do not have an unlimited license to pursue their own self-interest at any cost; indeed, the primary constraint on state sovereignty is that domestic policies should not undermine the sovereignty of another state. Legislation that exclusively or primarily will have effects in other states, such as the financial regulations common to secrecy jurisdictions, is therefore not the exercise of sovereignty, but an encroachment on the sovereignty of others (Norwegian Government Commission, 2009: 144–6).

For too long, the facilitating function of secrecy provided by secrecy jurisdictions has been considered an inalienable part of the way the global economy works. Nonetheless, incentives can be changed and the boundaries of the acceptable redrawn. The initiative to address the harmful structures of opacity aims at establishing a new standard for acceptable use of the normative power of sovereign states.

10.3 REFORM PROPOSAL: AN INTERNATIONAL CONVENTION ON FINANCIAL TRANSPARENCY

The Independent Norwegian Government Commission has proposed the establishment of an International Agreement or Convention on Transparency in International Economic Activity [hereafter the "Convention"] with the goal of "prevent[ing] states from developing secrecy structures which are likely to cause loss and damage to other jurisdictions" (Norwegian Government Commission, 2009: 16). One of the most important tasks for the Convention would be to first define unacceptable practice in this area.

According to the Commission (2009: 144–5), the Convention would:

> First . . . bind states not to introduce legal structures that, together with more specifically defined instruments, are particularly likely to undermine the rule of law in other states. Second, states which suffer loss and damage from such structure must have the right and duty to adopt effective countermeasures which will prevent structures in tax havens from causing loss and damage to public and private interests both within and outside of their own jurisdiction.

The rest of this section argues for the virtues of such a Convention in curbing the illicit flow of capital out of developing countries via secrecy jurisdictions.

There are many reasons for the international community to ratify such a Convention and work towards the elimination of secrecy jurisdictions. The first of these involves respecting the financial sovereignty of all states. As was argued above, state sovereignty is not unlimited, but rather is constrained by the need to respect the sovereignty of other states. Legislation that exclusively or primarily will have effects in other states, such as the financial regulations common to secrecy jurisdictions, is therefore not part of the sovereignty of secrecy jurisdictions. It is instead an encroachment on the sovereignty of those states which are affected by secrecy and related regulations. The Convention, by prohibiting secrecy regulations would therefore help uphold the sovereignty of states affected by those regulations.

In addition, of course, the world would be better off without secrecy jurisdictions given the many harmful effects they have in both developing and developed countries. An international agreement to do away with the secrecy structures would bring tremendous benefits to the majority, in the long term probably including secrecy jurisdictions themselves, and not least to developing countries.

There are, however, few legally binding rules in this area. The work of the OECD and the Global Forum on Transparency and Exchange of Information for Tax Purposes, which has had a degree of success, is about enforced standards, but not binding rules or law. Non-compliance risks the inconvenience of peer pressure and grey-listing which may lead to some degree of economic sanctioning. Earlier, compliance with standards required having laws, regulations, and procedures in place—on paper. With the financial crisis and the increased attention to lost tax revenue in rich countries, the G20 in particular has applied political pressure resulting in both the OECD/Global Forum and the FATF beginning to focus on more effective implementation of standards. Having the right laws in the books is no longer sufficient; they must be put to use, as well. Still, this new resolve may well prove to be no more than a dent in the secrecy apparatus. It is worth noting that in some areas implementation of standards seems to be of higher quality in the classical, small island secrecy jurisdictions than in some of the large OECD financial centers that provide "offshore" services (Findley, Nielson, and Sharman, 2013). Whether peer reviewing of these political and economic heavyweights will have any effect remains to be seen. Smaller jurisdictions—exposed to real pressure—may have reason to feel unfairly singled out.

More fundamentally, the traditional and prevailing response to the existence of financial secrecy and secrecy jurisdictions has been to adapt to it by demanding access to information from those jurisdictions. However, there are at least four reasons why this approach is less than ideal:

1. There are still, under current standards, limits as to what type of information can be requested and on what basis.
2. For a request for information to be successfully met the authorities in the secrecy jurisdiction must themselves have access to relevant information. In jurisdictions where there is legalized bank secrecy, few or no obligations to collect or store information regarding beneficial ownership, accounting records, and so on, the authorities may not be in a position to share any information.
3. Even when a request for information is successful, which it may not always be, the damaging secrecy structures and (lack of) regulations are left intact, ready to be exploited for criminal purposes.
4. Attempts to secure access to information have mostly been undertaken through multilateral organisations such as the OECD or the UN. These bodies include jurisdictions in whose interest it is to block progress in promoting transparency. Any attempt to reduce secrecy and do away with harmful regulations will be met with opposition, and often a "least common denominator" type of solution is the only alternative.

As opposed to the "adaptive" approach of trying to secure what information may be available—in reality tolerating the fact that secrecy and harmful structures exist—the idea of the Convention is to "do away with" secrecy. The Convention would thus try to address the root cause of the problem, not limit itself to an adaptation of the current reality.

A common objection to the idea of a Convention is that "we have the instruments, let's use them." However, as we have just seen, current instruments are focused on adaptation to a situation where secrecy structures exist, and where it is accepted that a jurisdiction can create tax structures and other arrangements with "predatory" characteristics, that is, they are constructed to apply to foreign companies only, and they undermine the sovereignty of other states. So while we may have instruments to increase the pressure on secrecy jurisdictions and increase access to information, even if they are used to the full extent they do not go to the root of the problem.

A related objection is that a process parallel to discussions in existing multilateral forums may undermine these ongoing efforts. The response is that the focus of a Convention would be different from current initiatives and processes. Rather than directing attention to the symptoms of the disease, the Convention would attempt to treat the disease. Another way of looking at the Convention is to consider it as a global framework, with globally expressed commitments, within which the more specific proposals and recommendations discussed in a tax or an anti-money-laundering or an anti-corruption setting could be promoted. Depending upon the success in gathering support for a Convention and the details included in its protocols, some interaction or coordination with other processes may be necessary. An overriding concern should in any case be to avoid duplication and conflicting purposes.

Another objection is associated with a general wariness about the time and effort it would require to develop "yet another" international agreement or Convention. But while there are conventions in the areas of tax, transnational organized crime, and anti-corruption, and plenty of global standards in between, none covers the whole—transparency and illicit financial flows. Moreover, the Convention would be an important addition to existing international initiatives to address transparency and illicit financial flows. For example, two initiatives currently gaining momentum within the international community are country-by-country reporting (CBCR) and automatic exchange of tax information (AEI). Both are thought to have deterrent effects with respect to the use of secrecy jurisdictions and to enable tax authorities to detect and act upon cases of non-compliance with international standards (OECD, 2013). These are indeed valuable goals and the idea of the Convention should not be thought of as a replacement to these other initiatives. However, while CBCR and AEI would make more important information available, they do not themselves take a stand, or force countries to commit to taking a stand, on the problems of tax evasion, aggressive tax avoidance, and so on. The Convention, on the other hand, would provide a clear and unambiguous standard on what is acceptable international practice—and by making this law in each jurisdiction, addresses transparency more directly than CBCR and AEI (although, again, these initiatives may develop into important complements to help realize the goal of the Convention). The Convention, by prohibiting secrecy regulation, would therefore add something valuable to existing international efforts to fight tax evasion.

Developing and mobilizing support for a Convention on transparency will certainly require time and resources. Considering the immense harm associated with illicit financial flows it may be worth the effort.

10.4 WHAT THE CONVENTION COULD LOOK LIKE

There are at least two, slightly different, strategies for developing a Convention, or perhaps they could be seen as phases.

One would be along the lines briefly mentioned above: to construct a global framework, comprising countries both on the *inflow* and *outflow* sides of the illicit financial flows equation, asking all to join in a common commitment. Most recommendations on measures necessary to curb illicit financial flows are directed either at the countries suffering from outflows—in particular developing countries—or at the countries receiving the outflows. For outflow countries there will typically be recommendations related to governance and capacity, and for inflow countries typically recommendations on transparency, regulation, and oversight. A convention with the purpose of embracing a majority of jurisdictions will likely have to have fairly general provisions and obligations.

Another strategy, or perhaps a second phase of a process starting out as a general and global framework, could be more ambitious, and two components in particular would be relevant: 1) an obligation not to introduce legal structures that are particularly likely to undermine the sovereignty of other jurisdictions, and 2) the right and duty of a jurisdiction to introduce countermeasures to prevent typical "tax haven structures" from causing loss and damage within or outside its own jurisdiction. Countermeasures or sanctions could in principle be introduced by a single state or collectively. To balance sanctions in a carrot-and-stick approach, the Convention might also include the provision of technical assistance or support for alternative income generation in jurisdictions that are highly dependent upon the financial sector for income or that are willing to move away from a business model based on opacity.

A phased approach makes sense in terms of Convention development and adherence to it. Protocols can be added gradually, and not all signatories need to commit to every protocol. The idea of the Convention as a global and rather general framework is appealing in terms of generating attention, comprehension, and as a basis for the gradual adoption of specific recommendations in the area of transparency. A Convention including protocols and obligations with the explicit purpose of protecting sovereignty through counter-measures will inevitably encounter more opposition and fewer states are likely to sign up to it. The potential for genuine and effective change, though, with a sizeable amount of states ratifying or respecting the Convention, is important.

It is perhaps worth noting that the US, through unilateral action, in the last couple of years has brought about radical change and important progress in terms of transparency. Aspects of both the Dodd-Frank Act, albeit not yet effective, the Foreign Account Tax Compliance Act (FATCA), and legal action against bank secrecy have forced changes internationally that seemed unlikely until very recently. No doubt, the prospect of substantial negative financial consequences of not complying with US demands has been effective.

Moreover, although the Convention might seem far-fetched or even impossible to some, there is precedent for similar marked change in international financial relations. The 1930s was a time of trade wars and protectionism, with stifling economic growth hurting small and poor countries in particular. Even though the negative consequences for the majority were well recognized there were always country representatives in international forums such as the UN who saw it in their interest to block progress. Consequently, a small group of like-minded countries came together to establish a free-trade area, and with the idea gradually gaining recognition it resulted in the establishment of GATT and eventually the World Trade Organization. Against all odds the initiative of a dozen countries was a tremendous success.

A first and quite fundamental step in a process leading to a Convention would be to garner support for the idea that an overall framework for global commitment to financial transparency is needed. This would rest on broad recognition that financial secrecy is damaging to the well-being of the global majority and that it undermines state sovereignty. It would also be based on the appreciation that it is possible to "ban" secrecy, rather than merely adapting to it. From there the specific requirements could be agreed to, gradually if necessary, whereby signatory states commit not to introduce legislation and practices considered to encroach on and undermine other states' sovereignty. A combination of regulation intended solely for foreign companies, combining no or low tax with lax requirements in terms of information, audits, oversight, and control, would be an example of such unwanted practice. As illustrated by the examples from free-trade and US unilateral action, when the policy makes sense or economic-political weight is brought to bear—major change is possible.

10.5 OTHER MEASURES

In addition to securing the elimination of secrecy jurisdictions, the Convention could also serve as a mechanism to unite other existing proposals for promoting transparency as a measure to combat illicit financial flows. These should include the following:

10.5.1 Country-By-Country Reporting

Currently, corporations are only required to account for trade with unrelated companies and are therefore able to conceal trade between affiliates of the same company. Country-by-country reporting (CBCR) calls on multinational corporations (MNCs) to report all sales, profits, and taxes paid in all jurisdictions in their audited annual reports and tax returns—including those within the company. It also requires them to list the countries in which they operate, and the names of their entities in each country.

The information provided by CBCR increases financial transparency and corporate accountability. Currently, citizens do not have enough information "to establish even whether an MNC operates in their jurisdictions, let alone what it is doing there" (Tax Justice Network, n.d.). It would also make tax-avoiding schemes, such as abusive transfer pricing, easier to identify. The result is likely to be two-fold: first, CBCR will provide a strong deterrent for MNCs to engage in transfer mispricing in the first place (Murphy, 2009: 21), and second, "the data needed to resolve many disputes in favour of the tax jurisdiction raising [a] transfer pricing enquiry will be available for the first time" (Murphy, 2012: 40). This greater transparency could therefore help improve tax collection and generate much-needed revenue in developing countries.

Signatories to the Convention should pass legislation requiring that MNCs publish country-by-country accounting reports that would be subject to audit on an annual basis (PWC, 2013: 29).

10.5.2 Automatic Exchange of Information

Measures such as CBCR (or the publication of beneficial ownership data) are important for increasing transparency with respect to financial information. Automatic exchange of tax information on a global level would enable authorities to detect and act upon cases of non-compliance with international standards (OECD, 2013).

The OECD's Global Forum process in particular is crucial in promoting multilateral exchange of information. In the St. Petersburg Summit the G20 endorsed automatic exchange of tax information and pledged to implement it among their members by 2015, calling on other jurisdictions to do the same. As part of the Convention on Financial Transparency, signatories could be required to provide certain types of financial information about non-residents to those residents' country of origin. The Convention could also establish a centralized system for collecting, storing, and analyzing the information provided (Tanzi, 2005).

10.5.3 Due Diligence Standards

Due diligence standards vary widely across jurisdictions, and secrecy jurisdictions sometimes rely on minimal due diligence in order to attract investment and maintain secrecy of financial information. The Convention could help address these weaknesses by creating a forum for establishing international due diligence standards, including, for example, a minimum acceptable standard, as well as methods for implementation.

10.6 OBSTACLES TO IMPLEMENTATION

As referred to above, various doubts and objections to the idea of a Convention have already been raised. There is no doubt that powerful vested interests will be opposed. They can, perhaps, be placed in three groups:

1) Those with economic benefit from secrecy, whether directly through criminal or illicit interests or indirectly through the harbouring or protection of such criminal money. Wealthy individuals and commercial actors with an interest in concealing their assets or businesses practices would also fall in this group.
2) Economic libertarians who believe low or no taxes, and lack of regulation and state control is beneficial to economic development, and that the opposite is an infringement on privacy and confidentiality.
3) Those that agree with the motives of financial transparency but believe that current instruments and on-going processes will produce the best result, or who are skeptical regarding the idea of conventions as such.

This essay argues that a Convention might be a good idea, and the arguments made here will have to convince a sufficient number of states to join in the process if it is to be successful. As illustrated by the origins of GATT, and the more recent conventions against land mines and cluster munitions, a small number of states can initiate a process leading to global acceptance and not all states have to ratify a convention for it to be respected in practice.

The economic self-interest of governments is a powerful driver of policy and in the case of financial transparency it is hard to argue in "outflow states" that the combination of no tax and secrecy makes sense economically or in terms of generating state revenue.

10.7 SUMMARY

Financial transparency is right, sensible, and important in countless ways. Financial secrecy facilitates crime and harms economic development, and transparency is now at the top of the international policy agenda, whether the context is budgetary problems in the North or outright exploitation of poor people in the South. The question is more about how to ensure transparency. Current efforts tend to focus on the sharing of information—but leaving the damaging structures of secrecy intact—and increasing political pressure has been brought to bear on typical tax havens. This paper argues that a more effective and comprehensive approach would be to introduce a Convention or international agreement on transparency that would outlaw the harmful practices altogether, and include in it protective measures against jurisdictions that do not respect such a Convention.

Opponents to the idea of a Convention will be many and powerful, but there are examples of similar efforts succeeding against high odds. A political process for transparency, centered on a Convention, would in any case have the potential to draw attention to the issue and push the transparency agenda forward.

REFERENCES

Cohen, Stephen B., 2013. "Does Switzerland's Tax Haven for Offshore Accounts Violate Internationally Recognized Human Rights?" Georgetown University Law Center.

FATF, 2012. The FATF Recommendations, http://www.fatf-gafi.org/topics/fatfrecommendations/documents/fatf-recommendations.html, accessed 30 July 2015.

Findley, Michael G., Daniel L. Nielson, and J. C. Sharman, 2013. *Global Shell Games: Experiments in Transnational Relations*. Cambridge University Press, Cambridge.

Henry, James S., 2012. "The Price of Offshore Revisited," Tax Justice Network. http://www.taxjustice.net/cms/upload/pdf/Price_of_Offshore_Revisited_120722.pdf, accessed 30 July 2015.

Murphy, Richard, 2009. "Country-by-country Reporting: Holding Multinational Corporations to Account Wherever They Are," Task Force on Financial Integrity and Economic Development.

Murphy, Richard, 2012. "Country-by-country Reporting: Accounting for Globalization Locally," Tax Justice Network. www.taxresearch.org.uk/Documents/CBC2012.pdf, accessed 7 September 2015.

Norwegian Government Commission on Capital Flight from Poor Countries, 2009. "Tax Havens and Development." Report from the Government Commission on Capital Flight from Poor Countries. Appointed by Royal Decree of 27 June 2008. Submitted to the Ministry of Foreign Affairs, on 18 June 2009. Translation from the Norwegian.

Government Administration Services. Information Management. Oslo, 2009.

OECD, 2013. "The Global Forum on Transparency and Exchange of Information for Tax Purposes, Progress Report to the G20 Finance Ministers and Central Bank Governors: Global Forum Update on Effectiveness and Ongoing Monitoring." September. OECD, Paris.

PWC, 2013. "Tax Transparency and Country-by-country Reporting: An Ever-changing Landscape." http://www.pwc.com/gx/en/tax/publications/tax-transparency-reporting-an-ever-changing-landscape.jhtml, accessed 30 July 2015.

Tanzi, Vito, 2005. "Globalization, Tax System, and the Architecture of the Global Economic System." IDB Papers, 2005. http://www.iadb.org/en/inter-american-development-bank,2837.html, accessed 7 September 2015.

Tax Justice Network, n.d. "Country by Country Reporting," http://www.taxjustice.net/topics/corporate-tax/country-by-country/, accessed 30 July 2015.

UNODC, 2004. *United Nations Convention Against Transnational Organized Crime and the Protocols Thereto*. United Nations, New York.

11

Lakes, Oceans, and Taxes

Why the World Needs a World Tax Authority

Vito Tanzi

11.1 INTRODUCTION

This paper deals with the ability of governments to collect the tax revenue that they desire, to perform the economic functions that citizens have come to expect them to perform in today's world. It explains why taxation is now facing challenges that, if not addressed, could progressively and significantly reduce the governments' ability to raise taxes. The paper will argue that fundamental changes in the "architecture" of the world's economic relations may be required. It will ignore the ideological debate, between those who argue that governments have become Leviathan monsters never satisfied with the tax revenue that they get and those who argue that governments should do more than they do to bring about societal changes and to address issues of poverty and human rights.

The paper has five sections. The first discusses the *supply* of and the *demand* for taxes in the period until about the decade of the 1980s, when globalization intensified. The second discusses developments, in economic structures, in policies, and in some relevant technology, that started having a growing impact on the governments' ability to raise taxes. These developments created what the author of the present paper has described as "fiscal termites" (Tanzi, 2001). These "termites" started to eat away at the foundations of the current tax systems (Tanzi, 2013). The developments described are affecting all countries. However, some countries, and especially poorer countries with mineral resources, may be more exposed to particular problems of global tax evasion than other countries. In some of these countries major cases of poor governance or corruption (at times by the countries' own leaders) have created particularly bad situations. The third discusses institutional or organizational changes, some affecting the existing economic architecture of the economic relations among countries that are needed to prevent the growing problems from getting worse and from significantly reducing the countries' ability to raise the revenue that they need. The fourth section describes what a World Tax Authority could do, if it came into existence. The final section provides some brief, concluding remarks.

11.2 TAXES AND THE GROWTH OF THE WELFARE STATES

Until the decade of the 1920s, the demand for tax revenue by governments had remained relatively modest, compared with modern times (Tanzi, 2011). During this period it would have been also difficult for governments to extract large tax levels from the population. Both the *supply* of taxes and the *demand* for taxes met at a low tax level. At that time, assistance to the poor was largely left to churches and charitable organizations and there was no attempt and little interest by governments to redistribute income, from richer to poorer income groups, or to offer protection against some risks to citizens.

With the passing of time, changes that were taking place in the structure of the economies of several countries, (large firms with thousands of dependent workers, more use of accounting, increased production of manufactured products, more trade with other countries, more people living in larger cities, less informality in the economy) increased the potential for raising higher tax revenues to allow governments to significantly increase their socially oriented activities.

Although there had always been some trade among countries, especially in basic commodities and in products that were available only from particular countries, and there had been also some movement of capital, (loans to governments and funds to finance major infrastructure projects), in this period most products and services were produced exclusively with the inputs of the countries in which they were produced and with the financing provided by domestic sources. Therefore, the value of the products reflected almost entirely the domestic value added, with the exception of the imported basic commodities that were required. There was little capital movement and there was no payment for *parts* of *final* manufactured products produced in some countries and assembled in another country. There were almost no payments for the use of intellectual or intangible property inputs (patents, trademarks, copyrights, insurance fees, services provided by headquarters of corporations, including those for research and development, and so on).

As a consequence of the economic architecture of the world that had prevailed until recent decades, the *tax bases* of sovereign countries could be compared to domestic lakes, the water of which could be exploited only by the national governments of the countries in which the lakes were located. There was no, or little, fear of foreign *tax competition*. The exploitation of the national tax bases by governments was limited only by the traditional resistance from the national taxpayers (domestic tax evasion, political resistance) and by the limitations of the national tax administrations.

While the push toward greater demands by governments, for higher tax revenue into gross domestic products had started before the Great Depression, the policies that were introduced during the Depression and soon after World War Two accelerated that process. The new economic role of the state required more public revenue and, after the Great Depression, tax levels started going up in several now-developed countries. The greater demands for tax revenue came at a time when the changed structures of the countries' economies could, more easily than in the past, accommodate those demands. The industrial countries had become less informal and less rural and were fast becoming industrial, creating large firms that hired thousands of workers. This made it easier to levy taxes, especially in economies that were still relatively close.

Until about the decade of the 1970s, capital movements had remained largely controlled. The rise of a globalized economy, with corporations that would operate and produce in several countries, would come later. In the 1970s or early 1980s large multinational corporations, that produced final products and also services, and not just basic commodities, started growing in importance. In the new century, some large multinational corporations came into existence that produced also *intangible* products using "intellectual property." Some of these corporations (Google, Apple, Microsoft, Facebook, Amazon) became enormous, measured by the market value of their sales, by their profits, and by the workers that they employed. By the first decade of the new century trade *among* multinational corporations accounted for more than half of total trade among countries. Before that time, trade among countries and especially among multinational corporations, in particular trade based on intellectual property and on intangible products, had been limited.

11.3 THE IMPACT OF GLOBALIZATION ON TAXES

The relatively tax-friendly environment that for several decades had made it possible for many industrial countries to increase their tax burdens, started to be challenged, especially in the 1990s. The challenges accelerated in the new century when national economies became much more open and imports and exports, as shares of GDPs, increased sharply, and when capital started to move freely across countries. A global financial system came into existence that, with the help of new technology, allowed trillions of US dollars to cross national borders every day.

The role of multinational corporations, which assembled *final* products from parts manufactured in several other countries, increased sharply. The inputs or parts were assembled in one country (China, Germany, the United States, etc.) from where the final products were sold worldwide. This arrangement created difficulties for the national tax administrations, because they could not determine the value of the imported parts that were product-specific so that it was impossible to determine what their value would have been if they had been traded in a competitive market. This exacerbated the problem of "transfer prices." Attempts to rely on the so-called "arm's length principle," recommended by the OECD, became increasingly anachronistic. Corporations acquired large scope in manipulating costs, to show higher profits in countries where tax rates were lower and lower profits in those where the tax rates were higher.

Financing through debt, rather than through equity capital, for which the interest payments made to the creditors were deductible costs while the payments of dividends were not, replaced much equity financing. This created the problem of "thin capitalization" which contributed to lowering the tax liability of many corporations. Furthermore, the loans could be obtained from tax havens, where the interest payments were not taxed. Cross-country use of intellectual property (patents, trademarks, copyrights, etc.) increased and the value of the use of intellectual properties was difficult to determine, leading to further abuses. Internet shopping became common and shopping for intangible products also increased the difficulties of identifying sellers and buyers. Some of the multinational enterprises that sold intangible products (Google, Apple, Microsoft, Facebook, etc.) became some of the largest enterprises in the world. It also became difficult to tax corporations that exploited natural resources, especially when the market prices of the commodities fluctuated.

The above developments created greater opportunities for tax avoidance and tax evasion, especially for global economic activities. They encouraged the growth of tax havens and the use of "tolling" and "triangulation" strategies, in which some products or services are sold to, or are bought by, controlled foreign enterprises and the prices are adjusted up or down to report lower profits. Berlusconi, the former prime minister of Italy, was found guilty of having presumably used such a system in the enterprise that he controlled.

The arbitrary use of "transfer prices"; of "tolling" and other "triangulation" techniques; the arbitrary valuation of intellectual property; the excessive use of loans instead of equity, and especially of loans obtained from affiliated sources located in tax havens; the manipulation of interest rates in the loans and of insurance charges; and other such maneuvers have given a strong incentive to enterprises, and to rich individuals, to use "tax planning" to reduce their tax liabilities. Now production decisions by corporations are much influenced by tax considerations and, in many enterprises, personnel that deal with tax planning have become, at times, more important than production engineers or other personnel. This has been the *demand side* of tax avoidance.

There has also been a *supply side* to this tax avoidance process. This has consisted in the growth of a tax advisory industry, made up of individuals working independently or through law or accounting firms, and of "tax havens" and "offshore centers" that have taken advantage of the situation to extract benefits or "rents" from what could be called the "world tax base." This base has progressively become interconnected and, like an ocean, has expanded to include all, or parts of, the previously independent national lakes that the national tax authorities had previously been able to exploit without foreign competition or consideration. In some sense the ocean that has been created by the now-connected lakes has taken some of the characteristics of a "common." As it is known, commons can be subjected to the "tragedy of commons," a tragedy that Garrett Hardin made famous, with a 1968 article in *Science*. As economists had long known, and as Hardin had made popular among non-economists with his article, "commons" tend to be exploited and at times *overexploited* by those who have access to them.

The exploitation of the "world tax base," or of the "world tax common" can take different forms. Smaller countries (Lichtenstein, Switzerland, Ireland, Holland, Panama, Cyprus, and some others) and some territories (the US state of Delaware, Isle of Man, and others) may be tempted to introduce domestic tax rules and low tax rates that have the goal of attracting to them a larger share of the "world tax base," that would have been taxed in the countries in which the enterprises or the individuals had actually produced the taxable base. In addition to the small countries, "tax havens," of which there are many, aim to attract to them parts of the world tax base. The net effect is that the world tax base is partly diverted from areas where tax rates are high, and from where that base has actually been generated, to places where tax rates are low or even zero.

Real economic activities move much less than tax bases (Tanzi, 1995). Antigua or Bermuda or even Ireland accommodate far less *real* economic activity than the tax bases that are attributed to them and that they can exploit. "Tax planning" by taxpayers (be these enterprises or individuals) exploits (at times legally, at other times less so) the opportunities that are offered to them, by complex or inadequate national laws, to shift taxable income to the places where the rates are low or are even zero. The losers tend to be the countries that, because of these maneuvers, lose revenue, or that encounter increasing difficulties to keep raising the revenue to which they feel they are entitled. This revenue loss can lead to increased public borrowing thus contributing to macroeconomic difficulties.

This problem has forced larger countries to abandon some of the basic principles that had guided tax policies in past decades, especially the principle that *income is income, regardless of the source*, and that all sources of income should be taxed at the same rates (Tanzi, 2014). Recent decades have been characterized by the progressive abandonment of the Haig-Simons or the Hicks principle, which required the uniform taxation of all income sources, and by a return to the taxes, that had existed in the distant past, when each source of income was taxed separately and often at different rates. The result has been that dividends, profits, interest incomes, capital gains, so-called "carried trade," and other sources of incomes that are especially important for rich individuals, are now often taxed at significantly lower rates than wages, thus contributing to, growing income inequality (Alvaredo et al., 2013). The share of total income going to individuals at the top one percent of the income distribution has increased dramatically since the 1970s, and has reached very high levels in the United States and in some other countries. The same has happened to the share received by capital in national income. This change in tax laws and in tax rates has also affected total tax revenues. Among twenty-nine European countries, twenty-five had lower shares of tax-to-GDP in 2010–11 than they did in 2000 (European Commission, 2013).

As we described earlier, these difficulties were increased by globalization, by the use of new technologies, and by changes in the structure of economies. When firms that account for large and growing shares of the economy (Google, Apple, Microsoft, Facebook, and others), and rich individuals that receive growing shares of total income pay little in taxes, as it has been reported by recent revelations and statistics, this must affect the levels of taxation that countries can easily collect. The "fiscal termites" have definitely been at work, eating away at the foundations of modern tax systems. If their action is not contained, or stopped, there could be negative consequences in the long run.

11.4 THE NEED FOR A GLOBAL TAX AUTHORITY

Over the past half century the concept of "public good," a concept that entered theoretical economics in the 1940s and 1950s, (with contributions by Paul Samuelson, Richard Musgrave, and others), acquired an increasingly *global* dimension (Kaul et al., 2003; Razin and Sadka, 1999). Global "public goods" now include world peace, the environment, or the absence of global warming, the status of the oceans, stability in the global financial system, global health (i.e. the absence of pandemics), global economic stability, a well-functioning trading system, alleviation of global poverty, absence of crimes against humanity, and so on. Globalization and closer connectivity among people have increased the importance of these "global public goods."

To protect or promote these global public goods in the absence of a world government, the international community has over the years created various international institutions that act as proxies for ministries that would exist under a world government (Tanzi, 2008). These institutions include: the United Nations, to deal with world peace; the World Bank, to promote the elimination of poverty and global economic growth; the IMF, to promote macroeconomic stability; the World Trade Organization, to promote smoothly working trading systems; the World Health Organization, to promote good health and the absence of epidemics, and so on. However, there remain gaps in the architecture of the world economic and social system. Two important gaps are the absence of an organization to regulate and deal with the recently created global financial system and an organization to regulate tax relations among countries, to prevent unfair tax competition and to limit the opportunities for global tax evasion. The rest of this paper deals with the latter gap.

In the previous section it was argued that the national tax systems, which had existed in the past, had been similar to *domestic* lakes that could be exploited only by the *national* governments of the countries in which they were located, without the fear of "poaching" by other countries' governments. In recent decades the lakes became progressively and increasingly connected and, slowly, started to resemble an ocean. This started to create a classic "common," making it possible for some countries and for some taxpayers to exploit it to their advantage. Some countries saw the possibility of increasing their revenue by exploiting the "common" and many taxpayers saw the possibility of reducing their tax burdens by moving (at times only virtually) their taxable incomes or other tax bases to low- or no-tax jurisdictions.

As with the experience of some "commons," and as described in the seminal work by Elinor Ostrom, that earned her the Nobel Prize in economics, in principle "coordination" among countries could prevent the exploitation of the "world tax base" from becoming a "tragedy of commons," without the need of a supervising or mentoring institution. Over past years some forms of tax cooperation has in fact developed among countries. These included: (a) double- taxation treaties among countries, which include some exchange of information; (b) directives issued by the European Commission; (c) the guidance issued by the Fiscal Affairs Committee of the OECD and related activities, and, more recently, (d) declarations denouncing tax avoidance/evasion by political groups such as the G20 and the G8 and unilateral actions by some countries. However, none of these has resolved the tragedy of the commons under discussion. Each will be discussed in turn.

Over the years countries have negotiated hundreds of bilateral tax treaties at considerable costs. For example, Mexico has negotiated forty-nine, and Brazil thirty-two such treaties. They have been directed mainly at protecting foreign investors against double taxation; were generally designed by the tax lawyers of the more advanced countries; and they had bilateral partners. There is now fairly general agreement among experts that these treaties have not helped the less developed countries and have done little to deal with "the tragedy of commons" described above. Rather, they have largely reduced the tax burdens on the foreign investors and the tax revenue of the poorer countries.

The various "directives," issued by the European Commission have been regional in character, being limited to the EU countries, and have had limited impact either on the coordination of tax systems within the EU, where they ought to have had an impact, or on the problems discussed in this paper. Tax competition and lack of tax harmonization remains a problem even within EU.

The role that the Committee on Fiscal Affairs of the OECD has played over the years has been more visible and more important, but not productive enough. First, the countries that are part of the OECD are only about 15 percent of the world's countries and they are the richest. Their interests inevitably tend to diverge from those of the poorer countries. Second, the Committee has been a forum for discussion and not for decisions. Third, *policy* issues have been much less discussed than *administrative* issues, because those who represent the countries in the regular meetings of the Committee on Fiscal Affairs come mostly from tax administrations and not from the policy-making ministries. Fourth, there has been a feeling, on the part of some observers, that in the past the OECD could have been more forceful, more imaginative, and more inclusive in discussing and in promoting solutions to growing tax problems. Some of its solutions, for example the strong defense of "transfer prices" or its approach to "tax havens," have been criticized. With its limited staff it has focused on solving past administrative difficulties, and less on anticipating future ones.

The recent reports about tax avoidance by large multinational corporations, such as Google, Apple, Starbucks, some large pharmaceutical companies, and others, and recent "estimations" (guesses?) of global tax evasion that run into the hundreds of billions of US dollars, and declarations issued by groups of countries that are part of the G20 or the G8, show a growing concern over this problem. But they do not suggest convincing solutions. Declarations have focused on better exchange of information among countries. Such exchanges might be *part of* a solution to the problem. However, they are not likely to solve the problem (Tanzi and Zee, 2001). There have been useful hearings held in the US Congress and in other legislative bodies that have highlighted some of the developing problems and have called attention to the quantitative dimensions of global tax avoidance. These hearings have increased pressures on some tax havens but have not made much impact yet toward a solution.

These agreements among *some* groups of countries, or unilateral or bilateral measures, have not led so far and are not likely to lead to effective rules about unfair tax competition by some countries and prevent aggressive tax planning by many multinational corporations or rich individuals. They are not likely to deal with the problem or to prevent it from becoming progressively more serious. The actors are just too many and their incentives are too divergent for coordinated or spontaneous solutions to emerge. Something more significant is needed.

Realistic solutions to the problem would have to include some or several of the following reforms: (i) extension of the residence principle to reduce the possibility that simply changing an address can reduce tax liability for some taxpayers; (ii) a greater use of source taxation, as was suggested in Tanzi (1995); (c) some fundamental reform of corporate income taxation, for example, better defining the tax base and using formula apportionment of profits; (d) easier exchange of information among countries; and (e) greater reporting requirements for corporations and individuals to all the countries in which they operate. These and other possible measures would need a powerful and competent global mentor and referee that can carefully analyze the specific reforms proposed, determine which have merit, refine them, and suggest the practical ways in which they could be implemented. Such a mentor can only be some super-national World Tax Authority.

In a paper published more than a quarter century ago that called attention to trends that at that time were still not yet easily visible, the author predicted that future developments would "make it difficult for countries to maintain their present levels and structures of taxation." The paper concluded, "that the day may come when the countries [would need to] create an "International Revenue" *to collect taxes* that could not be collected by separate governments and to allocate them either to the provision of international public goods or back to the countries. Such an international institution might also collect information on taxpayers for the benefit of the members' tax administrations" (Tanzi, 1988: 277).

Section 11.5 discusses in some detail a realistic and useful role that a World Tax Authority could play. Such an institution would add an important element to the architecture that now lubricates and facilitates the economic relations among countries. It would add a missing "proxy" for a ministry that a World Government, if it existed, would need to have.

11.5 WHAT WOULD A WORLD TAX AUTHORITY DO?

If a World Tax Authority (WTA) were created, what would be its mandate? Naturally, there are several possibilities and functions that could be given to such an Authority. They range from relatively modest and realistic, to highly ambitious and unrealistic. The mandate that would be given to such an institution would depend not only on what some think that the world needs but on how much power the countries, and especially the governments of the more powerful ones that would have to authorize, endorse, and finance such an institution, would be willing to delegate to it. Taxation is undoubtedly one of the most political of all of governments' activities. Therefore, the greater are the powers that one would want to give to the new institution, the lower are the chances that it would ever see the light of day. To have any chance of being born, the new institution must be seen as useful to help the countries' governments to solve problems that they want to solve, but not so powerful as to usurp the power that the countries' legislatures and policymakers now have.

The *initial* responsibility given to a WTA should be relatively modest in order to increase its acceptability to leading countries, and not just to representatives of civil society. If the institution came into existence and proved to be useful, those countries might be willing to give it increased responsibilities over time. To be useful, a WTA should be as representative as possible of the *whole* global community. It should not be seen as the agent of specific groups, be these rich or poor countries. It would need to include a far larger number of countries than does the OECD or the EU. Ideally all countries and all independent jurisdictions should belong to it.

Many commentators from the right tend to see taxes as evil instruments and tax competition as a benign activity that keeps down tax levels. Those who hold these views would inevitably fear that a World Tax Authority could become an instrument for Leviathan governments hungry for higher taxes. They would oppose the creation of a WTA and their effort would attract financial support from conservative, rich individuals and from some corporations. It might be mentioned that, in June 2001, a report to the "High Level Panel on Financing for Development" (the Zedillo Report), that had been prepared by the president of Mexico for the high-level Monterey Meeting, had included, in the original draft, a proposal for the creation of a "World Tax Organization" based on Tanzi (1999). A well-organized campaign by opponents to the proposal managed to have it removed from the final report and from any discussion at the meeting. The WTA had to wait for a better time to be born. A too-ambitious proposal would face similar opposition and risk a similar fate today.

It is highly unlikely that the major countries, which would have to agree to the creation of such an institution, would agree any time soon to the creation of one that would have the power to *levy* taxes on the citizens of sovereign countries, as had been proposed in Tanzi (1988). That time may come one day, but that day is likely still some time far in the future. However, even without the power to tax, a World Tax Authority could perform many useful tasks that would be helpful at this time to the community of nations. It is worth repeating that, if such an Authority were seen to be useful and efficient in what it did, countries might, over its future life, give it more responsibilities.

Tanzi (1999) made a list of some of the tasks and functions that such an institution could perform. The list is reproduced below with some updating and some elaboration. The main goal of such an institution would be to reduce *unfair* tax competition, *unfair* exploitation of the "world tax base," and to help reduce the growing problem of tax avoidance and tax evasion that is connected with global activities. Domestic tax problems would not be among the responsibilities of the WTA although the institution should have the expertise and the mandate to provide technical assistance, especially to poorer countries, when they required it, as for example in their dealings with multinational corporations.

The *first* task that a WTA would undertake on a regular basis would be the identification of major trends and problems in taxation, at the international level, for all groups of countries. Today there is no regular, formal identification of these trends and problems, even though there are occasional publications that report on some of them. Among these reports, those by the IMF, the OECD, the CIAT, and the European Commission are useful, as well as reports by the Tax Justice Network, articles by Bloomberg Net and publications by government sources, by accounting firms, and by academics.

The *second* task would be that of compiling and making available relevant tax information and statistics for as many countries as possible. The availability of this information has grown over the years but it is still highly deficient. There is now no official institution that has such a responsibility *for the whole world*, although some private and public institutions attempt to do some of it (see, for example, OECD, 2013; PWC, 2013).

The *third* task would be to publish a periodic, regular *World Tax Development Report* that would present the tax statistics, identify the trends and the major problems, identify best practices, and suggest solutions to developing problems. This task could be prepared with, and facilitated by the collaboration of institutions such as the OECD, the IMF, the World Bank, the EU, the CIAT, and other relevant institutions. It could also include the contributions of major accounting firms.

The *fourth* task would be to develop basic principles and codes of behavior for countries that would aim at minimizing the creation of cross-country, negative externalities originating from the tax policies of some countries. These principles could not eliminate the freedom that individual countries now have in pursuing tax policies that are desirable for them and in setting the rates for some taxes. However, they would make the countries' policymakers more sensitive to the cross-country consequences that their policies might have. These cross-country externalities have become progressively more frequent in recent years and more damaging to the national interests of some countries. Some of them occasionally attract the attention of the World Trade Organization.

The *fifth* task would be the creation of an international tax forum in which the policymakers and the tax experts that represent the different countries would meet and where they could exchange views and ideas on *general* tax matters that are not often pushed by paid lobbyists, who reflect the interests of specific groups.

The *sixth* task would be to establish an international forum for the discussion of *specific countries' tax policies* and for informal arbitration, when the actual or the proposed tax policies of a country or a group of countries have, or are believed to have, *significant* negative impact on other countries and when they are challenged by the representative of those other countries. Strange as it seems, such a forum does not exist today. In principle the outcome of the tax arbitration could lead to penalties for the countries that produce the negative externalities. However, the possibility of such penalties might not be acceptable today to many countries. Alternatively, and perhaps more realistically, it could lead to the issuing of official statements that aim at creating influencing behavior, by *shaming* particular countries.

The *seventh* task would be to promote specific rules and to identify limits for exchanging information on taxpayers among countries. Such an exchange might raise difficult logistic and practical difficulties, and even constitutional problems for some countries. There is also the danger that requests for information, on particular taxpayers, may not always be promoted by legitimate objectives on the part of the requesting countries. Requests are cheap to make but may be costly for the countries that must provide the information, when that information is not routinely available to them and may be difficult to provide it in a format (and in a language) that would be useful to those who request it. Imagine the United States and China exchanging information each in its own language and each using its own definition of taxable income. See Tanzi and Zee, 2001, for elaborations of these points. Therefore, the exchange of information that is seen by many as the solution to many of the current problems requires specific and well-thought-out rules, to prevent fishing expeditions and unreasonable requests by some countries. It must also be recognized that at times requests may be based on political or commercial objectives rather than legitimate needs. Therefore, some filters must exist.

The *eighth* task would be for the experts in the WTA to study various solutions that are suggested by tax experts, including the ones mentioned earlier, to deal with global tax problems. Once the experts at the WTA have settled on the solutions that they consider best, they would promote them and would push the countries to adopt them, providing them with technical assistance, when needed and requested.

Finally, and most importantly, a World Tax Authority would create a system of regular "surveillance" over the behavior of countries' tax policies. Such a system does not now exist. The complaints about unfair tax competition are often unilateral and ad hoc and major tax reforms by individual countries take place without any global assessment. Such "surveillance," with the results discussed by representatives of *all* countries and made public in a summing up of the discussion, would encourage better behavior by member countries and reduce tax competition, when it risks becoming *unfair*.

The "surveillance" function would be similar to the one that now exists at the IMF, over macroeconomic policies, or at the World Trade Organization, over trade policies. As mentioned above, it could be combined with a system of guided arbitration, when the policies of a country lead to complaints by other countries. The basic point is that the existence of a World Tax Authority would make the tax policies of a country everyone's business and not the exclusive business of that country. The impact that such an institution could have would depend on its prestige, the quality of the staff that it would attract, on the resources available to it, on the level of the representation of the countries in its decision-making, and on the impact, legal or simply reputational, of its decisions.

The question of whether to have an arrangement that would give one country one vote, as in the UN General Assembly, or to weigh the vote by the economic size of the country (as the IMF is supposed to do), if occasional voting is required, would be one of the most important issues to decide, should such an institution come into existence. The more democratic arrangements would probably reduce the power of the institution and the chance that it could effect meaningful change.

11.6 CONCLUDING REMARKS

This paper has dealt with the increasing difficulties that many countries are encountering to keep collecting, in an equitable and efficient way, the levels of taxes that they need to finance their public spending. The paper has traced some important historical developments: in the structure of the countries' economies; in the expectations of what governments should do for their citizens; and in the economic relations among countries. Over the years these developments (a) progressively increased the need for public resources, (b) facilitated the collection of higher tax levels and, in more recent decades, because of globalization and of some technological changes, (c) created growing difficulties in maintaining or increasing their tax levels. These difficulties were largely connected with tax competition and with increasing global tax evasion.

The paper has argued that, given the above-mentioned problems, there may be a need for establishing a World Tax Authority, that would not, in the first instance, collect taxes—although a time might come for such a role to finance global "public goods"—but that would help bring order to the tax policies of countries, especially to those that have cross-country implications. In the absence of such an institution, some of the problems connected with unfair tax competition, with international tax avoidance, and with the "poaching" of other countries' tax bases are like to intensify, contributing to progressively more serious macroeconomic difficulties for some countries and to the reduction of some governments' ability to deal with domestic social problems.

REFERENCES

Alvaredo, Facundo, Anthony B. Atkinson, Thomas Piketty, and Emmanuel Saez, 2013. "The Top 1 Percent in International Perspective," *The Journal of Economic Perspectives* 27 (3), summer: 3–20.

European Commission, 2013. *Taxation Trends in the European Union*. Brussels.

Kaul, Inge, Pedro Conceicao, Katell le Goulven, and Ronald U. Mendoza, 2003. *Providing Global Public Goods: Managing Globalization*. Oxford University Press, New York.

Musgrave, Richard, 1969. *Fiscal Systems*. Yale University Press, New Haven.

OECD, 2013. *Revenue Statistics of OECD Countries*. OECD, Paris.

PWC, 2013. "Paying Taxes 2013: the Global Picture." http://www.pwc.com/gx/en/paying-taxes/assets/pwc-paying-taxes-2013-full-report.pdf, accessed 7 September 2015.

Razin, Assaf and Efraim Sadka, 1999. *The Economics of Globalization: Policy Perspectives from Public Economics*. Cambridge University Press, New York.

Tanzi, Vito, 1988. "Forces that Shape Tax Policy," in Herbert Stein (ed.) *Tax Policy in the Twenty-First Century*. John Wiley and Sons, New York.

Tanzi, Vito, 1995. *Taxation in an Integrating World*. The Brookings Institution, Washington, DC.

Tanzi, Vito, 1999. "Is There a Need for a World Tax Organization?" in Assaf Razin and Efraim Sadka (eds) *The Economics of Globalization*. Cambridge University Press, New York.

Tanzi, Vito, 2001. "Globalization, Technological Developments, and the Work of Fiscal Termites," *Brooklyn Journal of International Law* XXVI, no 4.

Tanzi, Vito, 2008. "The Future of Fiscal Federalism," *European Journal of Political Economy* 24: 705–12.

Tanzi, Vito, 2011. *Government versus Markets: The Changing Economic Role of the State*. Cambridge University Press, New York.

Tanzi, Vito, 2013. *Dollars, Euros and Debt: How We Got into the Fiscal Crisis, and How We Get out of It*. Palgrave Macmillan, London.

Tanzi, Vito, 2014. "The Challenges of Taxing the Big," *Revista de Economia Mundial*, Special Issue on International Public Economics, summer.

Tanzi, Vito and Howell Zee, 2001. "Can Information Exchange Be Effective in Taxing Cross-Border Income Flows?" *Liber Amicorum Sven-Olof Lodin*. Kluwer, London.

12

Tax Competitiveness—a Dangerous Obsession

Nicholas Shaxson and John Christensen

12.1 INTRODUCTION

Some people wonder why the world's big powers don't send in the gunboats and close down the tax havens. These places, after all, suck out their tax revenues, make it harder to regulate their financial institutions, and host a global criminal underworld. With some $20 trillion or more in financial wealth sitting out there,[1] offshore and untaxed or lightly taxed, and growing at over 10 percent annually, it's a good question.

There are several answers, each with major implications for developing countries.

The simplest answer is that it's complicated. There's no easy way to shutter those myriad tax and secrecy loopholes. Try to crack down, and an enabling army of highly paid accountants, lawyers, bankers, and company formation agents will create new loopholes and pathways through the evolving international system. This game of cat and mouse throws up more confusion and complexity. Developing countries with under-resourced tax administrations are particularly hard-hit, and the problem is getting worse.

A second reason is that there is no interest group more rich and powerful than the rich and powerful, who are the main users and beneficiaries of the offshore system of tax havens or secrecy jurisdictions. The losers are ordinary taxpayers in rich and poor countries alike who don't have the political power or expertise to challenge the skilled enablers. Again, this is most difficult for

[1] A widely cited estimate of $7.8 trillion is provided by Gabriel Zucman (2013, 2014.) Henry (2012) provides higher estimates of $21–32 trillion; and see *The Price of Offshore, Revisited*—supplementary notes, Tax Justice Network, June 5, 2014, providing suggestions why Zucman's estimates may be too low. For the growth rates, see Tax Justice Network (2014), or Kar and LeBlanc (2013) each estimating 10 percent growth rates or more.

poorer countries, which are victims of looting by their élites who stash their wealth offshore, and therefore resist change.

To grasp a third answer, it helps to try and guess how many Nigerians or Indonesians stash their illicit cash in London or Zurich—then guess how many wealthy Swiss or British individuals stash theirs in Lagos or Jakarta. The discrepancy illustrates the point: the offshore system is engineering a gigantic net one-way flow of capital from poor countries to rich ones: something that conventional globalization theories never seriously addressed. Nearly every secrecy jurisdiction is either a rich Western country (such as Switzerland or Luxembourg) or is a satellite of one—such as the Crown Dependencies and Overseas Territories of the United Kingdom which include such offshore giants as the Cayman Islands, Jersey, and Bermuda.

A fourth and more complex answer can be found by asking a further question: how have things got to this state? It certainly wasn't always like this.

12.2 THE GENESIS OF TAX COMPETITION

To find answers to *this* question—how and why the tax havens have metastatized and grown so much faster than the global economy—we'll point to a statement by G7 leaders in Lyon in May 1996. Buried in their text was a then little noticed request for the OECD, a club of rich countries, to investigate a phenomenon known as "Tax Competition." That is the subject of this chapter.

Tax "competition" occurs when jurisdictions—whether independent nations or states inside a federation—dangle tax incentives to tempt investment, hot money, financial activities, or even wealthy individuals away from other jurisdictions, often nearby. There are three main ways that this happens: falling tax rates come down; the tax base (that is, what gets subjected to tax) shrinks, and enforcement gets weakened, often deliberately. Each move either directly takes a chunk out of other countries' tax systems, or puts pressure on them to follow suit and make their own cuts: in a "race to the bottom." This "competition" goes way beyond tax: it is also found in the areas of financial secrecy, financial deregulation, tolerance for criminal money, and more.[2]

The five main arguments of this chapter are as follows.

First, tax "competition" is wholly pernicious, with no meaningful redeeming features of any kind. This is true not just at a global level, but also at a purely

[2] Tax inducements come in a variety of forms: reduced statutory tax rates, tax loopholes, tax holidays, export zones, secrecy facilities that prevent other states taxing locally earned income; and deliberately lax tax enforcement. The incentives may be in domestic tax laws or tax treaties, or negotiated individually. The details can be complex: they may, for example, aim to give tax resident companies a competitive advantage over foreign competitors by letting them use foreign tax havens to escape home-country and foreign taxes.

self-interested national level, particularly for larger economies, where pursuing a "competitive" tax system is generally a recipe for national self-harm.

Second, some elements of the academic literature on this topic, arguing that the processes are modest or benign, are based on elementary misunderstandings and fanciful assumptions, or are irrelevant. These ideas are however seized upon by politicians and vested interests.

Third, the term "tax competition" is a misnomer—and this is highly consequential. It has nothing to do with market competition but is more like currency or trade wars—and should be rebranded as "*tax wars*," echoing the Brazilian term *Guerra Fiscal* (fiscal war). "Tax wars" better describes the processes and conveys the harm. We will use the term in this chapter.

Fourth, the process is driven very substantially by a false belief system that asserts that tax wars are a good thing at both a global level and at a national level—with the latter proposition expressed as: "our country must be tax competitive." Boeing's threats not to carry out safety checks on its aircraft if it doesn't receive adequate tax breaks provides an example of the level of credulity (CTJ, 2014). This false belief system is rarely subject to robust challenge.

Fifth, the tax subsidies that large corporations derive from this process do not stop when nominal rates reach zero: many corporations already enjoy negative effective rates derived from a range of rent-seeking subsidies they secure—and matters seem likely to deteriorate.[3]

Our arguments apply to rich and poor countries but developing countries have least to gain and most to lose, collectively and individually, from participating in the race.

12.3 LESSONS FROM THE LAST WAR ON TAX WARS

In 1998, then armed with the G7 mandate, the OECD released a seminal report "*Harmful Tax Competition: An Emerging Issue*," focusing quite heavily on tax havens.[4]

To begin with, the odd-sounding document raised few headlines. One of few who did pay attention was a US tax policy lobbyist called Daniel Mitchell,

[3] See, for example, CTJ, April 2012. They found that 30 large US companies enjoyed an average effective federal income tax rate of minus 3.1 percent in 2008–11, despite $205bn in pretax US profits. See also Peters and Fisher (2004).

[4] See OECD, 1998. The report honed in on low or zero tax rates, various kinds of secrecy, and a lack of genuine economic activity associated with income generated. All OECD member states, except for the tax havens of Switzerland and Luxembourg, approved the document. The episode is extensively covered in Sharman (2006).

a self-declared libertarian then working at the Heritage Foundation in Washington, DC.

Mitchell wasn't overwhelmed at first. "I thought, 'Ah, just a bunch of crazy European socialists,'" he later told us.[5] "For me, international tax—transfer pricing, interest allocations, and so on—was almost as bad as excise taxes on milk in Mongolia." But he and a couple of colleagues began to take a look.

An avid admirer of Ronald Reagan, Mitchell found his interest was piqued when the Bill Clinton administration in its last budget in February 2000 supported the OECD's new stance by proposing to require reporting of payments to tax havens and to deny foreign tax credits to income reported from designated tax havens. Four months later, the OECD unveiled a blacklist, with the threat of "defensive measures"—or sanctions, which bore similarities to the Clinton proposals.

This was a bombshell. "Our side was caught with our pants down," Mitchell admitted. By October 2000 he and Andrew Quinlan, a colleague, had set up the Center for Freedom and Prosperity, a lobby group hosted at the Cato Institute in Washington, DC, to spearhead the campaign against the "international bureaucrats" at the OECD. Their guerrilla campaign was to prove a wild success.

Before exploring what happened next, it's important to understand a little more about tax wars.

12.4 THE PROBLEM

Academic researchers, for their sins, disagree on the extent to which tax wars are harmful. Some even suggest they are beneficial.

The immediate problem is simple enough to explain. Governments do not tax financial capital and its representatives heavily for fear that they will flee—but workers are far less mobile: they can be taxed heavily and few will migrate elsewhere. The end result is that effective tax rates on financial capital—and by extension the wealthiest members of society—get cut, while tax rates on workers and consumers tend to rise to compensate. When one jurisdiction cuts, others feel pressured to follow suit, and the problem keeps evolving in one direction. Even if overall tax levels do not fall, the damage is felt on the tax structure inside individual jurisdictions, where the poor end up paying more.

[5] Dan Mitchell, interview by Nicholas Shaxson and John Christensen, Cato Institute, Washington, DC, 16 January 2009. For a fuller account of Mitchell's views, see Shaxson (2010), the chapter 'Ratchet' in Shaxson (2012).

Tax wars are not just the product of impersonal forces, however, but are nurtured and networked, as US expert Greg LeRoy explains of the process inside the United States:

> This system has a long history and many moving parts. It traces back to at least the 1930s and the Great Depression, and really matured by the 1970s. By then, most of the key actors were in place: secretive site location consultants who specialize in playing states and cities against each other; "business climate" experts with their highly politicized interpretations of tax and jobs data; and an organized corporate network orchestrating attacks on state tax systems.
>
> (Leroy, 2005)

Developing countries face similar pressures, of course, though the battles usually happen in private and we rarely hear about them.

Figure 12.1 shows the dramatic effects since 1980 on corporate tax rates in countries at different income levels.

The story does not end here, however.

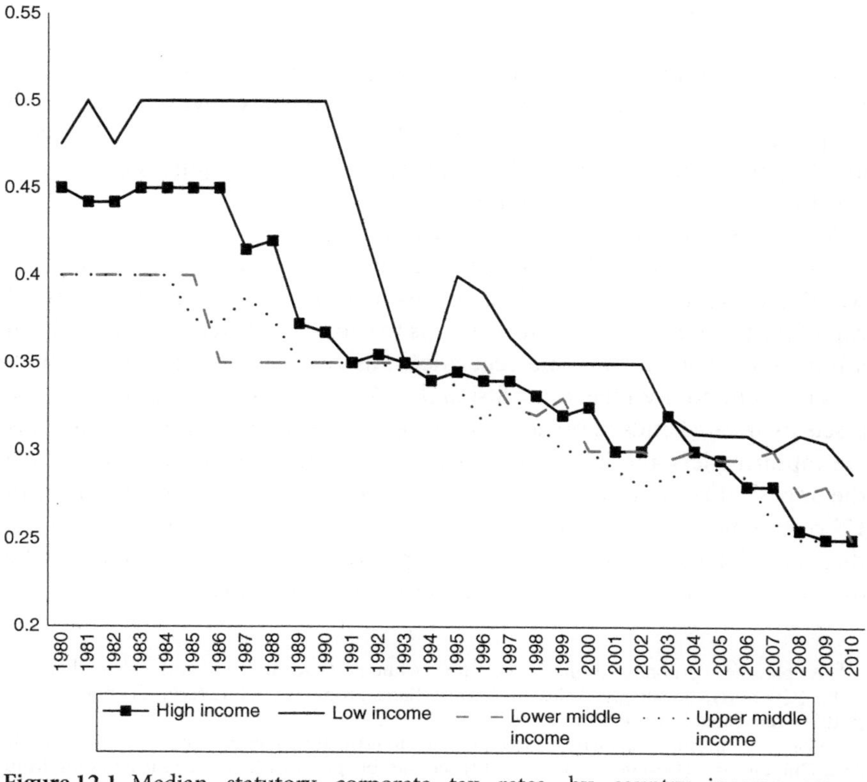

Figure 12.1 Median statutory corporate tax rates, by country income group, 1980–2010

Source: Keen and Konrad (2013)

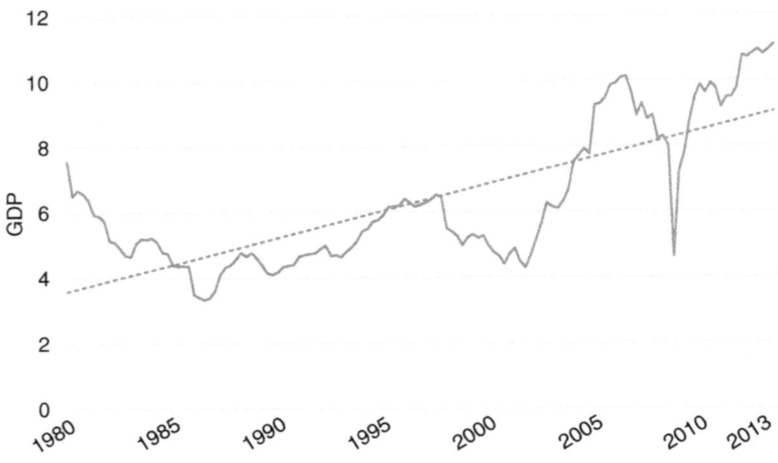

Figure 12.2 US corporate profits before tax to GDP, 1980–2013
Source: Derived from Federal Reserve Bank of St. Louis, FRED database

Despite plummeting tax rates, tax revenues have generally held up: for OECD countries, corporate tax revenues and total tax revenues rose from 2.4 percent of GDP and 31 percent of GDP respectively in 1980 to 2.9 percent and 34 percent in 2010. Mitchell, and many academics and pundits, have used this to argue that tax competition is benign.[6]

Yet this is to misunderstand the situation.

First, as Figure 12.2 above suggests, corporate pre-tax profits around the world have soared since the 1980s, as workers have lost battles with owners of capital; as technology has boosted returns to capital; as TNCs have used global arbitrage to shake off tax and regulations; as rising commodity prices have boosted commodity-related profits; and amid transfers of widespread public assets to private hands in privatization programs. Tax wars mean governments are capturing less and less of this corporate bonanza. Figure 12.3 shows how the impact of tax wars shows up in the structure of national tax systems, with US corporate taxes plummeting from a third of all taxes in the 1950s to less than a tenth today—with worker-related payroll taxes basically making up the difference. The evidence suggests similar trends in other countries.[7]

[6] A plot of corporate profits (after tax, without IVA and CCAdj) as a share of GDP. (Quarterly, Seasonally Adjusted Annual Rate. From Federal Reserve Economic Data (FRED), calculated 9 April 2014.

[7] Corporate profits as a share of GDP are hard to estimate for many countries, on available data. One estimate (Devereux, 2006, Fig. 12) sees taxable profit in OECD countries rising from 6.1 percent in 1965–85 to 9.9 percent in 1986–2004 (and presumably substantially more since then.) Evidence for developing countries is scant. For example, Abbas et al. (2012) note on p. 15: "We do not have data on corporate profits, which are likely to be different, because the gross

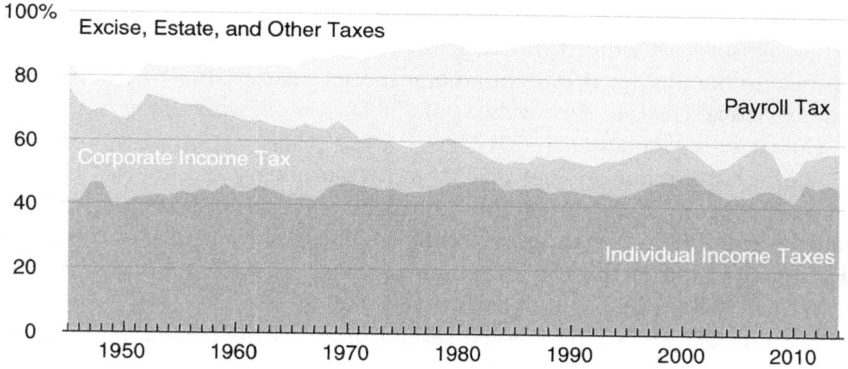

Figure 12.3 Sources of US federal tax revenue, 1945–2014

Note: "Other Taxes" category includes profits on assets held by the Federal Reserve.
Source: Graph provided to authors by Center on Budget and Policy Priorities, March 30, 2015, based on OMB Historical Table 2.2 https://www.whitehouse.gov/omb/budget/Historicals

Yet even this stark picture masks the full effects.

As corporate and other capital-related tax rates fall below top individual income tax rates, wealthy individuals convert their wealth and income into corporate forms, to enjoy the lower corporate rate. Effective tax rates on the wealthy fall further, and "corporate" tax revenues get an artificial boost in the data. Next, governments try to stop the wealthy converting to corporate forms by cutting top income tax rates towards corporate rates. Effective tax rates on the wealthy fall further, and the tax system gets compressed into still more regressive forms. This secondary impact of tax wars on top of income tax rates—which have nearly halved from some 70 percent in the United States and United Kingdom since towards the 1970s—may well be at least as great as the direct, measured impacts on the taxes on capital—if not more so.

Developing countries may have been hardest hit, as the IMF noted in May 2014: spillovers are "especially marked and important for developing countries—at least twice as large as for OECD countries, with respect to the tax base."[8] Or, as Thomas Rixen puts it in his own summary of tax wars and their consequences: "the adverse effects [of tax wars] are strongest in developing countries" (Rixen, 2011a).

operating surplus includes profits from unincorporated businesses, and because there are various other accounting differences, especially in the financial sector."

[8] The IMF adds: "These countries typically derive a greater proportion of their revenue from corporate tax... and the empirics reported here suggest that spillovers are especially strong for them... Compared to OECD countries, the base spillovers from others' tax rates are two to three times larger, and statistically more significant." See IMF (2014: 1).

Special tax incentives are widely regarded as an unusually pernicious form of tax subsidy.[9] Another IMF study on tax and developing countries notes: "A race to the bottom is evident among special regimes, most notably in the case of Africa, creating effectively a parallel tax system where rates have fallen to almost zero" (Abbas et al., 2012).

But the race isn't only happening *between* developing countries: OECD countries' tax policies directly impact them too. Figure 12.1 above shows that while the catfight at the OECD may seem like an esoteric, distant battle for officials in developing countries, this is far from the case: they are impacted directly.

Yet this *still* isn't the end of the story.

The OECD's 1998 report noted several other harms emanating from tax wars and their progeny, harmful tax regimes. They distort real and financial investment flows, it said, making capital flow to where it can achieve the highest level of subsidy, rather than to where genuine economic productivity is highest, in a clear negation of the pro-trade arguments of the British economist David Ricardo. They undermine the integrity and fairness of tax structures, and discourage tax compliance. They destroy jobs by shifting the tax burden away from capital and towards labor. They also increase administrative costs for individuals, for companies, and for tax authorities.[10]

To summarize, tax wars undermine democracy by encouraging governments to choose tax systems their voters never asked for and never would ask for. They are re-engineering the global economy to provide tax subsidies to large TNCs, enabling them to undercut their smaller, more nationally focused rivals in markets on a factor—tax—that has nothing to do with genuine economic productivity and efficiency, and everything to do with extracting wealth from taxpayers elsewhere. Given that smaller players are typically the job creators and genuine innovators, this re-engineering of the corporate landscape damages employment, curbs true entrepreneurialism, boosts short-termism and rent-seeking, distorts markets, and makes capital allocation even less efficient. The changes are, for corporations, like refined sugar in the human body—empty financial calories with adverse long-term health effects (Quentin, 2014).

To summarize this summary: tax wars are irredeemably noxious, from pretty much any angle one can think of—even from a purely selfish national perspective.

[9] Special incentives not only hurt revenues: they distort tax systems, they can be corruptly obtained, they require large administrative resources, and they are likely to attract rent-seeking activity over productive long-term investment.

[10] The OECD (1998: 70) explicitly stated these harms: "Harmful preferential tax regimes can distort trade and investment patterns, and are a threat both to domestic tax systems and to the overall structure of international taxation. These regimes undermine the fairness of the tax systems, cause undesired shifts of part of the tax burden from income to consumption, shift part of the tax burden from capital to labour and thereby may have a negative impact on employment."

12.5 HARD REALITIES VERSUS IDEOLOGY

This raises a key question, seldom asked: why do nations engage in the race?

Do they face a genuine "prisoner's dilemma" forcing them to join in the race for reasons of naked self interest—while (possibly) still recognizing that at a global level the race is harmful? Or are they being bamboozled by a false belief system luring them into the game cheerled on by lobbyists, when in reality there is no overall penalty from not playing?

This chapter argues that it is generally the latter, particularly for larger countries and for developing countries.

Although the academic literature correctly argues that nations tend to behave as if they face a "prisoner's dilemma" implying that each should individually engage in the race to the bottom on tax, this paper argues that they are engaging on the basis of a set of misunderstandings. Most importantly, those driving policy to engage in the race are confusing the fortunes of one sector or sectors of their economy with the interests of their nation as a whole. To "compete" on tax involves that sector being substantially cross-subsidized by other economic actors; but overall, at a national level, this provides no net benefits (and causes harm): they are generally better off not playing. The prisoner's dilemma need not exist.

So if this belief system is false, where does it come from, and how is it sustained?

We would argue that the "competitiveness" agenda is an outgrowth of a wider tax-cutting agenda that has become so embedded in many countries that its foundations are no longer seriously examined, despite the fallacies at its heart. For instance, it is routinely argued that—because of tax wars, individual countries *must* cut taxes on capital to stop it fleeing elsewhere; *ergo*, corporate tax-cutting is virtuous, as it brings investment and hence growth. And if corporate tax-cutting is virtuous, then tax wars, forcing corporate tax rates down, must be beneficial too.

A moment's thought is enough to reveal the circularity in this argument—an argument that starts with an invalid assumption. We suggest that this intellectual whirlpool is a key wellspring from which both the ideology and the process of tax wars have emerged and sustained themselves for decades, fed partly by erroneous conclusions from strands of academic research, nurtured by the appealing words "competitive" and "competitiveness," and fired up by over-hyped and widely misunderstood totems such as Ireland or Hong Kong.

Box 12.1 explores this, using the UK and Ireland to narrate how the false consciousness can emerge.

In all this, however, there is some good news.

The idea that nations must bow down to international capital's demands not to be taxed is bogus. Tax sovereignty can generally be regained, with no penalty for the nation as a whole and with considerable potential benefits.

Box 12.1 The UK's "Competitive" Tax Regime: A Scorecard

The current UK coalition government has made "competitiveness" an emblem of its economic strategies, under a slogan that Britain (or "UK PLC," as some corporate tax-cutters like to put it) is "Open for Business."[11]

Tax is a centerpiece of the strategies. The United Kingdom from 2010 began to reshape its corporate tax regime to "compete" with tax havens like Bermuda, the Netherlands, Ireland, Switzerland, and Luxembourg. It is slashing the headline corporation tax rate from 28 percent in 2010 to a target of 20 percent in 2015, along with a new "patent box"[12] and other reforms, notably a move away from a "worldwide" tax system (where a country taxes its TNCs on its worldwide income with credits for foreign taxes paid) towards a more "territorial" one (where it taxes only their domestically sourced income).

The UK media, dazzled by "competitiveness" arguments and by cheerleading from the UK government, from the accountancy profession, and even from some academics, has rarely questioned the moves, and cite many expected benefits to the United Kingdom. At the time of writing the UK economy is growing faster than its European peers, leading to quite common arguments that the new "competitive" tax regime was a (or the) key reason.[13]

Yet there are two things wrong with the scorecard.

The first problem is that the evidence so far does not fit this story. Reuters investigations could only identify a handful of companies that have relocated for tax reasons.[14] It found that the gross jobs and tax yields have been pitiful, and possibly negative. Of the companies that provided data, Reuters identified fewer than 100 jobs definitely created as a result of the tax transformations; and one tax-driven relocation was expected to see 600 job cuts. Companies, when asked, were not able to identify a single genuinely tax-driven new investment project. As for gross tax benefits: for 2013 Reuters found one $200,000 payment, while several relocations saw the companies involved earn corporation tax credits and "tax

[11] UK Prime Minister David Cameron's fondness for the Twitter hashtag #GlobalRace illustrates how pervasive and soundbite-led the competitiveness agenda has become in the UK.

[12] The patent box regime, phased in from 2013, applies a 10 per cent tax rate to the portion of the company's profits that can be attributed to the patent. To qualify, the company must have invented the patent or perform "significant management activity" relating to its development. See UK Government (2013). See also Houlder (2010) and Houlder (2014).

[13] See, just for one among a multitude of examples, Warner (2014). He argued that the UK's recent economic growth fortunes had been better than Europe's "largely" because of changes to the tax system, discounting factors such as the large fall in the Pound Sterling currency since the financial crisis; the spectacular then ongoing party in the UK housing market, the fact that deep recessions are typically followed by recovery and—helping account for Britain's relatively higher growth in Europe—the myriad structural problems in Europe accompanying currency union.

[14] See Bergin (2012) and Bergin (2014). The companies that have identified as having moved were Aon Plc, CNH Global N.V., Delphi Automotive Plc, Ensue Plc, Liberty Global Plc, Noble Corp. Plc. and Rowan Companies, WPP, Shire Pharmaceuticals, Fiat, and United Business Media. When Fiat said in January 2014 it would shift its tax domicile to Britain, Reuters reported that the move "would have no impact on headcounts in Italy or elsewhere" (Reuters, 2014).

assets" for that year: a negative flow. These are the *gross* benefits: but the costs—the taxes lost to corporations that never intended to leave or would have invested anyway—have been high: as one tax adviser summarized in 2011: "every other UK multinational that had no intention of leaving the UK is ecstatic (*Accountancy Age*, 2011)." The UK government itself estimated that the cuts to the headline rates alone would lose the UK Treasury £7.8 billion annually by 2016/17; other estimates have ranged as high as £10 billion annually. The Institute for Fiscal Studies said of the patent box component that it was poorly targeted, expensive, and would foster little innovation.[15] The subsidy is also attracting scrutiny from the European Commission, and Ireland and possibly other havens are considering modifying their own tax regimes to undercut the UK again.

The failure of a bid by the US pharma company Pfizer for the UK-based AstraZeneca, designed as an unashamedly tax-fueled move, has at least flushed out some of the fallacies behind the cheerleading. It was widely recognized in the UK financial press as not only an unproductive and purely rent-seeking deal, but also likely to destroy significant numbers of UK jobs and to destroy value too, as is so often the case in tax-motivated mergers. John Gapper wrote in the *Financial Times*: "Companies put together purely for tax reasons—with no industrial or cultural logic behind them—will be fragile . . . this does not create stronger enterprises or bring wider economic benefits" (Gapper, 2014).

An older and more widely hyped example of tax "competitiveness" is Ireland. Ireland's tax regime has certainly attracted some financial activity. But this is not at all what it seems, as the footnote here explains.[16]

(*continued*)

[15] See Seely (2014); and see also the calculations in Murphy (2014).

[16] Since the 1990s Ireland has grown faster than most OECD countries. However tax is far less important for this "Celtic Tiger" growth than is popularly supposed. The central reason for Ireland's growth is its unique position as an English-speaking gateway for US TNCs into Europe: the only English-speaking country in the Eurozone. This isn't easily replicable elsewhere, particularly in poorer countries with governance and reputational risks which make them singularly ill-placed to attract such "conduit" flows. Old transatlantic cultural, economic, and even family links and a favourable time difference boost the Irish offering. A third factor is that Ireland has been an enormous net beneficiary of European subsidies, such as under the Common Agricultural Policy. A fourth factor was large-scale immigration to Ireland, whose education and training had been subsidized by other countries elsewhere—and simple population growth was a major component of headline GDP growth, pre-crisis. What is more, when crisis hit in 2008 the "Celtic Tiger" was exposed as having been made significantly of paper. For a more detailed exploration of the role of corporate Taxes in the "Celtic Tiger" see "Did Ireland's 12.5 percent corporate tax rate create the Celtic Tiger?" Fools Gold blog, 10 March 2015. Its housing boom was out of proportion to nearly all the other property bubbles, pre-crisis, artificially boosting GDP growth figures: and the subsequent bust has been legendary. What is more, Ireland is now feeling the pinch from the UK's moves: (see, for example, Accounting Web, 2013.) For discussion of the importance of taxes to Ireland, see Stewart, 2011. Similarly, the UK to a degree plays a role as a gateway into Europe; as is Hong Kong as the premier "offshore" gateway into China. For some pointers on Iceland, see TJN (2008). It is almost inconceivable to think that many developing countries, with the partial exception of the unusual Indian Ocean island of Mauritius, could have a hope of reproducing such strategies.

Box 12.1 **Continued**

A second key point with the scorecard, highlighted by the UK's shift from a "worldwide" towards a "territorial" tax system,[17] is that such a shift, even though it directly involves only rich countries, transmits harmful ricochet effects to developing countries.

Until recently the UK had extensive "Controlled Foreign Company" (CFC) rules stipulating that if a UK TNC shifts certain forms of income into other jurisdictions and tax havens, the United Kingdom can still tax those offshore profits. So UK TNCs had less incentive to dodge taxes in a developing country: a tax bill reduced elsewhere would be topped up back home in the UK. But from 2010, following heavy lobbying[18] behind the scenes, the United Kingdom began drastically to water down these CFC provisions, effectively encouraging TNCs to use tax havens. UK-based TNCs are now effectively encouraged to shift profits out of developing countries, knowing that their reduced tax bills will not be topped up again in the UK. These tax moves alone have been estimated to cost developing countries some £4 billion annually, equivalent to nearly a third of the entire UK aid budget—though the UK Treasury, when asked to conduct a "spillover analysis" of the impact on developing countries, declined (Actionaid, 2012).

In the United States, a sustained campaign is underway to move from a largely "worldwide" tax system towards a more territorial one, in the name of "competitiveness."[19] Given the dominance of US TNCs, such moves could transmit far greater harmful "competitive" impulses across the world, draining massive resources from many developing countries. An IMF working paper notes that developing countries:

[17] Under so-called "worldwide taxation," corporations resident in a country are taxable by that country on relevant parts of their income from all over the world, normally with deductions or credits for taxes paid elsewhere, and often "deferral" of tax until the income is repatriated to the home country. By contrast, so-called "territorial taxation" involves countries taxing only that income that arises domestically, and leaving other countries to tax income in their jurisdictions. The US is currently the most important "worldwide" taxation country, though in fact it and most countries have a mix of territorial and worldwide taxation. Matheson et al. (2013) discuss the implications of US moves towards territorial taxation and note that several recent proposals for US tax reform propose or consider moving towards territorial taxation: for instance, the Simpson-Bowles Commission recommended it; the Volcker Report (by the President's Economic Recovery Advisory Board) considered it favorably; US House Ways and Means Committee Chairman Camp's proposed legislation would adopt a territorial system together with a minimum tax on foreign earnings. Yet they note that: "Little, if anything has been said about the potential impact on LICs of changes in the framework for global taxation adopted by major industrial countries."

[18] The changes were pushed forward with little opposition by business liaison groups whose 30 members had an estimated 3,000 tax haven subsidiaries between them already. See Brooks (2011).

[19] See, for example, Kotlikoff (2014) or Devereux (2012). Devereux, of the Oxford University Centre for Business Taxation is one of the most-cited academics in the area of tax wars. We explain below why the Centre seems fundamentally conflicted in these debates. Also see Kleinbard (2014), "Competitiveness Has Nothing to Do with It," USC CLASS Research Papers Series No. CLASS 14–26, USC Legal Studies Research Papers Series No. 14–34.

> are likely to feel increased pressure to lower their corporate income tax and withholding tax rates in order to attract foreign capital.... without this shelter provided by a worldwide system, [this] may add to the already notable degree of tax competition among developing countries... Low income countries should keep a close eye on international tax changes proposed and adopted by the largest economies. (Matheson et al., 2013.)[20]

The process of tax wars has a vulnerable point: the belief system that underpins it. This appear to us to be by far the best entry point from which Cameron's "#globalrace" can be tackled, with potentially enduring results: we make recommendations on this at the end of the chapter.

The lobbyists' counter-attack against the OECD's 1998 project illustrates just how important the belief system is.

12.6 THE FIGHTBACK

As the OECD project got underway, the Center for Freedom and Prosperity helped drum up a campaign of emails and messaging in Washington, rallying an alliance against the "Global Tax Police" and the "Parisian Monstrosity"—that is, the OECD (Sharman, 2006: 85).

The havens' cause was helped immeasurably by the fact that the OECD project was couched in terms of an attack on tax "competition," rather than on tax havens per se. Armed with the dog-whistle words "competition" and "competitive" (not to mention "freedom," "liberty," and "enterprise") the alliance went on the attack.

Here is Mitchell, in his folksy style, explaining how he thinks countries "compete":

> Say you only had one gas station in a town. That one gas station could charge high prices; it could maintain inconvenient hours; it could offer shoddy service. But if you have five gas stations in a town, all of a sudden those gas stations need to compete with each other.
>
> ...
>
> Now imagine you are a governor of Massachusetts. You'd love to shut down New Hampshire—because it's competition.... If governments are trying to impose high tax rates, people actually have options to move either themselves, or their money, across borders.
>
> (Mitchell, 2009)

[20] See also IMF (2014: 37–9).

This alluring argument, in fact, has a long academic tradition. It dates back to a 1956 paper by the US economist Charles Tiebout, who argued that tax "competition" between jurisdictions resembles competition between firms in a market, beneficially sorting populations into optimal communities with tax mixes tailored to suit them.[21] Governments are "cartels" or natural monopoly suppliers of services, requiring "competitive" discipline. Some of the academic literature, and many populist politicians, still explicitly accept Tiebout's logic.[22]

The model, however, is nonsense. Consider a company that cannot compete. It may go bankrupt and disappear: for all the pain involved, this "creative destruction" is a source of the dynamism of markets. But what is the result if a country cannot "compete?" A *failed state*? No: nobody would—or could—"shut down New Hampshire." What is more, public goods (such as appropriate environmental legislation) clearly cannot usefully be allocated via markets; "competition" among states merely introduces market competition on public goods through the back door and will lead to market failures, as Hans-Werner Sinn describes in his paper on "systems competition" (Sinn, 1997).

The race to the bottom, a macro political-economic phenomenon, is nothing to do with the microeconomic phenomenon of economic competition between firms in markets.[23] Yet—perhaps largely because they share the same word in English—the two utterly different processes get conflated.

Tiebout's model requires spectacular, heroic assumptions. Jurisdictions must be comprised of perfectly mobile, perfectly informed and farsighted citizens, willing to rip their children out of schools and relocate costlessly in great shoals to more tempting jurisdictions at the drop of a tax inspector's hat. The model ignores commuting to different tax zones; it assumes there are no tax havens; and that neither public goods nor negative externalities (such as pollution) spill into other jurisdictions—and so on.

21 See Tiebout (1956). Later work expanded Tiebout's study to incorporate firms as well as individuals: e.g. White (1986).

22 Examples of "Tiebout populism" abound. For instance, US President Bill Clinton argued that each nation is "like a big corporation competing in the global marketplace" (Krugman, 1994). More recently, Swiss President Ueli Maurer said in January 2013: "Locational competition exists within our own borders. This leads to good infrastructure, to restraint in creating red tape and to low taxes.... That is not only the case in business, but also in politics... Progress and prosperity are not only achieved through competition in the private sector, but also through competition among systems of government and business locations" (Maurer, 2013). The International Financial Centres Forum (IFC Forum), a prominent lobby group for tax havens, states: "Businesses operate best when in competition. The same is true for governments. Government cartels to maximise income through attacks on (tax) competition should be discouraged, just as similar behaviour to constrain competition between corporations is rightly curbed" (IFC Forum, 2013).

23 As Martin Wolf, chief economics correspondent of the *Financial Times*, notes: "the notion of the competitiveness of countries, on the model of the competitiveness of companies, is nonsense." See Wolf (2005: 260, 261, and 268). The chapter "Sad about the State" explores these issues in some depth, with a particular focus on taxation and competitiveness.

In feverish Washington, DC, of course, nobody was stopping to think too hard about any of this. This was *competition*, right? Our country is competing in a global marketplace! Competition is under attack from bureaucrats in France working for a Global Tax Police!

The fact that the fallacies behind these ideas were unable to break through the frenzy is all the more remarkable, given just how fragile the pro-tax wars belief system is.

12.7 COMPETITIVE THRILLS AND THE INVESTMENT MYTH

Many people in this area argue that even if the process is the destructive arm's race at a global level, it still makes sense for individual jurisdictions, and particularly smaller ones, to participate out of pure self-interest. Yet even this argument, it seems, is founded on basic misunderstandings.

Four years before the OECD project emerged the US economist Paul Krugman wrote an article entitled "Competitiveness: A dangerous obsession," in which he argued that there is literally no such thing as national "competitiveness," at least in the way it is traditionally wielded. Pull the concept apart, and national competitiveness seems to be "a funny way of saying 'productivity'," he said—not productivity relative to competitors, but merely domestic productivity.[24]

> People who believe themselves to be sophisticated about the subject take it for granted that the economic problem facing any modern nation is essentially one of competing on world markets—that the United States and Japan are competitors in the same sense that Coca-Cola competes with Pepsi—and are unaware that anyone might seriously question that proposition.
>
> . . .
>
> It is simply not the case that the world's leading nations are to any important degree in economic competition with each other, or that any of their major economic problems can be attributed to failures to compete on world markets. The growing obsession in most advanced nations with international competitiveness should be seen, not as a well-founded concern, but as a view held in the face of overwhelming contrary evidence. And yet it is clearly a view that people very much want to hold . . . Competitive images are exciting, and thrills sell tickets.

Though his arguments focused on trade, much could be applied in the area of tax.

A lot of the thinking in this area, which Mitchell exploited ruthlessly in Washington, rests on an elementary economic howler: confusing the fortunes of the corporate sector with the fortunes of a whole economy.

[24] Krugman (1994). In January 2011, he added "everything I said then remains true" (Krugman, 2011).

For a TNC, a tax might feel like a cost. But for a country, *tax is not a cost but an internal transfer*.

Corporate tax cuts subsidize corporations at the expense of costs elsewhere in the economy: either higher taxes for others, or higher borrowing, or reduced public services. Wealth transfers from schools and highways to private corporations and their shareholders do not obviously or automatically make a country more "competitive." This elementary insight is, astonishingly, absent from many studies.

12.8 BUT "COMPETITIVE" TAX CUTS BRING INVESTMENT!

The story does not end here, of course. Mitchell and many others argue that cutting taxes on capital should attract or retain enough foreign "investment" to justify the immediate tax losses.

Again, it's a theory that is alluring but wrong, particularly for large economies, and *especially* for developing countries.

Threats by business owners to relocate for tax reasons are legion, and the rhetoric of "tax us too much and we will flee" drives timid and inexperienced politicians to do the bidding of mobile international capital, every day, around the globe.[25]

But talk is cheap. The evidence shows that not only is there rarely substance behind the threats, but those that *do* flee were usually contributing little anyway—and they nearly always relocate for non-tax reasons. Business leaders, apparently speaking against their own interests, back this up. Warren Buffett (2011) said:

> I have worked with investors for 60 years and I have yet to see anyone—not even when capital gains rates were 39.9 percent in 1976–7—shy away from a sensible investment because of the tax rate on the potential gain.

Paul O'Neill, former head of the aluminium giant Alcoa and US Treasury Secretary under President George W. Bush, said:

> As a businessman I never made an investment decision based on the tax code... If you are giving money away I will take it. If you want to give me

[25] Type "tax" and "competitive" into a search engine and the sheer range and relentlessness of such threats may become apparent. Or, for a collection of hyperventilating articles about how taxes cause "exodus" of rich people and their money, see "Huge Flight of Rich after French Tax Hikes? Nope." Mark Thoma, Economist's View blog, 13 March 2013, http://economistsview.typepad.com/economistsview/2013/03/-huge-flight-of-rich-after-french-tax-hikes-nope.html, accessed 15 July 2015.

inducements for something I am going to do anyway, I will take it. But good business people do not do things because of inducements.[26]

More broadly, survey after survey finds that genuine foreign greenfield investment—the good stuff that brings jobs, supply chains, and long-term engagement and skills transfers to an economy—pays relatively little attention to tax.[27] Oil companies invest where the oil is, not where the tax breaks are; and Syria won't attract car factories just by offering tax breaks. The first-order concerns are usually political stability and the rule of law; healthy and educated workforces; strong infrastructure and good access to markets and resources. All these are substantially tax-financed, directly and indirectly.

For developing countries, the limited literature finds that gross FDI benefits from tax-cutting are limited,[28] and are frequently associated with large

[26] See ITEP (2011). See also Box 12.1, showing how the UK's "competitive" tax changes seems to have had little impact on genuine economic investment, at potentially great cost.

[27] The OECD states: "There is a consensus in the literature about the main factors affecting (foreign) investment location decisions. The most important ones are market size and real income levels, skill levels in the host economy, the availability of infrastructure and other resource that facilitates efficient specialisation of production, trade policies, and political and macroeconomic stability of the host country . . . [tax incentives] play only a limited role" (OECD, 2007). Though there is presumably *some* effect, empirical studies have yielded contradictory and inconclusive results. For example, Hines (1999) contends that each percentage reduction in the CIT rate yields a 2 percent increase in FDI. A more recent meta analysis suggested that a 10 percentage-point reduction in a country's effective average tax rate increases its long-run stock of FDI, by some 30 percent (De Mooij and Ederveen, 2008.) Yet the IMF (2014) notes that over half of this may be mergers and acquisitions alone: portfolio shuffling rather than greenfield investment; much of the rest is likely to be non-merger portfolio shuffling or jobless profit-shifting, as Box 12.1 describes. Yet these studies also miss a factor that is particularly pertinent for developing countries: much "foreign" investment is in reality "round-tripped" local investment, dressed up as foreign investment. Hines does not take this into account; few such studies do. Other studies find lesser effects on gross FDI flows. For example, US states are a useful place to measure the FDI effects of tax wars, due to the quantity of good available historical data. A 2013 study into 50 years of US state tax incentives is summarized: "There is . . . no conclusive evidence from research studies conducted since the mid-1950s to show that business tax incentives have an impact on net economic gains to the states. . . . nor is there conclusive evidence from the research that taxes, in general, have an impact on business location and expansion decisions" (Rubin and Boyd, 2013, summarized in Tax Analysts, 2013).

[28] Abbas et al. (2012) state that: "Empirical evidence on corporate income tax developments in developing economies remains scant." For more fine-grained examples, an IMF study on the Eastern Caribbean Currency Union found that tax-cutting led to annual tax losses of 9–16 percent of GDP but did not seem to boost FDI flows; tax concessions were not among the top 15 of the 40 areas companies said were critical for investment (Chai and Goyal, 2008). A survey on Kenya found that 61 percent of 159 businesses surveyed cited the regional market and Kenya's overall political and economic stability as the core factors underpinning their investment—versus just one percent who cited special concessions from the Export Processing Zone, a cornerstone of Kenya's exports strategy. See ActionAid and TJN-Africa (2012, Appendix 3). See also IMF (2006) and Kinuthia (2010, Table 13). For sub-Saharan Africa, the limited literature finds that special tax regimes and incentives cost revenues, but do not generally attract useful FDI. A January 2014 IMF Working Paper summarizes: "Taxation does not significantly affect foreign firms' locations, while the other main aspects of investment climate (infrastructure, finance, human capital, and institutions) do" (Kinda, 2014). In Latin America, tax cuts seem to have been associated with some

revenue costs. Developing countries are generally more vulnerable to the tax losses, since they depend more on corporate taxes than OECD countries do, and also face stronger pressures to cut taxes.[29]

What is more, foreign investment that is tax-sensitive is—almost by definition—footloose and therefore poorly embedded in the local economy. So skittish, tax-sensitive capital is likely to be corporate profit-shifting and portfolio-shuffling that is most likely to be rent-seeking and wealth-extracting, rather than genuinely wealth-creating.

These issues are, again, particularly acute for developing countries. Why would an investor flighty enough to require tax concessions not also be scared away by standard developing-country issues such as difficult governance, and conflict or contract risk? In the words of one UK tax expert: "in sub-Saharan Africa issues such as the rule of law and infrastructure mean tax is not that relevant."[30] (This is analogous to the reason why tax havens are almost always located in or symbiotically linked to rich OECD countries.)

increased FDI, though again this is typically in short-term portfolio flows, not long-term investments. See Wibbels and Arce (2003). Estache and Gaspar (1995) found that any benefits flowing from tax incentives offered by Brazilian states were significantly outweighed by the resulting revenue losses. Studies in Malaysia and Thailand found that the tax incentives were of little value to the target firms, which would have invested regardless of the available subsidies (Boadway, Chua, and Flatters, 1995). See also Halvorsen (1995).

[29] Key reasons why developing countries may be more vulnerable than rich countries to tax wars include:

a) They tend to rely more heavily on corporate income taxes than OECD countries, since base-broadening is much harder when the "base" consists of large numbers of relatively poor taxpayers, and when tax administrations are weaker;

b) Corporate tax losses represent a geographical transfer from poor countries to corporate shareholders in rich countries—which is not the case when this happens within the OECD constellation;

c) Typical developing country markets market are smaller, face a more elastic supply of international capital and has a smaller base of local investors, as well as a greater need to overcome country reputational issues—so they face stronger pressures to take outsize gambles on offering tax subsidies;

d) In developing countries tax administration and enforcement are weaker, and the creation of special tax regimes are more vulnerable to special-interest lobbying and corruption. As one account puts it, tax policymaking is not part of the daily cut and thrust of public political debate as in OECD countries but instead tends to be "narrow, specialised and concentrated in non-public spaces: the manoeuvrings of small pressure groups lobbying for exemptions from import duties, or individual large companies bargaining with ministers and tax officials about their assessments and liabilities." See Moore (2004).

For more evidence on tax wars, tax incentives and developing countries see Keen and Simone (2004); and OECD (2007); Keen and Mansour (2009); African Development Bank (2011); Rixen (2011); Abbas and Klemm (2013); *Revenue Mobilization in Developing Countries*, IMF Fiscal Affairs Department, 8 March 2011. https://www.imf.org/external/pubs/ft/wp/2012/wp1228.pdf, accessed 15 July 2015.

[30] This is closely related to the reason why almost no developing countries have ever become successful tax havens or secrecy jurisdictions, unless underpinned by a larger Western power: skittish tax- or secrecy-sensitive capital rarely migrates to badly governed countries, as the thought experiment about Nigeria and Indonesia above suggests.

This reveals another fundamental, elementary problem with much of the academic research.

Because tax is a transfer within an economy, not a cost, and because tax-based lures are likely to attract the "wrong" kind of foreign investment, it is hard to see the point in measuring how much "investment" or FDI tax incentives bring in, without *also* taking into account the associated tax and other costs. Yet many studies use FDI or "investment" flows as their main or even sole benchmark for success—even though holistic economy-wide performance measures, such as overall long-term economic growth, are what matters.[31]

One might consider alternative holistic approaches to assess "competitiveness," such as the World Economic Forum's Global Competitiveness Index. But even if one accepts their model of "competitiveness," tax-cutting does not obviously help[32] here either: Figure 12.4 illustrates this.

There are, however, many studies purporting to show that general tax cuts, or corporate tax cuts, boost growth. Yet all the studies we've seen claiming these results are fraught with problems and typically use complex models hedged with unworldly qualifications and assumptions.[33] Some

[31] Evidence backs this elementary insight. For instance, Klemm and Parys (2009) state: "Lower corporate income tax rates and longer tax holidays are effective in attracting FDI, but not in boosting gross private fixed capital formation or growth." It may be that because it is so hard to disentangle growth effects from corporate tax cuts amid all the noise of other factors, some researchers fall back on what is easier to measure: namely FDI and other investment responses.

[32] The World Economic Forum's Global Competitiveness Index ranks 144 countries using 12 "pillars" of competitiveness which include institutions, infrastructure, the macroeconomic environment, health and primary education; higher education and training; labor market efficiency; financial market development; technological readiness; market size; business sophistication; and innovation. Most of these require tax financing. Michael Porter, another widely cited competitiveness "guru," stresses that some aspects of a tax system, such as its complexity, can have negative impacts on a nation's competitiveness, and although he is no great fan of taxation he does not advocate tax cuts as a general proposition either: he recognizes that these involve trade-offs that may or may not be worth it. As Porter puts it: "Many benefits of locating elsewhere, such as low wages or taxes, are visible and immediate, whereas the drawbacks are frequently subtle and apparent only over the long term" (Porter and Rivkin, 2012).

[33] For a more recent study claiming that corporate taxes hurt growth, see Arnold, 2008. Yet all the studies we've seen finding similar results contain potentially fatal flaws.

For one thing, corporate taxes have averaged 2.6% of GDP for OECD countries on average since 1965. Even a swingeing ten-point cut in effective corporate tax rates would affect merely 0.25% of GDP; it would be surprising if such a tiny factor could have a measurable impact on long-term GDP growth, particularly since tax is not a cost to an economy but a transfer within it, and given the multitude of other ingredients that contribute to growth. Possible explanations for the findings:

a) a failure to disentangle correlation and causation; and use of selective data, particularly by organizations financed or part-financed by industry players; or by individuals who have bought into tax-cutting ideologies;

b) corporate tax cuts typically come as part of government stimulus packages enacted when economies are at low point of an economic cycle—exactly the moments when subsequent growth will naturally be greater than average: we've not seen a study that properly takes this into account;

research—including from some of the most respected and widely cited institutions in the field—is skewed by money, ideology, and corporate lobbying.[34]

And of course there are many studies that find no such effect, or a reverse effect.[35] The tax-cutters struggle to explain how very highly taxed countries

c) studies mostly ignore very long time frames: tax-funded railways or education, for instance, pay off over many decades;

d) most of the cited studies to date rely heavily or entirely on pre-2008 data, which for many countries involved growth rises later revealed, post-crash, as ephemeral and substantially the product of bubble economies;

e) Many studies do not properly disentangle locally financed TNC investment from the foreign-financed variant (see, for example, Devereux and Griffith, 2002: 79–102);

f) Crucially, a large number of these papers rely on complex models often dependent on fairytale assumptions, as noted. Here is an example, somewhat randomly selected. "In common with other such measures, we ignore complications which would arise if we allowed the hypothetical investment to be risky. We consider the tax system only as it applies to a mature manufacturing firm—so the measures do not reflect the position for services or for hi-tech industries. The measures presented here also apply only to an investment in plant and machinery, financed by equity; we do not present estimates for investment in other assets (land or inventories, for example), nor for other forms of finance. We do not consider the treatment of losses or other forms of tax exhaustion. We analyse only source-based corporate income taxes—we do not include taxes levied in the country of residence of the parent company, nor do we include any source-based taxes paid by corporations that are not based on profit. We generally exclude industry-specific measures and we do not allow for any forms of tax shifting. We have not included personal taxes levied on corporate source income" (Devereux, 2006).

What is more, studies looking at headline GDP growth rates almost never take effective account of distributional issues within economies—a huge issue tremendously impacted by tax wars. See also Chinn (2015) and (Fisher et al. (2012).

[34] One of the most influential bodies is the Oxford Centre for Business Taxation in the United Kingdom. Its origins and staffing, however, raise questions about its independence in this particular debate. For example, *Accountancy Age* in 2005 reported on an interview with Christopher Wales, then a managing director with Goldman Sachs, who was the driving force behind setting up the center. The article notes: "Wales' mission was to ensure a simple, but fair taxation system that allows UK businesses to compete effectively and profitably in a global marketplace. The culmination of this mission, he says, was the creation and launch of the Oxford University Centre for Business Taxation on 4 November this year. Based at the Saïd Business School and backed by £5m-worth of funding from the influential Hundred Group of Finance Directors, the center has been set the goal of using academic weight, alongside HM Revenue & Customs and business expertise and assistance, *to achieve a more competitive tax system for British businesses*" (*Accountancy Age*, 2005; our emphasis added). This chapter suggests that one cannot advocate a "competitive" tax regime while also showing academic independence on the subject. At the time of writing, Wales was still a member of the Oxford Centre's advisory board, while also working for PWC.

[35] See, for example Hungerford (2013) or, for a summary of various papers, Huang and Frentz (2014). While some argue that corporate tax cuts have "dynamic" Laffer-type effects where tax cuts boost business, thus helping support revenues, we are not aware of studies in this area that incorporate the other side of the balance sheet: "dynamic" effects that presumably occur as a result of other taxpayers elsewhere having to bear the brunt of the lost corporate taxes. This counterweight would be especially strong in demand-deficient OECD countries today, with businesses sitting on trillions in uninvested cash piles—due substantially to low consumer demand for their products. Tax cuts for corporations would seem especially harmful in this

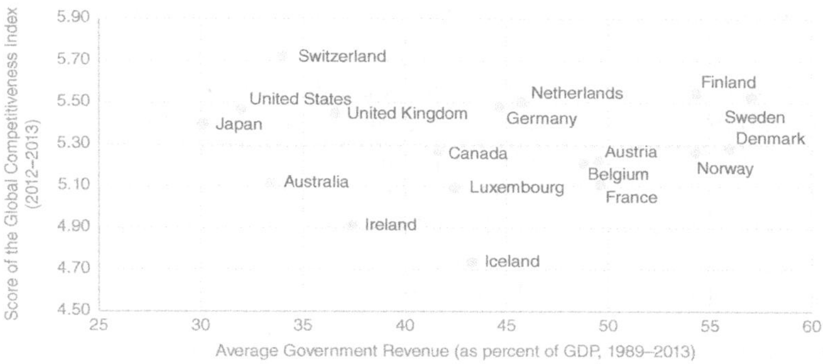

Figure 12.4 Average government revenue and score of the Global Competitiveness Index 2012–13

Source: Christensen and Shaxson, using World Economic Forum for the GCI score and Conference Board data[36]

(such as Scandinavian countries) have historically grown at similar rates to much lower-tax comparable countries such as the United States or Japan;[37] or the similarly powerful observation that the high-growth "golden age" quarter-century after the Second World War was a period of tax rates (and effective corporate tax rates) that are astonishingly high by modern standards; and that falling taxes since then have been accompanied by lower and narrower economic growth.[38]

Amid the clouds of claims, counter-claims, and deliberate obfuscation in the academic literature, it seems most likely that overall tax levels, or the rate or level of corporate taxes, have a rather neutral effect on economic growth—consistent with the fact that tax is not a cost to an economy but a transfer within it.

These arguments, too, hardly mattered in the political fight that the OECD had ignited in 1998.

environment: adding to idle corporate cash piles through tax cuts is likely to be like pushing on a string, while the "lost" tax revenues sap government spending and hence overall demand. At the time of writing, US corporations alone were estimated to be sitting on some US$5 trillion of cash or equivalent on their balance sheets (Sánchez and Yurdagul, 2013).

[36] The sample of countries included those with comparable levels of GDP per capita, and excluding micro-states which often have their own "tax haven" growth dynamics. The cut-off was to use states with GDP per capita (PPP) of above $20,000 on average from 1989–2013. Source: Conference Board data tables.

[37] For another graph of long-term relative economic performances, see, for example, Wolf (2012).

[38] There *is* evidence, however, that lower overall tax levels correlate with worse human development including higher inequality. See, for instance, Brooks and Hwong (2006).

12.9 THE BUSH ADMINISTRATION CHANGES TACK

By September 2000, three months after the OECD blacklist came out, the tax havens and their friends were coordinating their defenses closely. The havens promised to challenge the OECD publicly, and lobbied bilaterally among sympathetic OECD states. In March 2001 they formed the International Tax and Investment Organization (ITIO)[39] to marshal the fight. Mainstream publications such as the *New York Times*, the *Financial Times* and *The Economist* began to cover the story, but the audience was always, Sharman explains:

> Disproportionately élite, centring on politicians, national and international bureaucrats within the transnational tax policy community, the financial services industry, academics, and think tanks, but only rarely NGOs, and still less the mass public.

The European tax havens of Switzerland and Luxembourg were vociferous, joining the line that "competition" was under attack. Several other OECD governments including Australia and Austria said essentially the same thing.[40]

Initially, the new administration of George W. Bush did not seem to oppose the initiative, and in February 2001 US Treasury Secretary Paul O'Neill signed a G7 finance ministers' communiqué endorsing the project, making the apparently unremarkable statement that "I support the priority placed on transparency and cooperation to facilitate effective tax information exchange."

But once the lobbying began, the Treasury began to receive a deluge of letters from the usual anti-tax conservatives in Washington. The CFP got support from the US Congressional Black Caucus—which one might have thought would take the side of ordinary African-American (and perhaps ordinary African) taxpayers, against the havens—but in this case was persuaded to take the side of "some of our closest neighbors and allies" in the Caribbean: Cayman, Bermuda, the British Virgin Islands and their like.

The lobbyists had a solid card to play too. The OECD project rather looked like a campaign against smaller countries: what a Cayman representative called "big bully syndrome" was easy to demonstrate, since many OECD member states that are major tax havens themselves avoided the blacklist. The OECD was exposed as "a bunch of racist hypocrites," as Mitchell politely put it. By now, the OECD was firmly on the back foot.

Surrender came very soon. On May 10 the US Treasury announced that it would no longer support the OECD initiative, and O'Neill wheeled out the Tiebout argument: "The United States simply has no interest in stifling the

[39] Later renamed as the International Trade and Investment Organization (ITIO).

[40] *The Economist* magazine noted: "Some officials at the OECD now regret ever using the phrase 'harmful tax competition.' As one of them puts it, 'As an economist, how can you ever say anything bad about competition?' "

competition that forces governments—like businesses—to create efficiencies" (O'Neill, 2001). It was a stunning victory for the havens.

Sullivan (2007) explains what ensued:

> After O'Neill's announcement, the OECD efforts to curb "harmful tax competition" slowly dissolved into a series of toothless pronouncements, a mixture of cheerleading and scorekeeping that continues to this day [written in July 2007]. Beginning in 2001 the OECD started to abandon its confrontational approach. Tax havens were now "participating partners." The original July 31, 2001, deadline to avoid defensive measures came and went without a murmur, and the OECD later publicly admitted that it had no intention to pursue them in the future.
>
> The OECD also downsized its goals. Its entire focus became information exchange on request with tax havens on civil tax matters. Even this was undermined by something called the "Isle of Man clause." Under this proviso, agreed to by many of the havens, no reforms were required until every listed state and every OECD member state—including Luxembourg and Switzerland—committed to do the same. In 2003 this condition was extended to include third-party competitors such as Hong Kong and Singapore. Therefore, in Sharman's words, tax havens "were in effect not committed to anything."

Sharman summarizes more pithily: "The OECD had to give up its ambition to regulate international tax competition."

12.10 SO WHO WAS PULLING THE STRINGS?

The last war on tax wars provides a crucial lesson, via a question. Did Mitchell and the havens win because of the raw economic and political muscle of large corporations and wealthy individuals? Or did they win through rhetoric, lobbying, argument, and bluster? Sharman's study explores this in some detail, and his conclusion is perhaps surprising:

> There is little evidence that corporate interests played the most important, or even *an* important, role in the defeat of the OECD campaign. Private sector interests were deliberately shut out of the agenda-setting stage.
>
> . . .
>
> Two of the OECD's most important opponents, the predominantly Caribbean ITIO and the Center for Freedom and Prosperity, cannot be reduced to fronts for business interests. Both were poor and depended on a media-based rhetorical strategy. Interviews with those across the spectrum confirm that when the Bush administration defected from the OECD initiative in 2001 this was a product of ideologically motivated persuasion and not narrow money politics.[41]

[41] Sharman (2006: 51). Mitchell confirmed to the authors in an interview in Washington, DC, his organization's small funding base, including from the controversial Koch Foundation,

This episode strongly supports a view that tax wars are, while obviously in part a product of direct pressure from corporate and other vested interests, significantly driven forward by an carefully crafted and effective, yet fundamentally erroneous, belief system.

And in this fact lies a great opportunity. A concerted, large-scale pushback against a belief system is eminently achievable: far more so than would be a campaign trying to turn back the tide in a world of genuine unalloyed national self-interest. We now discuss how this might be attempted.

12.11 RECOMMENDATIONS FOR DEVELOPING COUNTRIES

We have two sets of recommendations for how developing countries can equip themselves to address global tax wars. Other chapters in this book outline many possible approaches, so we will focus on those most closely aligned with the tax wars problem.

A *first part* focuses on measures that can be successful relatively fast, and implemented directly by non-OECD countries.

- Tax wars tend to occur most actively on a regional or sub-national, rather than a global, level. Regional cooperative groupings, such as the African Tax Administration Forum, or the European Union's Code of Conduct Group, are essential for coordinating and combating race-to-the-bottom policies and reaching regional agreements on minimum tax bases, rates, and more. The ultimate version would be a World Tax Authority, though we recognize the political difficulties of achieving (Tanzi, 1999).
- A single ministry—the Finance Ministry or equivalent—should have exclusive competence over granting tax concessions, which should only be made through tax laws. This helps coherent policymaking and stops departments with no direct stake in the revenue consequences handing out tax favors.

though he would give no further details of that. Andrew Quinlan, director of the Center for Freedom and Prosperity (CFP) highlighted a key pressure lever when he claimed in 2002 that "just ten days of lobbying" would be enough to get the US to cut off its $60 million annual funding to the OECD (Sharman, 2006: 141). The OECD has remained timid on the subject ever since. In 2013, following the economic crisis, amid widespread austerity and public outcries about corporate tax avoidance in many OECD countries, the OECD produced a new project to tackle the problems, its so-called Base Erosion and Profit Shifting (BEPS) process. Perhaps bloodied by the failure of its ill-fated Harmful Tax Competition project fifteen years earlier, the report paid relatively little explicit attention to tax competition and instead focused on offering technical solutions to the problems of taxing TNCs. Once bitten, twice shy.

- All tax concessions, incentives, and rate cuts should face proper democratic scrutiny: regular and updated cost–benefit analyses; debated annually in parliament. There should be full, easy-access public transparency, including identifying the official or officials who provide each exemption, with the justifications they used. Special exemptions for individual players[42] should be prohibited.
- Donors must not tie aid packages to tax benefits for donor home country firms.[43]
- In the design of federal states and in regional groupings, it must be remembered that there is always likely to be a "spoiler" state (or states); the more tax competencies that are devolved to smaller geographical units, the more intense and harmful the tax wars are likely to be. Where tax policy requires unanimity, one or two member states can easily block progress: qualified majority voting can overcome this obstacle.
- Natural resource extraction can be taxed at very high rates. Natural resources belong to the people and won't disappear: even if they aren't exploited today then they are saved costlessly in the ground. As well as the usual recommendations for broad, fine-grained contract and revenue transparency, transparent bidding and open tendering, a further proposal would help civic engagement. Governments or civil society groups should also publish annually *simple* per-unit total tax revenue shares from the resource. This should better harness public engagement, and throw the onus onto extraction companies and governments to publicly justify contract terms and costs.[44]

[42] A useful and longer set of recommendations is provided in the OECD's draft principles on tax incentives for developing countries (OECD, 2013). We would not disagree with any of them.

[43] A publication from the IMF, OECD, World Bank, and United Nations notes: "Another form of exemption that has proved especially problematic for many developing countries is the practice of exempting from taxation donor-funded projects—sometimes in all respects, not merely from tariffs on importation. This further stretches the limited administrative capacities of many developing countries, risking leakage of 'donor' goods into the economy without taxation. Where donors are willing to provide direct budget support, insisting on such exemptions makes little sense" (IMF, OECD, World Bank, UN, 2011).

[44] Gross revenues per barrel (or per unit) produced as a share of total gross sales value. There are of course many complex reasons why revenue shares may change: complex geology requiring expensive recovery; political risk at the time of contract signature; cost recovery phases, and more. Yet one might say "so what?" This transparency requirement—e.g. that "our country only received *x* percent of the value of the mineral produced" puts the onus squarely on the government and the extracting companies to justify the revenue share: currently, the onus is on civil society and so on to justify any complaints. This highly simple, understandable, and visible measure potentially becomes a cause for civil society actions and public pressure. Such revenue share breakdowns are, in fact, already available from subscription-only publications such as *Petroleum Economist* or *Wood Mackenzie*, but they are rarely harnessed for political purposes.

A *second part* of our policy proposals rests on our finding that tax wars are driven very significantly by a demonstrably false belief system. We propose an organized, networked, and radical body or task force to counteract this belief system.

This would involve the creation of, say, a "Competitiveness Institute," or some such, with poles in developed and developing countries. This would seek to be an insurgency into the heartlands of the economics profession: expert-led, radical, and proactive in counteracting the false belief system,[45] aiming to replicate the scale of success of organizations such as the Institute for Economic Affairs (IEA) in Britain or the Heritage Foundation in the United States.

It would seek to transform the language of debate. It would shun elegant mathematical models based on unworldly assumptions and would instead create high-level research and analysis that brings inequality, democracy, justice, history, and the needs of developing countries firmly and explicitly into the frame. It would contact and actively challenge journalists, politicians, and pundits who misuse the language of "competitiveness" and misunderstand the nature of tax wars.

The logic of our arguments, plus the fact that changes in developed countries directly impact developing countries, mean that this body must have a central pole in the heartlands of the tax-cutting and "tax competitiveness" ideology—that is, the United States and United Kingdom. Donors and actors interested in engaging on developing countries therefore need to allocate at least some attention and resources towards winning the arguments in rich countries. Such an institute should, of course, also have a clear mandate to focus substantially on developing countries, and to build up regional centers of excellence. And, since the arguments about tax wars' harm are simplest and clearest at the global level, the institute would pay special attention to global-level institutions such as the OECD, the IMF, the World Bank, and the United Nations.

More broadly, "competitiveness" is potentially a prism through which to view many issues: the arguments outlined here can be extended, with some modification, into other theatres such as financial regulation, wage policies,

[45] Think tanks focusing on competitiveness already exist—such as the Institute for Strategy and Competitiveness at Harvard Business School. Several nonprofits in the US, such as *Good Jobs First*, have taken a strong interest in tax wars, yet are narrowly focused, geographically or thematically speaking. We have seen few efforts by think tanks to engage seriously and comprehensively with this agenda from the perspectives of this paper, which would be regarded as radical for many. Models for the radical stance of such a body might include the influential Tax Justice Network, headquartered in the UK, and Citizens for Tax Justice, headquartered in the US and with a long-standing and effective focus on providing research, analysis, and data to counteract the dominant "competitiveness" agenda. (Disclosure: both authors work with the Tax Justice Network.)

criminal law, and many others. This could open the possibility for a range of new alliances and rich new research agendas.

Great opportunities have opened up since the global financial crisis emerged to harness widespread discontent with neoclassical economics, illustrated in the flourishing of a new, post Washington Consensus economics movement[46] seeking to move the profession away from elegant but narrow mathematical models into a richer realm that considers inequality, history, philosophy, democracy, anthropology, and ethics. We believe a serious and wide-ranging alternative to the Washington Consensus can be built here.[47]

A focus on "competitiveness" could, in a sense, also become "Phase Two" in the global battle for "tax justice." Phase One, a successful decade-old intellectual and activist insurgency, has focused on the international spillovers radiating out from tax havens and abusive tax and secrecy regimes, gaining the attention of world leaders. Phase Two would complement and expand the international spillovers by focusing also on how setting up harmful tax or secrecy or financial regulatory facilities do not just hurt other nations, but can be a recipe for domestic self-harm too. This could dramatically expand the constituencies for reform beyond those concerned primarily with the welfare of citizens in other jurisdictions, towards those concerned with their own jurisdiction—which means practically everybody.

[46] For a short summary of the issues, see for example Skidelsky (2014).

[47] As Davies (2014) notes: "rhetorics and theories of *competition and competitiveness* have been central to neoliberal critique and technical evaluations from the 1930s onwards." A new focus on the "competitiveness" of financial centers, for example, would look at financial regulatory arbitrage and unpick the domestic and foreign harms that can flow from the pursuit of a "competitive" financial center. There are clear affinities between tax and financial regulation from a competitiveness perspective, yet there is almost no research on this. Genschel and Schwarz remark: "The literature on tax competition develops in virtual isolation from that on regulatory competition. Basic similarities are obscured by conceptual differences. Thus the distinction between source/origin-based and residence/destination-based taxation corresponds closely to the distinction between mutual recognition and national treatment in regulation with broadly similar implications for cross-border arbitrage and international competition." In this they cite Schmidt, 2007. For one example of a member of the tax justice community seeking to engage and build alliances on financial regulatory arbitrage, see "Letter to Michel Barnier and Eight Finance Ministers," 1 July 2013, by 25 civil society organizations in the US and Europe, in response to the ministers' letter to US treasury Secretary Jacob Lew, 18 April 2013 (<http://www.taxjustice.net/cms/upload/pdf/International_G20_Letter_Derivatives_7-1-13.pdf> accessed 15 July 2015). Both letters concerns the extraterritorial aspects of the US Dodd-Frank law regulating financial derivatives. Such examples of civil society and tax justice groups engaging on financial regulation are relatively rare. A focus on "competitiveness" links up, too, with what we have called the "Finance Curse"—where hosting an oversized financial center can create a range of unexpected domestic harms, rather like the "Resource Curse" that can afflict mineral-dependent economies (Shaxson and Christensen, 2012).

REFERENCES

Abbas, S. M. Ali and Alexander Klemm, with Sukhmani Bedi and Junhyung Park, 2012. "A partial race to the bottom: corporate tax developments in emerging and developing countries," IMF Working Paper WP/12/28.

Accountancy Age, 2005. "Profile: Christopher Wales, Brown's Buddy at Goldman Sachs," 8 December.

Accountancy Age, 2011. "Should we rejoice at the return of WPP?" 30 March.

Accounting Web, 2013. "Ireland fears UK tax competition," Accounting Web, 24 April, http://www.accountingweb.co.uk/article/uk-tax-overhaul-potential-threat-irish-investment/540826, accessed 8 September 2014.

ActionAid (with Richard Brooks), 2012. "Collateral damage: How government plans to water down UK anti-tax haven rules could cost developing countries—and the UK—billions." ActionAid. http://www.actionaid.org.uk/sites/default/files/doc_lib/collateral_damage.pdf, accessed 8 September 2014.

ActionAid and TJN-Africa, 2012. "Tax competition in East Africa: A race to the bottom?" ActionAid International and Tax Justice Network—Africa. http://www.actionaid.org/sites/files/actionaid/eac_report.pdf, accessed 17 August 2015.

African Development Bank, 2011. *Domestic Resource Mobilisation for Poverty Reduction in East Africa: Lessons for Tax Policy and Administration.* http://www.afdb.org/fileadmin/uploads/afdb/Documents/Project-and-Operations/Tanzania%20case%20study%20final.pdf, accessed 7 September 2015.

Arnold, Jens, 2008. "Do tax structures affect aggregate economic growth? Empirical evidence from a panel of OECD countries," OECD Working Paper No. 643, 14 October. http://www.ecn.ulaval.ca/~sgor/cit/arnold_oecd_2008/arnold_oecd_2008.pdf, accessed 17 August 2015.

Bergin, Tom, 2012. "UK record challenges link between corporate tax cuts and jobs," *Reuters*. 17 October. http://uk.reuters.com/article/2012/10/17/uk-britain-tax-jobs-idUKBRE89G0UD20121017, accessed 8 September 2014.

Bergin, Tom, 2014. "Britain becomes haven for U.S. companies keen to cut tax bills," *Reuters*, 9 June. http://www.reuters.com/article/2014/06/09/us-britain-usa-tax-insight-idUSKBN0EK0BF20140609, accessed 8 September 2014.

Boadway, R., D. Chua, and F. Flatters, 1995. "Investment incentive and the corporate tax system in Malaysia," in A. Shah (ed.) *Fiscal Incentives for Investment and Innovation*. Oxford University Press, New York.

Brooks, Richard, 2011. "The principles of tax policy: written evidence submitted by Richard Brooks," UK Parliament, Session 2010–2011, 31 January 2011. http://www.publications.parliament.uk/pa/cm201011/cmselect/cmtreasy/memo/taxpolicy/m46.htm, accessed 8 September 2014.

Brooks, Neil and Thaddeus Hwong, 2006. "The social benefits and economic costs of taxation," Canadian Center for Policy Alternatives. http://www.taxjustice.net/cms/upload/pdf/Benefits_and_Costs_of_Taxation.pdf, accessed 17 August 2015.

Buffett, Warren, 2011. "Stop coddling the super-rich," *New York Times*, 14 August. http://www.nytimes.com/2011/08/15/opinion/stop-coddling-the-super-rich.html?_r=0, accessed 17 August 2015.

Chai, Jingqing and Rishi Goyal, 2008. "Tax concessions and foreign direct investment in the Eastern Caribbean Currency Union," IMF Working Paper WP/08/257,

November. http://www.imf.org/external/pubs/ft/wp/2008/wp08257.pdf, accessed 17 August 2015.

Chinn, Menzie, 2015. "The information content of the ALEC-Laffer-Moore-Williams economic outlook ranking," Econbrowser. http://econbrowser.com/archives/2015/07/the-information-content-of-the-alec-laffer-moore-williams-economic-outlook-ranking, accessed 7 September 2015.

Clausing, Kimberley, A., 2012. "The future of the corporate tax," prepared for the NYU/UCLA conference on The Income Tax at 100, October 2012. http://www.law.nyu.edu/sites/default/files/ECM_PRO_073857.pdf, accessed 17 August 2015.

CTJ, 2012. "Big no-tax corps just keep on dodging," Citizens for Tax Justice, 9 April. http://www.ctj.org/pdf/notax2012.pdf, accessed 17 August 2015.

CTJ, 2014. "Should it bother us that Boeing says it needs a tax incentive to make its planes safe?" Citizens for Tax Justice, 13 January. http://www.ctj.org/taxjusticedigest/archive/2014/01/should_it_bother_us_that_boein.php#.U57AU42Sw0N, accessed 8 September 2014.

Davies, 2014. *The Limits of Neoliberalism: Authority Sovereignty and the Logic of Competition.* Sage, New York.

De Mooij, Ruud A., and Sjef Ederveen, 2008. "Corporate tax elasticities: A reader's guide to empirical findings," *Oxford Review of Economic Policy* 24 (4): 680–97.

Devereux, Michael P., 2006. "Developments in the taxation of corporate profits in the OECD since 1965," Oxford University Centre for Business Taxation, WP 07/04, revised December. http://eureka.bodleian.ox.ac.uk/3393/1/WP0704.pdf, accessed 17 August 2015.

Devereux, Michael P., 2012. "The best reform of corporation tax would be its abolition," *Financial Times*, 3 December.

Devereux, Michael P. and Rachel Griffith, 2002. "The impact of corporate taxation on the location of capital: A review," *Swedish Economic Policy Review* 9. http://spot.colorado.edu/~utar/DevereuxGriffith.pdf, accessed 17 August 2015.

Estache A. and Vitor Gaspar, 1995. "Why tax incentives don't promote investment in Brazil," in A. Shah (ed.) *Fiscal Incentives for Investment and Innovation.* Oxford University Press, New York.

Fisher, Peter et al., 2012. *Selling Snake Oil to the States: The American Legislative Exchange Council's Flawed Prescriptions for Prosperity.* http://www.iowapolicyproject.org/2012docs/121128-snakeoiltothestates.pdf, accessed 7 September 2015.

Gapper, John, 2014. "Shareholder value means more than a tax break," *Financial Times*, 30 April.

Halvorsen, R., 1995. "Fiscal incentives for investment in Thailand," in A. Shah (ed.) *Fiscal Incentives for Investment and Innovation.* Oxford University Press, New York.

Henry, James S., 2012. *The Price of Offshore, Revisited: New Estimates for Missing Global Private Wealth, Income, Inequality and Lost Taxes,* Tax Justice Network. http://www.taxjustice.net/cms/upload/pdf/Price_of_Offshore_Revisited_120722.pdf, accessed 8 September 2014.

Hines, J. R., Jr, 1999. "Lessons from behavioral responses to international taxation," *National Tax Journal* 52: 305–22.

Houlder, Vanessa, 2010. "Patents tax break poorly targeted, says IFS," *Financial Times*, 30 November. http://www.ft.com/intl/cms/s/0/d2685736-fcb3-11df-bfdd-00144feab49a.html, accessed 17 August 2015.

Houlder, Vanessa, 2014. "Patent box holds key to Pfizer-AZ deal's attraction," *Financial Times*, 29 April. http://www.ft.com/intl/cms/s/0/c7dc2092-cfb7-11e3-a2b7-00144feabdc0.html#axzz3ChkaFQ2r, accessed 17 August 2015.

Huang, Chye-Ching and Nathaniel Frentz, 2014. *What really Is the Evidence on Taxes and Growth? A Reply to the Tax Foundation*, US Center on Budget and Policy Priorities, 18 February. http://www.cbpp.org/cms/?fa=view&id=4094, accessed 17 August 2015.

Hungerford, Thomas L., 2013. "Corporate tax rates and economic growth since 1947," Economic Policy Institute, 4 June. http://www.epi.org/publication/ib364-corporate-tax-rates-and-economic-growth/, accessed 17 August 2015.

IFC Forum, 2013. "What is tax competition?" International Financial Centres Forum. http://www.ifcforum.org/tax-competition.php, accessed 8 September 2014.

IMF, 2006. *Kenya, Uganda and United Republic of Tanzania: Selected Issues*, IMF, 1 December.

IMF, 2011. *Revenue Mobilization in Developing Countries*, IMF Fiscal Affairs Department, 8 March. http://www.imf.org/external/np/pp/eng/2011/030811.pdf, accessed 17 August 2015.

IMF, 2014. "Spillovers in international corporate taxation," IMF Policy Paper, 9 May. http://www.imf.org/external/np/pp/eng/2014/050914.pdf, accessed 17 August 2015.

IMF, OECD, WB, UN, 2011. *Supporting the Development of More Effective Tax Systems, Report to the G-20 Development Working Group*. http://www.oecd.org/ctp/48993634.pdf, accessed 17 August 2015.

ITEP, 2011. "Taxes and economic development 101," Institute on Taxation and Economic Policy, Policy Brief, September. http://itepnet.org/pdf/pb42.pdf, accessed 17 August 2015.

Kar, Dev and Brian LeBlac, 2013. *Illicit Financial Flows from Developing Countries: 2002–2011*, Global Financial Integrity. http://www.gfintegrity.org/report/2013-global-report-illicit-financial-flows-from-developing-countries-2002-2011/, accessed 17 August 2015.

Keen, Michael and Kai A. Konrad, 2013. "The theory of international tax competition and coordination" in Alan J. Auerbach, Raj Chetty, Martin Feldstein, and Emmanuel Saez (eds), *Handbook of Public Economics*, Volume 5. Elsevier, Amsterdam and Oxford.

Keen, Michael and Mario Mansour, 2009. *Revenue Mobilization in Sub-Saharan Africa: Challenges from Globalization*, IMF Fiscal Affairs Department, July. http://www.frp2.org/english/Portals/0/Library/Tax Policy/Revenue MOb.pdf, accessed 17 August 2015.

Keen, Michael and Alejandro Simone, 2004. *Is Tax Competition Harming Developing Countries more than Developed?* IMF Fiscal Affairs Division, reprinted by Tax Analysts. http://www.taxjustice.net/cms/upload/pdf/Keen_TNI_copyright_tax_competition_developing.pdf, accessed 17 August 2015.

Kinda, Tidiane, 2014. "The quest for non-resource-based FDI: Do taxes matter?" IMF Working Paper WP 14/15, January.

Kinuthia, Bethuel Kinyanjui, 2010. "Determinants of foreign direct investment in Kenya: New evidence," Africa Studies Center, Leiden and University of Nairobi, School of Economics, August.

Kleinbard, Edward D., 2014. *We Are Better Than This: How Government Should Spend Our Money*. New York: Oxford University Press.

Klemm, Alexander and Stefan van Parys, 2009. "Empirical evidence on the effects of tax incentives," IMF Working Paper 09/136, 1 July.

Kotlikoff, Lawrence, 2014. "Abolish the corporate income tax," *New York Times*, 5 January.

Krugman, Paul, 1994. "Competitiveness: A dangerous obsession," *Foreign Affairs*, March/April.

Krugman, Paul, 2011. "'Competitiveness'" Blog for the *New York Times*, 22 January. http://krugman.blogs.nytimes.com/2011/01/22/competitiveness/?_php=true&_type=blogs&_r=0, accessed 17 August 2015.

Leroy, Greg, 2005. *The Great American Jobs Scam: Corporate Tax Dodging and the Myth of Job Creation*. San Francisco, CA: Berrett-Koehler Publishers.

Liu, Li and Roseanne Altshuler, 2013. "Measuring the burden of the corporate income tax under imperfect competition," *National Tax Journal* 66 (1), March: 215–38. http://ntj.tax.org/wwtax/ntjrec.nsf/175d710dffc186a385256a31007cb40f/785c5ab0ca-c6167985257b35007320ca/$FILE/A08_Altshuler.pdf, accessed 17 August 2015.

Matheson, Thornton, Victoria J. Perry, and Chandara Veung, 2013. "Territorial vs. worldwide corporate taxation: Implications for developing countries," IMF Working Paper WP/13/205, October.

Maurer, Ueli, 2013. "Diversity, competition and 'resilient dynamism,'" address by Swiss President Ueli Maurer at the World Economic Forum Annual Meeting 2013, 23 January. http://www.vbs.admin.ch/internet/vbs/en/home/documentation/reden/liste/detailspeech.47544.nsb.html, accessed 17 August 2015.

Mitchell, Dan, 2009. "The liberalizing impact of tax havens in a globalized economy," presentation at Capitol Hill, 23 March.

Moore, Mick, 2004. "Taxation and the political agenda, north and south," *Forum for Development Studies*, 1 June. http://www2.ids.ac.uk/gdr/cfs/pdfs/FDS-01-04-Art-Moore.pdf, accessed 17 August 2015.

Murphy, Richard, 2014. "George Osborne's £10 billion a year tax giveaway to big companies," Tax Research UK, 30 January. http://www.taxresearch.org.uk/Blog/2014/01/30/george-osbornes-10-billion-a-year-tax-giveaway-to-big-companies/, accessed 8 September 2014.

OECD, 1998. *Harmful Tax Competition: An Emerging Global Issue*, approved by the OECD Council, 9 April. OECD, Paris.

OECD, 2007. *Tax Incentives for Development—A Global Perspective: Experiences in MENA and non-MENA Countries*. June. http://www.oecd.org/mena/investment/38758855.pdf, accessed 17 August 2015.

OECD, 2013. *Draft Principles to Enhance the Transparency and Governance of Tax Incentives for Investment in Developing Countries*. http://www.oecd.org/ctp/tax-global/transparency-and-governance-principles.pdf, accessed 8 September 2014.

O'Neill, Paul, 2001. "Confronting the OECD's 'harmful' tax approach," *Washington Times*, 11 May.

Peters, Alan and Peter Fisher, 2004. "The failures of economic development incentives," *Journal of the American Planning Association*, Winter 2004, 70 (I): 27–37. https://www.mackinac.org/archives/2009/nr043009-petersfisher.pdf, accessed 17 August 2015.

Porter, Michael E. and Jan W. Rivkin, 2012. "Choosing the United States," *Harvard Business Review*, March. https://hbr.org/2012/03/choosing-the-united-states, accessed 17 August 2015.

Quentin, David, 2014. "The UK Law Commission consultation on the fiduciary duties of investment intermediaries: Response from the Tax Justice Network," 24 March. http://www.taxjustice.net/2014/03/24/tjn-response-uk-law-commission-investment-intermediaries/, accessed 17 August 2015.

Reich, Robert, 2011. "American competitiveness, and the President's new relationship with business," *robertreich.org*, 22 January. http://robertreich.org/post/2863461038, accessed 8 September 2014.

Reuters, 2014. "Fiat Chrysler creates Dutch holding, sets tax domicile in UK," *Reuters*, 29 January. https://hbr.org/2012/03/choosing-the-united-states, accessed 17 August 2015.

Rixen, Thomas, 2008. *The Political Economy of International Tax Governance*. Palgrave Macmillan, Basingstoke.

Rixen, Thomas, 2011. "From double tax avoidance to tax competition: Explaining the institutional trajectory of international tax governance," *Review of International Political Economy* 18 (2) S:197–227. http://dx.doi.org/10.1080/09692290.2010.481921, accessed 17 August 2015.

Rixen, Thomas, 2011a. "Tax competition and inequality: The case for global tax governance," *Global Governance: A Review of Multilateralism and International Institutions* 17. http://papers.ssrn.com/sol3/papers.cfm?abstract_id=1488066, accessed 17 August 2015.

Rubin, Marilyn M. and Donald J. Boyd, 2013. "New York State business tax credits: Analysis and evaluation," http://www.capitalnewyork.com/sites/default/files/131115__Incentive_Study_Final_0.pdf, accessed 17 August 2015.

Sánchez, Juan M. and Emircan Yurdagul, 2013. "Why are corporations holding so much cash?" St Louis Fed, January. http://www.stlouisfed.org/publications/re/articles/?id=2314, accessed 17 August 2015.

Schmidt, S. K., 2007. "Introduction: mutual recognition as a new mode of governance," *Journal of European Public Policy* 14: 667–81.

Seely, Antony, 2014. "Corporate tax reform," UK House of Commons Library, Standard Note: SN5945, 23 May.

Sharman, Jason, 2006. *Havens in a Storm: The Struggle for Global Tax Regulation*. New York: Cornell University Press.

Shaxson, Nicholas, 2012. *Treasure Islands: Tax Havens and the Men Who Stole the World*. London: Vintage.

Shaxson, Nicholas, and John Christensen, 2012. "The finance curse: How oversized financial centres attack democracy and corrupt economies," Tax Justice Network. http://www.taxjustice.net/cms/upload/pdf/Finance_Curse_Final.pdf, accessed 8 September 2014.

Sinn, Hans-Werner, 1997. "The selection principle and market failure in systems competition," *Journal of Public Economics* 66: 247–74. http://www.cerium.ca/IMG/pdf/1-1-The_selection_principle_and_market_failure_in_systems_competition.pdf, accessed 17 August 2015.

Skidelsky, Robert, 2014. "Post-crash economics," Project Syndicate. 18 June. http://www.project-syndicate.org/commentary/robert-skidelsky-knocks-the-scientific-halo-off-mainstream-economists-teaching-and-research, accessed 8 September 2015.

Stewart, James, 2011. "Corporation tax: How important is the 12.5% corporate tax rate in Ireland?" IIIS discussion paper, submission to HM Treasury on Rebalancing the Northern Ireland economy, HM Treasury, March. Trinity College, Dublin.

Sullivan, Marty A., 2007. "Lessons from the last war on tax havens," http://archive.freedomandprosperity.org/Papers/sullivan-taxnotes.pdf, accessed 17 August 2015.

Tanzi, Vito, 1999. "Is there a need for a world tax organisation?" in Assaf Razin and Efraim Saka (eds) *The Economics of Globalisation: Policy Perspectives from Public Economics.* Cambridge: Cambridge University Press.

Tax Analysts, 2013. "Billions of tax dollars later, no new jobs for New York," Tax Analysts, 9 December. http://www.taxanalysts.com/www/features.nsf/Articles/DC64E543F3D1B2DE85257C3C00530CB6?OpenDocument, accessed 17 August 2015.

Tax Justice Network Blog, 2008. "Mitchell's miracle in Iceland," 2 July. http://taxjustice.blogspot.ch/2008/07/mitchells-miracle-in-iceland.html, accessed 17 August 2015.

Tax Justice Network, 2014. *The Price Of Offshore, Revisited, Supplementary Notes, June 2014,* Tax Justice Network. http://www.taxjustice.net/wp-content/uploads/2014/06/The-Price-of-Offshore-Revisited-notes-2014.pdf, accessed 17 August 2015.

Tiebout, C., 1956. "A pure theory of local expenditures," *Journal of Political Economy* 64 (5): 416–24.

UK government, 2013. "Making corporate taxes more competitive," UK government. 11 October. https://www.gov.uk/government/policies/making-corporate-taxes-more-competitive, accessed 8 September 2014.

Warner, Jeremy, 2014. "Europe is jealous as Britain rediscovers the Laffer Curve," *Daily Telegraph,* 9 June. http://www.telegraph.co.uk/finance/comment/jeremy-warner/10887847/Europe-is-jealous-as-Britain-resurrects-the-Laffer-Curve.html, accessed 17 August 2015.

White, Michelle J., 1986. "Property taxes and firm location: Evidence from proposition 13," in Harry S. Rosen (ed.) *Studies in State and Local Finance.* Chicago. http://www.nber.org/chapters/c8898.pdf, accessed 17 August 2015.

Wibbels, Erik and Moisés Arce, 2003. "Globalization, taxation and burden-shifting in Latin America," *International Organization* 57 (1), Winter 2003: 111–36.

Wolf, Martin, 2005. *Why Globalization Works.* Yale University Press, New Haven, CT.

Wolf, Martin, 2012. "Taxation, productivity and prosperity," Martin Wolf's Exchange, *Financial Times,* 31 May. http://blogs.ft.com/martin-wolf-exchange/2012/05/31/taxation-productivity-and-prosperity/, accessed 17 August 2015.

Zucman, Gabriel, 2013. "The missing wealth of nations: Are Europe and the U.S. net debtors or net creditors?" *Quarterly Journal of Economics* 128 (3): 1321–64.

Zucman, Gabriel, 2014. "Tax evasion on offshore profits and wealth," (draft) prepared for *Journal of Economic Perspectives.* http://gabriel-zucman.eu/files/Zucman2014JEP.pdf, accessed 17 August 2015.

13

A Fair Deal in Extractives

The Company Profit-related Contract

Johnny West

13.1 INTRODUCTION

It has become a truism that many of the big oil and mining companies dwarf the governments they deal with in terms of turnover, technical expertise, and sometimes effective personnel. The impact can clearly be seen in contractual arrangements in the extractive industries which result in projects that can take a decade before the government sees any significant revenues, and which all too often in the last decade have resulted in company super-profits while the poor countries which host the projects are left with too little to show for it.

This problem exists equally at the stage of negotiating contracts and enforcing them. Under-resourced civil services in many countries in the global South are simply unequipped to handle the best that money can buy on the company side in terms of lawyers, accountants, and other technical experts. "Asymmetry of information" is the euphemistic phase often used (International Monetary Fund, 2012).

My proposal is to shift all extractive industry contracts to a new basis: explicitly modeling company returns on capital, and making them the central feature of fiscal terms. Contracts would be accompanied by a financial model agreed to by both parties which capped company return on investment at a stated level within a certain range. Implementation would be flexible, as turbulent market conditions changed initial assumptions and forced re-evaluation. The financial model would be reviewed jointly every year in the crucial early stages of the project, and every two or three years subsequently. Adjustments would happen to other fiscal terms in the contract to bring company profits up or down to the agreed level of internal rate of return, or IRR.

These contracts would serve the legitimate concern of investors, to ensure that their money can earn reasonable returns, while aligning more closely with the central political reality of natural resources in the modern world—that, apart from in the United States, they are collectively owned by the peoples of the countries where they are found. Economic rent, or super-profits, therefore naturally belong to the owners of the resource, the people. As operators, the companies should be entitled to a "cost-plus" arrangement where they are rewarded for their expertise and capital but not deemed to be owners of the resource.

These deals, which are extremely complex and involve hundreds of moving parts, represent a huge challenge to governments particularly of the global South as they try to monitor what is happening, and what the cost base of the companies really is across chains of affiliates in dozens of jurisdictions. Gearing assessment of the contracts, and public attention, to the return on investment made by companies is a better way of understanding core dynamics than the current obscure combination of multiple fiscal terms. It would challenge governments to really understand the contracts they have signed and ensure that they are properly implemented, something which is very far from the case right now.

Adapting the structure of contracts in this way would not be technically complex. The elements to do it already exist in current contractual forms widely used, such as economic equilibrium clauses and terms to define possible imposition of resource rent taxes, or windfall taxes. Reorienting contracts to consider what company profits actually are would expose the enormous base claimed by companies to proper scrutiny, and contribute in a major way to tracking flows of finance in extractives from the upstream into the channels of global capital. It might also result in some projects being deemed simply not profitable enough for both parties.

13.2 THE PROBLEM

This problem has been extensively written about and debated in recent years, not least because of the commodities boom over the last decade which generated trillions of dollars of value coming out of the global South. One aspect of it is well understood, so well understood in fact that it is often taken to be the whole thing. A paraphrase would run like this: extractives companies frequently have turnovers larger than the GDPs of countries they negotiate with. Governments have varying degrees of experience and capacity in dealing with these industry titans but frequently suffer from what is politely called "asymmetry of information" at the negotiating table, with the result that contracts are unfair and lock in super-profits for the multinational companies while effectively denying hundreds of millions of people a fair whack of the benefits of their own natural resources.

This is true as far as it goes but is too limited in scope. For example, it is widely understood to be true in the case of Africa, particularly now that many African countries have become early stage oil and gas countries for the first time—Mozambique, Tanzania, Uganda, Kenya, Niger, Ghana, Mauritania, possibly even Somalia. But it may also be the case in long-established large producers. When ExxonMobil decided to sign exploration contracts in the Kurdish region of Iraq in 2011, expressly against the wishes of the federal government in Baghdad, word has it that the company had a legal staff of 60, both in-house and from several of the world's leading energy practices, working on the question of whether it could be held in breach of its service agreement. Iraq has been producing oil since 1927, OPEC was founded in Baghdad and a class of competent technocrats kept the wells pumping all the way through the country's wars and the implosion of its infrastructure. But the oil ministry was simply no match for ExxonMobil's lawyers. Iraq may be a spectacular example at the edge of the spectrum but the turbulence which so often goes hand in hand with an economy dependent on natural resource corruption—often summarized as "the Resource Curse" (Sachs and Warner, 1997)—means that many countries with a long oil history may because of war, entrenched elites, or bad governance, be at any particular point in time at a significant disadvantage relative to the smoothly functioning systems and institutional excellence of a well-run multinational. Think Azerbaijan and the newly independent states of the former Soviet Union signing deals with BP and Chevron in the early 1990s, Iran at various points in the last half century, or perhaps Libya now.

But two other aspects of this dynamic are less well understood. The first is how acutely it affects the way agreements are carried out—how much money governments get even relative to what is in the contracts they have signed, or at least what they *think* is in the contracts they have signed. The second is the misconception that there is a necessary link between the rise of "resource nationalism" and an increase in what governments get on behalf of their citizens.

At the end of 2013 I spent a morning listening to officials from several different agencies of an African government explain the difficulties they were having figuring out why they were getting so much less in royalties from an iron ore deal than they thought they would. The royalty, at 3 percent, was already on the low side. But with market prices through most of the year hovering at around $130 per tonne, one would have thought—and they did think—that they should be receiving about $3.90 per tonne shipped. Instead, the company was handing about $2.25 per tonne over to them, representing a 40 percent drop from what they were expecting. Several explanations for tranches of this difference had been offered by the company. The company freely acknowledged, for example, that it was selling the ore at a discount to one of its own affiliates to refine. The government officials believed they should have the right to charge royalty at an agreed market rate, a standard provision in many agreements where an "arm's length price" is established, but it was not clear without being able to look at the text of the contracts and their accounting procedures whether this right was in this contract or not, and the officials themselves were not sure. In any case, they had no consistent access to market prices. But there were other explanations for other parts of the difference that they did not understand.

The conventional wisdom of taxation around extractive industries has been that some "fiscal tools," as they are known, or means for governments to raise revenue, are easier to assess and administer than others. In this time-honored discussion royalties are always on the easy end of the spectrum. To compute a royalty, you take the amount of stuff that comes out of the ground. You look at how much it sells for on the open market. You apply your percentage royalty of, say, 5, 10, 15 percent. And you are done. No messing about with what company costs were, or what expenses can be written down when. A royalty, governments are often advised, may not maximize your revenues to the last penny, but at least you know what you are getting and any high school math student can calculate it, the argument runs. But this example provides a serious check on that orthodoxy. And it is by no means unique (International Monetary Fund, 2012).

The scale of revenues missing in action from existing contracts is huge. In 2013, the Africa Progress Panel's (2013) Africa Progress Report headed by Kofi Annan reported an estimate of some $39 billion of calculated taxes on extractive industries the previous year, or almost as much as the continent received in aid.

The means by which these funds never make it to African, Asian, Latin American, and for all we know European and North American treasuries is well documented in other parts of this book. Special Purpose Vehicle companies, high-secrecy low-tax jurisdictions, abuse of transfer pricing, and so on. Enough to make a socially progressive libertarian weep, in fact, because it all adds up to the free market being a figment of our imagination. But the scale of it is spectacular in the oil, gas, and mining industries. In 2012, the Norwegian chapter of the international alliance Publish What You Pay tried to enumerate the number of legal vehicles affiliated to BP around the world and ended up having to guess between 1,600 and 1,700. Their report says BP's communications department at its headquarters in London were unable to offer a precise number of legal vehicles the group owned. If you search for the US mid-cap oil company Anadarko on the excellent open source database of corporate entities around the world, http://www.opencorporates.com, you will find 336 entries carrying the name in thirty-three jurisdictions. There are undoubtedly more in countries whose company registers have yet to make it to the Internet.

Civil society is beginning to catch up to the problem and "beneficial ownership," or which company owns which and who exercises real control, has become a live issue in the transparency agenda in the last couple of years. But outside private sector accounting circles, there is precious little awareness of how corporate chains work, certainly not among the governments and the public. The Extractive Industries Transparency Initiative in 2014 in its Pilot Project Beneficial Ownership (2014) reported a pilot in ten of its member countries to begin to chart beneficial ownership. But voluntary efforts at tracking this issue, unaided by mandatory disclosure in easy-to-access formats, are likely to be always behind the curve.

13.2.1 Didn't OPEC Take Care of That?

The misconception that OPEC and resource nationalism leveled the game in the oil industry in the second half of the twentieth century rests on a severe underestimate of the role played by costs claimed by the company to be recovered before profits are taxed. This is not to deny that there has been a clear shift in balance away from the old Western "Seven Sister" companies and towards the new national oil companies, or the increased take that OPEC and other producers have achieved. But those gains have not been quite so extensive or clear cut as is often imagined. Broadly speaking, the last half century have seen a series of nationalist claims for ownership and management of natural resources to be at first fiercely resisted and then often quietly and diplomatically mitigated, worked around, and eroded to the extent made possible by politics and an imbalance of technical expertise (Stevens, 2008).

For example, the history of the forms of contracts in the oil and gas industry is often described as a progression from concession agreements, where the countries held no ownership, to production-sharing agreements initiated in the first years of OPEC, where both companies and governments owned some of the oil, to the addition of state participation in the form of oil companies such as INOC in Iran or PDVSA in Venezuela, culminating finally in service agreements such as those signed by Mexico and Iraq under which the government owns all the oil and simply pays companies a fee to extract it. In this narrative, each successive stage is represented as a further step in the path towards national control of resources. Problem solved!

What is seldom understood is that the form of contact is irrelevant to the financial result. Or, to be more accurate, that any of these forms of contract can be engineered to produce any financial result. On the one hand it is true that historically concession agreements were used for decades by Western oil companies to run the oil fields of the Middle East as fiefdoms. But they are now used by both the United Kingdom and Norway in the North Sea, and Norway is known for optimizing income out of its fields. On service agreements, Iraq trumpeted in 2009 and 2010 that it had succeeded in drawing the oil companies into contracts that did not transfer ownership of a single drop of oil. And yet the Deutsche Bank report "Iraq: The Mother of All Oil Stories" (Sankey et al. 2010) study of one of these agreements, ExxonMobil's in West Qurna, concluded that it could be reaching a return on investment of 20 percent a year, higher than many projects where it holds a share of production and can formally book the barrels on the New York stock exchange. Iraq's state budget for 2013 included a line item of about 20 billion dollars labeled as oil company costs. The service fee the companies got was given very wide publicity (ExxonMobil gets $1.90 per barrel in West Qurna). The cost structures claimed by the companies were not.

And it is in fact precisely in contexts where resource nationalism has "won" that the potential for costs to constitute a huge tranche of revenues all but inaudibly flowing out of countries is greatest. In 2005, Libya announced production-sharing contracts where the government share of profit on oil reached 92 percent and the companies were reduced to just 8 percent (*Oil and Gas Journal*, 2005). This appears to be a triumph of national will compared to earlier sharing arrangements which could be in the 30 percent range for the company. But the smaller a company's share of what are declared as profits, the greater its incentive to spirit away extra dollars within the cost structure which it submits to the government for full reimbursement before any profits are split. Without getting too far into the details, in the Libyan agreements at just 8 percent profit share, there are times in the life cycle of an oil field where adding just one extra dollar of "cost" per $100 barrel could increase net revenue flows to a company by nearly a quarter, whereas in the first production-sharing contracts in Indonesia the highest value padding an extra dollar of cost could reach is around the 5 percent mark. The Iraqi case is complicated because reliable figures for fees paid are hard to come by and costs are not broken down by company. But in theory there are cases, such as with BP in Rumaila, where an extra dollar of artificial cost could boost net revenues by 50 percent.

This is not just theoretical. A senior Libyan state oil official confirmed to me after the 2011 revolution that the 2006 agreements had in fact resulted in roughly the same flow of *money* to the international companies as previous generations of contract, it was just that more of it was labeled as cost and less of it as profit. In the Iraqi case, a senior executive at Italian oil firm Eni told reporters, perhaps in an off-guard moment, that the company had changed its mind and agreed to go ahead with accepting much lower remuneration fees than it had bid for on the understanding that there would be flexibility in claiming costs.

The devil, then, is in the detail, the detail is inordinately complex, and often beyond the capacity of governments, particularly in developing countries, to monitor.

The traditional approach to this question of complexity has been to suggest introducing simpler taxation systems.

Simple in theory is good, but what if it just fails to deliver as much to governments? One of the reasons so many African countries are up in arms over company super-profits is that many of the contracts they signed before the commodity boom started in the first years of the 2000s had flat-rate royalties and other instruments instead of sliding scale, which would have allowed the countries to capture more of the super-profits when they arrived with higher prices. Those deals were simple—and wrong. Simple in theory can also turn out to be less simple in practice, as we have seen with a royalty that has lost 40 percent of the value the government expected from it along the way. And the fact is that these industries *are* overwhelmingly complex. Both price and cost bases are volatile. Technology is an ever-changing factor and the lead times on investments, as projects become ever more complex, can now stretch into decades. Governments and even countries can come and go, China rises, Europe stalls, the United States finds shale gas. A more obscure perhaps but more decisive element in the structure of many projects is the fact that there are over 200 jurisdictions on the planet with their own legal systems (Ernst & Young, 2014). This means, for example, that it is not possible to introduce uniform forms of contract around the world, which could then be readily understood and compared.

But if it is hard to remove the complexity of these deals, and if this complexity is an inherent part of how unbalanced and unfair extractive industry deals happen, what is left?

13.3 PROPOSAL

Our proposal is simple, radical, and perhaps a little counterintuitive. We propose embracing that complexity to make it work for us.

We should create a new norm around oil, gas, and mining contracts that concentrates not on what the government will receive, but on what the companies get. More specifically, contracts should assure companies of a specific rate of return on their investment, or take what might be called a "cost-plus" approach. This would satisfy the legitimate sphere of investor concern, the return on investment of their resources. Then the government gets the rest.

Rates of return vary according to level of perceived risk and slightly different metrics are sometimes used. One approach is called the "cost of capital" and seeks to determine if a company's investment in any given project will be as high as the next best thing they could have done with the capital they are investing in it, which in most cases is a combination of their own reserves, project financing, and human resources. In many industries around 10 to 12 percent a year is considered a normal cost of capital.

An oil, gas, or mining contract working on this basis could still use any combination of fiscal tools normally used—royalties, profit share, state company participation, corporate income tax, and so on. But these would all be designed to achieve a certain company profit rate, defined as the internal rate of return, or IRR for short. This IRR would be specifically agreed to from a financial model for the project signed by both parties at the start of the project which also included the estimated costs of production and sales prices of the commodity. Inevitable market fluctuations mean the targeted IRR would need to be revised every so often, perhaps annually during the critical early stage of capital expenditure by the government, and every two to three years once a project went into production. Specific tools such as royalty rates and profit splits would then be specifically adapted to adjust to any shortfall or excess in taxation in the preceding period, and a new version of the financial model of the project agreed between the two parties. Ideally, the company would be required to sign an affidavit or other legally binding document in its headquarters' jurisdiction stating that the agreed model was accurate to the best of its knowledge.

The IRR would become the single most publicized metric of such deals. Newspaper headlines would announce that an IRR of 12 percent had been agreed. The president or prime minister might phone the oil minister and ask why there were reports that an IRR might have risen to 18 percent on review. An auditor general, on the other hand, might be concerned that a reported IRR of only 8 percent was suspiciously low and want to see more invoices. Even assuming a relatively effective implementation, there would still be variations between one contract and country and another, and over time within the same project, and probably still be disputes. The IRR-based contract would not be a panacea.

But it is important to stress three things. First, the question of risk is factored into a cost of capital calculation so that it fully abides by the risk–reward mantra companies often offer as a justification for not changing the status quo. The second is that companies already perform these calculations themselves. Oil and mining companies vet potential new projects very closely, and in the oil industry techniques to assess what a threshold of resources worth developing are in any given field are in wide use. Companies use IRR already in their internal calculations, as do the international financial institutions and some governments. Third, in order for such styles of contract to work, governments would have to access significantly more company data on costs and on the scale and quality of resource in the project than they have to date.

Before we examine each of these in detail, however, it is worth zooming out a bit, to flesh out the argument of why contracts need to focus on company costs, not government revenues, and how that could address the revenue shortfalls and unbalanced deals that have prevailed in these industries.

There are two fundamental features about natural resource management. The first is political. Almost everywhere in the world except the United States, natural resources are owned by the people and managed for them by the state. In many countries this is written in at constitutional level, and, whether one agrees that it should be so or not, it hardly needs further clarification.

The second is economic. Natural resource industries are governed by the economic concept of rent, and more specifically the Ricardian concept of rent, which is based on the idea that the cost of producing the same thing which sells for the same price can vary wildly (Ricardo, 1817). This sounds more complex than it is. Oil has been selling at about $100 per barrel for much of 2010–13. But it costs as little as seven dollars a barrel to produce oil in Saudi Arabia whereas in some parts of Canada it can cost $70 a barrel to produce, close to the highest costs in the world (also known as the marginal barrel). In everyday parlance, we might say that at $100 a barrel there was therefore $93 profit per barrel in Saudi Arabia and $30 in Canada. But economists would frame this differently, saying that there was $30 of profit in both countries, but that in addition, Saudi Arabia enjoyed $63 of "rent." The idea is that as the Saudis would presumably have been happy to sell oil for much lower prices as long as they could still turn a profit. All revenues earned above the point at which they decided it was worth getting the oil out of the ground is rent or, quite literally "money for nothing."

Rent in this economic sense naturally lies with the owner of the asset. What contracts that define a company's return on investment would do, then, is to join these core concepts together. Since the people, as represented by their governments, own the assets, they should collect all the rent. The companies would then perform a service for which they would earn a profit acknowledged to be in a reasonable range. Sierra Leone or Australia should collect rent. Total and Shell should not.

Switching between contractual terms might seem arcane. But what such a change would promise is the potential to align contractual obligations properly with the real and just patterns of ownership of natural resources for the first time. And with that comes the possibility of more greatly mobilizing national and international political energy than what is in play today, not just to ensure that better deals are negotiated but also, critically, that they are effectively monitored once they are underway.

The global transparency movement around extractive industries has just got to a place for the first time where contract transparency, the idea that the contracts themselves should be disclosed, has become a mainstream demand. So far only seven countries around the world have published most or all of their contracts with oil, gas, and mining companies. Another dozen or so have agreed to disclosure of some agreements. It is a strange and confusing time on the issue, as indeed on the transparency agenda more broadly. A move to include an obligation to publish contracts within EITI as part of its new standard in 2013 was blocked by fierce opposition from companies that sit on its board at the same time as many individual contracts are published at companies' own request when they are raising finance from shareholders on listed exchanges, for example, or being acquired (OpenOil, 2014).

It seems likely that contract transparency will advance over time and become unexceptional, as the reporting of revenue payments did before it. But then what? How will anyone in the public space make use of these long and turgid documents? Work is underway. Activists are recruiting pro bono support from lawyers and other professionals to begin to make sense of the contracts and grasp their basic structures. It will not be long before financial modeling follows textual analysis into the public domain and then, for the first time, civil society will be in a position not just to react to or query official figures and prognostications but to be proactive and produce reasonable projections of their own.

But as long as these are contested and unofficial, the monopoly on timely and accurate information and therefore authoritative commentary will rest with government officials within their own countries. While they may find challenges keeping up with the sheer resource levels and technical competence of counterparts from some of the best resourced and managed companies in the world, when it comes to civil society these officials certainly feel pretty comfortable, as a rule, that they know enough to dominate the debate and keep the upper hand. The standard description of asymmetry of information between multinationals and host governments needs to be expanded, as it is in fact an asymmetry which exists at three different levels, with companies at the top, governments in the middle and citizens at the bottom.

But company profit ratios written into the contract, with a countersigned financial model attached, would put everyone more or less on the same page. It is true there would need to be a tremendous skilling up compared to current levels to allow most governments to understand what was going on, an issue we will return to later. But all deficiencies would become "known unknowns" in the words of Donald Rumsfeld, some of them skill sets, some of them data sets, some of them institutional dysfunctionalities blocking proper communication between a dozen different government agencies at national and subnational level (Robinson et al., 2006).

The company's IRR would evolve into the single best measure of whether a country was getting a fair deal or not, a function currently occupied by default by a different metric known as "government take" which is inappropriate for a number of reasons. Use of government take sidelines consideration of cost structures in terms of the incentives they could provide companies to maximize reported costs. It also ignores the critical question for most countries of when in the 25- or 50-year life cycle of an extractives project the treasury could start to see money rolling in.

It is important to understand that IRR-based contracts would be a standardized metric, not a standardized number. Differences would still quite legitimately exist due to differences in geological potential and what is called "above ground risk"—building physical infrastructure to get resources to market if need be, the governance climate, market oscillations, and political disturbance.

Once the benchmark was established, leaders would drive their negotiating and implementing teams towards it. Public campaigns would be built around it and considerable resources would be unleashed. If the economics of modeling were standardized, and official models of real contracts published, it is something thousands of high school math students could follow as coursework. Nearly two decades after the transparency movement began to work on extractive industries, public understanding of the workings of the system and the business models could finally coalesce into the stuff of kitchen table talk. Geek kitchen table talk, to be sure, but viable nonetheless for significant numbers of trouble-making intellectuals, which would in itself count as a vast increase in the number of pairs of eyes on the problem than exists in most countries of the world today.

This would be bolstered by strong international support. Programs by Norway, the United Kingdom, and other countries to help developing country governments get more tax from extractive contracts have already succeeded strongly at a relatively small scale. Now we could expect to see them scaled up and given global coherence. There would be no shortage of funders bidding for that glory—if Bretton Woods did not step up to the task of a vastly expanded tax collection support program, UNDP would, or one or more of the bilateral agencies, or the newer foundations emanating out of Silicon Valley.

Such support by OECD countries would not be entirely disinterested, for another aspect of pinning companies down to defined returns on capital in the host country is to bound the parameters of how they can channel value and funds from upstream countries to tax havens around the world. The timing now for this proposal on contracts works almost perfectly with other initiatives on mandatory tax disclosures about to come into effect in North America and the European Union. The Dodd-Frank clauses in the United States and their cousin EU directives on transparency and accountability will oblige companies by 2016 to provide detailed flows of payments made by oil and mining companies to any government anywhere in the world as part of their disclosure to maintain listed status in financial markets. If total profit per country is pinned down in the upstream by IRR-based contracts, we would then have both ends of the money chain in extractive industries. The chains of jurisdictions and special purpose vehicles in the middle, sometimes dozens of stages long, would still be hard to sort out and might take long processes of advocacy around tax havens and many years. But we would have the beginning and the end of those chains.

13.4 OBJECTIONS

There are three main objections posed to the concept of extractives contracts explicitly geared to company profits and return on capital.

The first and most serious is that such a system requires a serious upgrade in the capacities of many civil services in the global South, and, by raising the bar, offer more loopholes in fact to companies, who could lower their stated profit rates. Second, that basing contracts on company profits in this way would be such a departure from the accepted way of doing business that it would simply not be practical. Lastly, that such an emphasis on restricting company profitability when commodity markets are so volatile might result in deals not getting done and investors walking away. We deal with each of these in turn.

13.5 THE MORE LOOPHOLES ARGUMENT

Assessing a company's profit rate in an oil or mining project involves two interlinked challenges: access to data and complexity of calculations. Just to take the value of sales, for example, prices in world markets change daily. And many grades of crude oil or minerals are not priced directly but either allocated a discount or premium against benchmarks. Not to mention currency fluctuations. Add all this together and over the course of a year it is quite conceivable that for one project you need over a thousand data points, and a facility for calculating their relationships, to address just this one element. And the price of the commodity itself is relatively straightforward compared to other goods and services, many of them highly technical, which may not have assessable market prices at all.

A further problem is the sheer volume of goods and services going into extractives projects. An audit which the government of Uganda commissioned from Ernst & Young on the Australian oil company Hardman was leaked to the Internet by the London-based activist group Platform (Ernst & Young, 2009). Although it covered five years (2001 to 2006), the interesting thing is the number of suppliers and presumably items given that the project under review was very early stage exploration. Nearly a decade later, Uganda is still looking at first oil from its fields in the Albertine Basin in 2017 at the earliest and Hardman themselves are long gone from the country, replaced by Heritage who were replaced by Tullow. So the audit period is for very early stage exploration costs, set up in country, and covers less than $40 million of expenses submitted to the government, a mere trifle in the scale of many oil projects. Nevertheless, Hardman submits expenses for 104 separate suppliers from twelve jurisdictions, including the British Virgin Islands (for rigs) and Panama (for "wellsite equipment hire"). In a vanishingly rare example of these processes brought to light, Ernst & Young found serious flaws in the invoicing and procedures. Some of the expenses were owed to employees and Hardman kept original records 10,000 km away in Perth, Western Australia. Some cases of abuse are almost amusing because egregious, such as when company executives charged the government of Uganda for golf clubs imported to near their site on the shores of Lake Albert, ostensibly as part of a community outreach project involving sports. Villagers in the region have about 20 percent access to electricity, the nearest golf club is over 100 km away, and in any case no such outreach plan had been built into the contract, meaning associated costs would not be deductible. Other infringements might be much harder to catch. What would be the normal capacity of Ugandan civil servants to gauge how accurate costs are for technical items such as well boring, seismic equipment or wireline logging services? Or more general headings such as "consultancy services" "geology services" and "safety consultants." Consider also that Uganda at this stage has no experience of oil production.

Contracts explicitly based on assessing company profits would require building a much better idea of their cost bases across multiple jurisdictions, and a better handle on world markets and norms. Some critics would argue that to make this intricate web of commerce the core architecture of a contract is to invite trouble.

The counter-argument has two main elements. First, contracts involve most of this complexity already, but in a way which is hidden. Governments around the world already lose tens of billions of dollars a year. And most of the simplicity of the contracts touted by "pragmatists" turns out to be theoretical. A royalty is not as straightforward as it seems, and in any case there are other considerations than simplicity in selection of fiscal tools. Royalties, for example, are both front-ended and regressive in technical terms, meaning they are good at providing some income to governments as soon as production begins but bad at capturing super-profits. Flat rates applied to any tool rather than a sliding scale may be simpler—but wrong, as in the case of many African contracts in the last decade. Second, capacity is directly linked to political will and public awareness. If company returns are promoted as *the* measure it will focus technical expertise. Of course companies would have an incentive to try and minimize their stated profits—but they already have that anyway.

In short, focusing contractual terms on company profits would raise the governments' game. Also, by stipulating that the contract would be accompanied by a mutually agreed-to financial model, to be revised at predefined intervals, the parameters of slippage would be bound and advertised from the start of the project.

13.5.1 Unviable Legal Innovation

The second objection is more legalistic. It suggests that a new form of contract would be hard to work out and promote within the norms of the oil and mining industries. From a purely technical point of view, such contracts would be unworkable.

In fact, many contracts already include company profits as input. Many versions of a resource rent tax (RRT), or windfall tax, rely on assessing company profitability. These clauses run standard contract terms under normal market conditions but then use language to say that the government reserves the right to introduce an extra tax on their earnings when their rates of return are above a certain percentage and it looks like they are earning super-profits. All the IRR-based contract would do is to turn this into the normal end result, not an exceptional event brought about by market booms. Company profits fixed at a ceiling would be the new business as usual.

Technically speaking, in fact, a contract that capped company profits front and center could be passed through another commonly used clause known as an economic equilibrium clause. The equilibrium clause has traditionally been designed to safeguard the interests of the investor by ensuring that any changes in legislation introduced by the host state that increase costs will be balanced by adjustment of financial terms elsewhere in the contract. For example, if a new law raised the standard rate of corporate tax, or established a minimum wage, the company could calculate its increased costs as a result of these measures and ask for redress by, for example, a lower royalty rate or higher profit share that was calculated to bring back the same revenues as were lost (Cameron 2013). The IRR-based contract in essence would be an economic equilibrium clause in the reverse direction. It says that the terms are what they are but if, for any reason, company profit passed a certain threshold, the other fiscal terms could be adjusted *in the other direction* to ensure the government captured all the rent again, by raising the royalty or lowering the profit share.

Many governments have considered renegotiation of extractives contracts in the last five years because they have failed to benefit from the largest commodity boom in history. Switching terms to an IRR-based arrangement would be hard in most cases, especially with extractives companies which are not shy in using litigation, and their superior knowledge of it, to pursue their interests. But this is not something specific to this particular proposed change. *Any* proposed change seeking to better the deal for governments will likely evoke the same response. What may be possible in many countries is a build over the next two or three years which works in two stages. First, governments can invoke clauses in many contracts which define their right to information from the companies to gain access to the companies' own financial models. In some cases this alone might lead to a government decision to seek renegotiation, either because company profits were demonstrably too high or because they refused to reveal them. Secondly, new mandatory disclosure requirements such as the Dodd-Frank Act and the EU Accounting and Transparency Directives will put information into the public domain which allow richer analysis of company payments, and indirectly profits, across countries, allowing governments to contest company models.

13.5.2 What If the Investor Walks Away?

The last objection is that the imposition of caps on profits might simply make investors walk away in some cases. This is clearly true, especially in regions which are marginalized from the global economy and whose governments have few other development options. The question is whether that would be a bad thing.

Extractive industries tend to be global, as governments are parochial. Experience has shown there is little chance, for example, that new or marginal producers such as in East Africa, for example, have either the market position or political will to bargain collectively. Progress is more likely to come from large-scale single-country producers with a strong national management if they re-engage with the international industry, such as Mexico, Iran, or Venezuela.

But in any case there is a broader point to be made about the "walk-away" argument. The metrics applied to the economic impact of oil and mining industries on developing economies are not development friendly. In recent years, responding to sometimes intense attention from civil society and the sensitive issues of corruption and bad governance, the mining industry and the Bretton Woods institutions have developed a discourse around the contribution the industries make to economic growth. But it is nearly always measured in terms of Foreign Direct Investment (FDI) or Gross Domestic Product (GDP), which mean next to nothing in terms of inclusive growth or better quality of life for ordinary citizens.

In 2011, for example, Niger achieved 16 percent GDP growth, twice as high as China, because its oil came "online," or into production. At the same time there was a crisis in food supply that led several hundred thousand people, some 10 percent of the country's population, to be at risk of malnutrition and even starvation. "Africa Rising" is a storyline touted by many companies, development banks, and investors but it has seen many cases of jobless growth. Countries which have population bulge and a host of other development challenges see almost no broader impact from the extractives sectors than any monies they may contribute to the treasury. Sustainable development has become a watchword and there is a cottage industry of economists and development professionals devoted to trying to maximize other kinds of benefit: shared infrastructure where a company needs roads or electricity, for example, in an area which doesn't have any; "local content," or how the arrival of a big spending investor could stimulate the local private sector; training to ensure not just manual labor but skilled jobs in the projects go to national citizens. But top-level evidence for consistent contribution by the industries in these other areas is hard to come by.

Added to that is the question of whether all the social, environmental, and political impacts of these projects are really factored into the decision to go ahead and pull stuff out of the ground—and the terms of the contract which govern that. Contracts have acquired more politically correct and sensitive language in recent years about the rights of local communities and protection of the environment. But in many low governance environments, which not un-coincidentally can also be economies with a high degree of dependence on extractive industries, there are serious questions about whether these clauses and obligations are really respected.

Put all of that together and the heat of debate around who is getting a fair deal takes on a new dimension. In arguments over the slicing of the pie, the "fair deal" discourse, there is an assumption that the pie is big enough for both sides to get what they need from it (Itriago, 2009). But it may be that, especially when you factor in the real total footprint of these industries, there is simply not enough in a given project to compensate both the company and the government to the extent they need. There is reason to believe that this is the case with many projects that are in various stages of implementation right now but it is masked. But if the company profit margin is put out front, and the two parties cannot agree on what it should be or what the chances of achieving it under various market conditions are, it may be that it would simply be better to leave it in the ground. Most governance frameworks have a value chain for extractive industries where the decision to extract exists as the first major decision point. In reality, though, it is hardly ever invoked (Barma et al., 2012). In this sense the company profit oriented contract could actually take heat out of a lot of mistrust that exists right now, since the basis for discord is that the pie is big enough for a significant cut for everyone but this is an assumption that is rarely subjected to rigorous and independent analysis.

13.6 CONCLUSION

Contracts governing the production of commodities that scar the landscapes of scores of countries, determine their economic development, and generate trillions of dollars a year are misaligned with the political reality of natural resources—they are owned by the peoples of the countries where they are found. Companies enjoy far greater capacity and resources than most governments and are able to bend both the terms of the contracts and their implementation to their own commercial advantage. The result is a hemorraging of public funds to shell companies and waves of jurisdictions around the world.

A simple readjustment of the terms of the contract to focus on and cap company profits in any given project would put national ownership front and central but allow the necessary flexibility to attract international expertise and capital.

REFERENCES

Africa Progress Panel, 2013. *Africa Progress Report: Equity in Extractives, Stewarding Africa's Natural Resources for All.* pp. 1–120.

Barma, N., Kaiser, K., Tuan, M. L., and Vinuela, L., 2012. *Rents to Riches? The Political Economy of Natural Resource-led Development.* World Bank, Washington, DC.

Cameron, P., 2013. "Reflections on Sovereignty over Natural Resources and the Enforcement of Stabilization Clauses" in K. P. Sauvant (ed.), *Yearbook on International Investment Law & Policy 2011–2012.* Oxford University Press, New York, pp. 311–44.

Ernst & Young, 2009. *Review of Exploration Activities in Block 2 Licensed to Harman Petroleum Resources Limited* [Online] Available from http://www.carbonweb.org/showitem.asp?article=376&parent=39, accessed 30 March 2015.

Ernst & Young, 2014. *Global Oil and Gas Tax Guide.*

Extractive Industries Transparency Initiative, 2014. *Pilot Project Beneficial Ownership* avaiable at https://eiti.org/pilot-project-beneficial-ownership, accessed 24 March 2015).

International Monetary Fund, 2012. *Fiscal Regimes for Extractive Industries: Design and Implementation*: 1–81. Fiscal Affairs Department, IMF, Washington, DC.

Itriago, D., 2009. "Lifting the Resource Curse: How Poor People Can and Should Benefit from the Revenues of Extractive Industries." Oxfam Briefing Paper 134.

Oil and *Gas Journal*, 2005. "Impressive Libya Licensing round Contained Tough Terms, no Surprises," 103 (15) [Online] Available from http://www.ogj.com/articles/print/volume-103/issue-15/exploration-development/impressive-libya-licensing-round-contained-tough-terms-no-surprises.html, accessed 30 March 2015.

OpenOil, 2014. "Oil Contract Repository" [Online] Available from http://openoil.net/2014/11/11/openoil-launches-repository-385-oil-contracts-from-54-countries-one-click-away/, accessed 30 March 2015.

Ricardo D., 1817. *On the Principles of Political Economy and Taxation.* John Murray.

Robinson, J. A., Torvik, R., and Verdiec, T., 2006. "Political Foundations of Resource Curse," *Journal of Development Economics* 79: 447–68.

Sachs, J. D. and Warner, A. D., 1997. "Natural Resource Abundance and Economic Growth," Center for International Development and Harvard Institute for International Development, Harvard University.

Sankey, P., Clark, D., and Micheloto, S., 2010. "Iraq: The Mother of All Oil Stories," Global Markets Research, Deutsche Bank.

Stevens, P., 2008. "National Oil Companies and International Oil Companies in the Middle East: Under the Shadow of Government and the Resource Nationalism Cycle," *Journal of World Energy Law & Business* 1 (1): 5–31.

14

Self-Help and Altruism

Protecting Developing Countries' Tax Revenues

Michael C. Durst

14.1 THE ORIGINS OF BASE EROSION AND PROFIT SHIFTING: POSTWAR WONDER DRUGS AND WONDROUS TAX PLANNING

Until the middle of the twentieth century, relatively little uncertainty surrounded the question of where, geographically, the income of international businesses was derived. The kind of activity which dominated international commerce—raw materials extraction and manufacturing—tended to involve obvious physical loci of production. In most cases, therefore, the common-sense division of income among different group members seemed at least roughly self-evident. During the 1920s and 1930s, under League of Nations auspices, the world's economic powers articulated a principle for the apportionment of taxable income among the different members of multinational business groups under which it was, essentially, assumed that (i) the group members would arrange, among themselves, a division of income which would roughly coincide with the relative contributions of different group members to the economic value-added generated by the group; and (ii) the resulting apportionment of income among group members would be roughly similar to that which would be obtained if the group members were not commonly owned, but transacted with one another independently. There was general acceptance of the notion that tax authorities should not interfere with what was seen as the naturally occurring "arm's length" intra-group divisions of income unless substantial tax avoidance was apparent; and this principle was incorporated, in various ways, in national legal systems, and bilateral income-tax treaties, around the world. The arm's length approach to the international division of income—essentially a multilateral agreement among countries for benign neglect of questions of income apportionment—appears to have served pre-War tax administration relatively well, and to have engendered little if any controversy in practice.

The situation changed markedly after World War Two. Pharmaceutical companies, including several based in the United States, had developed patents for unprecedentedly effective medications ("wonder drugs") of various kinds, with highly profitable markets around the world. The pre-War traditions of arm's length income attribution suggested, moreover, that those particular legal entities within multinational groups which held legal ownership of the group's patent rights could be attributed large proportions of the income derived from the group's global activities. US pharmaceutical groups responded to this opportunity by establishing wholly owned subsidiaries, originally known as "base companies," in zero-tax jurisdictions (primarily Switzerland and Puerto Rico) and assigning those subsidiaries the legal ownership of their patent rights. As a result, much of the income from the sales of pharmaceuticals around the world flowed to the tax-exempt base companies, typically in the form of royalties paid by other members of the commonly controlled group who were involved in manufacturing the group's pharmaceuticals, and selling the pharmaceuticals in lucrative markets around the world. The proportion of the group's income that was taxable in the United States, where the group's products typically had been developed, was dramatically reduced.

In the early 1960s, the Kennedy Administration, alarmed at the apparent losses of federal revenue resulting from the use of base companies, asked Congress to take action to stem the outflow of corporate tax revenues. In response, Congress first considered replacing the arm's length approach with an alternative "formulary" approach, similar to that which had been in use since the early 1900s among the US states, under which income would be apportioned according to the relative amounts of physical business activity observed within different jurisdictions. Congress ultimately decided, however, in the Revenue Act of 1962, to instead curtail income-shifting through the use of base companies by enacting the "controlled foreign corporation" (CFC) rules of what became subpart F of the US Internal Revenue Code.

As originally envisioned, the CFC rules of subpart F were supposed to provide broadly that if a subsidiary of a US group is subject to taxation in a zero- or low-tax country, and the subsidiary receives payment from related parties of a kind indicating a transfer of income earned in other countries—including, for example, royalties for the use of intellectual property and interest on indebtedness—the amount of the payments will be treated as subject to taxation in the home country of the multinational group. Effectively drafted and enforced CFC rules generally should take the profit out of base company structures, since the income intended to be shifted to the tax-haven country and thereby largely or fully exempted from taxation would end up being taxed at the presumably relatively high rates of the home country of the multinational group.

A key functional aspect of CFC rules is that, while their immediate effect is to transfer taxable income, which otherwise would be destined for zero- or low-tax countries, to the home country of the multinational group, the long-term effect is to discourage the shifting of income in the first instance from countries where the income is earned to zero- and low-tax jurisdictions. For example, a US-owned multinational group might lose interest in shifting income earned in, say, Kenya, to a zero- or low-tax affiliate in, for example, Luxembourg, if the transferred income will be treated under US CFC rules as taxable at high rates in the United States. Therefore, in practice, CFC rules protect the corporate tax bases not only of the country that enacts them, but also of all countries around the world from which multinationals might attempt to shift income.

There is therefore, very importantly, an altruistic element to the enactment CFC rules: to the extent they are effective, they tend to protect not only the country that enacts them, but other countries as well, against base-erosion transactions effected by multinationals based in the enacting country. The US CFC rules therefore always have been open to the charge that they operate perversely from the standpoint of US economic interests. They direct little if any incremental revenue to the United States, and at the same time they make unavailable to US multinationals, opportunities available to other countries' multinationals to shift to zero- and low-tax jurisdictions income earned from operations in countries around the world.

It is therefore often argued that US CFC rules place US-based multinationals at a disadvantage relative to their competitors, without offering countervailing benefits to the US Treasury. The "competitive disadvantage" argument has had powerful political legs in the United States, and almost from their enactment in 1962 the US CFC rules have been progressively weakened so that today they pose very little disincentive to the shifting of income around the world by US-owned multinationals. Initially, the erosion of the US CFC rules was based on exploitation of apparently unintended ambiguities in the 1962 statutory language. However, each time tax practitioners identified a particular gap in the coverage of the CFC rules, the "competitive disadvantage" argument discouraged congressional efforts to plug the gap; and so as additional verbal defects in the rules were identified, the CFC rules tended to become less effective over time. Then, in 1997, the US Treasury issued tax regulations—the "check the box" regulations—which originally were designed to simplify certain of the domestic provisions of the tax code but also, apparently inadvertently, enabled US-based multinationals effectively to avoid the operation of the CFC rules at will, essentially by organizing their foreign affiliates in particular ways under foreign laws distinguishing, for local purposes, among different kinds of corporate entities. The US Treasury soon recognized its mistake and sought to amend the regulations to remove their unintended international effects; but, citing the competitive disadvantage argument, US multinationals succeeded in mustering congressional pressure to prevent the amendment of the new regulations. The net result is that since 1997 the US CFC rules have had little effect and US-based multinationals today remain almost entirely free, under US tax laws, to shift income earned around the world to affiliates organized in zero- and low-tax jurisdictions.

Around the world, a number of countries, other than the United States, which are home to multinationals have enacted CFC rules similar in structure to US subpart F as originally enacted in 1962. The effectiveness of CFC regimes varies from country to country, ranging from those of Japan, which appear largely to curtail Japan-based multinationals from engaging in income shifting to the Netherlands, which has enacted no CFC rules at all. Overall, while some countries' rules are more stringent than those of the United States, in general CFC rules around the world appear to have been quite porous, enabling multinational groups to shift income largely at will, from wealthy and developing countries alike. And around the world, the altruistic nature of CFC rules seems to have affected governments' willingness to adopt them. (In this connection, a particularly revealing recent event has been the decision of the United Kingdom to amend its CFC rules with the general goal of preventing UK-based multinationals from shifting income from the United Kingdom, but not from other countries in which the multinationals conduct business.) In light of the chronic weakness of the world's network of CFC rules, it is not surprising that the shifting of profits from countries in which multinational groups conduct business has proliferated over the decades.

Today, base erosion transactions can take a number of different and sometimes exceedingly complicated forms. Despite their variety and transactional intricacy, however, all of the contemporary base erosion transactions do contain an element in common. They all, in one way or another, involve tax deductions claimed by group members in countries where they conduct business for payments made to other group members that are resident for tax purposes in zero- or low-tax countries.

Many of today's base erosion transactions involve the lending of money between commonly owned members of a multinational group. For example, a group might establish a financing subsidiary in a zero- or low-tax jurisdiction, which then extends loans to other affiliates operating in higher-tax jurisdictions. When the high-tax borrower pays interest to the zero- or low-tax lender, the borrower enjoys a reduction of tax in the country where it operates, but the lender faces no corresponding increase in its tax burden. The group as a whole therefore enjoys a reduction in its overall tax liability. This asymmetry creates a tax incentive for groups to establish loans among commonly owned affiliates beyond the levels that might be necessary to meet the group's business needs.

Others of today's base erosion transactions are relatively close variants of the royalty holding-company structures that the US Congress originally sought to address in 1962. In these transactions, a multinational group transfers cash to an affiliate in a zero- or low-tax country, which the affiliate uses either to create, through financing R&D efforts of other companies, or to purchase valuable intangibles to use in the group's business. Other affiliates transfer income from places where they conduct business to the zero- or low-tax group member in the form of royalties.

Other base erosion transactions, often very complicated in legal structure, have arisen during the last two decades; these often are referred to in tax practice as "restructuring" or "supply chain" transactions. These transactions involve the establishment of what have come to be called "hub" or "principal" companies in low- or zero-tax countries, which agree contractually with other members of the group to bear the financial risk for activities performed by the other group members, such as the performance of R&D services, centralized purchasing services, or the service of managing manufacturing operations. Under these structures as well amounts typically are deducted against relatively high tax rates in countries in which affiliates perform business operations without corresponding tax inclusions elsewhere. And in each case the available tax advantages pose a strong incentive to establish and employ entities in zero- and low-tax jurisdictions in ways that do not appear to be required by the group's non-tax business needs.

By the 1990s, base erosion planning had become virtually universal among the world's multinationals, regardless of where they are based. Indeed, given the effectiveness of these transactions in reducing companies' effective tax rates, and their apparent widespread acceptance among governments around the world, corporate finance departments almost certainly would have been perceived by many of their shareholders as derelict if they had not steered their groups toward participating in base-erosion arrangements.

14.2 THE RECENT POLITICAL ASSAULT ON BASE EROSION

Given the substantial effect of base erosion on public revenues around the world it may seem remarkable that base erosion structures have not until quite recently attracted much public attention around the world. The longstanding public indifference probably testifies in large measure to the topic's relative lack of accessibility owing to its legal and financial complexity. Perhaps as well, the perception of the booming global economy as a tide raising all boats discouraged questioning of the mechanisms by which the private sector ensured its vast growth during the second half of the twentieth century.

Nevertheless, by about 2005 influential journalists had begun to write exposés of transactions in which wealthy taxpayers, including multinational companies, were avoiding taxation through the use of complex transactions designed by prominent lawyers and accountants, often with apparent government acquiescence. Originally the investigative journalism appears to have been triggered by a spate of tax-avoidance transactions involving very wealthy individuals based in the United States who found ways of reducing their US taxes on gains attributable to the high-technology boom of the 1990s. Although some of the early journalism focussed on international tax avoidance, most focussed on issues arising from anomalies in US tax law. Soon, though, especially after the questionable corporate behavior of the 2008 international financial crisis became apparent, journalistic attention, as well as the attention of some prominent international nongovernmental organizations (NGOs), turned increasingly toward the global activities of multinational corporations, and therefore to the kind of income shifting that had become increasingly pervasive in the global tax system since the end of World War Two.

The reports about tax avoidance in the immediate post-crisis years tended to fall into two categories. NGOs generally focused particularly on the erosion of the corporate tax bases of the poorer developing countries. The general message of their reports has been that multinational companies doing business in developing countries have managed through profit shifting to pay little corporate income tax while the employees of the companies and the consumers of their products have been subject to a grievous lack of public services and infrastructure. This has been perceived by some as displaying an overdrawn tone of moral opprobrium toward the multinational business groups operating in developing countries, thereby oversimplifying the decades-old matrix of economic and political factors that have generated the global network of tax avoidance that the NGO reports seek to describe. There can be no doubt, however, that these reports attracted significant attention from policymakers.

The most immediate impetus to the current activity in the OECD and G20, however, was not the NGO reports focusing on developing countries but instead a series of news articles focussing on erosion of the tax bases of the wealthier developing countries. One result of these news articles was a detailed report on base erosion involving US-based multinationals released in 2010 by the staff of the Joint Tax Committee of the US Congress, which received widespread attention in tax policy circles. Then, in 2012, a series of news articles appeared in the United Kingdom describing the tax affairs of three US-based multinational groups, Starbucks, Amazon, and Google. These reports claimed that although all three groups conducted substantial business activities in the United Kingdom, all but a small portion of the groups' UK income was removed from the country through the payment of royalties and other amounts. This prompted not only public protests, but also parliamentary hearings which received extensive media coverage both in the United Kingdom and abroad. As a result of the UK news stories and legislative hearings, strong public support appears to have developed, especially in the United Kingdom and some other European countries, for legislative action to curtail base erosion.

The OECD's BEPS report, and the G20's ratification of the report, plainly constitute a response to the recent exposure given to international profit shifting by both NGOs and the media. The OECD report portrays profit shifting as a threat to governmental finance around the world; notably, although the membership of the OECD consists of some of the world's wealthiest countries, the report mentions particularly the damage caused by base erosion to the finances of developing countries. The report recommends that national governments adopt a number of measures designed to curtail base erosion transactions, several of which are described below. The issuance of the BEPS report represents a fairly dramatic change in direction for the OECD, which as recently as 2010 had issued guidelines for member countries, which some saw at the time as a ratification of base erosion practices and certainly did not express the criticism that is contained in the BEPS report. Currently, national governments around the world are evaluating the possibility of national legislation that would implement the OECD report's recommendation; the extent to which these evaluations will lead to substantial legislative changes is to date uncertain.

14.3 THE CENTRAL ROLE OF TAX COMPETITION

An understanding of the problem of erosion of the corporate tax base of developing countries requires consideration of the critically important topic, already touched on, of tax competition. Because the corporate income tax falls squarely on income from business investment, economists across the political spectrum often criticize the corporate tax as posing especially strong disincentives to business investment and economic growth. As an empirical matter, it is not entirely clear that corporate income taxes inhibit economic growth more than other taxes, such as the personal income tax or value-added taxation. Nevertheless, there can be little question that the apparent economic disincentives resulting from the corporate tax are far more visible than the disincentives which may result from other forms of taxation. Corporate managers tend explicitly to weigh their companies' potential investments quite explicitly by reference to the investments' expected after-tax rates of return. Legislators and other policymakers therefore often perceive that the lower the corporate tax rates in their jurisdiction, the better the investment will be.

The result for many years has been competition among different tax jurisdictions to lower their corporate tax rates—the so-called "race to the bottom." Competition to reduce corporate tax burdens has long been visible among the US states, which operate within a single economic market and generally are geographically contiguous. In recent decades, with the globalization of the economy and the increasingly prominent economic role of multinational firms, tax competition has become increasingly prominent at the international level as well. There has, for example, been a marked tendency of countries around the world to lower their statutory tax rates over the past decade. The global growth of base erosion and profit shifting can similarly be seen as a manifestation of international tax competition.

Indeed, corporations almost certainly have, through the use of base erosion and profit shifting, reduced their effective tax rates around the world by far more than most countries would be willing to reduce their statutory tax rates. As a political matter, it is easier for governmental actors who are inclined toward tax competition to tolerate base erosion and profit shifting than to explicitly reduce the country's statutory tax rate. Explicit reductions in tax rates typically require recourse to cumbersome legislative processes. Moreover, proposals to reduce corporate tax rates can carry substantial symbolic freight, as they typically will be perceived as undesirable by organized labor as well as labor's political allies. Base erosion, in contrast, has tended to spread by the proliferation of regulatory measures that often do not require explicit legislative approval (notwithstanding that legislators could, if they were so inclined, intervene to stop them). Moreover, these measures typically have been cloaked in verbal complexity (as witnessed, for example, by the verbosity of the US and OECD transfer pricing rules) and euphemistic terminology (such as "arm's length" transfer pricing rules, which seems to imply the automatic operation of market forces instead of the artificial shifting of income to zero- and low-tax countries; and the "check the box" regulations, which present themselves on their face as an innocuous administrative simplification). In short, by tolerating and even promoting the use of base-erosion transactions, governmental actors can respond to the perceived pressure of tax competition without the detailed public scrutiny which explicit legislative measures might attract.

14.4 PROPOSED SOLUTIONS TO BASE EROSION

Discussions of international tax policy typically focus on four kinds of legislative measures which countries around the world could adopt in order to curtail base erosion:

(i) *A strengthened international net of CFC rules:* The OECD's BEPS report advocates that countries which are home to multinational business groups strengthen their CFC rules on a coordinated basis. The apparent goal is that these countries—predominantly countries in the G-20 and the OECD—would prohibit their multinationals from shifting income, to zero- and low-tax countries, from the tax bases of *all* countries, from the wealthiest and most industrialized to the poorest developing countries. This idea has conceptual appeal. A comprehensive global network of CFC rules would end base erosion once and for all, since all countries that are home to multinationals would remove any tax incentive for their multinationals to shift income to zero- and low-tax jurisdictions, from every country in which the multinationals conduct business operations.

However, the widespread adoption of strengthened CFC rules by the host countries of the world's multinationals is likely to face political obstacles. Adopting and implementing these rules could fairly be characterized as, in part, an exercise of altruism by the wealthier countries in favor of the poorer developing countries, the tax bases of which are vulnerable to income shifting, but which tend not to be home to large multinationals. It is to be hoped that recognition of the altruism inherent in strengthened CFC rules would not in itself pose a decisive political impediment to their adoption. The altruism inherent in the strengthened rules might, however, be seen as aimed too broadly and therefore as economically inefficient. A particular country's strengthened CFC rules would have the effect of prohibiting the country's multinationals from shifting income not only from developing countries but from all the countries, wealthy and poor, in which the multinationals conduct business. A wealthy country might be willing to place burdens on its multinationals in order to prevent them from stripping income from poor developing countries, but might not wish to impose similar burdens on its companies in order to protect the fiscs of other wealthy countries. This tendency of a country's CFC rules to protect the wealthiest, along with the poorest, of the country's trading partners is likely to limit many countries' willingness to tighten their CFC rules substantially in response to the OECD's recommendations.

(ii) *Formulary apportionment and quasi-formulary measures*: Countries around the world might choose to curtail base erosion by adopting rules under which a specific proportion of a multinational's total global income can be taxed by the countries where that firm conducts business, according to a formula based on the total proportion of the global group's payroll expenses incurred in, and sales revenues derived in, each country. This kind of formulary approach has been used for about a century to apportion income among the US states and Canadian provinces; and a number of commentators, including this author, have advised countries to adopt it in order to protect their tax bases from erosion. Under a formulary approach, multinationals would no longer be able to shift income to zero- and low-tax countries in amounts disproportionate to their observable business activities in those countries. Formulary apportionment would therefore disallow income-shifting to zero- and low-tax countries in which multinationals perform little if any activity.

Proposals for formulary apportionment at the international level have been exceedingly unpopular among business groups. The OECD roundly condemned formulary apportionment in its comprehensive review of transfer pricing policies in 1995, and no country has ever given it serious consideration. The primary arguments proffered in opposition to formulary apportionment have been (i) that different countries inevitably would adopt inconsistent formulas, leading to "double taxation" as taxpayers faced conflicting tax claims; and (ii) formulary apportionment would involve undue administrative complexity. The author and others have questioned these claims, suggesting that formulary apportionment would involve less difficulty arising from conflicting tax claims by different countries, and less administrative difficulty than currently arise today under arm's length pricing. Formulary approaches have, perhaps, gained some greater respectability than they have enjoyed historically: OECD personnel, while continuing to discount the notion of adopting formulary apportionment for international use, have recently argued that some practices under the arm's length approach need to be modified to achieve better correlation between the amount of income apportioned to a country and the business activities actually conducted there. In addition, the International Monetary Fund has expressed an intention to study the possibility of international formulary apportionment. While these developments perhaps suggest that international formulary apportionment will be accepted in the long term, it still seems unlikely that formulary apportionment will play a significant role in effecting international tax reform in the immediate future.

Nevertheless, a simplified (and admittedly highly approximate) transfer pricing regime, which to some extent involves formulary principles, has been used by Brazil for a number of years and could serve as a model for developing countries, even in the near term. Brazil essentially requires various kinds of businesses that operate in the country to maintain minimum levels of taxable income there—for example, minimum returns on sales from distribution operations, and minimum returns on cost for manufacturing operations. This approach affords an effective block against the erosion of the national tax base; the downside, however, is that inbound multinational companies often complain that their tax burdens are inconsistent with their actual operating results. No other country has formally adopted the Brazilian approach, and until recently it has been something of a pariah in polite discussions of international tax policy, although arguably it has gained respectability in recent years, having been the subject of a comprehensive analysis in a 2013 United Nations study of possible transfer pricing practices for developing countries.

Many developing countries do not have access to the personnel and financial resources necessary to attempt seriously to enforce conventional transfer-pricing rules, and experience in the wealthier countries suggests that even well-funded efforts at transfer pricing enforcement can prove highly problematic. As explained later in this chapter, however, some form of transfer-pricing enforcement is likely to be necessary if developing countries are to be able to protect themselves against the wide range of transactions by which multinationals today are able to shift profits from a country's tax jurisdiction. Therefore, notwithstanding the criticism they are likely to receive from various quarters, developing countries and the organizations that advise them should give careful and open-minded consideration to the use of the Brazilian model in ensuring reasonable levels of taxable income from locally based distribution and manufacturing operations. Possibly, some type of methodology that is similar to but more flexible than the Brazilian approach—for example, establishing minimum margins and markups on a presumptive basis, subject to exception if the taxpayer can demonstrate unforeseen economic hardship in its local-country operations—might prove useful.

(iii) *Limitations on deductions*—For many years, countries have sought to protect their tax bases by limiting taxpayers' deductions for the kinds of payments that typically fuel base erosion. Most common are restrictions of deductions for interest, especially when the interest is paid to creditors that are related to the debtor, or when the creditor is located in a zero- or low-tax country; some countries also have enacted limitations on the deduction of other kinds of payments, including royalties. In general, however, the limitations on deductions that are in effect around the world have constituted only a porous barrier against tax base erosion. As part of its BEPS recommendations, the OECD has urged that countries strengthen their limitations on outbound deductions, especially on interest paid to related-party lenders.

As opposed to the partial altruism behind CFC rules, deduction limitations are essentially self-help remedies. That is, deduction limitations protect directly the revenue bases of the same countries that have chosen to adopt the measures—and their enactment is within the control of those countries.

Deduction limitations have a long heritage of application around the world, and their increased use by countries in response to the OECD's BEPS recommendations likely would be perceived as within the bounds of conventional tax policymaking. In drafting deduction limitation statutes, developing-country governments can refer to a number of statutory models which are currently in use in countries with different styles of tax statutes. For these reasons, I have suggested in the past that developing countries place the adoption of deduction-limitation statutes covering payments of interest, royalties, and service fees high on their lists of priorities for reducing revenue losses to BEPS.

Some caution, however, should attend any expectation that deduction limitations can on their own adequately protect the tax bases of developing countries. First, drafting deduction-limitation statutes requires, in each instance, the making of numerous important distinctions. For example, should the statutes curtail deductions only for payments made to zero- or low-tax countries, or only to members of the taxpayer's own commonly controlled groups? Similarly, should limitations apply, say, to all of a taxpayer's interest payments, or only to interest payments in excess of a specified percentage of a taxpayer's income before payment of interest? These and other distinctions have complicated the drafting of deduction-limitation statutes in other countries; they complicate the process of dealing with interest groups during the drafting of statutes; and the distinctions might make the statutes difficult to administer, especially in developing countries, which may have very few personnel to devote to tax enforcement.

In addition, although deduction limitations can potentially address those forms of base erosion which depend on payments of interest, royalties, and service fees, they cannot address base erosion through some of the more sophisticated "hub company" tax planning techniques, which depend on directing payment for tangible goods—namely, products destined for resale around the world, and raw or intermediate materials used in manufacturing operations—to affiliates in zero- or low-tax countries. To curtail base erosion of this kind, it will be necessary for the countries hosting the distribution or manufacturing operations to ensure those operations earn sufficient taxable income, either by the application of conventional transfer pricing enforcement techniques, or perhaps by Brazilian-style minimum margins or markups if these are seen as easier to administer.

(iv) *Withholding taxes*—For many years the tax laws of countries around the world have imposed withholding taxes on outbound payments of certain amounts, including deductible payments of interest, dividends, and sometimes service fees. For example, a country's laws might require that a taxpayer paying interest or royalties to foreign recipients pay withholding taxes at a rate of, say, 15 or 20 percent of the gross amount of the interest or royalty. Separately, taxpayers typically are entitled to deduct the amount of the payments from their taxable incomes. Historically, tax policymakers and practitioners have not tended to view withholding taxes as enforcement tools restraining excessive deductions; instead, withholding taxes generally have been justified by the view that allowing taxpayers full deductions for interest, royalties, and perhaps service fees tends to understate the amount of net income that properly should be considered as generated in the country from which payments are made. For example, some took the view that payments of interest or royalties include within them value-added derived from economic activity in the countries from which the interest or royalties are paid, so that removing the interest or royalties entirely from the country's tax base to some extent deprives the country of its proper measure of tax revenues. According to this line of thought, withholding taxes are viewed as compensation to the country from which payments are made—the "source country"—for the excessive removal of locally generated value-added from the country's tax base.

Over the years, withholding taxes have fallen from favor among tax policy-makers. Because they are imposed on the gross amounts of payments made, rather than on the basis of a taxpayer's net income, withholding taxes are not correlated with a taxpayer's ability to pay and therefore depart from commonly held perceptions of a properly functioning income tax. Accordingly they are sometimes seen as impediments to international commerce, and in recent decades it has become common for countries to agree in income tax treaties to reduce or eliminate withholding taxes in cross-border transactions with one another. In some instances developing countries have curtailed or relinquished their rights to collect withholding taxes both through bilateral treaties and by offering inbound investors exemption from withholding taxes on a case-by-case basis.

Perhaps reflecting continuing conceptual discomfort with withholding taxes, the OECD has not included them among its recommendations for curtailing BEPS. Nevertheless, withholding taxes should pose clear and effective economic disincentives to the payment of interest, royalties, and service fees in connection with base erosion transactions. Moreover, despite their having fallen into intellectual disfavor, their long and continued use should provide withholding taxes with the protection of international legitimacy.

Withholding tax laws tend to be relatively simple in their structure, and the language used tends to be similar throughout the world. Because of their fairly uniform structure across countries, they should be well suited to coordinated implementation by developing-country governments within, perhaps, a geographic region, thus offering a means of dampening tax competition. Further, although withholding taxes are sometimes the subject of administrative difficulty—for instance in evaluating whether a particular payment falls within the definition of one of the particular categories of payments to which the withholding tax applies—in general they are straightforward to enforce. In particular, the claiming of a deduction by a taxpayer typically serves as a strong signal to the tax authority that a withholding tax may properly be due. For all of these reasons, the revitalization of withholding tax regimes, by statutory enactment and by the renegotiation or, where necessary, partial abrogation of treaties which now prohibit the levying of withholding taxes, should be seen as a high priority by governments that want to protect their tax bases against erosion.

14.5 THE WAY FORWARD FOR DEVELOPING COUNTRIES: A POLITICAL AND ETHICAL PERSPECTIVE

The NGO commentary that helped to trigger the current global interest in BEPS reform tends to direct moral opprobrium at the multinational corporations that engage in income-shifting transactions, as well as the lawyers and accountants who assist them. From one perspective this may have merit: multinational groups do routinely enter into business arrangements in developing countries from which, the companies know they will derive little if any corporate tax revenue. Blame also has been directed at the governments of countries that are home to the multinationals both for failing to maintain effective CFC regimes, which would protect developing countries against base erosion, and for propagating an "international consensus" on tax policies that tends to encourage the relinquishment of withholding taxes by developing countries, as well as to perpetuate international transfer pricing rules which developing countries cannot feasibly enforce.

The criticisms that have been made of multinational companies, and their home governments, have been productive in drawing increasing public attention to the fiscal problems faced by developing countries in the world economy. However, to assign responsibility for developing countries' corporate-tax shortfalls solely to decision-makers within multinational companies and their home governments would be simplistic and counterproductive. Developing-country governments have long had at their disposal mechanisms such as withholding taxes and deduction limitations, by which they could afford their countries' tax systems a large degree of protection from base erosion. Not only have developing countries generally not availed themselves of these measures, in some cases they have allowed their historical systems of withholding taxes to erode. Moreover, developing countries routinely trade away their rights to tax multinational businesses, in many instances offering tax holidays or other exemptions to companies willing to make inbound investments.

Much of the apparent reluctance of developing-country governments to protect their countries' tax bases almost certainly can be attributed to tax competition. Inbound investments by multinational companies often have high public profiles in developing countries. Political leaders in developing countries can expect a great deal of criticism if they are seen to have failed to attract inbound investment—much more criticism than they are likely to receive for forgoing tax revenues in order to attract the investment. The fear of losing inbound investment if corporate tax burdens are enforced, moreover, is not entirely unfounded. The plain arithmetical logic of corporate income taxation holds that the higher the tax burden, the lower will be the investor's expected after-tax return from a contemplated investment; hence, higher tax burdens almost certainly do, in fact, lead to some diminution in the demand for investment.

Indeed, the belief that enforcing corporate tax obligations will unduly discourage business investment—whether justified or not—has influenced tax policy in countries at all stages of economic development. For example, fear of tax competition plainly is responsible for the shrinking role of corporate taxation in the fiscal systems of the United States and other developed economies; this concern also undoubtedly has contributed to the failure of many of the wealthier countries, including the United States, to maintain effective CFC regimes. Policymakers in many settings around the world appear to have reached the conclusion that while corporate income tax laws should not be repealed entirely, the corporate tax nevertheless has serious undesirable side effects and the tax's effective rate of incidence should be kept low.

To the extent that this judgment is valid, one might expect the same logic to apply with respect to the economies of the poorer developing as well as the wealthier countries. The problem, however, is that whereas the wealthier countries generally are able to shift the national tax burden from the corporate income tax to other forms of taxation, including individual income and consumption taxes, developing countries tend to be far less able to do so. The domestic economies of the poorer developing countries often are based very heavily on informal activity, such as home-based manufacturing and small-scale retail sales operations, with few books and records available to facilitate tax administration. Developing countries, therefore, are likely to be much less able than wealthier countries to replace forgone corporate tax revenues with revenues from individual income and consumption taxes. Further, the costs, in terms of unmet human needs, of revenue shortfalls in developing countries may be greater than the costs of similar shortfalls in wealthier societies. For these reasons, a trade-off of corporate tax revenues in order to enhance the local investment environment might be defensible, in terms of the overall enhancement of well-being within a country, for wealthier countries but very difficult to defend for poorer developing countries. At least until alternative sources of revenue can be developed effectively, developing countries are likely to have substantially greater need to raise revenues under their corporate tax rules.

The question therefore is how, in the face of the continuing economic pressures that historically have given rise to base erosion, developing-country governments are going successfully to curtail it. It should be plain at this point that the problem is not primarily one of designing technically sound legislative measures; such measures—notably withholding taxes and deduction limitations—have been available for many decades. The problem is instead very largely political in nature. Put simply, developing-country policymakers will need to find ways to overcome fears of suppressing inbound investment in order to garner the political will to enact effective base-protection measures.

The difficulty of raising the necessary political resolve should not be understated. Although it is only in recent years that the problems of developing countries in raising corporate tax revenues have come to the attention of the public, tax experts, including those involved in international development work, have understood the dilemma facing developing countries for many years. These experts have devoted substantial energy and knowledge to helping developing countries develop more effective tax systems, but the problems posed by BEPS remain largely unresolved. Given the longstanding nature of the political barriers faced by developing countries in addressing BEPS, as well as the severe stress that fears of being seen to discourage inbound investment can place upon political decision-makers, it seems unlikely that any single policy initiative, alone, can be effective—or that the problem is likely to be solved in the very short term. Instead the solution is likely to result from the application of a number of different policy measures acting in concert, probably over a substantial period of time.

14.6 A SUGGESTED PROGRAM FOR RESEARCH AND GOVERNMENTAL ACTION

Following are some measures that appear to have promise, based on the analysis offered above, for assisting developing countries in mitigating their losses of corporate tax revenues to base erosion and profit shifting. This list may be seen as a suggestion toward a research and policy agenda for (i) the governments of both the developing and the wealthier countries, (ii) multi-governmental economic organizations including the IMF, the World Bank, and the OECD, and (iii) civil society organizations that seek to work toward redressing the current dilemma faced by many developing countries in addressing revenue losses from base erosion and profit shifting. The list undoubtedly is not comprehensive. It is hoped, however, that the suggested program will provide a useful indication of the combination of actions, by different parties, which is likely to be required if the base erosion problems with which developing countries are now dealing can be satisfactorily redressed.

(i) *Enactment of self-protective measures by developing countries, and international forbearance with respect to the sometimes-unpopular remedies such as withholding taxes and fixed transfer pricing margins and markups.* A *sine qua non* for the effective control of profit shifting from developing countries would appear to be the enactment by developing countries of targeted measures to prevent or strongly discourage the transfer of tax-deductible payments to subsidiaries of multinational groups that have been established in zero- and low-tax countries. One potentially useful form of targeted measures would include direct limitations on deductions for certain payments of interest, royalties, and service fees. These kinds of measures have a good deal of international respectability among tax policymakers and in fact are recommended explicitly by the OECD in its BEPS report. For reasons explained above, however, complexities in the design of deduction limitations may limit the extent of their usefulness. As a practical matter, therefore, alternative measures—including strengthened withholding tax statutes, and presumptively required margins and markups, under rules similar if not identical to those of Brazil, for distribution and manufacturing operations—may be necessary if a country's protections against base erosion are to be reasonably comprehensive.

The most important obstacle to the adoption of self-protective measures by developing countries is likely not to be foreign opposition, but instead domestic fears of discouraging inbound investment. Nevertheless, the attitudes of international policymakers and multi-governmental organizations also may be influential. In this connection, policymakers in both national governments and multi-governmental organizations should carefully consider adopting a posture of greater receptivity to measures, including withholding taxes and prescribed margins and markups, which admittedly can depart markedly from taxation based on the close estimation of net income, but nevertheless can pose substantial practical advantages in the context of developing-country tax administration. It may well be that the conceptual trade-off, between precision and administrability, on which the "international consensus" against relatively approximate means of levying income taxes historically has been based, achieves undesirable results in the heavily resource-constrained environment of developing-country tax administration.

(ii) *Continuing analytical assistance by international economic agencies in weighing trade-offs between protection of developing countries' revenue bases and the encouragement of inbound investment.* International organizations have sought for a number of years to convince developing-country governments, through economic analysis, that the sacrifice of corporate tax revenues in order to attract inbound investment typically is unattractive to developing countries. There probably is a limit to the potential effectiveness of this kind of economics-based advocacy because, first even the most scientific of economic analyses must weigh variables that can be measured only subjectively, and second the perceived political imperative within developing countries to promote inbound investment may in many instances be so compelling as to overwhelm any willingness on the part of government officials to acknowledge countervailing considerations. Despite these limitations, however, the educative function of international development agencies, in advocating the need for balance in assessing the trade-off between tax revenues and incentives for investment, is indispensable for the development of reasoned economic policies and should continue.

(iii) *Development of alternative tax sources from inbound investment, including excise taxes designed to replace portions of the corporate levy.* Around the world, governments have relied to varying extents on alternative means of deriving income taxes from particular multinational industries for which the measurement of net income, under conventional corporate income tax rules, poses especially severe administrative difficulties. Prominent examples include excise taxes on (a) telecommunications services, including mobile telephone services, which tend to be economically important in developing countries and often are provided by foreign-owned carriers; (b) premiums paid for insuring local-country risks (as insurance policies in developing countries very often are reinsured by foreign companies, making measurement of net income from the insurance services very difficult); and (c) services performed by banks and other financial institutions, the complex affairs of which render income taxation virtually impossible to administer in many cases. Unlike corporate income taxes, excise taxes are not subject to reduction through deductible payments made from a country. The selective replacement of corporate income tax levies with excise taxes might significantly improve a country's net revenues from its business-tax base.

(iv) *Enactment of laws prohibiting deviation from regular income tax laws in negotiating natural resource concessions and other agreements with investors.* It has become common in the process of drafting contracts between governments and inbound investors, including natural resource concession agreements and telecommunications licenses, to treat as open for negotiation (as part of the "fiscal terms" of the agreements) full or partial exemptions from both income and withholding taxes at regularly applied rates. Given that those negotiating on behalf of governments may face strong domestic political pressure to conclude agreements, and also that the lead government negotiators may be officials responsible for economic development rather than for taxation, governments may well tend to agree to tax concessions which are far greater than necessary to induce the desired inbound investment. To counter these tendencies, it would be sensible for national legislation to prohibit the modification of regularly applicable tax rules in the course of agreements with particular inbound investors or other taxpayers. Legislation of this kind would not unduly constrain the range of negotiations: Although tax rules would not be subject to modification, the primary commercial terms, which typically are at the center of negotiators' attention, would remain fully subject to negotiation, and if investors perceive the country's tax rules as unduly demanding, they can seek compensating concessions in the primary business provisions of the agreements. Governments would, however, be protected against erosion of their tax bases in the course of typically pressurized negotiations.

(v) *Continued international assistance in taxing the informal economy*. The crux of developing countries' special vulnerability to corporate base erosion and profit shifting is the tendency of developing-country economies to include relatively large informal sectors, thereby limiting the revenues that can be raised from alternatives to the corporate tax. Accordingly, efforts to raise greater revenues from domestic sources, even in the presence of much off-the-books economic activity, may be essential to reducing developing countries' susceptibility to BEPS. International organizations and other sources of aid are already devoting significant effort to assisting developing countries in the generation of government revenues from domestic sources. Growing recognition of the special damages incurred by developing countries from the need to rely heavily on revenues from international transactions should encourage the intensification of this ongoing technical assistance.

(vi) *Regional coordination of tax policies and practices*. Regional coordination of tax policies—for example, agreement among countries in a region that they will apply withholding taxes on particular kinds of payments at minimum rates, that they will not provide tax holidays or otherwise offer investors exemption from generally applicable revenue laws, or that they will impute income to inbound distribution or manufacturing operations at specified minimum levels—could help significantly to dampen tax competition among developing countries. Any attempt to constrain economic competition by agreement among sovereign countries is, obviously, fraught with difficulty, and it cannot be assumed that negotiation of multilateral tax agreements will prove politically feasible. Nevertheless, even by devoting serious efforts to the drafting and public discussion of agreements of this kind, regional tax administration and economic development organizations could make significant contributions to the articulation of best tax policies and tax administration practices for developing-country governments.

(vii) *Altruistic forbearance in dealing with developing-country tax systems by multinational companies*. The current fiscal plight of many developing countries reflects in large measure those countries' relative lack of bargaining power in international economic and political markets. In particular, the pressure of competition for inbound investment has in some cases induced developing countries virtually to abandon efforts to protect their revenues. This kind of market-based difficulty in self-protection has not, of course, been unique to the area of taxation; the desire to attract inbound investment also has been associated with failures in achieving, for example, adequate environmental protection and worker health and safety regulation. It may well be that the remediation of some countries' current fiscal difficulties will be possible only with some degree of voluntary forbearance by multinational companies in their dealings with developing-country fiscal authorities. Altruistic actions by multinationals in various areas are far from unknown, for example in matters involving child labor, the purchase of materials derived from endangered species, and participation in bribery and other corrupt practices. In the context of taxation, multinational companies might agree voluntarily, when dealing with the governments of countries with per capita incomes below specified levels, to refrain from accepting tax holidays or other exemptions from regularly applicable taxes, and to refrain from political advocacy in opposition to income-stripping limits, withholding taxes, or other base-protection measures.

(viii) *Continued advocacy by NGOs and the media.* Advocacy by NGOs, and investigative reporting by the press and other media appears to have been essential in raising public interest in the problems associated with tax base erosion, including the special difficulties faced by developing countries. To some extent the NGO and media reports might be seen as unfairly impugning the motives of some participants in global economic activity; and in some instances the rhetoric used may have conveyed an unduly simplified picture of the difficulties faced by developing countries. Nevertheless, the work of the NGOs and media has been essential in bringing a serious problem faced by developing countries to greater public attention and it is important that this work continue. The inaccessibility of tax laws owing to their complexity and the ability of economically motivated interest groups to achieve high degrees of access to legislative and regulatory decision-makers, suggest that advocacy by NGOs and probing media reporting are likely to remain essential if international tax policies are to be considered in a manner that reflects the interests of all affected parties.

14.7 CONCLUSION

The erosion of corporate income tax bases, of countries around the world at all levels of economic development, has a long history and reflects pervasive political and economic pressures. In wealthier countries this erosion might be seen as a reasonable trade-off for a more inviting climate for business investment. For the poorer developing countries, however, which have relatively little ability to replace corporate tax revenues with revenues from other forms of taxation, shortfalls in corporate tax revenue can impose serious constraints on social and economic development.

As the economic and political causes of corporate tax base erosion are variegated and complex, successfully confronting the phenomenon is likely to require recourse to many policy instruments. Moreover, given that base erosion to some extent reflects the often dominant bargaining power of multinational companies in their dealings with developing-country governments, solutions probably will require the companies voluntarily to step out of their market roles and relinquish some of their bargaining power in the course of those dealings. Further, although the dominant motivation for the protection of developing-country revenues must come from the developing countries themselves, numerous actors, including not only governments and multinational businesses, but also international economic organizations, NGOs, and the media will need to play significant roles. It is hoped that the suggestions offered in this chapter will be useful to those in all these settings who would develop programs for the research and implementation of effective policy measures to redress the loss of tax revenues by the poorer developing countries.

ACKNOWLEDGMENT

A prior version of this chapter has been published by Bloomberg BNA Inc. and is printed by permission with all rights reserved.

SELECTIVE BIBLIOGRAPHY

Data on different countries' relative reliance on corporate tax revenues:

USAID, "Collecting Taxes" database, http://egateg.usaid.gov/collecting-taxes, accessed 17 August 2015.

Sources of historical discussion of "international consensus" in tax policy:

Avi-Yonah, Reuven S., 1997. "The Rise and Fall of Arm's Length: A Study in the Evolution of U.S. International Taxation" (originally published 1995 in the *Virginia Tax Review*; updated version published as a University of Michigan Law School working paper in 1997 and available online at http://law.bepress.com).

Avi-Yonah, Reuven S. and Kimberly A. Clausing, 2007. "A Proposal to Adopt Formulary Apportionment for Corporate Income Taxation: The Hamilton Project," Brookings Institution, Washington, DC.

Durst, Michael C. and Robert E. Culbertson, 2003. "Clearing away the Sand: Retrospective Methods and Prospective Documentation in Transfer Pricing Today," *Tax L. Rev.* 57: 37.

Langbein, Stanley I., 1986. "The Unitary Method and the Myth of Arm's Length," *Tax Notes* 17 (February): 629–38.

Wells, Bret and Cym Lowell, 2012. "Tax Base Erosion and Homeless Income: Collection at Source Is the Linchpin," *Tax L. Rev.* 65: 535.

NGO reports on base erosion in developing countries:

Action Aid, 2012. "Calling Time: Why SABMiller Should Stop Dodging Taxes in Africa." http://www.actionaid.org.uk/sites/default/files/doc_lib/calling_time_on_tax_avoidance.pdf, accessed 9 September 2015.

Christian Aid, 2009. "False Profits: Robbing the Poor to Keep the Rich Tax-Free." https://www.christianaid.org.uk/Images/false-profits.pdf, accessed 9 September 2015.

US media reports on tax base erosion:

Drucker, Jesse, 2013. "IRS Auditing How Google Shifted Profits," *Bloomberg.com*, 13 October.

Duhigg, Charles and David Kocieniewski, 2012. "How Apple Sidesteps Billions in Taxes," *The New York Times*, 28 April.

OECD and G20 reports on base erosion and profit-shifting:

G20, 2013. "Tax Annex to the St. Petersburg G20 Leaders' Declaration," September.

OECD, http://www.oecd.org/ctp/beps.htm, 16 August 2015.

US legislative report on income-shifting:

Staff of the Joint Committee on Taxation, 2010. "Present Law and Background on Possible Income Shifting and Transfer Pricing." https://www.jct.gov/publications.html?func=startdown&id=3692, accessed 9 September 2015.

Media reports and other materials related to base erosion questions in the United Kingdom:

Duncan, Hugo and Tamara Cohen, 2012. "Starbucks 'Treats Tax Like a Church Collection Plate': Treasury Chief Secretary Attacks Coffee Chain," *Daily Mail*, 9 December.

Kleinbard, Edward D., 2013. "Through a Latte Darkly: Starbuck's Stateless Income Planning," *Tax Notes*, 24 June.

KPMG, 2012. "Controlled Foreign Companies: A Summary of the New Rules," September. http://hb.betterregulation.com/external/Controlled%20Foreign%20Companies%20-%20a%20summary%20of%20the%20new%20rules%20-%20Sep%2012.pdf, accessed 9 September 2015.

Syal, Rajeev and Patrick Wintour, 2012. "MPs Attack Amazon, Google and Starbucks," *The Guardian*, 2 December.

Description of Brazil's Transfer Pricing Rules:

Falcao, Tatiana, 2012. "Brazil's Approach to Transfer Pricing: A Viable Alternative to the Status Quo?" Bloomberg BNA Transfer Pricing Rep., 12 February.

United Nations, 2013. "Chapter 10, 'Country Practices,'" *United Nations Practical Manual on Transfer Pricing for Developing Countries.*

Discussions of formulary apportionment as alternative to arm's-length transfer pricing rules:

Avi-Yonah, Reuven S. and Kimberly A. Clausing, 2007. "A Proposal to Adopt Formulary Apportionment for Corporate Income Taxation: The Hamilton Project," Brookings Institution, Washington, DC.

Avi-Yonah, Reuven S., Kimberly A. Clausing, and Michael C. Durst, 2009. "Allocating Business Profits for Tax Purposes: A Proposal to Adopt a Formulary Profit Split," *Florida Tax Rev.* 9: 497.

Durst, Michael C., 2013. A series of articles suggesting statutory and regulatory language to implement formulary apportionment, published in *Bloomberg BNA Transfer Pricing Report* over approximately 12-month period commencing 16 May 2013; republication in book format forthcoming.

Recent discussions by author of special problems of developing countries:

Durst, Michael C., 2013. "The OECD's Base Erosion Plan and Developing Countries," *Bloomberg BNA Daily Tax Report*, 30 July.

Durst, Michael C., 2013. "Protecting the Tax Bases of Developing Countries: Next Steps," *Bloomberg BNA Daily Tax Report*, 29 November.

Reviews of public finance and natural resources for developing countries:

Barma, Naazneed, Kai Kaiser, Tuan Minh Le, and Lorena Vinuela, 2012. "*Rents to Riches? The Political Economy of Natural Resource-led Development.*" World Bank. https://openknowledge.worldbank.org/handle/10986/, accessed 17 August 2015.

Daniel, Philip, Michael Keen, and Charles McPherson (eds), 2010. "The Taxation of Petroleum and Minerals: Principles, Problems & Practice." International Monetary Fund and Routledge.

15

Ten Ways Developing Countries Can Take Control of their Own Tax Destinies

Krishen Mehta and Erika Dayle Siu

15.1 INTRODUCTION

The question of how developing countries get a fair deal on tax justice is an important and sensitive one. This question goes to the heart of how a country can attract foreign direct investment (FDI) while maintaining fiscal sovereignty in the pursuit of development. On the other hand, it is also important to understand that the question of ethical tax practices by multinational companies (MNCs) is not an easy one. We recognize some of the complex issues that go into decision-making by MNCs. Factors in such decisions include the risks of capital expropriation, government challenges to the repatriation of profits, foreign exchange risk, time consistency risks (or how future governments could view existing contracts), reputational and public license risk, customers' responses, and so on. In the context of such shared interests, it is not productive to create a façade of an evil empire of MNCs or their advisors. But what a developing country *can* do is to take control of its own tax destiny.

In this paper, we describe ten ways developing countries have taken control of their own tax destinies, and which are consistent with the theme and objectives of this book. These methods are certainly not one-size-fits-all, and each country context is different. However, the fiscal policies outlined below may serve as useful models for developing countries in striking the balance between encouraging FDI and maintaining fiscal sovereignty.

15.2 BE VERY CAUTIOUS ABOUT SIGNING TAX TREATIES

There are over 3,000 bilateral tax treaties in existence at the present time, and one-third of them have been signed by developing countries (OECD,

2014: 18). They divide up (for tax purposes) about $600 billion of investment flows between the countries concerned, often at the expense of the revenue base of the developing countries. If not properly negotiated and structured, treaties often protect MNCs at the expense of developing countries (IMF, 2014: 25). Moreover, there is evidence that signing tax treaties doesn't always result in greater FDI as expected, and may even result in revenue losses to developing countries (Sauvant and Sachs, 2009; IMF, 2014: 25–6). Although substantial revenue losses can be caused by treaty abuse (whereby affiliate corporations are set up as conduits in treaty partner states by corporations in non-partnering states, allowing them to indirectly take advantage of treaty benefits) there are more fundamental issues of taxing power relinquishment at play when entering into tax treaties.

When a developing country negotiates a tax treaty based on an international model, it is expected to commit to reducing or sometimes eliminating withholding taxes on outflows of cash in the form of payments of interest, royalties, dividends, and other service fees.[1] Such treaties also include commitments to: restrict the scope of their tax jurisdiction primarily to active income from a fixed place of business;[2] use specific dispute resolution measures that often include mandatory arbitration;[3] and include non-discrimination clauses, which oblige them to grant the same deductions for taxpayers resident in the treaty partner country as they do for their own residents.[4] Non-discrimination clauses, without a Limitation on Benefits or other anti-abuse clause, can prevent countries from placing caps on the deductibility of interest payments, which can be used for profit-shifting purposes.

In light of these disadvantages, a number of developing countries are now choosing not to sign these bilateral tax treaties, and yet they continue to do business with many countries across the globe. For example, the United States and Brazil have an extensive trade and investment relationship, even though there is no bilateral income tax treaty between the two countries. Since 2011 Argentina and Mongolia have cancelled or re-negotiated some of their bilateral income tax treaties (McGauran, 2013: 8).

In the case of renegotiation, inclusion of a Limitation on Benefits clause could provide the necessary foundation to challenge a claim of treaty benefits in cases of abuse. For example, the 2006 US Model Income Tax Convention, Article 22, restricts residents of Contracting states to "qualified persons," who have a connection with the Contracting state as provided by the Article. However, negotiation and administration of these clauses can be complex.

[1] OECD Model Tax Convention on Income and Capital, Arts. 10–12 [hereinafter OECD Model]; UN Model Double Taxation Convention between Developed and Developing Countries, Arts. 10–12 [hereinafter UN Model].

[2] OECD Model, Art. 5; UN Model, Art. 5.

[3] OECD Model, Art. 25; UN Model, Art. 25.

[4] OECD Model, Art. 24; UN Model, Art. 24.

Given the resource drain of negotiation and administration, and the inherent asymmetry of bargaining power between developed and developing economies, many countries may do better to avoid entering into these agreements. In any case, many of the aims of tax treaties can be accomplished through unilateral legislation in domestic law (Thuronyi, 2010).

15.3 DO NOT FALL INTO THE TRAP OF TAX COMPETITION AND TAX INCENTIVES

Since the mid twentieth century, many countries, both developed and developing, have forgone tax revenues in the form of tax incentives and reduced tax rates in the expectation of attracting new business investment (Lent, 1967). At times, these incentives have been characterized as compensation for above-normal capital risks, at other times, as enhancements to "business climate." However, as globalization and the mobility of capital have increased, tax competition between states has resulted in a race to the bottom (OECD, 1998; OECD, 2014). Studies of this trend have demonstrated that tax competition impedes (rather than promotes) long-term economic development and often pits impoverished countries against each other (James, 2009). Ultimately, the winners have been the MNCs rather than the citizens and governments of developing countries.

Another reason that governments often end up giving away too much is due to the imbalance of wealth and power between large MNCs and that of the host country. Many developing countries, desperate to attract foreign direct investment, often accept unfair conditions imposed by powerful MNCs when negotiating contracts due to fears that the companies will take their business elsewhere. When many large multinationals boast revenues larger than GDPs of developing countries—compare Exxon Mobil and Thailand; or Ford and Morocco; or Wells Fargo and Angola; or Apple and Ecuador; or Pepsi and Oman, to name a few—the asymmetry of economic power can be significant, not to mention that these MNCs are often headquartered in world economic powers, such as the United States (Trivet 2011). In countering this imbalance, identification of a country's value-add to specific industries is essential. Location savings in the form of lower operating and labor costs, as well as greater potential for emerging consumer demand are often only present in developing countries. Moreover, in the case of natural resources, there is an even higher claim for source country uniqueness and entitlement to the benefits of extraction.

However, if such tax incentives are already in place, it is important to adopt laws to evaluate their effectiveness. For example in July 2013, the US State of

Rhode Island passed the Economic Development Tax Incentives Evaluation Act,[5] requiring regular evaluation hearings every three years for existing tax incentive programs and an evaluation after the first five years for new programs. The hearings would include analysis of data on economic impacts of the incentives and recommendations for improvement in meeting stated objectives.[6] Such evaluations are critical in ensuring that tax incentives offer long-term benefits for development in return for forgone public revenues, instead of short-term payoffs.

Concession of fiscal sovereignty in the form of tax incentives for FDI has even more long-term negative effects. Such revenue giveaways create impairment to domestic innovation and development when they disadvantage local firms. If the same tax incentives and concessions are not available to domestic (and often smaller) firms, competition on an equal footing is impossible, creating a double standard between international and domestic companies without adding any significant social value. As a result, it may have been better to not offer such incentives in the first place.

15.4 IMPOSE WITHHOLDING TAXES ON PAYMENTS TO NON-RESIDENTS

Why are withholding taxes important? Put simply, they strengthen the negotiating position with MNCs if for no other reason than that the government holds the cash. Withholding taxes operate as an initial presumption of minimal profit (typically in the 10–25 percent range) and require the resident entity making the payment to a nonresident entity to withhold a set percentage of the payment and remit that amount to tax authorities. Typically, taxpayers may claim credit for this payment against total income taxes due at the end of the filing period. Withholding taxes also capitalize on the time value of money: When the government share of the payment is deducted at the payment phase instead of collected at a later time, the value of the tax revenues is greater. Moreover, withholding taxes are also important enforcement tools, and simple to administer.

Unless withholding taxes are final, they may be refunded partially or completely at the end of the filing period by reductions to the base, through deductions or losses. Thus, despite their effectiveness at the front end, withholding amounts may be siphoned out through deductions and losses at the back end of the tax cycle. Final withholding taxes are designed to curb such losses. For example, Indonesia assesses a final withholding tax on various

[5] R.I. Gen. Laws, Sec. 44–48.2 et seq.

[6] R.I. Gen. Laws, Sec. 44–48.2–5.

payments to nonresident entities, including dividends, interest, royalties, and service fees (20 percent); fees for construction (2–6 percent); sale of Indonesian stock exchange shares (0.1 percent); real estate rental payments (10 percent) and transfer gains (5 percent); interest on savings deposits (20 percent) and bonds (15 percent); and lottery prizes (25 percent).[7]

As the reach of the digital economy expands, a few countries are also assessing withholding taxes on nonresident providers of digital services and online advertising. For example, under Vietnam's Law on Enterprise Income Tax, payments to a foreign contractor from online advertising and online training to a resident is subject to withholding tax.[8] India is also considering the same, given the recent *Right Florists* ruling against the taxability (under current law and treaty) of online advertising services provided by non-resident companies, Google and Yahoo.[9]

Withholding taxes on payments for royalties, dividends, interest, and services are widely used in developing countries. However, as mentioned earlier, without careful planning, withholding taxes can often be reduced or eliminated directly through withholding limitations or indirectly through tax jurisdiction restrictions in permanent establishment provisions of tax treaties.[10] In the case of Vietnam's withholding law on payments to foreign contractors for online advertising, a permanent establishment is deemed by requiring a foreign website provider to operate through a Vietnamese advertising service supplier.[11] In other cases, adoption and/or reinstatement of withholding taxes may require some treaty renegotiation, and developing countries have the sovereign right to do so.

15.5 ADOPT SAFE HARBORS AND OTHER SIMILAR MEASURES TO SIMPLIFY TAX ADMINISTRATION AND COMPLIANCE

Safe harbors are "tax thresholds" that can often broaden the tax base by simplifying the tax regime.[12] Safe harbors can also reduce administrative

[7] Indonesian Income Tax Law, Art. 4(2).

[8] Vietnam Ministry of Finance, Circular No. 60/2012/TT-BTC, Art. 4, examples 4 and 6, (12 April 2012). Under the Law on Enterprise Income Tax, income received by a foreign contractor from online advertising and online training provided by a non-resident company to a resident is subject to withholding tax in Vietnam.

[9] *ITO v. Right Florists Pvt Ltd* (ITAT Kolkata), April 12, 2013.

[10] OECD Model, Arts. 10–12; UN Model, Arts. 10–12.

[11] Vietnam, Ministry of Finance, Gen. Dept. of Taxation, Official Letter No. 1939/TCT-HTQT, 12 June 2013.

[12] "A safe harbor is a statutory provision that applies to a given category of taxpayers and that relieves eligible taxpayers from certain obligations otherwise imposed by the tax code by substituting exceptional, usually simpler obligations." OECD Transfer Pricing Guidelines para. 4.94.

burdens, and offer predictability to both companies and revenue authorities, and reduce litigation. They can also help boost foreign direct investment. Presumptive tax regimes, caps on deductions, and fixed profit margins in transfer pricing regulations provide various thresholds for simplifying tax systems.

Presumptive taxation uses an established measure of business activity to establish a broad base for taxation (Tanzi and de Jantscher, 1997; Tauber and Telasse, 1996; Miscossi and Parascandolo, 2010). For example, a presumptive tax (presumably at a much lower rate) can be levied on the gross receipts of a taxpayer without subtracting for expenses, losses, or deductions. Payments to nonresident companies located in low- or no-tax jurisdictions are deducted as expenses, and erode the tax base. A presumptive tax on gross receipts would effectively disallow such profit shifting.[13] Under the Brazilian income tax law, eligible companies with gross income BRL 78 million or below may calculate their income tax liability under the presumed profit regime, which provides presumed profit margins for various industry categories ranging from 1.6 to 32 percent. Income tax is imposed at the rate of 15 percent on the presumed profit. Another simplified regime (*Simples nacional*) is optional for micro-[14] and small[15] enterprises and allows for joint collection of certain federal, state, and municipal taxes.[16] Under this regime, the corporate tax is assessed on gross income with rates ranging from 4 percent to 22.90 percent. India has also recently set new guidelines with respect to IT-enabled services, establishing a 20 percent deemed mark-up on services up to $US 80 million, and 22 percent above that.[17]

In addition, caps on deductions for various payments to nonresident related parties provide simplicity for both the taxpayer and the government and protect the tax base from profit shifting. The overall principle of a deduction cap is that any charges paid for service or management fees or interest payments must be appropriately tied to the underlying benefit received by the resident entity. For example, generally a management fee of 2 percent is considered acceptable and can be built in as a safe harbor provision in the overall tax laws regulating deductible expenses. If a company has a 10 percent

[13] In the mid-twentieth century, presumptive taxes were argued as an "optimum" tax by Luigi Einaudi. Einaudi's theory was that an income tax based on average income would stimulate production due to the incentive to produce higher than average without being subject to higher than average taxation, thus resulting in a marginal tax rate of zero.

[14] Gross income cannot exceed BRL 360,000. In addition, the following are disqualified from simples: incorporated entities; entities with a non-resident shareholder; entities with other legal entities as shareholders; entities facilitating certain professions, such as engineers, accountants, etc. See Einaudi.

[15] Gross income cannot exceed BRL 3.6 million.

[16] Supplementary Act No. 123 of 14.12.2006.

[17] India Income Tax Rule No. 10TD.

profit on sales, it should not be allowed to charge a 10–15 percent management fee and thus, strip the entire profit out of the country.

There are various examples, which indicate that developing countries have options on what deductions to allow, and how much to limit those deductions. For instance, China takes the position that management fees should be considered as a shareholder cost, and are, therefore, not deductible.[18] Mexico limits payments made to nonresident related parties for interest, royalties, and technical assistance under its income tax law according to the taxability of the income in the third country as well as the debt to equity ratio of the resident entity.[19] Brazil limits deductions for interest paid to related parties according to the London Interbank Offered Rate plus a margin determined annually by the Ministry of Finance (currently 3 percent).[20] Brazil also limits deductions for payments of patent and trademark royalties and fees for technical, scientific, and administrative assistance to nonresidents between 1 and 5 percent based on the net related income of the payer and requires registration of the license agreement with the National Institute of Industrial Property (INPI) and the Brazilian Central Bank.[21] Again, however, tax treaties with non-discrimination clauses may limit deduction caps as they require the same deductions for resident and nonresident treaty partners.[22]

Given the theoretical and practical barriers for developing countries in administering transfer-pricing rules, some emerging economy countries have adopted safe harbors within the OECD Transfer Pricing methods. For example, Brazil adopted fixed margins under its transfer pricing laws, which are based on the OECD transaction-based methods: Comparable Uncontrolled Price (CUP); Cost Plus Method (CPM); and Resale Price Method (RPM).[23] For the CPM and RPM, Brazilian TP laws provide fixed margins for *gross* profits and mark-up rather than searching for comparable prices.[24] For CUP, the prices for exports and imports of commodities traded on internationally recognized mercantile and futures exchanges are determined by the Price under Quotation Method for Imports (PCI) and the Export with

[18] China (PR) Income Tax Law, Art. 49.

[19] Mex. Income Tax Law, Art. 28, paras. 27, 29, 31.

[20] Brazil Law No. 12,715/12. The rate is for 6-month term US deposits.

[21] Law 3.748/58; Art. 353 RIR/1999. Such payments by Brazil branches to foreign head offices are not deductible.

[22] OECD Model, Art. 24(4); UN Model, Art. 24(4).

[23] Transactional profit-based methods, such as the profit-split method and the transactional net margin method, are disallowed. Federal Law n. 9,430/1996 and subsequent amendments.

[24] For RPM, the quoted resale price is reduced by the authorized gross profit margin, resulting in a parameter price, which is used for the calculation of overall net profit. For the CPM, the predetermined cost-plus mark-up will be added to the cost of the product and will set the maximum value of imports and minimum value for exports.

Price under Quotation (PECEX) Method for exports, both based on the average quotation price of the global market.[25]

Fiscal sovereignty implies that each country exercises its right to decide how to define its taxable base and what deductions from the tax base are acceptable in meeting national economic, social, and environmental development objectives. The use of safe harbors in broadening the tax base and simplifying tax rules for taxpayer compliance and administration can be a useful tool in exercising fiscal sovereignty that works for everyone.

15.6 USE THE PROFIT-SPLIT METHOD MORE WIDELY TO DETERMINE TAXABLE PROFITS

The profit-split method is a way of addressing difficulties in valuing cross-border transactions and transfer-pricing arrangements. Basically, the profit-split method adds up the profits from a group of transactions for all related parties, then divides those profits among the related parties according to certain proxy measures of economic activity. These measures include headcount, sales, functions performed, risk borne, and assets employed by each party. This method partly resembles formulary apportionment, in that it divides up profits based on criteria, which reflect genuine economic activity. The key difference is that formulary apportionment divides overall profits between jurisdictions; while the profit-split methods divides transactional profits among related parties.

The OECD transfer-pricing guidelines include the transactional profit-split method, and it is widely used in certain insurance and banking business activities, such as in round-the-clock global trading of financial instruments.[26] In the OECD guidelines, the transactional profit-split method is encouraged where parties to a transaction make unique contributions, for which comparability does not exist. Profits are then split based on the functions performed by the parties, including assets used and risks assumed. The profit-split method is also encouraged (and is often used) to determine underlying profits under advance pricing agreements (APAs) while they are being negotiated.[27] At the same time, the OECD guidelines caution that the information required for profit splits is often difficult to access from foreign affiliates and may not be

[25] Federal Law n. 12,715/2012.

[26] OECD Transfer Pricing Guidelines, paras. 2.108 et seq. (2010); OECD, 2010 Report on the Attribution of Profits from Permanent Establishments, paras. 115 et seq.

[27] The OECD Transfer Pricing Guidelines state that under certain conditions, APA terms can be established by estimating an appropriate profit-split ratio. See para. 4.126.

consistent due to variations in currencies and accounting practices.[28] Country-by-country reporting in the form of a standard template would ameliorate this informational deficit and enable greater use of the profit-split method. Thus, the OECD has called for discussion on greater reliance on profit splits in light of the difficulties in securing information on comparable data as required under other transfer-pricing methods.

15.7 NATURAL RESOURCE MANAGEMENT: REVIEW AND RENEGOTIATE BASED ON RETURN ON INVESTMENT

Various models exist in determining the appropriate management of natural resources. For example, in the petroleum industry models range from complete state ownership in national oil companies (NOCs) to partnerships with private international oil companies (IOCs) (Daniel, Keen, and McPherson, 2010; IMF, 2012). For example, Saudi Arabia completely nationalized its oil and gas sector in the 1970s, and other countries, such as Azerbaijan, Algeria, Nigeria, and Angola operate contractual regimes, where the country owns the minerals and the oil company receives a payment to extract them (Nakhle, 2010). Then the oil company can buy the mineral at the world price, which is easy to ascertain. Under production-sharing arrangements (PSA), the IOC owns a share of the oil produced. Other countries, such as the United States, the United Kingdom, Canada, and Norway operate concessionary systems, where the IOC owns all of the oil extracted and the government share is yielded through royalties, income taxes, and other natural resource levies. Regardless of the revenue collection structure, it should be designed based on actual return on investment. All are important if we want to advance the fight against poverty and provide healthcare, education, and basic infrastructure to the countries concerned.

When natural resource management includes partnerships with private companies, it is important for resource-rich countries to negotiate (and re-evaluate) contracts judiciously to protect their revenue streams that are vital to a country's development and national fiscal sovereignty. The source country has maximum leverage at the time of signing or renewing an agreement. The well-known development success story of Botswana illustrates the importance of re-evaluation of mining contracts through a provision allowing for "re-negotiation due to changed circumstances." What began in the late 1960s as a

[28] OECD Transfer Pricing Guidelines, para. 2.114.

15/85 joint venture between the Government of Botswana and De Beers matured by 1975 into an agreement in which Botswana has a 50 percent share of the De Beers Botswana Mining Company and where Botswana receives no less than 65–70 percent of the profits (Alfaro, Spar, and Allibhoy, 2005). This renegotiation was by no means a deal breaker, but instead a reflection of changing economic and environmental reality. New diamond deposits had been discovered and De Beers had aspirations for expansion. Almost four decades later, De Beers continues to boast of its equal partnership with Botswana and the resulting benefits to the country's development.[29]

In this case, renegotiation was the key factor in creating a lasting win-win relationship. However, evidence from one study indicates that more than half of contracts negotiated by non-OECD countries contain stabilization clauses that insulate foreign investors from changes in legal circumstances, while only 17 percent of contracts negotiated by OECD countries contain such clauses (Shemberg, 2009; Sangwani, 2011). It is understandable that private investors are and should be concerned about political risks and time consistency, however, surely there is more to be gained from contract negotiation when many non-OECD countries contain such vast deposits of natural resources.

It is also important to remember that private producers are often multinational corporations that structure their investments with branches and subsidiaries in low- or no-tax jurisdictions. This structuring provides considerable opportunity to shift profits out of the country, including through transfer mispricing and indirect transfers of interest in mineral licenses or other exploration, extraction, and production equipment. A tax system design that is practical yet targeted to extract rent is critical to effective natural resource management. Once these laws are in place, it is important to ensure that they are not superseded by private contractual provisions.

As the recent *Tullow* ruling in Uganda illustrates, tax authorities have launched successful challenges against the application of preferential contract provisions that attempt to supersede tax laws enacted through a democratic process.[30] The *Tullow* case involved a dispute on the assessment of over $US 400m in capital gains taxes, which the private producer claimed were exempted through a provision in the PSA contract. The tribunal agreed that the exemption applied to the transfer that produced the tax assessment, but held that the exemption in the PSA signed by a government minister could not supersede tax laws passed by Parliament. The tribunal opinion stated: "The framers of the 1995 Constitution of Uganda thought it wise that the people's

[29] See Debswana: Mining Diamonds, Enriching the Nation, Report to Stakeholders 2013, available at http://www.debswana.com/Media/Pages/Reports.aspx.

[30] See *Tullow Oil v. Uganda Revenue Authority*, Uganda Tax Appeals Tribunal, Tax App. No. 4 of 2011 (June 16, 2014).

representatives should be the most suitable persons to impose the taxes they should pay. So be it."[31]

Finally, another critical element in natural resource management is transparency. Resources of a country ultimately belong to the people first, before the government or the private producer, and hence the contracts over the extraction of those resources should be made public. Adoption of transparency rules included in the Extractives Industries Transparency Initiative is an important step forward and as of this writing, these rules have been adopted in forty countries.

15.8 ADOPT MORE DISCLOSURE AND ATTESTATION RULES

Disclosure rules that require attestation by senior corporate officers and verification by independent public accountants provide an important risk assessment function for tax administrations and also encourage taxpayer compliance. Such rules have increasingly been adopted by developing countries. For example, the Dictaman Fiscal requirement is part of Mexico's tax statutes.[32] This rule operates at two levels: the company leadership and the independent auditor. The company is required to confirm that it has done a transfer-pricing study and has internal documentation on all major transactions. Furthermore, the rule requires the company to file an information return on all transactions above $1 million, which includes who the company is trading with, where it has its affiliates, why, and so forth. If the company is trading with a related entity in a tax haven the company cannot deduct even a single dollar unless it can establish that the transfer pricing has been done correctly. (Mexico's tax authorities also maintain a "blacklist" of about 50–60 tax havens.) A senior officer of the company must formally attest to this documentation.

Another requirement in Mexico is that the transfer-pricing documentation be approved by an independent public accountant through the Statutory Audited Tax Report (*Dictamen Fiscal*). The statutory auditors also have to attest that the company representation on both the internal documentation and the information return is reasonable and valid to the best of their knowledge. As a result of this requirement, the auditors take due diligence seriously: none can risk being disbarred from doing business in Mexico. Other countries, such as the Czech Republic, have also begun to

[31] See *Tullow Oil v. Uganda Revenue Authority*, Uganda Tax Appeals Tribunal, Tax App. No. 4 of 2011, at 52 (June 16, 2014).

[32] Mex. Income Tax Law, Article 76-IX.

develop greater transfer-pricing disclosure rules for large corporations engaged in related party transactions. Such disclosure is certainly an important step forward for tax administration risk assessment, but could be strengthened by attestation requirements by senior corporate officers and independent auditors.

15.9 HAVE ANTI-ABUSE RULES AND BETTER TRAINING FOR TAX ADMINISTRATORS

Countries need to act in their own self-interest and take control of their own destinies, and not wait for the OECD or the BEPS process to help.[33] Several countries already have anti-abuse provisions in their domestic tax laws to address tax avoidance. For example, Kenya has a general anti-avoidance rule that allows adjustment of a resident taxpayer's taxable profits in two main cases: (1) where business is carried on with a related non-resident and no or less than ordinary profit is produced; (2) where the (or one of the) main purpose(s) of a transaction is avoidance or reduction of tax benefit to be realized within the subsequent three years.[34] In order to prevent treaty abuse, Mexico monitors transactions between resident and non-resident related parties. In cases of potential abuse, Mexican tax authorities may request non-resident taxpayers to demonstrate juridical double taxation in order to claim treaty benefits.[35] Under this provision, the taxpayer must state under oath that the income is also taxed in the residence jurisdiction and provide the legal provisions as documentation.[36]

Some anti-abuse rules require more capacity than others to administer and thus, may be better suited to certain environments. For example, controlled foreign company rules are primarily useful in capital-exporting countries as they prevent base erosion by eliminating the deferral of taxation of income

[33] Several reports have already noted that despite the consultations held in Africa, Asia, and Latin America, the G20-OECD BEPS process fails to account for several primary sources of base erosion in developing countries. See G20-DWG BEPS Report, at 8. Developing country BEPS issues, not in the Action Plan, include "wasteful tax incentives, the lack of comparability data in developing countries and tax avoidance through the indirect transfer of assets located in developing countries." See G20-DWG BEPS Report, at 5.

[34] Kenya Income Tax Act, 1973.

[35] Mex. Income Tax Law, Art. 4.

[36] However, this rule does not apply in the following cases: (1) the non-resident's country has a territorial tax system; (2) the non-resident is exempt from tax under a tax treaty between the non-resident's country of residence and Mexico; or (3) where there is a transfer of shares under corporate restructuring rules referenced in a tax treaty between the non-resident's country of residence and Mexico.

generated from a foreign entity that is either directly or indirectly controlled by the resident taxpayer. Under Mexican law, all income from a controlled foreign entity that is established in a "preferential tax regime" is taxable in the current year regardless of whether the income has been distributed.[37]

In order to enforce such provisions, sufficiently paid and adequately trained staff are necessary. Opportunities to share best practices with other developing countries are also valuable. The G8 countries have committed to help developing countries in building capacity to collect the taxes owed to them, and many countries have been engaging in such efforts for some time through seminars and technical assistance (G8, 2013). In addition, budget support to fund salaries could also be helpful in retaining skilled employees, who are often recruited by private multinational legal and accounting firms that can offer multiples of government wages. The tax revenues gained from such investments now could cover salary maintenance in the future.

15.10 TAX THE INFORMAL ECONOMY AND REDUCE OUTFLOWS FROM INFORMAL BANKING, TRADE MISPRICING, AND OTHER MEANS

The more vigilance and transparency there is to control the informal economy, the more it will send a message of competence in negotiating with MNCs on inbound investment. Some developing countries have an informal economy that is 50 percent or more of GDP.[38] This not only forgoes valuable tax revenues for development, but also inhibits labor and consumer protection by the state. In order to protect fiscal and policy sovereignty, States must bring as much economic activity into the formal economy as possible. Adoption and enforcement of tax, banking, and customs regulations are critical to this process. Many developing countries have created presumptive tax regimes to formalize the economy. *Simples nacional* in Brazil applies to micro- (under $160,000 turnover) and small (under $1.5 million turnover) businesses and

[37] Income is subject to a preferential tax regime if the tax paid in the foreign jurisdiction is less than 75% of the income tax that would have been paid in Mexico. The following exceptions apply: (1) engagement in an active trade or business and passive income represents no more than 20% of income; (2) royalty payments (made at arm's length) are exempt where the intangibles have either been created by the foreign entity or acquired through an arm's length transaction; and (3) lack of effective control over the foreign entity administration, distribution of profits, or investments. Mex. Income Tax Law, Art. 6.

[38] See Abhinav Yashkar, "Estimating the Size of the Indian Underground Economy Using Fuzzy Logic," *International Journal of Emerging Technology and Advanced Engineering* (ISSN 2250–2459, ISO 9001:2008 Certified Journal, Volume 3, Issue 8, August 2013).

allows for joint collection of certain federal, state, and municipal taxes.[39] Under this regime, the corporate tax is assessed on gross income with rates ranging from 4 percent to 22.9 percent. Nigeria has also recently introduced legislation targeted at its informal economy.[40]

Banking regulations should ensure that money flows through formal banking channels and not through informal banking channels, such as the *hawala* system that enables the outflow of valuable resources with no paper trail. Domestic cash flows should also be regulated. Some countries have a policy that purchases of consumer goods above a certain amount, say $10,000, must be paid through formal banking channels rather than in cash; or that recipients of payments in cash over $10,000 must be reported to the government tax administration.[41] The premise of these laws is that such payments can only be made from income that has been previously reported and taxed. As a result, the informal economy cannot function as freely and more resources are channeled into the formal economy.

Banking regulations should go hand in hand with ensuring that there is adequate oversight in customs administration. Since many *hawala* transactions are conducted in the trade context, over-invoicing and under-invoicing are often ways to reconcile accounts after the informal transactions take place. Tax avoidance also takes place by routing trade—often unnecessarily—through low- or no-tax jurisdictions. A number of emerging economies have major segments of their exports flowing through Dubai, Mauritius, Cyprus, or other tax havens. This practice needs to be stemmed so that the tax base of the formal economy can be strengthened. Such internal rigor will be viewed in a positive light when a country is negotiating for its fair share of tax revenue from the MNCs or from its treaty partners.

15.11 FORM REGIONAL ALLIANCES

There is an African proverb that says, "If you want to go quickly, go alone. If you want to go far, go together." It is important to not only act judiciously in your own interests but also to foster regional alliances on tax and trade

[39] Supplementary Act No. 123 of 14.12.2006; <http://www8.receita.fazenda.gov.br/SimplesNacional> accessed 15 July 2015.

[40] Nigeria, PITA Act 2011, Sec. 36(5) states that where the income of the taxpayer cannot be ascertained, the taxpayer shall be assessed under a presumptive tax regime.

[41] See, e.g., 26 U.S.C. § 6050I.

matters. While capacity-building partnerships are certainly valuable, through organizations such as the African Tax Administration Forum (ATAF), and the Inter American Center of Tax Administrations (CIAT), political engagement cannot be understated. Regional economic communities in the global South, such as the East African Community (EAC), the Association of South East Asian Nations (ASEAN), and the Andean Community (CAN) have been taking steps in trade and other economic integration to enable greater flows of resources and increase economic development. In each of these economic communities, customs unions with common tariff schedules have been adopted while across EAC partner states corporate income tax rates are now uniform.[42] CAN countries have developed a multilateral double-taxation agreement among member countries as well as a Model Tax Convention for tax treaties with other non-member countries.[43]

Economic integration is by no means a painless process, as much political will and compromise is necessary in advancing economic growth and sharing in its prosperity. However, regional economic integration builds strength in a globalized economy. The European Union has twenty-eight countries, a common market, and the largest global economy at $18.45 trillion (nominal GDP). Imagine the power of other regional economic communities acting similarly in their own interests. Companies will not walk away when countries invoke the power of the group and negotiate from a position of strength.

15.12 CONCLUSION

Claiming and maintaining fiscal sovereignty requires an inventory and assessment of each country's resources, manufacturing base, and markets as well as an understanding that these resources are critical to the survival of multinational companies in a globalized economy. Against this backdrop, countries should seek to build partnerships on equal footing based on mutual understanding of how each party's priorities can inform the investment relationship. Tax policies that broaden (and not erode) the tax base and that increase

[42] All corporate tax rates are set at 30 percent. See Income Tax Act , Ch. 340, Uganda; Income Tax Act , Ch. 470, Kenya; Income Tax Act , Ch. 332, Tanzania; Income Tax Act, Law no. 16/2005 of 18/08/05 as amended, Rwanda; Income Tax Law no. 1/02 of 24/01/2013, Burundi.

[43] Decision 40/1971 of the Commission of the Cartagena Agreement established a multilateral treaty to avoid double taxation (Annex I) and also a Model Convention for the CAN member states (Annex II). This Decision was updated by Decision n. 578 of the Andean Community Commission in 2004, approving a new version of the multilateral DTA now renamed to "Scheme for the Avoidance of Double Taxation and Prevention of Fiscal Evasion," in force since January 1, 2005.

transparency and certainty for investment is a step in the right direction. For this reason, taking control of one's own tax destiny is an important imperative for every country.

REFERENCES

Alfaro L., D. Spar, and F. Allibhoy, 2005. "Botswana: A Diamond in the Rough," Harvard Business School Paper No. 9-703-027, p. 7.

Daniel P., M. Keen, and C. McPherson (eds.), 2010. *The Taxation of Petroleum and Minerals: Principles, Problems and Practice*. IMF, Washington, DC.

Einaudi, L. 1959. *Cronache economiche e politiche di un trentennio: 1893–1925*.

G8, 2013. Lough Erne Declaration, https://www.gov.uk/government/publications/g8-lough-erne-declaration/g8-lough-erne-declaration-html-version, accessed 27 July 2015.

IMF, Fiscal Affairs Department, 2014. "Spillovers in International Corporate Taxation." IMF, Washington, DC.

IMF, Fiscal Affairs Department, 2012. "Fiscal Regimes for Extractive Industries: Design and Implementation." IMF, Washington, DC.

James, S., 2009. "Tax and Non-Tax Incentives and Investments: Evidence and Policy Implications," Investment Climate Advisory Services of the World Bank Group. World Bank, Washington, DC.

Lent, G., 1967. "Tax Incentives for Investment in Developing Countries," IMF Staff Papers, 14 (2): 249–323.

McGauran, K., 2013. "Should the Netherlands Sign Tax Treaties with Developing Countries?, SOMO Report, p. 8.

Miscossi, S. and P. Parascandolo, 2010. "The Taxation of Multinational Enterprises in the European Union: Views on the Options for an Overhaul," CEPS Policy Brief No. 203.

Nakhle, C., 2010. "Petroleum Fiscal Regimes: Evolution and Challenges," in P. Daniel, M. Keen, and C. Macpherson (eds.) 2010, *The Taxation of Petroleum and Minerals: Principles, Problems and Practice*, pp. 89–94. London and New York: Routledge.

OECD 1998. "Harmful Tax Competition: An Emerging Global Issue." OECD, Paris.

OECD 2014. "Part 1 of a Report To G20 Development Working Group on the Impact of BEPS in Low Income Countries." p. 18. OECD, Paris.

Sangwani, N., 2011. "Stabilisation Clauses and the Zambian Windfall Tax," *Zambia Social Science Journal* 1 (1): 107–17.

Sauvant, K. and L. Sachs, 2009. *The Effect of Treaties on Foreign Direct Investment: Bilateral Investment Treaties, Double Taxation Treaties, and Investment Flows*. Oxford Scholarship Online, Oxford.

Shemberg, A., 2009. "Stabilization Clauses and Human Rights," IFC and United Nations Special Representative of the Secretary-General on Business and Human Rights Research Project.

Tanzi, V. and M. de Jantscher, 1987. "*Presumptive Income Taxation: Administrative, Efficiency, and Equity Aspects,*" IMF WP/87/54. IMF, Washington, DC.

Tauber, G. and H. Telasse, 1996. "*Presumptive Taxation in Sub-Saharan Africa: Experiences and Prospects,*" IMF WP/96/5. IMF, Washington, DC.

Thuronyi, V., 2010. "Tax Treaties and Developing Countries," in M. Lang et al. (eds), *Tax Treaties: Building Bridges between Law and Economics*, pp. 441–55. Amsterdam: IBFD.

Trivet, V., 2011. "25 US Mega Corporations: Where They Rank If They Were Countries, *BusinessInsider.com*. <http://uk.businessinsider.com/?r=US&IR=T> accessed 15 July 2015.

Index

Boxes, tables, and figures are indicated by an italic *b, t,* and *f* following the page number.